ISBN 978-1-5280-7776-7
PIBN 10927667

1 MONTH OF
FREE
READING

at
www.ForgottenBooks.com

By purchasing this book you are eligible for one month membership to ForgottenBooks.com, giving you unlimited access to our entire collection of over 1,000,000 titles via our web site and mobile apps.

To claim your free month visit:
www.forgottenbooks.com/free927667

English
Français
Deutsche
Italiano
Español
Português

www.forgottenbooks.com

Mythology Photography **Fiction**
Fishing Christianity **Art** Cooking
Essays Buddhism Freemasonry
Medicine **Biology** Music **Ancient
Egypt** Evolution Carpentry Physics
Dance Geology **Mathematics** Fitness
Shakespeare **Folklore** Yoga Marketing
Confidence Immortality Biographies
Poetry **Psychology** Witchcraft
Electronics Chemistry History **Law**
Accounting **Philosophy** Anthropology
Alchemy Drama Quantum Mechanics
Atheism Sexual Health **Ancient History**
Entrepreneurship Languages Sport
Paleontology Needlework Islam
Metaphysics Investment Archaeology
Parenting Statistics Criminology
Motivational

OBERLIN COLLEGE

ANNUAL REPORTS

OF THE PRESIDENT AND THE TREASURER OF OBERLIN COLLEGE FOR 1916-1917

PRESENTED TO THE BOARD OF
TRUSTEES AT THE ANNUAL
MEETING NOVEMBER 16, 1917

PUBLISHED BY THE COLLEGE
NOVEMBER 30, 1917
OBERLIN, OHIO

CONTENTS

ANNUAL REPORTS FOR 1916-17

CALENDAR

1917

Sept. 18, Tu.—First day of registration of students in all departments.

Sept. 19, We.—Second day of registration; academic year begins in all departments.

Nov. 16, Fr.—Annual Meeting of the Board of Trustees.

Nov. 29, Th.—Thanksgiving Day; a holiday.

Dec. 19, We.—Beginning of winter recess.

1918

Jan. 3, Th.—End of winter recess.

Jan. 25-Feb. 2—Final examinations, the College of Arts and Sciences.

Feb. 6, We.—Second semester begins.

Feb. 22, Fr.—Washington's Birthday; a holiday.

Feb. 28, Th.—Day of Prayer for Colleges.

Mar. 27, We.—Beginning of spring recess.

Apr. 3, We.—End of spring recess.

May 22, We.—Commencement, the Graduate School of Theology.

May 30, Th.—Memorial Day; a holiday.

June 7-June 14—Final Examinations, the College of Arts and Sciences.

June 16, Su.—Baccalaureate Service.

June 17, Mo.—Semi-Annual Meeting of the Board of Trustees.

June 18, Tu.—Annual Meeting of the Alumni.

June 19, We.—Eighty-fifth Annual Commencement.

June 21, Fr.—Summer Session begins.

Aug. 8, Th.—Summer Session ends.

COLLEGE YEAR OF 1918-19

1918

Sept. 17, Tu.—First day of registration of students in all departments.

Sept. 18, We.—Second day of registration; academic year begins in all departments.

Nov. 15, Fr.—Annual Meeting of the Board of Trustees.

Nov. 28, Th.—Thanksgiving Day; a holiday.

Dec. 20, Fr.—Beginning of winter recess.

1919

Jan.   3, Fr.—End of winter recess.

Feb.   5, We.—Second semester begins.

Feb. 22, Sa.—Washington's Birthday; a holiday.

Feb. 27, Th.—Day of Prayer for Colleges.

May 21, We.—Commencement, the Graduate School of Theology.

May 30, Fr.—Memorial Day; a holiday.

June 15, Su.—Baccalaureate Service.

June 16, Mo.—Semi-Annual Meeting of the Board of Trustees.

June 17, Tu.—Annual Meeting of the Alumni.

June 18, We.—Eighty-sixth Annual Commencement.

TRUSTEES, TRUSTEE COMMITTEES, AND ADVISORY COMMITTEES

THE BOARD OF TRUSTEES

REV. HENRY CHURCHILL KING, D.D., LL.D., PRESIDENT

ADVISORY COMMITTEES

Student Life and Interests, of Men

AMOS C. MILLER, '89, Chairman, Chicago, Ill.
EDGAR FAUVER, '99, Middletown, Conn.
JAMES H. GRISWOLD, '98, Cleveland, O.
ANDREW H. NOAH, Akron, O.
HEATON PENNINGTON, JR., '10, Cleveland, O.
EDWARD L. WERTHEIM, '07, New York, N. Y.
BEATTY B. WILLIAMS, '99, Mt. Vernon, O.

Student Life and Interests, of Women

HARRIET L. KEELER, '70, Chairman, Cleveland, O.
MARY A. AINSWORTH, '89, Moline, Ill.
MRS. ELIZABETH KEEP CLARK, '69, Evanston, Ill.
MRS. FLORA BIERCE DEE, '93, Chicago, Ill.
KATHARINE WRIGHT, '98, Dayton, O.

II. DEPARTMENTAL COMMITTEES

Ancient Languages

DAN F. BRADLEY, '82, Chairman, Cleveland, O.
A. B. BRAGDON, Monroe, Mich.
JAMES B. SMILEY, '89, Cleveland, O.

Botany

AMOS B. McNAIRY, Chairman, Cleveland, O.
HENRY C. COWLES, '93, Chicago, Ill.
DAVID C. FAIRCHILD, h.'16, Washington, D. C.

Chemistry

SEABURY C. MASTICK, '91, Chairman, New York, N. Y.
HARRY AINSWORTH, '84, Moline, Ill.
WILLIAM E. CHAMBERLIN, '87, Washington, D. C.
IRWIN S. OSBORN, Cleveland, O.

Economics

ALEXANDER HADDEN, '73, Chairman, Cleveland, O.
THOMAS N. CARVER, h.'05, Cambridge, Mass.
E. DANA DURAND, '93, Minneapolis, Minn.

Education

AMOS C. MILLER, '89, Chairman, Chicago, Ill.
FREDERICK W. BUCHHOLZ, '89, Chicago, Ill.
FREDERICK A. HAZELTINE, '89, South Bend, Wash.
JESSE F. WILLIAMS, '09, Cincinnati, O.

English Language and Literature

JOHN M. SIDDALL, '98, Chairman, New York, N. Y.
CLARK B. FIRESTONE, '91, Lisbon, O.
EDWIN O. GROVER, Chicago, Ill.
HENRY J. HASKELL, '96, Kansas City, Mo.
MRS. MAY ELLIS NICHOLS, '85, Brooklyn, N. Y.

Fine Arts, the Art Museum, and the Art Collections

JOHN L. SEVERANCE, '85, Chairman, Cleveland. O.
MRS. ELISABETH SEVERANCE PRENTISS, Cleveland, O.
KENYON COX, h.'12, New York, N. Y.
A. AUGUSTUS HEALY, Brooklyn, N. Y.
ARTHUR S. KIMBALL, h.'15, Oberlin, O.
IRVING W. METCALF, '78, Oberlin, O.

Geology

CHARLES B. SHEDD, '68, Chairman, Chicago, Ill.
WALTER N. CRAFTS, '92, Oberlin, O.
ARTHUR G. LEONARD, '89, Grand Forks, N. Dak.

German Language and Literature

MERRITT STARR, '75, Chairman, Chicago, Ill.
WILLIAM I. THOMAS, Chicago, Ill.
HENRY T. WEST, '91, Gambier, O.

History

CHARLES H. KIRSHNER, '86, Chairman, Kansas City, Mo.
GRANVILLE W. MOONEY, '95, Cleveland, O.
MERRICK WHITCOMB, Cincinnati, O.

The Library and Bibliography

WILLIAM C. COCHRAN, '69, Chairman, Cincinnati, O.
WILLIAM H. BRETT, Cleveland, O.
SHERMAN D. CALLENDER, '95, Detroit, Mich.
ALEXANDER HADDEN, '73, Cleveland, O.

Mathematics

JOHN L. SEVERANCE, '85, Chairman, Cleveland, O.
WELLS L. GRISWOLD, '94, Youngstown, O.
ALBERT M. JOHNSON, Chicago, Ill.

Oratory and Debate

WALTER T. DUNMORE, '00, Chairman, Cleveland, O.
FREDERIC M. BLANCHARD, '93, Chicago, Ill.
DAVID P. SIMPSON, '92, Cleveland, O.
WAYNE B. WHEELER, '94, Washington, D. C.

Philosophy and Psychology

HENRY M. TENNEY, Chairman, Lakewood, O.
DENTON J. SNIDER, '62, St. Louis, Mo.
FRANK N. SPINDLER, '94, Stevens Point, Wis.

Physical Education, Athletics, and Gymnasium, for Men

WILLIAM P. PALMER, Chairman, Cleveland, O.
MADISON W. BEACOM, '79, Cleveland, O.
CLAYTON K. FAUVER, '97, New York, N. Y.
FREDERICK R. GREEN, '94, Chicago, Ill.
CHARLES W. SEIBERLING, Akron, O.
A. BURNES SMYTHE, Cleveland, O.

Physical Education, Athletics, and Gymnasium, for Women

HOMER H. JOHNSON, '85, Chairman, Cleveland, O.
CHARLES E. BRIGGS, '93, Cleveland, O.
JACOB D. COX, Cleveland, O.
MRS. AGNES WARNER MASTICK, '92, Pleasantville, N. Y.
MRS. AUGUSTA JEWITT STREET, '11, Louisville, Ky.

Physics and Astronomy

JOHN R. ROGERS, '75, Chairman, Brooklyn, N. Y.
GUSTAVUS A. ANDEREGG, '99, Oak Park, Ill.
R. T. MILLER, JR., '91, Chicago, Ill.
ROBERT A. MILLIKAN, '91, Chicago, Ill.
ORVILLE WRIGHT, h.'10, Dayton, O.
HARRY ZIMMERMAN, '93, Fremont, O.

Political Science
THEODORE E. BURTON, '72, Chairman, New York, N. Y.
WILLIAM M. BENNETT, '90, New York, N. Y.
DAVID J. NYE, '71, Elyria, O.
LEWIS H. POUNDS, '82, Brooklyn, N. Y.
THEODORE REMLEY, '96, Kansas City, Mo.

Romance Languages
LUCIEN T. WARNER, '98, Chairman, Bridgeport, Conn.
ARTHUR S. PATTERSON, '95, Syracuse, N. Y.
HARRY H. POWERS, Boston, Mass.

Sociology
GEORGE S. ADDAMS, '90, Chairman, Cleveland, O.
JOHN R. COMMONS, '88, Madison, Wis.
HASTINGS H. HART, '75, New York, N. Y.
HOWARD STRONG, '02, Minneapolis, Minn.
CHARLES S. MILLS, h.'01, Montclair, N. J.

Zoology
MAYNARD M. METCALF, '89, Chairman, Oberlin, O.
CHARLES A. KOFOID, '90, Berkeley, Cal.
LOUIS L. NICHOLS, '87, Brooklyn, N. Y.
ALTHEA R. SHERMAN, '75, McGregor, Ia.

REPORT OF THE PRESIDENT

Annual Report for 1916-17

Presented by the President to the Trustees at the Annual Meeting, November 16, 1917

To the Board of Trustees of Oberlin College:

GENTLEMEN—As President of the College, I have the honor of presenting herewith my sixteenth annual report—closing fifteen years of my own administration—the report of the work of the College for the academic year 1916-17.

The President's report aims to give a fairly complete survey of all the more important aspects of the college year under review. It is based upon the reports of other officers and teachers, and goes upon the assumption that the President owes it to the Trustees and constituency of the College, himself to give them a digest of all the other reports, and so to bring into one connected account all the work of the College. For details, of course, reference must be made to the reports of the other administrative officers.

The *outstanding facts* of the year may perhaps be said to be: the effect of America's entrance into the world-war upon the college life and work; the death of Dr. Charles J. Ryder of the Board of Trustees; the completion and dedication of the Dudley Peter Allen Memorial Art Building; the action of the Board of Trustees, appropriating the larger part of the income from the Hall bequest—first becoming available for the college year 1917-18—for increase of salaries; the extended discussion of the interests of the men students of the College by a joint committee of Faculty and students; some strong additions to the Faculty;. the comple. tion of Mr. Gilbert's plans for the buildings of the Graduate

School of Theology; the removal of Society Hall from the campus; some extensive changes making still more useful the Administration Building and the Men's Building; many changes in a number of buildings, ordered by the state for better protection against fire; and the beginnings of our plans for a careful psychological study of all students.

Attention is called to the topical division and frequent headings of the report, to the full table of contents (pages iii-v), and to the index to all reports (pages 393-396) as well as to the special table of contents of the Treasurer's report (pages 305-306), and to the index of all funds in the charge of the Treasurer. (pages 371-374). These various helps should make it easy for any reader quickly to find the precise points upon which he desires information.

The report adheres to the personal rubric adopted several years ago: Trustees, Donors, Administrative Officers, Faculty, Alumni, Students. For college life and work are primarily personal, and these groups of persons really constitute the College. There naturally follow two sections dealing with the Relations to Other Educational Institutions and to The Vicinage of the College, and the usual concluding sections upon Gains and Needs.

I

TRUSTEES

Death

One member of the Board of Trustees has died during the year—Dr. Charles Jackson Ryder of Stamford, Connecticut. Dr. Ryder died at his home Monday night, September 24, 1917, at the age of sixty-nine, having been born in Oberlin on Christmas Day, 1848. His serious illness began late in February of the present year.

Dr. Ryder was a graduate of Oberlin College, of the class of 1875—the class that has the remarkable record of having had six of its members upon the Board of Trustees of the College. He graduated from the Theological Seminary in 1880, receiving the degree of Bachelor of Divinity, and the College conferred upon him the degree of Master of Arts in 1887, and the honorary degree of Doctor of Divinity in 1894. He was a brother of Professor William H. Ryder of Andover Theological Seminary, himself a member of the class of 1866, and brother-in-law of Dr. James Brand, for so many years pastor of the First Congregational Church of Oberlin. Between his graduation from college and the theological seminary, Dr. Ryder was for two years in charge of the Fisk University Jubilee Singers in their remarkable European tour under the auspices of the American Missionary Association, 1875-77. From 1880 to 1885 he was pastor of the Congregational Church of Medina, Ohio, and in 1885 he entered the service of the American Missionary Association and held successively the positions of Field Superintendent, Eastern District Secretary, and Corresponding Secretary. He had thus had thirty-two years of continuous service with the American Missionary Association, and had been a large factor during these years in its great work for the neglected races in the United States. He had been a member of the Board of Trustees of Oberlin College, in continuous service since 1900, and had always been loyally devoted to its interests. A man of rare sympathy and high unselfishness, he was loved and esteemed in every relation, and will be personally missed to a degree true of few men,— literally by hundreds who have been associated with him. The Trustee minute concerning Dr. Ryder has been prepared by his classmate, Mr. John R. Rogers, and should find place here.

Dr. Ryder's life work was done in connection with the American Missionary Association. For some years he has been Senior Secretary of the Association.

The success of Dr. Ryder in his work is known to all who are interested in efforts to help the backward races of our country. Four characteristics stand out in his personality.

His sincerity was recognized by all who looked into his face.

His love for humanity was exceedingly strong. Few men have touched so many lives for good.

His optimism knew no discouragement.

These characteristics united in an utter devotion to, and absorption in his work. He literally "toiled terribly" through many years.

He loved his college with a deep affection.

He considered his membership in this Board one of his greatest honors and responsibilities. His genial personality and wise counsel will long be missed by us.

Wherefore, Be It Resolved, That we, the Board of Trustees of Oberlin College, record our high appreciation of the character of Dr. Ryder and his services to this Board and to the world. That while we mourn with thousands of his friends, we rejoice in a "life race well run, life's work well done, life's crown well won."

Election of Members

At the annual meeting of the Board of Trustees, November 17, 1916, Dr. Charles J. Ryder, Mr. Charles B. Shedd, and Mr. Lucien T. Warner were unanimously reëlected as members of the Board for the full term of six years, beginning January 1, 1917. At this meeting also the Secretary reported that the Alumni had elected as Alumni Trustee for the same term, Hon. Theodore E. Burton, of the class of 1872. The Trustees whose terms expire January 1, 1918, are Dr. E. Dana Durand, Judge Alexander Hadden, Mr. Homer H. Johnson, and Mr. Charles H. Kirshner. Dr. Durand is the Alumni Trustee in this group. As already indicated the death of Dr. Charles J. Ryder creates a vacancy in the group of Trustees whose term expires January 1, 1923, and this vacancy should be filled at the annual meeting.

Important Official Actions

The annual meeting of the Board of Trustees occurred November 17, 1916, and the semi-annual meeting June 11, 1917.

The records of these meetings show the regularly recurring but important business of the Board: the appointment for the year of the standing Trustee and Advisory Committees, recorded elsewhere; the review of the Prudential Committee actions for the year; the granting of degrees and diplomas according to the recommendation of the General Faculty; and the approval of the entire list of Faculty changes and appointments recommended by the General Council. All of these Faculty changes are put on record in a later section of the report, dealing with the Faculty.

At the annual meeting a minute was adopted in memory of Mr. Frederick Norton Finney, who had died during the year, as recorded in last year's report.

At that meeting there was also the usual careful consideration of the annual reports of the President, the Treasurer, and the Investment Committee. The Treasurer also made his regular special report giving a classified list of all the college investments.

The recommendations of the General Council for a new scale of salaries for teachers, officers, and employes of the College, to be put into effect as soon as the income from the bequest of Mr. Charles M. Hall should become available, were presented to the Trustees at the annual meeting, and in general approved by them, and referred to a special committee for report at the semi-annual meeting. As finally adopted, the new scale of salaries is as follows:

1. For instructors, $1,000 the first year, $1,100 the second year, $1,200 the third year and thereafter.

2. For assistant professors and present associate professors, $1,500 for three years, $1,800 for three years, $2,100 thereafter.

3. For teachers hereafter appointed or promoted to the rank of associate professor, $2,400 a year.

4. For full professors, whether heads of departments or not, $2,500 for three years, $2,750 for three years, $3,000 thereafter.

5. For the President, not less than $8,000.

6. For other administrative officers, as follows: the Dean of the College, $4,000; the Dean of the Graduate School of Theology, $3,800; the Director of the Conservatory, $3,600; the Librarian, $3,400; the Secretary of the College, $3,400; the Treasurer, the regular salary of full professors; the Superintendent of Buildings and Grounds, $2,100; the Assistant in the Treasurer's Office, $2,100; the Secretary to the President, the regular salary of instructors; the Reference Librarian, $1,000; other administrative officers, the regular salary of the teaching rank to which they are assigned.

7. For other officers and assistants in administration, including stenographers and the library staff, a regular scale of $600 for the first year, $720 for the second and third years, $840 for the fourth and fifth years, $960 thereafter.

8. For other employes of the College, a scale to be determined later by the Prudential Committee.

There was also adopted at the annual meeting a form of agreement between the Trustees of Oberlin College and the executors and trustees of the Hall estate under the terms of the last will and testament of Mr. Charles M. Hall, providing that the square known as the college campus shall be always kept free of buildings, the present buildings on the campus to be removed within fifteen years from the date of the will.

The Trustees further approved at the annual meeting, in accordance with the recommendations of the Assistant to the President, a revision of the plan for Advisory Committees. The revised list of Advisory Committees occurs at the usual place in the opening pages of the Annual Reports.

At the semi-annual meeting of the Board of Trustees, on the recommendation of the Faculty and of the Trustee Committee on Honorary Degrees, authority was voted for the granting of the following honorary degrees at the commencement exercises, June 13, 1917: Doctor of Laws upon James Levi Barton, Senior Secretary of the American Board of Commissioners for Foreign Missions, upon Cass Gilbert, Architect, of New York City, and upon Herbert Clark Hoover, United States Food Administrator, *in absentia;* Doctor of Letters upon Henry Joseph Haskell of the editorial staff of the *Kansas City Star* and of the Oberlin class of 1896; and the degree of Master of Arts upon Mary Louise Graffam, Missionary of the American Board at Sivas, Turkey, and of the Oberlin class of 1894, *in absentia.*

To provide for increases in salary in the Graduate School of Theology, corresponding to those in the other departments of the College, the Trustees voted at the semi-annual meeting to approve the transfer, to the use of the School of Theology, of income to the amount of $7,585 from undesignated funds; the Treasurer's statement showing that the College had in hand such undesignated funds to the amount of more than $550,000, far more than sufficient to provide the income transferred.

A report of a special committee, recommending the establishing of military training as part of the regular curriculum of instruction in the College, was referred to the Faculty and Prudential Committee for consideration and later recommendation. It may be added at this point, that the Faculty have found it impossible, up to the present time, to secure the services of such an officer as seemed required if the work were to be done in a way to be accepted by the Government.

The Trustees further gratefully agreed to accept a trust fund from the estate of Col. John H. Beacom, a student of Oberlin College from 1875 to 1878, as an endowment fund for scholarships. This scholarship fund is made available for the College through the hearty coöperation of the brothers of Col. Beacom,—Judge M. W. Beacom of Cleveland and Mr. B. D. Beacom of Wellsville, Ohio.

There was also presented at the semi-annual meeting the general plans of the college architect, Mr. Cass Gilbert, for the new theological buildings, and the Trustees voted to approve of these plans and to authorize the architect to go forward with the working drawings.

The budget for the year 1917-18 as adopted by the Trustees is presented here in outline:

BUDGET FOR 1917-1918

(Less transfers of income between departments)

Income

University	$ 148,772
College of Arts and Sciences	199,724
Graduate School of Theology	41,620
Conservatory of Music	107,025
	$497,141

Expense

University	$ 148,772
College of Arts and Sciences	199,724
Graduate School of Theology	41,620
Conservatory of Music	107,025
	$497,141

The full financial transactions of the College for the year are not represented by these totals, and that these may be seen in brief comparison, the following table of complete receipts and expenditures except changes of investments and transfers made between Departments is here given:

Important Prudential Committee Actions

A brief summary of the more important actions of the Prudential Committee between the meetings of the Trustees, not elsewhere covered in this report, finds record here as usual, since the Prudential Committee is empowered by the Trustees to act for them *ad interim*.

As the care of the physical property of the College is a chief charge of the Prudential Committee, the records for the year naturally show many building changes and repairs which are summarized in the report of the Superintendent of Buildings and Grounds. Repeated votes, of course, appear concerning the erection and completion of the Art Building.

On account of the high cost of labor and of all building material, it has seemed plainly wise to postpone the erection of both the Allen Memorial Hospital and the Hall Auditorium. But the *sites* for both buildings have been secured. The Prudential Committee authorized the purchase from the Oberlin Hospital Association of the tract of land on West Lorain street opposite Cedar avenue, to be used as a site for the Allen Memorial Hospital. The purchase of the Town

Hall was also carried through by the Prudential Committee, and with the previous purchase of the Methodist Church property, assured an ample site for the Hall Auditorium. Other important purchases of properties coming within the general plan outlined by Mr. Gilbert, the architect of the College, were of the Martin property on East College street and Willard court, covering a considerable part of the half square directly east of the campus; of the Royce house on West College street; and of the Clark house on West Lorain street. The land for the proposed science quadrangle is now mostly in hand. As a first step toward the clearing of all buildings from the campus, in accordance with the will of Mr. Charles M. Hall, Society Hall was removed just before the end of the college year.

Very considerable changes have been made in the *Administration Building* and in the *Men's Building*. Through the generosity of Mr. J. D. Cox, the beautiful candelabra have been erected in front of the Administration Building, and ample storerooms for the different offices of administration have been provided in the third story of the building. In accordance with the recommendations of the joint committee of students and Faculty on the men's interests, the Men's Building has been very successfully divided into four entries, so far as the dormitory accommodations of the building are concerned, and two kitchenettes have been put in on the first floor. The plan for the four entries involved the division of the dormitory space into four parts, thus assuring smaller groups of students and helping to more intimate acquaintance within the group. The kitchenettes have made the Men's Building much more available to the men for smaller social gatherings, in which the men themselves should act as hosts, and in this way have distinctly furthered the purposes of the building.

Under the orders of the Industrial Commission of Ohio, *Peters Hall and Severance Chemical Laboratory* have been newly wired for electricity throughout, at a very considerable expense. The further orders of the Industrial Commission, for better protection against fire, have involved some rather costly changes in practically all our dormitory buildings.

The purchase of *library stacks* was authorized for the rooms in the Carnegie Library formerly occupied by the Olney Art Collection.

The Committee made further provision for the care of the health of the students in setting aside the Metcalf house at 268 Forest street for a *college infirmary,* to take charge of cases needing a little special rest and care, but not serious enough to be sent either to the hospital or to the contagious cottages.

Some much needed repairs of the hotel property were also voted. Provision has been made for the immediate partial carrying out of a part of a completed plan for an underground electric bell system. Preliminary steps have been taken by the Committee looking to a greatly needed trunk sewer for surface and cellar drainage, beginning in the Chapel square. The College has also shared in the repaving of West Lorain street, and in laying new walks on the west side of the Second Church square.

To provide necessary quarters for the *training camp* of the teachers course in physical education for women, the Committee authorized the purchase of the Black farm on Lake Erie in Berlin township, Erie county. It seems reasonable to expect that sufficient lots can be sold off from this farm to provide at a minimum cost the necessary accommodations for the summer camp. This camp will furnish the greatly needed opportunities for instruction in boating and swimming.

The *effects of the war* are reflected in various votes of the Committee: releasing certain teachers for special war service; offering our laboratories for the use of the Government; approving, at the request of the Government, of establishing a short emergency course for women in bandaging, massaging, etc.; remitting term bills in the case of students entering on Government service; coöperating with the students through the college boarding houses in raising a prison camps fund; authorizing an increased price for board in the college boarding halls and much heavier payments for coal.

The Prudential Committee have also given considerable attention to the whole matter of *salary increases* for all the employes of the College, and have shared with the General Council the responsibility of making recommendations concerning these increases.

After full consideration, approval by the Investment Committee, and personal conference with a number of other Trustees, the Prudential Committee finally authorized, at a special meeting called September 20th in Cleveland, the *agreement with the Hall trustees* for the adjustment of the payment of the tax on the third of the Hall bequest designated for educational work abroad, and for taking care of certain annuities and special bequests. This agreement makes possible a definite settlement of the estate, and secures for the College an earlier beginning of the income from the Hall bequest.

The Prudential Committee have also authorized, at various meetings, certain special *emergency appointments* not passed upon by the Trustees. A full list of these appointments is given, in connection with those made by the Trustees, in the section of the report devoted to the Faculty.

II

Donors

The Hall Bequest

The College began to share in the Hall bequest for the first time during the year under review, the Treasurer reporting the receipt of $100,000 from Mr. Hall's executors as a part of the $200,000 fund left for endowment of the college grounds. And with the college year 1917-18, the College expects to secure regular income from the Hall bequest. One hundred and fifty thousand dollars has been thus added to the income of the College in the annual budget for the current year. This is more than the entire present income from invested funds. This added income not only provides for the previous budget of the College without deficit, but also makes possible greatly needed increases in the salaries of the employes of the College, outside of the Graduate School of Theology, as well as an enlargement of the teaching staff in several departments. This income from the Hall bequest represents the largest single increase in the endowment of the College ever received in its history. And the increase in the value of Mr. Hall's estate since his death will finally make the growth in endowment from this single source still greater.

The Dudley Peter Allen Memorial Art Building

The new Art Building, located at the southeast corner of Lorain and North Main streets, has been completed during the year under review. It was erected in memory of Dr. Dudley P. Allen, of the college class of 1875 and for many years a member of the Board of Trustees of the College. The completion of the Art Building is the fruition of hopes long cherished, growing naturally out of the Art courses of various kinds, which have been offered by the College practically from its beginning, and particularly stimulated by the courses in history and appreciation of art, first begun by Mrs. A. A. F. Johnston and continued by Professor Charles B. Martin. It was most appropriate, therefore, that Dr. Allen's will should have provided for an endowment of $100,000 for the Mrs. A. A. F. Johnston professorship of art, a part of the income of this endowment being available also for purchases for the art museum.

The architect of the building was Mr. Cass Gilbert of New York; the chief contractor, the J. H. Parker Company, also of New York; the interesting decoration of the clerestory of the sculpture hall and the mosaics of the loggia were carried out according to the designs of Mr. Frederick J. Wiley. The art needs of the College put a difficult problem up to the architect, calling for provision for the exhibition rooms of the art museum, for classrooms for instruction in History and Appreciation of Art, and for studio rooms for instruction in Drawing and Painting. The building itself bears witness how satisfactorily and harmoniously these different objects have been wrought into the plan. The first floor of the main building and the mezzanine gallery are thus held for museum purposes and for the art library and the Director's office. The rest of the mezzanine floor is reserved for a larger and a smaller classroom and related rooms. The studio wing is devoted to the instruction in Drawing and Painting. And all this the architect has embodied in a building that, so far as its exhibition purposes are concerned, is lighted wholly from above and yet has no skylight showing. The building belongs to the later type of the northern Italian Romanesque, and is itself a work of art, giving an ideal setting for the art objects there to be housed. It will have its own constant ministry of beauty through all the years in which it shall stand. The way in which the architect has made use of color in the exterior of the building, the perfect proportions everywhere secured, the beauty of the wrought iron work throughout the building, the charm of all its minor details, and the lovely court between the main building and the studio wing, suggest some of the charms of this noble building. The arrangements for heating, ventilating, and cleansing the air of the building are very complete, and the so-called daylight system of electric lighting has been installed for the galleries. The walls which will be most used for exhibition purposes have been sheathed with pine for the more convenient placing of exhibits.

The site of the building includes the former site of the Baptist church and of a number of other buildings, and its expense, $36,650, was wholly met by the gift of Mr. John L. Severance. The entire cost of the building, including the extensive preparation of the grounds and the laying of the brick walks, was $197,000, and has been wholly provided by the generous gifts of Mrs. Elisabeth Severance Allen Prentiss, Mrs. Prentiss adding recently $26,000 to her previous gifts. The furnishing of the building cost about $7,000, and was provided by a previous gift of Mr. Louis H. Severance. Most of the casts in the building have been recently purchased, at an expense of about $2,000, from a part of the income from the Johnston endowment. Exclusive of the casts, therefore, there has been devoted to the site, the building, the furnishing, and the preparation of the grounds, $241,000. It is difficult to express how great an addition this means, both to the resources of the College and to its even unconscious ministry to the community. At the same time, the Trustees should face the fact, that every new building means a large demand on the general budget for running expenses.

A considerable part of the Olney art collection, the gift of Professor and Mrs. Charles F. Olney of Cleveland; the rugs, Chinese pottery, and paintings given by the will of Mr. Charles M. Hall; the Rookwood pottery and the most

interesting Persian silk rug given by Mr. Frederick Norton
Finney; and the various other art objects belonging to the
College find their place now in this building.

It is peculiarly appropriate that this building should be
erected in the honor of Dr. Dudley P. Allen, so character-
istically—as the memorial inscription calls him—a "lover of
the beautiful in nature and art." Dr. Allen's first gift to
the College, while still a medical student in Boston, was a
set of art photographs, and the esthetic aspects of the college life and its environment always especially called out his
interest and care, as his bequest of the Johnston professorship itself indicated.

At the dedication exercises addresses were made by the
donor, Mrs. Elisabeth Severance Allen Prentiss; by the architect, Mr. Cass Gilbert; by the Director of the Cleveland Art
Museum, Mr. Frederic Allen Whiting; by Professor Clarence Ward, the Director of the Art Museum; and by the
President. As the President said at those exercises, so he
may appropriately say here again: On behalf of the Board
of Trustees and of the Faculty of Oberlin College—and
hardly less for all its students and Alumni present and pros-
spective, and for the citizens of Oberlin—I now accept for
the uses of the College this noble building, dedicated to
"whatsoever things are lovely and of good report," and to
the memory of a man of such largeness of ideals and such
fineness of taste, as made his Alma Mater glad to bestow
upon him the highest honors and trusts in its possession. I
here publicly record our deep gratitude to its generous donor,
and rejoice with her in the high beauty of the building now
completed, which the genius of the architect has made possible. And as President of the College, I hereby undertake
for myself and my colleagues in the Trustees and Faculty,
so far as in me lies, to hold this building true to the purposes
for which it has been given; that, so long as it shall stand,
it may perpetuate and develop among the students of Ober-

lin College the ennobling appreciation of beautiful things, so characteristic of the man in whose memory it. has been erected. And may the blessing of God abide upon all the work which shall there be carried on.

The Gift of Mr. J. D. Cox

During the year under review the College received from Mr. J. D. Cox nearly $13,000, to replace the entire amount that the College itself put into the Administration Building; since Mr. Cox desired to make that building, erected in the memory of his father, entirely his own gift. This further gift of Mr. Cox, replacing other college funds, has made possible the purchase of the Black farm on Lake Erie for a summer camp for the teacher's course in physical education for women, already recorded; of a complete addressograph equipment for the Secretary's office; and of needed further filing cases and other equipment for various offices of the Administration Building, as reported by the Secretary. Mr. Cox became responsible also for certain other improvements in the building, including provision for ample storage rooms on the third floor. for the decoration of all the interior walls, and for the erection of the candelabra in front of the building. With the completion of these changes, the Administration Building becomes ideally fitted for its constantly enlarging work.

The Bequest of Colonel John H. Beacom

As already recorded in the review of the action of the Trustees, an agreement was entered into by the Trustees with the brothers of Col. Beacom—Judge M. W. Beacom of Cleveland and Mr. B. D. Beacom of Wellsville, O.—by which, in accordance with the will of Col. Beacom, a scholarship fund will be established that will probably amount to about $50,000. This is a most noteworthy addition to our scholar_

ship funds, which are all too small for the many and pressing demands upon them. The College is particularly glad
that there is thus to be established a John H. Beacom Endowment Fund, which will keep in memory and upon the
records of the College the long, brave, and devoted service
of a gallant soldier, himself a former student of the College.

The Bequest of Miss Holbrook

By bequest of Miss Laura Emeline Holbrook of Cleveland, O., a graduate of the literary course, of the class of
1852, there has come to the College, as noted in the Treasurer's report, the sum of $7,763.75. The bequest is unre-
stricted and will be added to university endowment.

Gifts Reported by the Treasurer

The gifts reported by the Treasurer are divided into
two classes: Gifts for Current Use and Gifts to Capital. The
whole amount of *Gifts for Current Use* in the year under review was $100,424.55. The largest sums in this amount were
payments on the Art Building and its site, and the gift for
the Administration Building from Mr. J. D. Cox, already
mentioned. The indebtedness of the College to the Carnegie
Foundation for the Advancement of Teaching is shown in
the amount which the College is now regularly receiving from
that fund for retiring allowances, amounting to $7,105.04.
Especial attention should be called to the fact that there
has come in from members of the Living Endowment Union
during the year $3,732.01. Only a small part of this was
definitely designated, and by vote of the Prudential Committee $3,410.51 was used for scholarship aid. The Union
thus gives great assistance at a much-needed point in the
work of the College. The need for scholarship funds is further emphasized by the necessity for seeking other current
gifts, aggregating for the year $2,121.50. The College is
especially grateful to the Oberlin Association of New York
for a special gift of $1,144.81 to meet the extraordinary ex-

penses for military and Red Cross training last year. A portion of this sum came in after the close of the financial year, and does not appear, therefore, in the Treasurer's report. The class of 1891 contributed $844.59 to purchase the library of their classmate, Professor Guy Stevens Callender of Yale University, for the Oberlin College library. The class also added $200 as endowment for the care of this collection. This makes an especially appropriate memorial for an able and devoted teacher.

The total amount of *Gifts to Capital* reported by the Treasurer is $111,587.75. The largest sums in this total are the payment by the trustees of the Hall estate of $100,000 as a part of Mr. Hall's bequest to establish an endowment fund for the care of the campus and other grounds, and the bequest of Miss Laura C. Holbrook, both already mentioned. The A. H. Noah loan fund has been increased by $1,000 through a further gift of Mr. Noah; and Miss Mary J. Brown and Miss Carrie Brown of Oberlin have given $2,000 to found the Anna B. Gray scholarship for women, at present carrying an annuity. The details of the further sums for endowment will be found in the Treasurer's report.

Gifts Reported by the Librarian

The Librarian reports that 5,227 volumes have been added by gift to the library during the year under review, out of a total of 10,997. The most important single gift was from ex-Senator Theodore E. Burton of the Board of Trustees and of the college class of 1872. This gift included the library of Professor Giles W. Shurtleff, for so many years a member of the Faculty of the College, and a large number of volumes and pamphlets from Mr. Burton's own private library. Professor Shurtleff's library adds much classical material to the library resources. From Mr. Burton's private library came an extremely interesting collection of books and pamphlets on South America. By Mr. E. Snell Hall of

Jamestown, N. Y., there was presented the library of his father, the Rev. Elliott Hall, numbering over 500 volumes; and other valuable books and pamphlets have come from the libraries of Dr. J. K. Greene and Dr. D. L. Leonard. Professor Currier heads the list of the Faculty, this year, in gifts to the library. The Librarian calls attention to the fact that in the gift of Mr. C. J. Clark there are included many early Ohio imprints valuable for their illustration of Ohio history.

Other Gifts

The College is further indebted to Mrs. Elisabeth Severance Prentiss for a large number of photographs taken by her father in the Nearer East; many of these are mounted on slides and can be used to advantage in stereopticon lectures.

Through the kindness of Judge Madison W. Beacom of Cleveland there have also come to the College a number of valuable objects of anthropological interest from the collection of his brother Col. John H. Beacom.

Through Professor Sherman there has come in some valuable manuscript and other material, illustrating most helpfully certain advanced courses in English Literature.

The Department of Botany reports as the most important gift of the year a set of forty New Zealand ferns, from Mrs. E. B. Hitchcock. This is a portion of the New Zealand exhibit at the Centennial Exposition in Philadelphia in 1876, and was given by the Commissioner from New Zealand to Mrs. Hitchcock's father.

The Department of Zoölogy mentions an interesting gift from Mr. J. C. Lincoln of Cleveland, offering two half scholarships for students taking work at the Marine Biological Laboratory at Woods Hole, Massachusetts. This gift placed Oberlin on the list of coöperating institutions and societies for the Woods Hole Laboratory, for the year.

The President desires here to acknowledge, on behalf of the Trustees and Faculty of the College, all the gifts now reviewed, and thus publicly to express to each individual giver the earnest thanks of the College.

The beginning of the income from the splendid Hall bequest, and the completion of the Art Building, would alone mark the year as most notable.

III

ADMINISTRATIVE OFFICERS

For the year under review only one change occurred in the administrative staff of the College—the appointment of Dr. Carl C. W. Nicol as Assistant Dean of College Men. With the present year Dr. Nicol succeeds Dean Cole as Acting Dean of College Men.

With the election of Professor Edward S. Jones to the Department of Psychology, appointed with special reference to the psychological study of students both as to their present work and their future life-calling, it had been intended to put the Bureau of Appointments in his charge. But as he was asked to undertake similar work for the Government, in the examination of soldiers, the College felt that they could not refuse him leave of absence for so important a service. The work of the Bureau of Appointments continues, therefore, in Professor Lord's hands.

Treasurer, Secretary, and Assistant to the President

The general officers of the College besides the President are the Treasurer, Secretary, and Assistant to the President, and their reports, as having to do with all departments of the College, naturally take precedence in the review of the year.

Report of the Treasurer

The *gifts* to the College reported by the Treasurer for the year under review have already been mentioned.

The Treasurer has made a few *changes* in the presentation of his report, which add still further to its clearness and interest. The main divisions of the report are for the first time made typographically to appear as such; and this single change makes the report much easier of consultation. It will be noticed that all Funds in the body of the report, as well as in the description of Funds, have been put in alphabetical order. Two reasons certainly justify the inclusion of a description of funds in the Treasurer's report at not too distant intervals: the donors of these funds are thus kept in mind in connection with the purposes for which they made their gifts; and the precise conditions under which the funds have been received by the College are also kept in remembrance. In the earlier statements of the report, there is included a carefully classified statement of the net income from general investments. A full classified account of the cost of operating the central heating plant also appears for the first time. The unusual price of fuel for the year past has much increased at that point the operating expenses of that plant. The Treasurer has also erected for the first time as a permanent account, student Loan Funds, in which all loan funds are brought together. This makes it possible hereafter to treat all such funds in the same manner.

The income and expense and accumulated deficits by departments is briefly shown as heretofore, and the balance sheet brings out clearly and succinctly the main financial facts concerning the College. Attention is called once more to the fact that the report has a careful table of contents and a full index, making it easy to refer to individual items.

In the examination of the report it should once more be borne in mind that it does not show the Hall bequest, as that estate was still unsettled for the year under review, nor the capital sums of Dr. Allen's bequest of $100,000 for instruction in the History and Appreciation of Art, and $100,000 for a hospital and a for a nurse fund, since these funds are administered through the Cleveland Trust Company.

The total funds in the hands of the Treasurer consequently do not show a great change from last year. They now amount to $3,029,937.30, excluding deficits, an increase of $296,209.64. The total endowment funds of the College, including neither funds carrying annuities nor scholarship and loan funds, are shown to have reached $2,457,637.72, an increase of $114,488.92. When the scholarship and loan funds, now amounting to $225,551.96 (an increase of $31,688.16), are added to these endowment funds strictly construed, the total endowment of the College, in the sense in which the term is ordinarily used, is $2,683,189.68, an increase of $146,177.08. Dr. Allen's bequests for endowment would still further increase this amount by $150,000, making *a total of endowment funds of* $2,833,189.68. The Treasurer estimates this year the value of buildings, sites, and equipment used for college purposes at $2,222,750. This, less the amount included in "Advances," added to the total of investments, makes the entire property of the College, as shown in the balance sheet, $5,183,685.55, an increase over last year's total of nearly $400,000. If the Allen bequests of $200,000 are included, as they should be for a true view of the resources of the College, the *total assets* would for the first time exceed five million dollars, and make an aggregate of $5,383,684.55, *exclusive of the Hall bequest.*

When these figures for the present year are compared with those of 1907 and 1902, it may be seen that the present figures show a gain in endowment and scholarship funds in ten years of $921,942.09, and a gain in total assets in ten years of $2,161,268.40. In fifteen years the endowment and scholarship funds have increased $1,395,848.49, and the total assets have increased $2,841,582.06. That means that both endowment funds and total assets have considerably more than doubled in fifteen years. It should be further noted that the income from the Hall bequest, included in the budget for the current year, represents a sum which would more than double again the total endowment of the College.

The *unfavorable facts* brought out in the Treasurer's report are: the accumulated deficits in the University, College, School of Theology, and Academy accounts, now amounting to $114,233.93; the considerable increase in ''Advances'' (page 345); the depreciation in general investments— $51,256.30; and the lower rate of interest earned for the year—4.325 per cent. It should be remembered that *the rate* is made lower by the fact that considerable non-interest bearing funds are taken into account. The *deficits* have been authorized in the last few years, on the ground, that neither drastic cuts in the budget nor too great interference with normal growth were justified, in view of the properly anticipated large income from the Hall bequest. This has become partially available for the first time for the year 1917-18.

Report of the Secretary

The report of the Secretary falls, as usual, into two main divisions: Publications and Office Work, Records, and Statistics.

The *publications* of the year have been those regularly issued, with a single exception—a special bulletin given to the announcement of the course in Public School Music. The Secretary is planning for the coming year to make more use of special bulletins of information, instead of sending the full catalogue to all inquirers. The college advertising of the year has been again chiefly of an indirect nature, through the use of the attractive college calendar, and the valuable news letters issued from the office of the News Bureau under the charge of Professors P. D. Sherman and F. B. Stiven. The Secretary hopes during the coming year to issue two bulletins bearing specially on men's interests: a bulletin giving information concerning the men's gymnasium and the facilities in Oberlin for both indoor training and out of door athletics and play, and a bulletin giving information concerning the Men's Building. It is also hoped that the long planned book of college legislation, to contain a careful codification of the votes of the Trustees and Faculty, may be published within the year. The Secretary has the pleasure of reporting that the need, expressed in last year's report, especially for an addressograph equipment for the office, has been met through the recent gift of Mr. J. D. Cox.

The Secretary's report on the *ballot for Alumni Trustee* shows that over a thousand nominating votes were cast, resulting in the nomination of five exceptionally strong candidates for the Board of Trustees. The result of the final ballot will be announced at the meeting of the Board.

The *statistics* for the year show that the College issued 249 degrees and diplomas. The total number of degrees and diplomas granted during the existence of the College is now 8,046. The total number of individual graduates from the different departments of the College since its foundation is 6,597, almost evenly divided between the sexes. The net total of living Alumni is 5,136, of whom 2,415 are men and 2,721, women. The number of *new* students for the year 1916-17 was 722. This makes the aggregate of all students who have been in attendance since the founding of the College to June 30, 1917, 42,331. The total enrolment of students for the year in all departments was 1,631. This number excludes entirely all so-called ''unclassified students,'' and is wholly of students of college or graduate rank, the Academy for the first time not appearing in the enrolment statistics of the College.

The Secretary presents the usual statistics concerning the *proportion of men and women* both in the entire institution and in the College of Arts and Sciences. The percentage of men in the entire institution for the year 1916-17 (in spite of the fact that the Conservatory enrolment is naturally very largely of women) was 35.01 per cent, a slight loss as compared with the previous year. The percentage of men in the College of Arts and Sciences was 40.2 per cent. The total attendance of college men was the largest in the history of the College. The Secretary calls attention to the fact that the last ten years have shown a surprising steadiness in the percentage of men in the College of Arts and Sciences. The war has, of course, markedly affected the proportion of men for the current year. The Secretary is probably right in his belief that only the establishment of engineering courses, or courses similarly appealing to men, could essentially change the proportion of men in the entire institution. The present situation, at any rate, suggests the wisdom of continuing the limitation of numbers in the college department for the present, and perhaps also is an indication that further special advertising could be used to advantage.

The Secretary includes as usual *figures for the fall term* of the present year, corrected to October 22nd. These figures show an enrolment of 925 in the College of Arts and Sciences, of 38 in the Graduate School of Theology, and of 330 in the Conservatory of Music. The net total for these departments was 1,293, as compared with 1,490 for the fall of 1916—a loss of 197. This is a smaller percentage of loss than was estimated in the budget for the current year. The loss of course is especially among the men.

In the enrolment of the institution, the Secretary's figures still show the usual large percentage of *students from outside the State* of Ohio. For the year under review 55.60 per cent come from outside the state, as against 55.81 per cent for the year previous. The five states sending the largest number of students are: Ohio, 724; Pennsylvania, 142; New York, 93; Illinois, 88; Michigan, 78. The most noteworthy change here is in the increase in the number of students coming from Pennsylvania. Two years ago Pennsylvania ranked fifth, with a total representation of 102, whereas she now ranks second, with a representation of 142.

Report of the Assistant to the President

Certain points naturally dwelt upon by the Assistant to the President have been already anticipated. The Assistant reports as one of the most gratifying features of the last three years, the gains in scholarship and loan funds, although the amount of such funds is still far short of the needs. He calls attention also to the continued and greatly valued help of the Living Endowment Union, all of whose undesignated income is appropriated directly to scholarship aid. In view of the fact that the Graduate School of Theology does not share in the income of the Hall estate, there is naturally emphasized in the report the two outstanding needs of the School of Theology: $50,000 additional endowment for the student employment fund, and new theological buildings. The need of the new theological buildings is accentuated by the recommendation of the State Building Inspector that the College discontinue the use of Council Hall for college purposes as soon as possible.

Heads of Departments and Associated Officers

The work of the administration of the College includes not only that of the general administrative officers now reviewed, but also that of the Heads of Departments and of the officers associated with them: the Dean of the College of Arts and Sciences, with the Dean of College Men, the Dean of College Women, the Registrar, and the Chairman of the Committee on Admission; the Senior and Junior Deans of the Graduate School of Theology; the Director of the Conservatory of Music, with the Dean of Conservatory Women; the Librarian, and the other general officers of the College—the Chairman of the Women's Board, the Director of the Men's Gymnasium, the Director of Athletics, the Director of the Women's Gymnasium, the Secretary of the Bureau of Appointments, the Director of the Summer Session, and the Superintendent of Buildings and Grounds.

The College of Arts and Sciences

Dean Cole's report of the central department of the College is presented in the usual form, and deals successively with the membership of the Faculty; Faculty actions; reports from the individual members of the Faculty; instruction; students; and needs. The nominal ratio of regular teachers to students for the year under review was one to 15.3, a slight improvement over the ratio of the preceding year; but, as Dean Cole says, this ratio probably indicates one of the greatest weaknesses of the College. That ratio ought to be brought down to one to ten or twelve.

The most important *actions of the college Faculty* concerned some radical changes in the schedule of classes; the establishment of majors in Fine Arts; management of the difficult questions relating to military and agricultural activities; and settlement of the controversy over practice teaching.

The problem faced in the revision of *the schedule* was to secure more class periods and a longer time before the mid-day Chapel, without encroaching further upon the afternoon hours, and, if possible, even lessening the time required by afternoon appointments, in order to leave a clear recreation period at the end of the afternoon. The problem was solved by the adoption of eastern standard time instead of central time, getting thus an extra hour of daylight in the afternoon; having all classes and the Chapel service begin on the hour instead of seven minutes after the hour; and allowing the scheduling of more classes on Monday, Wednesday, and Friday than had been before permitted, guarding, however, the early Monday hours.

The new endowment for the Johnston professorship of history and appreciation of art, and the completion of the new Art Building, both naturally led to the establishment by the Faculty of four *majors in Fine Arts,* a department in which there had been previously no major courses. The four majors are in the History of Art, in Architecture, in Painting and Sculpture, and in the Practice of Art with larger attention than in the other majors to studio work.

The Dean discusses the plans adopted by the College for provision for *military training for the men and Red Cross activities for the women* last spring. If such military training were to continue this year, it seemed necessary that there should be an instructor of wide training, and, if possible, of some direct experience with more modern phases of warfare; but, as has been already stated, it has not been possible up to the present time to secure a man who seemed fully qualified to meet the new demands, just because the Government is using apparently every fit available man in its own training camps.

As to the question of *credit for practice teaching,* as the Dean says, "it had always seemed to a majority of the Faculty that this kind of work was so technical and professional in character as to make it highly undesirable as part of a student's course for the A. B. To the students themselves, however, and to a strong minority of the Faculty it seemed a not unreasonable view that practice teaching should be regarded as a laboratory course for the practical illustration of the principles to be put into use in their later professional work, and as such should stand upon the same basis as laboratory work of any other sort.'' By an almost unanimous vote of the Faculty it was decided to permit the crediting of practice teaching to the extent of not more than two semester hours; though this does not mean that the Faculty have come to one mind upon the subject.

The *reports* of the individual members of the Faculty naturally bring out the gains and needs in each department. The reports in general give the impression of distinctly better quality in the work accomplished—the best of all gains. Four *needs* are practically emphasized by nearly all the Departments: the need of more classrooms, of additional library appropriations, of further equipment, and of a general lectureship which might be available for all Departments. Nothing comes out more clearly in the reports of the Faculty than the pressing need of a new and large recitation building, that would afford suites of rooms for the Departments (other than scientific), providing recitation rooms of different sizes, offices for consultation with individual students, and rooms for the exhibition of special material needing to be studied between classroom hours. Increased library appropriations are sought, not only for new books in the different Departments, but for the most important reviews and periodicals. Equipment, too, of the most varied kind is naturally called for, including phonographs for the Language Departments, maps and much illustrative material for the Departments of History and Economics, etc. A general lectureship would make it possible to bring outstanding men for special lectures in all Departments, instead of being restricted as college lectureships often are, to very limited fields. Some special points may be noted in individual Departments.

The Department of *English* notes the good effect of the institution of sub-Freshman sections in English Composition upon the writing of our students, and expects similar gains from the new introductory course in Literature.

The Department of *Romance Languages* records marked increase in the number of students in Beginning French and in Spanish, and the success of the French Club under the directorship of Professor Jameson. The Department now plans to give Spanish every year, instead of alternating as heretofore with Italian.

The Department of *German* notes the diminution of students in the German classes, especially in the second semester. That diminution is still more marked in the current year, but the Department does not expect it permanently to continue.

The Department of *Latin* reports a gratifyingly large enrolment in that Department, and a continued call for Latin teachers, and urges that the College take a supporting membership in the American School of Classical Studies at Rome.

The introduction of the four majors in the Department of *Fine Arts* has already been mentioned. Between 150 and 200 students are making use of the new Art Building. A large number of books from the main library have been transferred to the library of the Art Building, and these, with additional purchases, make a working library of about 1,000 well-selected volumes. More than 8,000 photographs and about 11,000 lantern slides are also installed in the library of the Art Building, and are now being catalogued and made available for convenient use under Director Ward's supervision. The most pressing need of the Department, of course, is endowment to carry the heavy running expenses of the building, and to permit bringing exhibitions and lectures to Oberlin. The year under review showed large and growing interest in the elementary course in Theory and Practice of Art. The studio wing of the new building has been furnished in accordance with the careful plans of Miss Oakes, and is proving most satisfactory.

The Department of *Mathematics* emphasizes the need of adequate equipment and furniture for the seminar room.

The present report from the Department of *Botany* covers the twentieth year of Professor Grover's work as head of the Department. In reviewing that period, Professor Grover pays special tribute to the previous work of Professor Albert A. Wright, and notes that since 1886 "twenty-two graduates of Oberlin have gone into college and university positions as teachers of Botany or Agriculture, or are in graduate schools of training for such work; while numerous others have entered Government service in Botany or Forestry, become landscape architects, florists, agricultural experts, fruit growers and farmers, or are teaching Botany in large high schools." The list of twenty-two college teachers and graduate students of Botany begins with R. A. Harper of the class of 1886, Professor and head of the Department of Botany at Columbia University, and ends with two members of the class of 1917, who are graduate students and assistants in Botany for 1917-18 in prominent universities.

Some notable gains were made in the Department of *Chemistry*. More students were registered in the Department than ever before, the increase being specially marked in the advanced classes. Twelve students in all completed either a major course in Chemistry or a major course in combination with some other Department. Under Professor Chapin a new plan of teaching second-year Chemistry was inaugurated, using a new text and manual on which Professor Chapin has been working for several years. Professor Holmes, the head of the Department, feels that the results of the new plan have been highly satisfactory. Professor Holmes urges the need of larger salaries for teaching assistants, and of more provision for research in teaching time.

The Department of *Geology* notes that students doing major work in Chemistry are electing Economic Geology to a considerably larger extent than earlier; and that within the past year not less than five leading institutions have definitely asked for graduate students of Geology from the College, and that others have written for advanced students who might become teachers.

The Department of *Physical Education* calls attention to the fact that three graduates who completed the major in Physical Education for men are all now engaged in Government service of some sort. The demand for graduates of the Teachers' Course in Physical Education for men continues to be much greater than the supply of candidates for positions.

Professor Williams of the Department of *Physics* urges the special needs of that Department. He believes the Department cannot really do the work that it ought to do, without greatly augmenting its material resources, increasing the teaching staff, and furnishing housing accommodations that can hardly be secured in Peters Hall. A new building for the Department of Physics seems to be one of the early building needs of the College. This call from the Department of Physics is perhaps all the more justified because, as Professor Williams says and as the President has often emphasized, the region in which Oberlin lies is likely to become a great industrial center, lying as it does where coal and iron ore meet. And it would be particularly appropriate that a part at least of the Hall bequest should go into providing for a much larger growth in the Department of Physics. Increased interest in the advanced courses in Physics and *Astronomy* has been shown, and the need of at least a modest provision for a suitable building for Astronomy, as well as for the new building for Physics, is urged.

The Department of *Zoölogy* reports that the enrolment in the class in General Zoölogy was the largest in ten years.

The laboratory directions for the course have been revised, enlarged, and printed as a loose-leaf manual. Some specially successful research work by students, both graduate and undergraduate, was done. The appointment of a college Mechanician for the coming year, and of a new Instructor in the Department of Zoölogy, are noted as decided advances. The Department urges that the College become a regular supporter of the Marine Biological Laboratory at Woods Hole.

The Department of *History* reports gains from the division of the large elementary course into sections, made possible by the appointment of an additional Instructor on part time. With the current year this part time Instructor is replaced by a full time Assistant Professor.

The Department of *Economics* outlines plans for the development of the Department with the expected increase in its teaching staff for 1918-19 and thereafter.

The Department of *Political Science* properly urges again the great importance of this Department, especially in present world conditions. The need of another teacher on full time is urged.

The Department of *Sociology* reports increasing numbers in the sociological courses.

In the Department of *Philosophy* Professor Kitch believes that a gain in interest in philosophical problems has come through a completer indication of the practical bearings of these problems. There are increased numbers in the advanced philosophical courses for the current year. The Department is offering a new course under the title "The Evolution of Social Forms, or the History of Etiquette."

The proposed extension in the Department of *Psychology,* for the current year, was partly defeated by the leave of absence granted to Professor E. S. Jones, almost immediately following his appointment. But an Instructor has been appointed, and the Department hopes that the enlarged plans are only delayed.

The Department of *Education* reports recognition of practice teaching as entitled to college credit, as the most important gain for the year.

Reference may be made directly to Dean Cole's report for the *general suggestions* of the Faculty which indicate some clear possibilities of gain in various directions. Attention may be called to a few special points. Suggestions are thus made of the possible gain: of supervised study for some of the Freshman and Sophomore work, with well prepared study coaches to assist; of more conference between Advisers as to the function and technique of the Adviser; of encouraging more research by Faculty and students; of a stricter standardization of so-called seminar courses; of larger influence of the College in town affairs; of definitely reorganizing the college year on a four-term basis. Professor Sherman specially emphasizes the growing need of a college theatre, in view of the fact that the Dramatic Association has reached a point, beyond which it cannot hope to make a larger contribution to community life without such a theatre.

In the Dean's consideration of the statistics concerning *instruction,* it appears that for the year under review, thirteen courses announced in the bulletin were not given, because they were not elected by a sufficient number of students. Five of these were Honors courses. On the other hand, four courses not announced in the bulletin were organized and given. In the two semesters of 1916-17 there were 506 classes and sections—26 more than for the preceding year. The average enrolment of all classes for the year 1916-17 was 22.7; the corresponding figures for the two preceding years were 23 and 23.1. There were six Departments in which the average size of classes and sections exceeded 30. Any figures concerning the average size of classes are necessarily somewhat misleading, since the average figure may be greatly affected by either a few very small courses or a few very large courses. The important point is to keep courses not definitely lecture courses down to numbers small enough to make instruction in them thoroughly effective.

In the section concerning *students*, the details concerning the scholarship of the students are fully given.

The *administrative work* of the Dean continued to be very heavy, for the year under review, because he was still carrying both the Deanship of the College and the active Deanship of the College Men. With the current year the Acting Deanship of College Men has been transferred to Professor Nicol, and some real relief is thus afforded Dean Cole, although the amount of work centering in his office, and for which he must have chief responsibility, is still probably too great.

The Dean again urges, as the most pressing of all the *needs* of the College of Arts and Sciences, an adequate recitation building, although there are a number of other needs only less urgent.

In making his report as Acting *Dean of College Men,* Dean Cole calls attention to the help given him for the year by Dr. Carl C. W. Nicol, who carried on the routine work in the office and assisted in the management of a number of disciplinary cases, and adds: "In the effectiveness of his work, and in the strength of the hold he secured upon the regard and respect of the men, Dean Nicol showed such ability and promise that he was unhesitatingly advanced at the end of the year to the position of Acting Dean, with entire responsibility for the office in the coming year." The most noteworthy feature of the year, from the point of view of the Dean of College Men, was the extended discussion, by a joint committee of Faculty and students, of conditions among the men students. The results of this discussion, as recommended to the Faculty, are thus summarized by Dean Cole:

1. To improve the rooming-house situation, it was recommended:

a. That the College establish two new rooming houses for men, each house to accommodate a group of about twenty men and to be under the house-government plan. This recommendation was adopted and the two groups were formed and accepted; but the whole plan was finally given up for the coming year because so many men from the groups went into federal service as to cause the disbanding of the rest, and the prospect of renting the houses, in view of the general falling off of attendance of men, was too remote to warrant trial of the plan until war conditions change.

b. That the dormitory section of the Men's Building be divided by permanent walls into four parts, each to accommodate from eighteen to twenty-two men; one section to be primarily for Seniors, one primarily for Freshmen, one primarily for officers of student organizations, and one to be undesignated; each section to be under the house-government plan, and the whole dormitory to be under a committee representing the several sections. This recommendation was accepted and has been carried out.

2. To improve the coaching of athletic teams it was recommended:

a. That a new assistant professorship be established in place of one of the instructorships in the department of Physical Education, the incumbent of which should be head coach of all teams.

b. That the College assume the part salary of two instructors, ordinarily amounting to $800 or $850, hitherto carried by the Athletic Association, leaving that amount free for the Association to use for supplementary coaching.

These two recommendations were adopted and have been put into effect for the coming year.

3. The question of forming a Men's League was left for consideration and action by the Men's Senate.

4. It was recommended, and voted, that the question of modifying the rule prohibiting the use of tobacco be laid over for two years, and then be considered on its merits; that meantime every effort be made to enlist student coöperation in securing adequate observance of the regulation.

There were in the immediate care of the *Dean of College Women,* during the academic year 1916-17, 644 women— 30 more than the preceding year. Through the coöperation of Miss Frances J. Hosford, former Dean of Academy

Women, who has been assisting Dean Fitch in her office, a careful record of all illnesses on the part of women, involving absences from classes has, for the first time, been kept and tabulated. This record shows an average of ten absences occasioned by illness for each woman. The fact that most impresses the Dean in this record is that over fifty per cent of these absences are due to comparatively slight illnesses, which are largely matters of hygiene. This seems to her, therefore, to be the place where effort for improved health must be chiefly made. There have been few cases of serious illness among college women. Both Dr. Fitch and Miss Hosford call attention to the unsatisfactory gas situation in Oberlin, as responsible both for difficulty with the eyes and attending headaches, and to a certain extent also for frequent colds. Dean Fitch speaks warmly of the work of Miss Dye, who was Secretary to the Dean for the year under review.

The records of the *Registrar* of the College of Arts and Sciences concern 1,077 students—48 more than for the preceding year. The usual exhaustive study is made of the losses and gains during the four years of the college course, for the class graduating last June. The percentage of graduation from the original membership of the class is slightly lower than that for 1916, and the percentage of loss at the end of the Freshman year is slightly larger than that for the preceding year. The Registrar believes that the higher standards adopted in scholarship account in part for the increased percentage of loss, but expects that with a fuller understanding of these standards and the methods now in use by the Committee on Admission, this loss will decrease. The Registrar's report includes a table showing the *choice of majors* of the last five classes. For the year 1916, the Departments registering the largest number of major students, in order, are English, History, Latin, Political Science, Physical Education, German, and Chemistry, Economies, and Sociology (the same number), and French and Mathematies (the same number).

The Registrar's records also show that 179 men withdrew in the second semester for some form of *service* to *their country*: 30 in the U. S. Naval Reserve, 5 in the U. S. Navy, 4 in the U. S. Army, 1 in the British Army, 8 in the American Ambulance service abroad, 2 in the Officers' Reserve Corps, 7 in the Cleveland Lakeside Hospital Unit, 1 in a Youngstown Hospital Unit, 1 in a Chicago Hospital Unit, 2 in the Medical Reserve Corps, 1 in industrial service, and 117 in agriculture. Twenty-two women also withdrew for agricultural work.

In connection with this statement of withdrawals from college for some form of service called out by the war, attention should be called to a report, printed elsewhere, from Mr. John E. Wirkler, Adjutant of the *Oberlin College section of the Intercollegiate Intelligence Bureau.*

The Intercollegiate Intelligence Bureau was organized in Washington in February, 1917, with the approval of the national government, with branches in most of the important colleges and universities, in order that these institutions might place at the disposal of the Government helpful information concerning its students and recent graduates. In connection with the Oberlin section, Mr. Wirkler reports that approximately 4,000 printed letters and census blanks were sent to present students, to all graduates from 1890 to 1916, to former students of the last three years, and to college officers and Faculty members. The resulting material has been made available in a card file of more than 6,000 cards. Since the establishment of the Bureau in Oberlin, Mr. Wirkler reports that 68 emergency requests, calling for one or more applicants, have been received, and these calls have permitted the Adjutant to bring to the attention of the national Bureau at Washington the qualifications of over 250 candidates. There is no machinery for reporting back to

the local Bureau the acceptance of the candidates, so that
it is difficult to give information as to the number of Oberlin
men receiving appointments through the Bureau.   The one
group of men who may be said organically to represent
Oberlin in the war is the Oberlin College Ambulance Unit
now at Allentown, Pa., which brought together a group of
45 men of the most recent generation of students for service
under the Government; though considerably more or less
unified groups are in other branches of service. A recent
study by the Adjutant seems to indicate that 268 present and
former students are active in some form of government service on account of the war: 77 in the Army, 45 in the Navy,
21 in Aviation, 58 in Ambulance Corps, 16 in Hospital service, 30 in Y. M. C. A. and relief work, 13 in special service,
and 8 in miscellaneous appointments. Of this number probably 44 are abroad. But it should be emphasized that these
figures by no means can be counted upon as indicating all
of the Oberlin graduates and non-graduates now in service.
Professor Sherman, as Secretary of the Oberlin Red Cross,
is supplementing this work, by seeking to put present Oberlin students and other friends into occasional communication
with Oberlin men already engaged in some form of national
service.

The report of the Secretary of the College as *Chairman
of the Committee on Admission* makes a study of the entire
enrolment of the College of Arts and Sciences. The report
shows that 337 students of Freshman rank came to the College from 218 different high schools, academies, and other
preparatory schools. At the same time, 60 students came to
us for advanced standing from 42 different colleges. The
number of men in the two upper classes in college has naturally been much affected by enlistment for the war; but the
Freshman enrolment is nearly normal, and the loss in attendance of men in the upper classes has been largely made good
by admitting a larger number of women. The result is that

the final attendance total in the College of Arts and Sciences for the first semester of the present year is 925, which shows a loss considerably less than was calculated upon in the making of the budget for the year. The army draft and other circumstances may change this favorable showing in the second semester. The British and Canadian experience, as well as that of other belligerents, has made so clear the need of keeping up the supply of younger men in the colleges and universities, even for the sake of the war and the after-the-war settlement, that the President ventured to emphasize this point in a letter to all Alumni in June.

The Graduate School of Theology

Dean Bosworth's report shows that the students in the Graduate School of Theology for the year under review numbered 52, of whom 2 were women. Of the fifteen men who received degrees at the last commencement, five have gone to foreign missionary work, two into the work of the Y. M. C. A. and Y. W. C. A., one is a member of a Hospital Unit in France, one in doing further graduate study, and six are pastors.

Dr. Ian C. Hannah began his stimulating work as Professor of Church History with the second semester of the year. For the current year the amount of *teaching* in the theological department has been somewhat reduced for several reasons. Dean Fiske is taking his sabbatical year, after ten years of hard and effective service, at present working in the libraries in and about Cambridge, Mass. Professor MacLennan, who offers a number of courses open to theological students, is also absent on leave for the year, but is undertaking educational work in one of the eastern army camps. And Professor Hutchins has been granted a special leave of absence for the first semester to assist the Y. M. C. A. in the organization of religious work in Camp Sheridan, at Montgomery, Ala. To replace in part the work so withdrawn,

Professor Walter Rauschenbusch, of Rochester Theological Seminary, was secured to give two two-hour courses for the first eight weeks of the semester, and Professor Frank H. Foster, Professor of Church History here from 1882 to 1892, to give a two-hour course in Homiletics for the last ten weeks of the semester. Professor Fullerton also is to offer a course of the same length in Biblical Homiletics.

The attendance of the theological department has been seriously affected by war conditions. Most of those whose earlier correspondence indicated that they were planning to enter the School of Theology this fall were called into army work, either as soldiers or as Y. M. C. A. secretaries. This has reduced the attendance at the present time to 38, 5 of whom are women. This figure will probably be increased a little at the beginning of the second semester. The attendance, though smaller, is as cosmopolitan as ever. Thirty universities, colleges, and theological schools are represented, and the home addresses of the students are in eighteen states and two foreign countries.

With the provision made by the Trustees for increase in salaries, the two outstanding *needs* of the School of Theology are suitable buildings, and the endowment of the Student Employment Fund, as already noted by the Assistant to the President.

The Conservatory of Music

The *Director* of the Conservatory is able to report that, after meeting all the expenses of the year, the Conservatory has found it possible to reduce the advances on Rice Memorial Hall by more than $11,000.

The String Department of the Conservatory gave an unusual number of concerts during the year under review. Dr. Andrews, Professor Stiven, and Professor Alderfer have continued the series of free organ recitals on the great organ in the Chapel, before increasingly interested audiences. Dr.

Andrews has besides given various recitals in different parts of the country.

The Director is gratified that the concerts in the Artist Recital course are proving increasingly attractive, not only to Oberlin, but to surrounding towns. The course is unquestionably of an unusually high order.

The outside work and publications of the Conservatory Faculty, and the changes in that body, are shown elsewhere.

In his courses in the History and Appreciation of Music, Professor Dickinson says, "I am trying more and more to show my classes how the culture derived from art is related to the larger life of the College, and also to the larger social and spiritual life of the world." A similar aim may properly be cherished in all our esthetic courses. The Organ Department of the Conservatory recognizes the great help that has come to the Department from the use of the great Chapel organ. Professor Heacox reports increasing satisfaction with the results of the keyboard training which was added to the courses in Harmony several years ago. The outcome of the experience of the last seven years in this work will soon be published in two volumes entitled "Keyboard Training in Harmony." With the current year the course in Public School Music is extended from two to three years, and this lengthening of the course brings up the question, as to whether graduates from it should not be given somewhat more formal recognition of their attainments upon completing this strong and dignified course for teachers. In incidental connection with this course in Public School Music, it is interesting to note that the Oberlin Board of Education has decided to give two units of credit in Music, beginning with the current year.

Many teachers in the Conservatory feel the need of endowment funds for scholarship aid. The need is hardly less great for scholarship aid in that Department than in the College and Graduate School of Theology. There would probably be some gain also in establishing a Conservatory

Bureau of Appointments, to help in the better placing of present and former students.

The *Dean of Conservatory Women,* Miss Frances G. Nash, reports that several favoring circumstances have made it possible for the present year to try the experiment of putting groups of first year conservatory women in two college houses—Allencroft and Ellis Cottage—and in a closely related private house. Forty-five in all are so provided for, and all board at Allencroft. So far the experiment seems to the Dean to be a real gain. Special satisfaction has been found in the use of Barrows House as a dormitory for conservatory women, and the house is increasingly becoming, under Miss Nash's plans, a valuable social center. The Dean feels that there has been closer coöperation than perhaps ever before on the part of the conservatory women in the Women's League and in all the common concerns of the women of the entire institution.

The Library

The *Librarian,* Professor A. S. Root, makes as usual a comprehensive report. The gifts to the Library have already been mentioned. The large number of volumes coming by gift to the Library is a constant surprise. But the Librarian makes an especial appeal for early printed books, as he says: "Every early printed book, every sixteenth century pamphlet, every book which marks an epoch in the scholarship of any given field, adds to the ability of the Library to help trace the development of knowledge. Our main dependence must be upon those who have these older books, which are becoming too expensive to be bought with the funds available for purchases. There must be among our graduates and among friends of the College many collectors of these books of earlier generations."

The gifts to the Library, with purchases and exchanges, have added during the year 10,997 bound volumes, making the entire number of bound volumes now in the Library 175,625. There were about 900 more additions of bound volumes than in the preceding year. Besides the bound volumes, the Library has 147,555 unbound volumes and pamphlets catalogued, and 5,950 unbound volumes of newspapers. The total number of catalogued pieces under the charge of the Librarian has now reached 361,094. The work of the cataloguing department was larger in amount than ever before, but even so, the department was not able to keep pace with the growing number of additions. The Librarian thus briefly summarizes the work of this department for the year:

> During the year 10,890 bound volumes were catalogued and 6,357 pamphlets and unbound volumes were catalogued. This involved the preparation of 46,942 new cards for the catalogue and the alteration, chiefly by the incorporation of additional information, of 18,382 cards previously written. 9,150 cards were withdrawn from the catalogue. These were largely written cards, mostly 2x5 size, which were replaced by the printed cards of the Library of Congress. Our card catalogue is now estimated to contain 519,161 cards.

The average daily attendance at the Library for the entire year, *including* the summer and all other vacations, was 700, a gain of 41 over the previous year. 5,093 persons, almost exactly the same as last year, drew 63,841 books for use outside of the building during the year. This figure also is very nearly the same as last year. The Librarian is looking forward with much satisfaction to the installation of two additional floors of stacks in the space previously occupied by the Olney Art Collection, though even this addition will hardly meet the needs of the library for more than three or four years.

Professor Root feels that his leave of absence, acting as Principal of the Library School connected with the New York Public Library, proved very much worth while, and he pays warm tribute to the work of Mr. Keyes D. Metcalf, of the New York Public Library and of the class of 1911, who was Acting Librarian in his absence.

Other General Officers

There remains to be reviewed the work of various other officers of the College, who have to do with certain aspects of the work of the entire institution: the Chairman of the Women's Board, the Director of the Men's Gymnasium, the Director of Athletics, the Director of the Women's Gymnasium, the Secretary of the Bureau of Appointments, the Director of the Summer Session, and the Superintendent of Buildings and Grounds.

The report of the *Chairman of the Women's Board,* Dr. Florence M. Fitch, records the fact that there have been under the care of the Deans of Women during the year under review 1,060 women. There have been no serious cases of discipline, and the women's interests have gone forward with unusual satisfaction on every side. The Women's League, which includes in its organization all the women of the institution, has finished its fourth year. Its significance in the life of the women, the Dean believes, has become so apparent that there is no uncertainty as to its continuance and increasing influence. Under the auspices of the League a very valuable vocational conference was held March 22-23, with speakers from outside presenting a number of new fields for women's work. The Home Girls Association was organized under the leadership of Miss Dye, Secretary to the Dean of College Women, and was officially recognized as a department of the League.

The Women's Advisory Committee, made up of Faculty women, continued its work through its five regular sub-committees: the Committee on Curriculum, the Social Committee, the Committee on Recreation, the Committee on Self-Supporting Students, and the Committee on Health. Under the auspices of the last Committee, of which Dean Nash is Chairman, arrangements were worked out for taking the Metcalf house at 268 Forest street as an infirmary for women students, as already described. Miss Thorp, a graduate nurse of Lakeside Hospital, is in charge of this infirmary. Dean Nash pays a specially high tribute to Miss Swazye, the visiting nurse of last year, who made 1,400 calls upon sick girls, and gave bed-side care to 467. The College was sorry to lose her services at the end of the year. 89 girls were cared for at the Browning house, which was used in part for an infirmary last year.

At the request of the Chairman of the Women's Board, Miss Hosford did most valuable work in personal conferences with the matrons of the various boarding houses. The aim in these conferences has been, as reported by Dean Fitch, three-fold: to secure an accurate report of the number of students in each house, and of its capacity and conditions, especially as to light and plumbing; to consult about individual students who are in need of special care along any line; and to give the matrons such encouragement and suggestions as may make their service more efficient. This is a piece of work that the Deans have long wished to be able to do, but which has become possible for the first time now through Miss Hosford. The matrons of the college halls are working out a uniform accounting system, and it is hoped that it may be possible soon to unify still further the business management of these halls. It seems impossible to solve satisfactorily the various problems involved in the halls of residence for the women without having more of these halls under the control of the College. It is especially recommended that the few college dormitories, which are still gas lighted, should be wired for electricity as soon as possible. At the request of the President, the Women's Board have made a careful study of the needs of the women, and of the

social life of the College, and their thoughtful and compre_
hensive report may be most properly included at this point.

The chief social problems are two—housing and rec.
reation.

It is the judgment of the Board that as rapidly as pos.
sible college residence halls should be supplied for all
women who wish to live in them. If the enrolment of the
women continues stationary at about 1,000, there would be
needed accommodations for approximately 750 to 800, the
remainder being young women whose homes are in town
or who work in private families or for other reasons
prefer to live in more quiet homes. There should, there.
fore, be added to our present equipment the enlargement of Barrows House and, if possible, of Shurtleff Cottage and the addition of six other buildings, accommoda.
ting an average of fifty to sixty. It would not be desirable, even if it were possible, to make so large a provision suddenly but probably one building could be added
every two or three years without embarrassing the situation of the town matrons.

The question of recreation seems naturally to devolve
upon women for study, although it concerns men as well as
women. The need of the men is perhaps even greater
than that of the women because women have more of the
home-making instinct and therefore utilize resources at
hand. The nation-wide interest in recreation and the recognition of its educational value make it suitable that the
college should plan for this means of enriching the life
of its students.

In Oberlin the social life of the students centers largely
in the boarding houses. On the whole, this has been desirable and furnishes much of the distinctive charm of the
Oberlin life, but it has its perils and limitations, and needs
to be supplemented, especially when the group is small and
not congenial and where one or two upper classmen are
isolated among younger students. There is danger of
too great freedom and lack of dignity because of the very
intimacy of the life. It is, also, difficult to combine the
good times of the household with suitable conditions for
receiving calls. Furthermore the natural desire ''to get
out in the free hour after dinner and do something'' tends

to make people restless. On the physical side, especially to relieve nervous strain, there is need for exercise in the form of play, for an opportunity to relax and lose self-consciousness; here lies the value of real amusements as contrasted with lectures and formal social engagements. For "the socially available" men and women there should be something more wholesome than picture-shows and evening strolls. For the student who is isolated or timid or abnormal there should be opportunity to be with other men or women in informal companionship, to meet and know the other sex in a natural, spontaneous, and yet impersonal way, and to carry a certain amount of responsibility for others' enjoyment and so to learn to forget one's self.

These recreational needs must be met by plans for the life of the men themselves, or the life of the women, and for men and women together both formally and informally. In this study we include merely informal social life. Formal occasions are not essentially recreational and do not call for any equipment other than that which is under the recreational needs, to be listed later. The requirements for the men are being considered by other committees. For the women there should be provided in all the larger halls a recreation room for women alone, distinct from the parlors which are open to men. There should be also a center open every evening to all women with some simple entertainment planned and a different committee as hostesses each evening. This would make possible the further development of class fellowship, of the organization of the town girls, general sings and other forms of social comradeship. Further athletic development would be of help here. There should be gatherings for organized play for miscellaneous groups and places for classes, societies, and other congenial groups to meet under influences which guard against crudeness and undue familiarity. For couples and groups of couples there should be quiet places to talk other than the street and a chance to do things together, which is the "best safeguard against unwholesome sentimentality." Rooms for games and reading, and small entertaining in groups would provide this opportunity.

The needs in the way of equipment are therefore:

1. A Director of Recreation to study the situation, to supervise, to utilize faculty coöperation, and to direct committees of students. She would also be able to enlist those students who especially need such experience. It would be desirable to have such a woman at once for part time at least. She might be able to combine with this some assistance in the gymnasium or teaching eurhythmic dancing in the Conservatory. Even our present resources could be utilized much more fully than they are if someone had·time to give to it; it it not right to ask much help from the gymnasium teachers who already have full schedules. Ultimately this director should have all her time for the recreational work.

2. More adequate lighting of the campus seats. It should be possible to make the campus a social center during the fall and spring where informal concerts by the band and mandolin clubs, class sings, story telling hours, and informal talks would provide entertainment. Country group dancing might also be introduced as an attractive feature, under proper supervision.

3. Lighting the tennis courts would increase their usefulness.

4. The Women's Building seems the most important addition to equipment. It should not be utilized as a dormitory and therefore would probably need some endowment. It should provide a center for the various activities and interests of the women and for the social life of couples and small groups of men and women. It might, also, serve temporarily for the mixed social life of the college.

5. Ultimately there should be a large social center open every afternoon and evening with an auditorium, equipped for moving pictures, for amateur dramatics and for entertaining lectures and readings. There should be rooms for organized games, bowling alleys, et cetera, and a floor for roller skating.

6. Swimming pools would contribute to wholesome recreation as well as to gymnasium work.

7. An artificial ice rink would be a most valuable asset in providing out of door recreation during the winter months. It has been suggested that if placed

near the ice plant, perhaps on the farm land of the Academy property, its maintenance would not be a heavy expense.

In submitting these recommendations the Women's Board would express its conviction that it is as important that the students be supplied with opportunities for thoroughly wholesome and uplifting recreation as that other needs, which we think of as more distinctly the responsibility of the college, should be met.

The Report of the *Director of the Men's Gymnasium,* Dr. F. E. Leonard, shows that 87.13 per cent of the men in all departments made some use of the gymnasium; and 97.42 per cent of college undergraduates. The corresponding percentages for 1915-16 were 87.42 and 96. This is a remarkable record. The percentage of undergraduates enrolled in *credit* classes was 48.71, as compared with 46.44 in 1915-16. The gymnasium also served four Boys' Clubs from the town, and a beginning was made in the way of accommodating boarding house groups for "play nights", as part of the movement for more wholesome recreation for our young men and women. The Director made a total of 207 physical examinations, including 34 reëxaminations. The men of the teaching and coaching staff continued their practice of meeting at regular intervals for a departmental luncheon, at which problems of policy and management were taken up and discussed informally. There were twelve such gatherings during the year. The chief advance noted in the Physical Education work was the appointment of an Assistant Professor in Physical Education in place of one of the three instructors.

The report of Dr. Leonard completes twenty-five years of his service as Director of the Men's Gymnasium—a period that has seen phenomenal gains in the physical education work of the College.

The *Director of Athletics,* Professor C. W. Savage, thus sums up the athletic history of the year 1916-17:

The unusual conditions occasioned by the world war, the loss of our regular foot ball coach, through illness, and the disciplining of sub-rosa fraternities, combined to give Oberlin the poorest record she has ever made in intercollegiate sports, and reacted unfavorably upon the interest taken in intramural activities.

The track season alone may be considered unusually successful. The Track Team, coached by Mr. Curtis, won the triangular meet with Case and Wooster; defeated Case in an impromptu dual meet hurriedly arranged to take the place of the meet cancelled by Ohio-Wesleyan, and easily won second place in the meet of the Ohio Intercollegiate Athletic Association at Columbus. In this meet, Captain Edwin H. Fall won the mile run, setting a new Ohio record at 4:20 3-5; and the Oberlin relay team won the beautiful one-mile relay cup. At the Western Conference Meet in Chicago, Captain Fall, single-handed, won fourth place for Oberlin by winning the one-mile run in the remarkable time of 4:16 4-5, a new Western Conference record; and by shortly afterward returning to the track and winning the two-mile run in 9:41.

Professor Savage feels that the unfortunate day mentioned in his last report as probable (when it would become necessary to abandon all forms of intercollegiate sport not financially profitable, such as tennis, track, soccer, cross country, and base ball, together with all intramural activities) has arrived, unless relief is found. That relief can come as the Director sees it, only by finding and setting aside an endowment for this phase of the work of the College, or by adopting a student athletic fee to be paid with the tuition, as is the case today in most of the Ohio colleges. The completion of the athletic fields remains as the paramount need, after the indebtedness of the Athletic Association has been cleared away.

Professor Savage reports a special meeting of the National Collegiate Association at Washington on August 2nd, called to decide the question of the continuance of intercollegiate sports during the period of the war. The resultant resolutions emphasize the ideals for which Oberlin has tried for years to stand: athletics of all instead of the few, no pre-season coaching, no training tables, professional coaching minimized, expenses reduced, and eligibility maintained. But it is unfortunate, as the report points out, that at just the time when the greater extension of athletic sports is advised as a war efficiency measure, Oberlin finds herself face to face with the necessity of curtailment.

Dr. Delphine Hanna, the *Director of the Women's Gymnasium,* expresses the satisfaction of the Department of Physical Education for Women in the purchase of the Black farm on Lake Erie, already referred to. She also outlines the proposed three months course for medical aides, for which the Government asked. The government plans for these courses for medical aides seem to have been held up for the present. The Director and Dr. Cochran have given a good deal of time to drawing up plans for a new gymnasium, so that the full result of their inquiries might be available for the architect, as soon as the means were at hand for this needed building.

The report shows that 520 women in the different departments of the institution took regular work in the gymnasium; and in addition to this number 138 members of the Gymnasium and Field Association, who were not doing gymnasium work, were supervised in their sports. Many women shared in field hockey, basket ball, base ball, class tennis, and tennis tournaments. The number of women who completed their two semesters of ten-mile walks was 83. 357 new students received physical examinations, and 200 were reëxamined. The Freshman required work seems to be going forward satisfactorily. Following the general recreational plan outlined last year, the Director reports that different houses were invited once a week for play hours at the men's and women's gymnasia; the leaders were provided from the departments of Physical Education and the Seniors doing major work in Physical Education. The number of students in the Teachers' Course in Physical Education for the year was 77. The Director feels that the Gymnasium and Field Association is making Dickinson House increasingly valuable as a recreation center for women, and believes that this will be still further helped by the fact that a tea room has been opened on the upper floor of Dickinson House, under the supervision of Mrs. Taylor, formerly matron of Barrows House.

Professor Lord makes a very suggestive report as *Secretary of the Bureau of Appointments*. He reports that with the entry of the United States into the war entirely new conditions arose, so that the work of the Bureau has been greatly changed and considerably increased. There have been many more calls for teachers than ever before, and many new lines of activity have been opened for our graduates. The Bureau has the unusual record of being able to report that not a single graduate registered with it is without employment. Some of the new features of the year have been the successful attempt to secure openings for men with a number of business houses; coöperation with the Chicago office of the U. S. Department of Labor; the unusual call during the latter part of the year and during the summer for women to replace men who had enlisted in government service; the very unusual demand for teachers, already mentioned; and a greater call than ever for teachers of Spanish. The Bureau was asked to make recommendations for 34 college positions, and the Secretary is sure that many more positions of this kind could be filled, if the College had more graduates with the Master's degree, to recommend. The Bureau has received almost twice as many calls this year as last—437 instead of 243. For the current year the Bureau plans to give much time to collecting and tabulating material to show what preparation is necessary for entrance to the various professions and occupations. This material might finally well find its way into a college bulletin.

The *Director of the Summer Session,* Professor S. F. MacLennan, reports an attendance of 111 students for the summer, of whom 15 were graduates. The attendance was 68 less than the previous year, and was undoubtedly much affected by war conditions. Thirty-four courses in all were given in this summer session, involving a total of 165 hours. The total number of instructors engaged was 14. On account of the reduced attendance, the summer session showed a small deficit.

The facts contained in the report of the *Superintendent of Buildings and Grounds,* Mr. Charles P. Doolittle, have been so largely anticipated in the consideration of the actions of the Prudential Committee as to require no discussion at this point.

The Work of the President

The work of the President has covered, as usual, administration, teaching, outside representation, publication, and financial work.

Much more time might profitably go to *administration* than is now possible. As the College grows, and the list of officers and teachers increases, much more time is really needed for personal conference on the part of the President, if the best results are to be obtained. This might ultimately mean that most of his teaching would have to be given up.

The President must naturally carry as one of his chief constant responsibilities the care for *the Chapel service,* which seems to him to deeply concern the inner life of the College. By vote of the Faculty, Dean Bosworth and the President each ordinarily take one of the Chapel services every week. The leadership of the other Chapel services devolves on other members of the Faculty, the ministers of the town, and invited speakers. There has been the usual variety in the

Chapel services of the year under review. Some special programs have been arranged from time to time, including song services, a memorial service for Alumni who had died during the year, addresses on the eighty-third anniversary of the founding of the College and on the anniversary of President Fairchild's birth, and a series of five services gathering around Handel's *Messiah*, arranged for the closing days of the fall term, just before Christmas. The students have had their vision enlarged during the year in connection with these Chapel services, by the presentation of many special causes in brief, thoughtful addresses. There has been thus brought home to them the significance of their own home Christian Association work, and of the work undertaken by the College in Shansi, China; of social settlement work, and of the Associated Charities; of Daily Vacation Bible Schools; of the Intercollegiate Prohibition Association; of the Federal Council of Churches; of Armenian and Syrian Relief; of the Y. M. C. A. work in prison camps; of the work of Constantinople College; and of the point of view of the English ''Fellowship of Reconciliation.'' Addresses on various aspects of the war have been made by a number of speakers, including Dr. Kelman of Edinburgh, Professor Porter of Yale, and Dr. John R. Mott. The President gave a series of addresses on ''What the College Stands for.''

The *teaching* of the President as usual involved six hours of teaching weekly, besides the regular Sunday Bible Class: three hours with the theological Seniors, two hours with the theological Middlers, and one hour with college Seniors. For the current year he is carrying the full two-hour course with the college Seniors.

The work of the President in *outside representation* is summarized as usual in a later section of this report with similar appointments of other members of the Faculty.

The President's *publications* for the year are also noted
in a later section, in connection with those of other members
of the Faculty.

Even with the prospect of the income from Mr. Hall's
bequest, the year has not been free from pressing financial
needs at a number of points, several of them still unmet. But
the *financial work* of the President and his Assistant are
naturally reflected in the preceding sections of the report
and need not be further summarized here.

IV

FACULTY

Faculty Changes

The various changes which have occurred in the Faculty
during the year covered by this report, as authorized by the
Trustees, or by the Prudential Committee, acting *ad interim*
for the Trustees, are presented, arranged by departments.

The College of Arts and Sciences

ENTERING ON WORK AFTER LEAVE OF ABSENCE

Miss Delphine Hanna, Director of the Women's
Gymnasium; Professor of Physical Education, after one
semester's absence for needed rest.

William DeWeese Cairns, Associate Professor of
Mathematics, after one year's absence for study and travel.

LEAVE OF ABSENCE

Miss Delphine Hanna, Director of the Women's Gymnasium; Professor of Physical Education, for the second
semester, for needed rest.

Simon Fraser MacLennan, Professor of Philosophy
and Comparative Religion, for one year, for study and
travel.

Edward Safford Jones, Assistant Professor of Psychology; Secretary of the Bureau of Appointments, for one

year, for special service in Psychology in connection with the United States Army work, with the understanding that the leave may be extended if necessary. (Prudential Committee, September 21, 1917.)

Miss Mary Megie Belden, Instructor in English, for one year, for further study.

Miss Hazel Kyrk, Instructor in Economics, for one year, for further study.

Louis Finley Keller, Instructor in Physical Education, for one year, for service in the United States Army, with the understanding that the leave may be extended if necessary. (Prudential Committee, September 21, 1917.)

RESIGNATIONS AND END OF TERM OF SERVICE

Charles Nelson Cole, as Acting Dean of College Men, after three years of service.

Louis Eleazer Lord, Professor of the Latin Language and Literature; Secretary of the Bureau of Appointments; resignation as Secretary of the Bureau of Appointments, after two years of service.

George Ross Wells, Associate Professor of Psychology, after five years of service.

Howard Cone Curtis, Instructor in Physical Education, after two years of service.

Miss Charlotte Dell Easton, Assistant in Geology, after two years of service.

Miss Rossleene Merle Arnold, Assistant in Chemistry, after one year of service.

Harold Haydn Clum, Student Assistant in Botany, after one year of service.

Howard Eugene Rothrock, Student Assistant in Geology, after one year of service.

Miss Nelle Marie Frederick, Student Assistant in Zoölogy, after one year of service.

Miss Vera Elizabeth Dye, Secretary to the Dean of College Women, after one year of service.

Miss Dorothy Ann McAuley, Stenographer in the office of the Bureau of Appointments, after one year of service.

PROMOTIONS

Miss Helen Finney Cochran, Associate Professor of Physical Education, permanent appointment.

Leigh Alexander, Assistant Professor of Latin and Greek, permanent appointment.

Carl Conrad Wernle Nicol, Assistant Professor of Psychology and Philosophy; Assistant Dean of College Men; to be Assistant Professor of Psychology and Philosophy; Acting Dean of College Men; for one year.

Harold Lee King, Instructor in History and Economics, to be Assistant Professor of History, for two years.

Mrs. Mary Taylor Cowdery, Instructor in French, permanent appointment.

REAPPOINTMENTS

Louis Eleazer Lord, Professor of the Latin Language and Literature; Secretary of the Bureau of Appointments; reappointment as Secretary of the Bureau of Appointments, for one year. (Prudential Committee, September 21, 1917.)

Miss Edna Louise Brownback, Instructor in English, for one year.

Mrs. Ellen Birdseye Hatch, Instructor in Physical Education, for one year.

Miss Lucy Tufts Bowen, Instructor in Physical Education, for one year.

Miss Emma Ottilie Bach, Instructor in German, for one year.

Lester Middleswarth Beattie, Instructor in English, for one year.

Louis Finley Keller, Instructor in Physical Education, for one year.

David Paul Maclure, Instructor in Physical Education, for one year.

Miss Louise Rodenbaeck, Instructor in German, for one year.

Miss Jessie Stephen, Instructor in Fine Arts, for one year, part work.

Rudolph Frederick Brosius, Instructor in English, for one year. (Appointed by the Prudential Committee, February 1, 1917, for the remainder of the year.)

Miss Mary Irene Dick, Assistant in Physical Education, for one year.

Paul Henry Fall, Assistant in Chemistry, for one year. (Prudential Committee, August 30, 1917.)

Ting Fu Tsiang, Student Assistant in Botany, for one year.

NEW APPOINTMENTS

Arthur Irving Taft, Assistant Professor of English, for two years.

Edward Hill Cox, Assistant Professor of Chemistry, for one year.

Edward Safford Jones, Assistant Professor of Psychology; Secretary of the Bureau of Appointments; for two years.

Jacob Speelman, Assistant Professor of Physical Education, for one year.

Howard Hall ,Preston, Assistant Professor of Economics, for one year. (Prudential Committee, August 24, 1917.)

Edwin Lathrop Baker, Assistant Professor of French, for one year, part work. (Prudential Committee, September 21, 1917.)

Robert Stanley McEwen, Instructor in Zoölogy, for one year.

John Frederick Dashiell, Instructor in Psychology, for one year. (Prudential Committee, August 24, 1917.)

Harold Church Spore, Instructor in Physical Education, for one year. (Prudential Committee, September 21, 1917.)

Miss Clara Hyacinthe Scott, Graduate Assistant in Philosophy, for one year.

Miss Louise Caroline Pollitz, Student Assistant in Geology, for one year.

Miss Dorothy Dix Williamson, Student Assistant in Zoölogy, for one year.

Miss Eunice Agnes Kinnear, Student Assistant in Botany, for one year.

Miss Ruth Martha McFall, Stenographer in the office of the Bureau of Appointments, for one year. (Prudential Committee, August 18, 1917.)

Miss Dorothy Ellsworth Birkmayr, Assistant in Fine Arts, for one year. (Prudential Committee, October 18, 1917.)

The Graduate School of Theology

LEAVE OF ABSENCE

George Walter Fiske, Junior Dean of the Graduate School of Theology; Professor of Practical Theology, for one year, for study and travel.

William James Hutchins, Professor of Homiletics, for the first semester, for work as Religious Director in Camp Sheridan, Montgomery, Alabama. (Prudential Committee, November 9, 1917.)

NEW APPOINTMENTS

Professor Walter Rauschenbusch, as Special Lecturer offering two two-hour courses for eight weeks of the first semester. (Prudential Committee, November 9, 1917.)

Professor Frank Hugh Foster, as Special Lecturer offering one two-hour course for ten weeks in the first semester. (Prudential Committee, November 9, 1917.)

The Conservatory of Music

ENTERING ON WORK AFTER LEAVE OF ABSENCE

Karl Wilson Gehrkens, Associate Professor of Public School Music, after one semester's absence for further study.

CHANGE OF TITLE

Mrs. Margaret Jones Adams, Instructor in Singing, to be Assistant Professor of Singing, part work.

Mrs. Ada Morris Hastings, Instructor in Pianoforte, to be Assistant Professor of Pianoforte, part work.

Mrs. Amelia Hegmann Doolittle, Instructor in Pianoforte, to be Assistant Professor of Pianoforte, part work.

Mrs. Bertha McCord Miller, Instructor in Ear Training and Harmony, to be Principal of the Children's Department and Assistant Professor in the Normal Course in Pianoforte.

Mrs. Charlotte Demuth Williams, Instructor in Violin, to be Assistant Professor of Violin, part work.

LEAVE OF ABSENCE

Miss Margaret Holmes Whipple, Instructor in Piano and in the Normal Course in Piano Teaching, for one year.

RESIGNATION AND END OF TERM OF SERVICE

Harold David Smith, Instructor in Pianoforte and Theory, for service in the Field Hospital of the regular army, after two years of service. (Prudential Committee, November 9, 1917.)

PROMOTIONS

Maurice Koessler, Professor of Violin and Ensemble, permanent appointment.

Bruce Headley Davis, Associate Professor of Pianoforte, to be Professor of Pianoforte, permanent appointment.

Karl Wilson Gehrkens, Associate Professor of Public School Music, to be Professor of School Music, permanent appointment.

Miss Gladys Ferry Moore, Student Teacher in Harmony and Ear Training, to be Instructor in Ear Training and Theory, for one year.

Harold David Smith, Student Teacher in Harmony, to be Instructor in Pianoforte and Theory, for one year.

REAPPOINTMENTS

John Edgar Snyder, Instructor in Organ and Theory, for one year.

Donald Morrison, Instructor in Violin, for one year.

NEW APPOINTMENT

Miss Lelah Enid Harris, Instructor in the Children's Department, for one year.

University

ENTERING ON WORK AFTER LEAVE OF ABSENCE

Azariah Smith Root, Librarian; Professor of Bibliography, after one year's absence as Acting Librarian of the New York Library School.

RESIGNATIONS AND END OF TERM OF SERVICE

Keyes DeWitt Metcalf, Acting Librarian, after one year of service.

Miss Margrethe Grace Mattison, Assistant in the College Library, after one year and two and one-half months of service. (Resigned November, 1916, Prudential Committee, April 5, 1917.)

Miss Mabel Harlow, Assistant in the College Library, after five and one-half months of service. (Resigned February 20, 1917.)

Miss Mary Martha DeFord, Assistant in the College Library, after eight and one-half months of service. (Resigned July 31, 1917; in service since November 18, 1916.)

REAPPOINTMENTS

Miss Mary Jean Fraser, Assistant in the College Library, for one year.

Miss Hattie Maude Henderson, Assistant in the College Library, for one year.

Miss Edith Melvina Thatcher, Assistant in the College Library, for one year.

Mrs. Mary P. B. Hill Wright, Custodian of the Art Collection, for one year.

Miss Laura Nell Chase, Assistant in the College Library, for one year.

Miss Helen Black Morton, Assistant in the College Library, for one year.

Miss Millicent Ione Shepherd, Assistant in the College Library, for one year.

Miss Dora Cargill, Stenographer and Clerk in the Office of the Treasurer, for one year.

Mrs. Charlotte J. Ormsby, Stenographer in the Secretary's Office, for one year, part time.

Miss Annette Persis Ward, Reference Librarian, for one year.

Joseph Anthony Humphreys, Stenographer and Assistant in the Office of the Assistant to the President, for one year.

Miss Elizabeth Johnston McCloy, Assistant in the College Library, for one year.

NEW APPOINTMENT

Miss Clare Graefe, Assistant in the College Library, for one year.

The length of the list of changes in the Faculty might seem to indicate that the main teaching body was actually changing more rapidly than is the case. The number of single items is increased by the fact that the list includes a considerable number of annual appointments, and of appoint-ments of student assistants, who are naturally not long in service. It will not be necessary to review all the items in this long list of Faculty changes, but attention should be called to certain cases not mentioned in previous sections of this report.

Leaves of Absence

The leaves of absence for the year reflect, in a number of cases, the demands of the war service. Assistant Professor Edward S. Jones, Instructor Louis F. Keller, of the College of Arts and Sciences, and Professor William J. Hutchins, of the Graduate School of Theology, are all absent in some service called out by the war. Dr. S. F. MacLennan, also, of the College of Arts and Sciences, is actually putting his leave of absence into educational work in one of the eastern army camps, as already noted. One of the resignations also, that of Instructor Harold D. Smith of the Conservatory, is occasioned by his call to army service.

Resignations and End of Term of Service

It has already been explained that Dean Cole retires with the present year as Acting Dean of College Men, and Dr. Carl C. W. Nicol succeeds him, and that Professor Lord con-tinues his service as Secretary of the Bureau of Appoint-ments, on account of Professor E. S. Jones' leave of absence. The College is sorry to lose, from its department of Psy-chology, Associate Professor George R. Wells, who goes to a full Professorship at Ohio Wesleyan University.

Promotions

The promotions recorded in all departments are all in regular course and well deserved. They include six permanent appointments of strong teachers.

Reappointments

The reappointments also in all departments are of tried teachers and officers and are in line with the regular procedure of the College.

New Appointments

The increase in the teaching force made for the current year is shown especially in the number of important new appointments in the College of Arts and Sciences. Six Assistant Professors and three Instructors are added to the teaching staff of the College of Arts and Sciences, and of these new appointments only two (that of the Assistant Professor of Psychology and the Instructor in Physical Education) replace previous appointments. The others are an outright addition to the teaching force.

Mr. Arthur I. Taft, Assistant Professor of English, is a graduate of Yale University, from which he also holds the degree of Ph.D. For the past six years he has been instructor in English in Yale, and last year was entrusted with a lecture course heretofore carried by the distinguished Professor Beers, who retired the previous year. Mr. Taft has the warmest commendation from the Yale Department of English.

Mr. Edward H. Cox, Assistant Professor of Chemistry, is a graduate of Earlham College, where he studied under Dr. Holmes, now the Oberlin Professor of Chemistry. He has had two years of successful teaching in the University of Louisville, and has done a large amount of very success-ful and valuable research in organic chemistry, fully equivalent to that ordinarily required for a doctor's degree. He was last year a graduate student at the University of Illionis.

Mr. Edward S. Jones, Assistant Professor of Psychology and Secretary of the Bureau of Appointments, is the son of Dr. J. P. Jones, the noted missionary to India, and is a graduate of Oberlin College in the class of 1910. Since graduation Mr. Jones has taken the degree of Ph.D. at the University of Chicago, done notable work in the Vocational Bureau at Cincinnati, headed by Mrs. Helen Thompson Woolley, and taught successfully in secondary schools and in college. Last year he was instructor in Psychology at Northwestern University, working both in the College of Liberal Arts and in the School of Commerce. Mr. Jones, as already noted, has been granted leave of absence since his appointment.

Mr. Jacob Speelman, Assistant Professor of Physical Education, graduated from the University of Missouri, in the class of 1916. His course in the University was premedical, and included the fine work given there in Physical Education. His athletic record is a strong one, comprising three years on the Varsity foot ball and basket ball teams, and the captaincy of the foot ball team in his senior year. He was also the champion heavy-weight wrestler and boxer of the University. Last year he was Director of Athletics at Lawrence College, Appleton, Wisconsin. His recommendations are excellent in every respect.

Mr. Howard H. Preston, Assistant Professor of Economics, is a graduate of Coe College, Cedar Rapids, Iowa, in the class of 1911. He received his A.M. degree from the University of Iowa in 1914, after a year of graduate study. He was assistant instructor in the same University the following year, and instructor in 1915-16. In 1916-17 he was instructor in the University of Texas, from which he comes to our assistant professorship. The letters of recommendation regarding Mr. Preston's personality and strength as a teacher are most satisfactory.

Mr. Edwin L. Baker, Assistant Professor of French, received the degrees of Bachelor of Arts and Bachelor of Music from Beaver College, Beaver Falls, Pennsylvania, and the degree of Bachelor of Arts from Trinity College, Hartford, Connecticut, in 1905. His graduate study was done at the Universities of Oxford and Madrid, and at the Sorbonne, in Paris. He has taught very successfully in secondary schools, in Beaver College, and at Pennsylvania State College, giving instruction in the two collegiate institutions in Romance Languages and in Music.

Mr. Robert S. McEwen, Instructor in Zoölogy, is a graduate of Western Reserve University, and a post-graduate, with a degree of Ph.D., from Columbia University. His whole training in Zoölogy was obtained in Columbia, where he has had a prolonged graduate course. His recommendations are of the finest type. His experience is limited to laboratory assistance, but there is every indication that he will make a highly successful teacher.

Mr. J. Frederick Dashiell, Instructor in Psychology, graduated from Moores Hill College, Indiana, with the degree of B. S. in 1908, and B. L. in 1909. He has also received from Columbia University the degrees of A. M. in 1910 and Ph.D. in 1913. He has taught as an assistant in Columbia University, as professor in Waynesburg College, and as instructor in Moores Hill College, Princeton University, and the University of Minnesota.

The appointments of Professor Walter Rauschenbusch and of Professor Frank H. Foster as special lecturers in the Graduate School of Theology, have already been mentioned. The other new appointments are in regular course and call for no special comment.

Organization

The work of the Faculty for the year under review was carried forward quite as usual, and through its regular organization. Perhaps the most important *new* work done by the General Faculty was through the Committees on Art Museum, Chapel Service, Illumination and Alumni and Town Participation in Commencement, Living and Social Conditions, Men's Building, Religious Interests, and Women's Board, though the work of the other Committees has gone forward on the usual lines.

Important Official Actions

The more important actions of the College Faculty are reviewed in the report of the Dean of the College of Arts and Sciences. Reference need be made here, therefore, only to the actions of the General Faculty. The General Faculty have done the usual amount of routine business in all the directions indicated in their standing committees, but most of their more important actions for the year come up naturally for discussion in connection with other sections of this report and may therefore be passed without further comment at this point.

Outside Work and Lectures

Various members of the Faculty besides the President have, during the year, represented the College, both officially and unofficially, in wide and varied forms of activity outside of the regular work of the College. These forms of activity are recorded, as illustrating the many-sided ways in which the officers and teachers of the College are rendering service beyond the College, not only in academic, but in unacademic lines. For the College owes a service to the community outside its strictly academic functions. The following list is intended to summarize the outside work, lectures, appointments, official connections, and special honors of the members of the Faculty during the year.

KING, PRESIDENT HENRY C.

Lectures, sermons or addresses at educational institutions: Dartmouth College, address at the inauguration of President Hopkins on ''The Function of the College''; Carleton College, two addresses in connection with the Fiftieth Anniversary; Blake Country School, Minneapolis, Minnesota; University of Minnesota, address at the Chapel; University of Michigan, Tappan lecture; North High School, Syracuse, N. Y.; University of Chicago, Convocation Sermon; Lorain High School, Lorain, Ohio, commencement address; Oberlin Business College, Oberlin, Ohio, address; Erie High School, Erie, Pa., address at the Senior Banquet; Western Theological Seminary, Pittsburgh, Pa., commencement address and an address at the Alumni Dinner; Flora Macdonald College, Red Springs, N. C., commencement address; Wake Forest College, Wake Forest, N. C., commencement address; Emory University, Atlanta, Georgia, commencement sermon; Bellevue High School, Bellevue, Ohio, commencement address; Miami University, Oxford, Ohio, baccalaureate sermon; Goucher College, Baltimore, Maryland, commencement address; Michigan State Normal College, Ypsilanti, Michigan, commencement address; Blissfield High School, Blissfield, Michigan, commencement address; Seashore Divinity School, Biloxi, Mississippi, nine addresses; University of Oregon, Eugene, Oregon, six addresses.

Miscellaneous lectures and addresses:

Before educational gatherings: Syracuse Public School Teachers of Syracuse, N. Y.; Phi Beta Kappa Society of New York and vicinity; Cincinnati Women Teachers' Association, at Cincinnati, Ohio; Annual College Night, at Erie, Pa.; University Club, at Erie, Pa.; Women's College Club of Youngstown, Ohio; Home Economics Association, at Cleveland, Ohio; National Union of Massachusetts Institute of Technology Clubs, at Cleveland, Ohio; Lorain County Schoolmasters' Club, at Oberlin, Ohio.

Before commercial organizations: Electric League of Cleveland; Executives Club of Buffalo.

Before other organizations: New England Society of Cleveland; Sandusky Men's Literary Club, on ''The War, Its Political and Spiritual Aspects''; address on behalf of the

League to Enforce Peace before the meeting of the American Hospital Association at Cleveland.

Addresses on special religious occasions:

Sermons before churches: Plymouth Congregational Church, Minneapolis, Minnesota; First Congregational Church, Oberlin, Ohio; North Congregational Church, Detroit, Michigan; Union Lenten Service, Oberlin, Ohio; Chicago Sunday Evening Club; short address at the Fiftieth Anniversary of the First Congregational Church of Atlanta, Georgia; at the rededication of the Presbyterian Church at Kinsman, Ohio; Congregational Church, Eagle Rock, California; First Congregational Church, Eugene, Oregon; First Presbyterian Church, Portland, Oregon, two sermons.

Other special addresses: Before the Y. M. C. A. of Oberlin College; before the Y. M. C. A. of the University of Minnesota; at the annual meeting of the American Board of Commissioners for Foreign Missions, at Toledo, Ohio; before a Y. W. C. A. group at Oberlin, Ohio, on ''South America''; to the Men's Club of the St. Nicholas Collegiate Church of New York; before the Toledo Ministers' Union; at the Congregational Church of Elyria, Ohio; before the Y. M. C. A. at Detroit, Michigan; before the Young People of the North Congregational Church, Detroit; at Dr. Joseph K. Greene's funeral, Oberlin; before the Student Volunteer Band, Oberlin; before the Oberlin Social Science Club, at Oberlin; before the Lorain County Y. M. C. A. Parents' meeting, at Oberlin; to the Lorain County Boys, at Oberlin; before the Student Women's Christian Fellowship mass meeting, at Chicago; before the Congregational Ministers' Union of Chicago; at the Oberlin Patriotic Meeting; at the funeral of Mr. Herbert Spore; before the Congregational Club of Cleveland and vicinity; before the Y. W. C. A. of Oberlin College; at the Federal Council of Churches, at Washington, D. C., on ''The Church's Responsibility and Opportunity''; before the Cleveland Presbyterian Union, on ''The Spiritual Significance of the War''; before the Northern Baptist Convention, Cleveland, on ''The Changing National and International Order''; at the funeral of Mrs. S. G. Wright; before the Congregational Ministers' Meeting at Los Angeles, California, on ''The World War''; five addresses on World Problems, before a conference of Y. M. C. A. Employed Officers of Michigan, at Torch Lake.

To these should be added the President's address before the American Missionary Association at Minneapolis, Minn., the President's address before the Association of American Colleges at Chicago, Illinois, the baccalaureate sermon for the Graduate School of Theology of Oberlin, the College baccalaureate sermon at Oberlin.

Addresses at alumni gatherings: joint meeting of the St. Paul-Minneapolis alumni; Toledo; Cincinnati; Detroit; Mahoning Valley Association of Oberlin Alumni at Youngstown, Ohio; Buffalo; Pittsburgh; Portland, Oregon; Alumni Association of Puget Sound, at Seattle, Washington; Oberlin Association of the Inland Empire, Spokane, Washington; Review of the Year at the general alumni meeting at Commencement, in Oberlin.

Addresses at Oberlin in connection with the work of the College, including the opening address of the college year; Chapel address on ''Discipline and the Fraternity Cases''; address at the Foot Ball Banquet, Oberlin; the annual ad-address to the Men's Senate; brief address at the College Sing; address to the matrons of the College houses; series of Chapel addresses on ''The Function of the College''; Chapel address on ''The Church''; address at the Slavic Banquet; address at the dedication of the Dudley Peter Allen Memorial Art Building.

The President's Sunday Morning Bible Class, through the year, on ''Life Problems''; with two special addresses on ''War and the Teaching of Jesus.''

Attendance at the Executive Committee of the Latin American conference, in New York; at the meeting of the Trustees of the Carnegie Foundation for the Advancement of Teaching, at New York; at a conference on educational work in missions, at New York; at the annual meeting of the Board of Missionary Preparation, in New York; at the annual meeting of the Association of American Colleges, in Chicago; at the Conference on Religious Work of the Y. M. C. A., at Garden City, L. I.; at the Commission on Missions, in New York; at the meeting of College and University Executives, at Washington, D. C.; at the conference of representative Congregationalists with Mr. Hoover on Food Conservation, at Washington, D. C.

Elected member of the Commission on a Union Theological Seminary in Montevideo, of the Committee on Coöperation in Latin America, and made Chairman of a committee to work out recommendations of the South American Deputation concerning lectures on Apologetics in Latin America; member of the Committee on Christian Education in Institutions of Higher Learning, of the Federal Council of the Churches of Christ in America, and of the Executive Committee of the General War Commission of the Churches; member of National War Work Council of the Young Men's Christian Association, and of the Sunday School War Council; member of the Mexican Coöperation Committee; member of the sub-committee on War Prohibition of the Committee of Sixty on National Prohibition; honorary member of the Chinese Students' Alliance in the United States of America; reëlected President of the American Missionary Association, member of the Council of the Religious Education Association, and of the National Council of the American Institute of Social Service.

ALEXANDER, ASSISTANT PROFESSOR LEIGH

Lecture (illustrated) on ''Pompeii and Some of Its Amusements,'' at the Congregational Church in Amherst, O., before the History classes of the Oberlin High School, and before the fifth and seventh Grades at the Prospect St. School, Oberlin; lecture on ''The Rhodes Scholarships,'' before the Freshman class of Oberlin College.

Attended the meeting of the Rhodes Scholarship Selection Committee for the State of Ohio, at Columbus, in December, and the conference of the Classical Association of the Middle West and South, at Louisville, Ky., in April.

Member of the Auditing Committee of the Classical Association of the Middle West and South, and of the Rhodes Scholarship Selection Committee for the state of Ohio.

ANDEREGG, PROFESSOR FREDERICK

Attended the meetings of the American Mathematical Society at Chicago, in December, and at Cleveland, in September; of the Ohio College Association and the Ohio State Association of Mathematics and Science Teachers (presiding at the latter) at Columbus, in April; and at the meeting of the Mathematical Association of America, at Cleveland, in September.

ANDREWS, PROFESSOR GEORGE W.

Organ recitals as follows: at Kinsman, O., Lancaster, Pa., York, Pa., Cleveland, 3 (including one with other artists), in Finney Memorial Chapel, Oberlin, 12; concert, with other artists, at Des Moines, Ia.

Paper on "Organ Teaching," at the Cleveland meeting of the Ohio State Music Teachers' Association.

Director of the Oberlin Musical Union—2 winter concerts and May Festival concerts; Organist of the Second Congregational Church, Oberlin; Conductor of the Oberlin Conservatory Orchestra.

BOHN, ASSISTANT TO THE PRESIDENT W. FREDERICK

Addresses at the meetings of the Alumni at Chicago, Detroit, Toledo, and Cincinnati; and miscellaneous sermons and addresses on a variety of subjects, educational and patriotic.

Represented the College at the meeting of the Association of American Colleges at Chicago, called to discuss the question of "The Relation of the Colleges to Military Preparation."

BOSWORTH, DEAN EDWARD I.

An Easter address before the Cleveland ministers; two addresses before an Intercollegiate Ministerial Conference at Rochester Theological Seminary; a paper read before the theological section of the National Council; a series of war sermons at the Old Stone Church, Cleveland; preaching at Harvard.

Attended Alumni meetings at Dayton, O., Boston and Springfield, Mass., and Rochester, N. Y.

BOWEN, INSTRUCTOR LUCY T.

Extension lectures as follows: "The Value and History of the Playground Movement," at Wakeman, O.; "The Value of Play," before the Ninety-five Club, Elyria, O., the Parent-Teachers Association of Kenton, O., the Women's Civic Club of Akron, O., the Physical Education Conference for Public School Teachers at Lorain, O.

BRECKENRIDGE, PROFESSOR WILLIAM K.

Organist in First Congregational Church, Oberlin.

BUDINGTON, PROFESSOR ROBERT A.

Addresses as follows: "Pasteur and His Work," before the Ninety-five Club, and before the Men's Class of the Sec.

ond Congregational Church, both of Elyria; "Eugenics," before the Woman's Council of Akron, O., and the Teachers' Association, Y. M. C. A., of Lorain, O.

Attended the meetings of the Ohio Academy of Science, at Columbus, O., in April, and presented a paper entitled "Amphibian Blood Transfusion."

Member of staff of the Marine Biological Laboratory at Woods Hole, Mass., during the summer.

CAIRNS, ASSOCIATE PROFESSOR WILLIAM D.

Spent most of Sabbatical year of leave of absence in study at the University of Chicago.

Taught in the summer session of the University of Missouri.

Lectured before one of the Mathematical Clubs at the University of Chicago, and before the Mathematical Conference of the summer session of the University of Missouri; presented a paper in a discussion on the program of the Mathematical Association of America in September.

Attended the winter and summer meetings of the American Mathematical Society and the Mathematical Association of America at New York in December, and at Cleveland, in September; the meetings of the Chicago Section of the same Society, in December and April, the meeting of the Central Association of Science and Mathematics Teachers at Chicago, in November, and the meeting of the Oberlin Association of Illinois, in Chicago.

Reëlected Secretary-Treasurer of the Mathematical Association **of America for 1917.**

CASKEY, PROFESSOR WILLIAM G.

Judge in the Illinois-Michigan debate at Ann Arbor, in April.

CHAPIN, ASSOCIATE PROFESSOR WILLIAM H.

Talks on Agricultural Chemistry before the Oberlin High School, and before the Farmers Institute at Pittsfield, O.; two talks on the Principles of Good Gardening, before meetings of the Oberlin townspeople, and five before the young women engaged in war gardening.

Attended a meeting of the teachers of Science and Mathematics, at Columbus, in April, and presented a paper on "Graham's Law of Gaseous Diffusion"; and a meeting of the American Chemical Society, at Boston, in September.

COCHRAN, ASSOCIATE PROFESSOR HELEN F.

Attended the meeting of the Association of Directors of Physical Education for Women, at Randolph-Macon Woman's

College, Lynchburg, Va., in April, and gave a report on Enlarged Thyroid Gland.

Councillor at Pinewood Camp on Burt Lake, Mich., during the summer, gave physical examinations and had charge of tennis.

COLE, DEAN CHARLES N.

Address at Alumni Meeting at Cleveland, in October; address at the general Alumni Meeting at Commencement, on "Men's Interests in Oberlin College."

Attended the meeting of the Association of American Colleges, in Chicago, in January, presenting a committee report discussing a paper by Dr. C. H. French, on the Efficient College; and the meeting of the Ohio College Association at Columbus, in April, presenting the report of the Committee on Educational Policy.

DICKINSON, PROFESSOR EDWARD

Paper on "Music in Public Worship," before the Ohio Music Teachers Association, at Cleveland, in June.

DOMROESE, ASSISTANT PROFESSOR FREDERICK C.

Attended the meeting of the Association of Modern Language Teachers of the Central West and South, at Indianapolis, in April.

ELDRED, INSTRUCTOR MABEL C.

Studied in the Summer School of Teachers College, Columbia University.

FITCH, DEAN FLORENCE M.

Addresses as follows: Before the Conference of Deans of Women in connection with the N. E. A. at Kansas City (2); at the Conference of Deans in connection with the A. C. A. Convention in Washington; before the Cleveland College Club, the Nineteenth Century Club, Oberlin, the Women's Club, Kansas City, High Schools in Kansas City and Amherst, O., Kent State Normal College, First Congregational Church, Lorain, O., and a union meeting of women and girls in Lorain; in connection with the work of the College, a series of five talks for Freshman Women, addresses before the Y. M. C. A., the Y. W. C. A., and the Women's League, as well as at smaller Oberlin gatherings.

Taught a class on China at the ten day Pacific Coast Student Conference of the Y. W. C. A. at Asilomar, Cal.

Attended the meeting of Oberlin Alumni at Kansas City.

Member of the ''Committee on the Recognition of Colleges'' of the Association of Collegiate Alumnae, and attended committee meetings in New York and Washington.

FULLERTON, PROFESSOR KEMPER

Papers before the Society of Biblical Literature and Exegesis, at Philadelphia, in December, and the American Oriental Society, at Boston, in April; lectures on Jerusalem before the Men's Club of Beaver, Pa., and the Congregational Church of Madison, O., and on Zionism before the Congregational Ministers' Association of Cleveland; a number of addresses and sermons before various organizations and in the various churches in Oberlin.

GEHRKENS, ASSOCIATE PROFESSOR KARL W.

Spent the second semester in study in New York City.

Several lectures in Professor Farnsworth's classes at Teachers College, New York; address on ''Democracy in Music Education'' for the Public Lecture Course in the University of Colorado, and three full courses of lectures in the summer session of that University.

Elected a Director of the Music Teachers' National Association, for three years, and appointed Chairman of the Committee on Public School Music; continued as Director of the Supervisors' National Conference, and member of the N. E. A. Committee on High School Music.

GEISER, PROFESSOR KARL F.

Attended the meeting of the American Political Science Association at Cincinnati, in December, and was appointed Chairman of the Section Program.

Taught in the summer session of Columbia University.

GROVER, PROFESSOR FREDERICK O.

Four talks and addresses on various subjects, in and about Oberlin.

Attended the annual field meeting of the Josselyn Botanical Society of Maine, at Moosehead Lake, in August.

HANNA, PROFESSOR DELPHINE

Studied the treatment of Infantile Paralysis in the New York American Baby Hospital, and in the Children's Hospital at Boston, during a part of the summer.

HANNAH, PROFESSOR IAN C.

Lectures on ''The Far East and the New Map of Europe,'' at the summer session of the University of Oklahoma, at

Norman; on "The History of Architecture" at the summer session of the University of Colorado, at Boulder; on "The New Map of Europe," at the annual meeting of the Williamsport, Pa., Teachers Institute.

Elected Fellow of the Society of Antiquaries, one of the Royal Societies of England.

HATCH, INSTRUCTOR ELLEN B.

Extension lectures as follows: on "Physical Training in the Grades," before the Wellington Public School Teachers; "The Value of Play," before the Civic Club at Rocky River, O.; "Playgrounds," before the Oberlin Prospect School Parent-Teachers Association; "Play and Games in Elementary Schools," before the Physical Education Conference for Public School Teachers, at Lorain, O.

Taught and studied in the Chautauqua Summer School of Physical Education.

HOLMES, PROFESSOR HARRY N.

Lectures as follows: "Colloid Research," before the Cleveland Section of the American Chemical Society; "The Formation of Crystals in Gels," before the Mellon Institute, Pittsburgh, the Franklin Institute, Philadelphia, the Johns Hopkins University, and the University of Nebraska.

Three research papers before the Kansas City meeting of the American Chemical Society: "Silicic Acid Gels," "Rhythmic Banding," and "Peptization and Gel Formation of the Ferric Arsenate and Phosphate."

Represented the Cleveland Section of the American Chemical Society as Councillor at the national meeting in Kansas City.

HUBBARD, PROFESSOR GEORGE D.

Addresses and talks as follows: "Knowledge and Faith" before the Men's Bible Class at Elyria, and the Community League at Fairview, O.; "Local Geology of Interest to Sportsmen," before the Oberlin Rod and Gun Club; "Soils, Their Origin and Nature," before the County Y. M. C. A.'s, at Pittsfield, O., and at Rochester, O.; "Possible Local Glaciation in Southern Vermont," before the Association of American Geographers, at New York City; "History of Development of the Great Lakes," before the Community Men's Club of Calvary Baptist Church, Cleveland; "Waste Lands in Ohio, Their Causes and Cures," before the Farmers' Institute, Pittsfield, O.; "History of Development of Niagara Falls,'' before the Farmers' Club, at Belden, O.; ''Drainage Developments in Southeastern Ohio,'' before the Ohio Academy of Science, and ''Preaching and Evangelism,'' before the Lorain Baptist Association.

Attended the meetings of the Geological Society of America, at Albany, N. Y., in December; the Association of American Geologists and the American Association for the Advancement of Science, at New York, in December and January; the Ohio Academy of Science, at Columbus, in April; the Entrance Committee Conference of the Ohio College Association; the Association of Ohio Teachers of Mathematics and Science; the Lorain Baptist Association, at Avon, O., in August.

Was called to Toledo three times to examine a shoreline property in litigation, and testify in court as to what happened physiographically along the shoreline during the historical period. Work on the Ohio Geologic Survey.

HUTCHINS, PROFESSOR WILLIAM J.

Gave a course in ''Fundamentals'' at the Y. W. C. A. Student Conference at Lake Geneva, Wis., in August.

Attended the meeting of the Oberlin Association of New York.

Y. M. C. A. Religious Director at Camp Sheridan, Montgomery, Ala., beginning in August, 1917.

JAMESON, ASSOCIATE PROFESSOR RUSSELL P.

Lecture on French Music, before the Cercle des Annales of Cleveland, with accompanying historical program.

Attended the sessions of the Modern Language Association, at Chicago, in December.

JONES, SECRETARY GEORGE M.

Attended the meeting of the North Central Association of Colleges and Secondary Schools, at St. Louis, in March.

JONES, ASSOCIATE PROFESSOR LYNDS

Paper, based on studies of the bird reservations of the coast of Washington (the studies having been undertaken at the request of the director of the Federal Biological Survey), before the Congress of the American Ornithologists' Union, at Philadelphia, in November; addresses concerning insects against which the farmers have to guard, before the Florence Township Grange, at Florence, O., the New London Farmers, and the Lorain County Farmers' Institute; on ''How to Attract Birds to the Home Grounds'' before the

Civic League of Akron, the Painesville Bird Club, and the Lorain Congregational Church; on ''The Economic Value of Birds'' before the Cuyahoga Falls Schools, and the Hiram Science Club; various addresses in Oberlin; spoke in Columbus, at the call of the local Audubon Society, in behalf of the effort to place the Bob-white upon the song bird list; the law passed. Advised with Superintendent Rawdon of Oberlin concerning the bird-house contest among the public school children.

Elected President of the newly organized Oberlin Branch of the Burroughs Nature Club for the present school year; continued as member of the Bird-lore Advisory Council.

KIMBALL, PROFESSOR ARTHUR S.

Director of the Choir of the Second Congregational Church, Oberlin.

LEHMANN, PROFESSOR FRIEDRICH J.

Director of the Choir of the First Congregational Church, Oberlin.

LEONARD, PROFESSOR FRED E.

Address on some phases of Hygiene and Physical Education before members of the Lorain, O., Sorosis.

Two courses, in Human Physiology and the History of Physical Education, at the Summer School of Harvard University, for five weeks in July and August.

Appointed, by the American Red Cross, regular instructor in First Aid, and conducted, between April 17th and May 31st, two classes for the Oberlin Women's Auxiliary.

LORD, PROFESSOR LOUIS E.

Lecture (illustrated) on Sicily, before the Scott High School of Toledo; paper at the meeting of the American Philological Association at St. Louis; address before the School-masters' Club at Ann Arbor.

Attended the meeting of the Classical Association of the Middle West and South, at Louisville, Ky., and was reëlected Secretary and Treasurer of that Association.

LUTZ, PROFESSOR HARLEY L.

Paper on ''The Operation of the Ohio Tax System as Illustrated by the Experience of Cleveland,'' before the Ohio College Association, at Columbus.

Appointed a member of a Committee on the Coördination of Taxation, of the American Economic Association; and

Chairman of a Committee on Taxation, of the new Ohio Academy of Social Sciences.

Attended the annual meeting of the American Economic Association at Columbus, and participated in the discussion of Professor Sprague's paper on "Taxes and Loans in War Finance."

LYMAN, PROFESSOR EUGENE W.

Conducted a class in New Testament study at the student conference of the Young Women's Christian Association at Lake Geneva, Wis., during the summer; and gave a course of lectures on Christian Ethics, at a Convocation of the Congregational ministers of Vermont, held at Middlebury College.

METCALF, ACTING LIBRARIAN KEYES D.

Attended the meeting of the Ohio College Association, at Columbus, in April.

MILLER, PROFESSOR EDWARD A.

Papers at the annual meeting of the Association of American Colleges, and before the departmental meeting of Philosophy, Psychology, and Education, of the Ohio College Association.

Two graduate courses, and one of the open lectures, in the summer session of the University of Chicago.

Attended the meetings of the Ohio Athletic Conference, at Columbus, in October and May, continuing as Secretary of the Conference.

Elected President of the State Association of Teachers of Education, and Chairman of the Committee on Legislation, of that Association.

MILLER, PROFESSOR HERBERT A.

Addresses as follows: "Foreign Travel in Cleveland" before the Oberlin Woman's Club; "Loyalty" at the Oberlin College Sing; Toast at the Twenty-fifth anniversary of Our Lady of Lourdes Bohemian Church, Cleveland; four talks to teachers of the First Church Sunday School, Oberlin; two community Forums, Oberlin; "Recreation for the Immigrant," before the Saturday Night Club, of Cleveland; "Immigration in Cleveland," before the Oberlin Nineteenth Century Club; "Responsibilities of the Franchise," before the Oberlin W. C. T. U.; "A Square Deal—the Man's Side," before the Oberlin College Y. W. C. A.; "Unorthodox Reform," before the Sociology section of the Oberlin

Woman's Club; "Militarism in the Schools," before the
Mothers' and Teachers' Club of Berea, O.; "The Neighbor
in Our Midst," before the Women's Club of Huron; "Russia," before the Sorosis of Medina, and the History section
of the Oberlin Women's Club; seven talks on the Liquor
Question, before the Y. M. C. A. Study Class; "Other Race
Prejudices," before the Oberlin Association for the Advancement of Colored People; "The Immigrant and the
War," before the Cosmopolitan Club of Fremont, and the
Norwalk Federation of Women's Clubs; "Responsibilities
of Patriotism," before the Oberlin High School; "Religious and Social Changes," before the United Brethren
Church of Wilkinsburg, Pa.; address before the Vacation
Bible School, at Lorain, O.; several speeches in connection
with the Oberlin Federation.

Attended the meeting of the American Sociological Society, at
Columbus, and the National Conference of Charities and
Corrections, at Pittsburgh.

President of the National Association of Cosmopolitan Clubs,
and of the Oberlin Federation for Village Improvement and
Social Betterment; Chairman of the Oberlin Committee
on War Gardens.

MOORE, PROFESSOR DAVID R.

Addresses on "Why the World War Began," before the Congregational Churches of Amherst and Elyria, and the Sunyende-
and (Business Men's) Club of Sandusky; on "Yuan Shi
Kai," at Wakeman; on Red Cross Work, at Pittsfield, O.;
on "Russia's Foreign Relations Since 1905," before the
College Club, Cleveland; on "Present Conditions in South
America," before the Ninety-five Women's Club, of Elyria; Decoration Day address, at Mount Eaton; on "Foreign
Influence in South America," in Oberlin summer session;
on "Japanese in South America," before the Oberlin
High School; on "German Political Philosophers," before
the History section of the Oberlin Women's Club.

Attended the annual meetings of the American Historical Association, and the Political Science Association, at Cincinnati; spent several days among source material at the
University of Chicago, and visited some classes during the
summer session of that University.

MOORE, ASSOCIATE PROFESSOR EDWARD J.

Attended the Cleveland meeting of the American Physical Society, in October.

Assistant Professor of Physics in the Extension Division of the
University of Chicago.

MOSHER, PROFESSOR WILLIAM E.

Addresses as follows: ''Germany and the German War,'' in
Cleveland and Elyria; ''Significance of Word Study in
Elementary Language Teaching,'' before the Association
of Modern Language Teachers of the Central West and
South, at Indianapolis, Ind.

Member of State Committee on Patriotic Education.

NICHOLS, ASSOCIATE PROFESSOR SUSAN P.

Attended the meeting of the Josselyn Botanical Society of
Maine, at Moosehead Lake, in August.

OAKES, ASSOCIATE PROFESSOR EVA M.

Spent five weeks in study at the Boothbay Art Colony, in
Maine, during the summer.

ROGERS, PROFESSOR CHARLES G.

Various addresses before Women's Clubs and High Schools.

Member of the teaching staff, in the department of Embryology,
at the Marine Biological Laboratory, Woods Hole, Mass.

SAVAGE, PROFESSOR C. WINFRED

Addresses before the Amherst (O.) High School, the Men's
Bible Class of the South Congregational Church, Rochester,
N. Y., at West Park Congregational Church, Cleveland,
before the Young People's Society of the Euclid Avenue
Congregational Church, Cleveland, the Lorain (O.) Teachers' Association, and the Chautauqua (N. Y.) Parents' Conference.

Attended the meetings of the National Collegiate Athletic Association, the Society of the Directors of Physical Education in Colleges and Universities, and the Athletic
Research Society, at New York, during the holidays; represented the College and the Ohio Conference Colleges at
a special meeting of the National Collegiate Association
at Washington, in August.

Retained on the American Intercollegiate Foot Ball Rules Committee by the National Collegiate Association.

Member of the Faculty of the Chautauqua School of Physical
Education during the summer of 1917.

SHERMAN, ASSOCIATE PROFESSOR PHILIP D.

Addresses and lectures as follows: ''Shakespeare's London'' (illustrated), at Amherst and Spencer, O., and before the Lincoln High School, Cleveland, the Afternoon Club of Wellington, O., and Oberlin High School; ''Sir Walter Scott and Waverly'' (illustrated), at the Second Congregational Church of Amherst, O., and before the City Federation of Clubs, Springfield, O.; ''The Modern Drama,'' before the Shakespeare Club of Norwalk, O.; ''Colonial Literature in New England,'' before the Oberlin Wommen's Club; ''The Reading of Shakespeare,'' before the Afternoon Club of Wellington, O.; ''The Use of Books,'' before the Oberlin High School; ''The Shakespeare Tercentenary,'' a memorial address, at Wellington, Canton, Marion, Galion, Sandusky, and Bellevue, O.; ''The Community Theatre'' at the Hotel Statler, Cleveland; ''Sir Walter Scott,'' before the Oberlin High School; ''Social Aspects of the Drama,'' before the Men's Club of the Congregational Church at Sandusky, O.; ''The Elizabethan Theatre,'' before the Literature department of the Oberlin Women's Club; ''Robert Burns,'' a memorial address, before the Scottish Societies at Amherst, O.; ''The Alhambra'' (illustrated), before the Oberlin High School, and at Sandusky, O.; ''Some Technical Aspects of Shakespeare's Stage,'' before the Afternoon Club at Wellington; ''Some Aspects of Russian Literature,'' before the Fortnightly Club of Elyria; ''Shakespeare's Ethics,'' before the Akron Civic League at Akron, O.; Commencement address at Spencer, O.

Readings at the Second Congregational Church of Elyria; before the Men's Clubs of the Ridgeville (O.) Congregational Church, and the First Congregational Church of Elyria; before the Afternoon Club of Medina, O., and the Sunyendeand Club of Sandusky; at the First Congregational Churches of Lorain and South Amherst, O., and the Oberlin High School.

Elected Chairman of the National Education Committee of the Drama League of America; to membership in the ''Blake Society,'' England; honorary membership in the Mid-West section of the Chinese Students Alliance of America.

Judge of the Essay Contest, Fremont and Lorain, O.; Oratorical contest, Youngstown and Akron, O.

SINCLAIR, ASSOCIATE PROFESSOR MARY E.

Attended the meeting of the American Association for the Advancement of Science, at New York, in December.

STIVEN, ASSOCIATE PROFESSOR FREDERIC B.

Organ recitals at the University of Toronto (one of an annual series), and in Ohio and Indiana.

Organist and Director of Music at the Euclid Avenue Christian Church, Cleveland.

UPTON, PROFESSOR WILLIAM T.

Organist and Choirmaster at Calvary Presbyterian Church, Cleveland.

WAGER, PROFESSOR CHARLES H. A.

Addresses before Elyria Clubs (2), the Men's Club of the First Congregational Church of Sandusky, and the Cleveland Alumni Association.

WARD, PROFESSOR CLARENCE

Lecture on ''The Cathedral of Reims,'' given under the auspices of the Archaeological Institute of America, at Kansas City, Nashville, St. Louis, Oxford, O., Indianapolis, Detroit, Madison, and St. Paul.

WILLIAMS, PROFESSOR SAMUEL R.

Papers as follows: ''Some Relations between the Magnetic and the Mechanical Properties of Steel and Nickel,'' before the Cleveland Engineering Society, at Cleveland, O.; ''The Effect of Transverse Joints on the Magnetic Induction in Iron and Nickel,'' at the meeting of the A. A. A. S., New York City; ''Magnetostriction and Its Bearing on Magnetic Theories,'' before the Ohio Academy of Science, at Columbus, O.

WIRKLER, ASSISTANT SECRETARY JOHN E.

Director and Manager of the Oberlin College Glee Club; Director of the First M. E. Church Choir, Lorain, O.

As a member of the Glee Club Male Quartette, appeared at six high school commencements, at Berlin Heights, New Haven, La Grange, Birmingham, Shiloh, and Greenwich; and on religious and political occasions at Chicago Junction, Wellington, Lorain (2), La Grange, Elyria, Amherst, and Oberlin.

Had charge of the Student Male Chorus at the celebration of
Washington's Birthday and at one of the Lenten Services,
both in Oberlin.

WOLCOTT, REGISTRAR F. ISABEL

Attended the annual meeting of the American Association of
Collegiate Registrars, at Lexington, Ky., in April, and was
Chairman of one of the topical conference sessions.

This list of the outside activities of the Faculty shows
that for the year under review Mr. Bohn, Dean Bosworth,
Professor Cairns, Dean Cole, Dean Fitch, Professor Hutchins,
and Professor Wager all shared with the President the representation of the College at Alumni gatherings in different
parts of the country. The record also makes plain that the
Faculty have felt the obligation that belongs to the scholar
to make available for as many as possible the results of his
own specialized researches. There is a long list of such addresses, therefore, as well as of highly specialized papers
before many scholarly bodies. It is difficult to select names
at this point, where so many have shared in the work.

The College has also made a considerable contribution
to the teaching force of the summer sessions of other colleges
and universities. The Faculty had a share, thus, in the summer teaching of the Chautauqua Summer School of Physical
Education, Chicago University, the University of Colorado,
Columbia University, Harvard University, the Marine Biological Laboratory at Woods Hole, the University of Missouri, and the University of Oklahoma.

The official positions held by members of the Faculty
in various scientific and educational bodies reveal the share
that the College is having in such coöperative work. The
College is honored in the honor paid to Professor Ian C. Hannah in his election as Fellow in the Society of Antiquaries,
one of the Royal Societies of England, and in Professor Sherman's election to membership in the Blake Society, England.

Publications

The list of publications of the Faculty is also intended to reflect not only distinctly educational and scholarly writings, but books and articles of a more popular sort, as illustrating again the breadth of community service so rendered by the College. The main publications of the Faculty for the year follow:

KING, PRESIDENT HENRY C.

> The Annual Report for 1915-16 of the President of Oberlin College.
>
> It's All in the Day's Work. (The Macmillan Company, New York.)
>
> Fundamental Questions. (The Macmillan Company, New York.)
>
> The Church's Responsibility and Opportunity. (Chap. III in ''The Churches of Christ in Time of War,'' published by The Federal Council of the Churches of Christ in America, New York.)
>
> What the College Stands for. (Bulletin of the Association of American Colleges, Vol. III, No. 1, Feb., 1917.)
>
> Missions and the World War: A Kingdom That Cannot Be Shaken. (*The Journal of Theology*, Jan., 1917.)
>
> Why America Joins the Allies. (Privately printed.)
>
> What the Country Expects of the Massachusetts Institute of Technology. *(Technology Review.)*
>
> What May the Nation Expect from the Christian Men of the Reserve Officers Training Camps? (*The North American Student*, July, 1917.)
>
> Some Advice to Young People about Their Libraries. (*The Advance*, Nov. 30, 1916.)
>
> Some Facts about Oberlin and My Hopes for Oberlin. (College Annual, 1917.)
>
> The Secret Fraternity Cases. (*Alumni Magazine*, October, 1916.)
>
> Professor Clarence Ward. (*Alumni Magazine*, March, 1917.)
>
> Good Thoughts in Bad Times. Baccalaureate Sermon for the Graduate School of Theology, May 13, 1917. (Privately printed.)
>
> Grounds of Hope in the Changing World-Order. College Baccalaureate, June 10, 1917. (Privately printed.)

ALEXANDER, ASSISTANT PROFESSOR LEIGH

New Circular of Information on the Rhodes Scholarships, prepared for the State Superintendent of Public Instruction to distribute throughout the high schools and colleges in the state of Ohio.

BOSWORTH, DEAN EDWARD I.

Thirty Studies about Jesus. (Association Press.)

The Christian Witness in War. (*The North American Student,* May, 1917, and reprinted in an addition of 50,000 by the Y. M. C. A. War Council, for use in the army and navy.)

BUDINGTON, PROFESSOR ROBERT A.

Some Consequences of Biological Study. (*School and Society,* Sept. 30, 1916.)

Zoölogical Editor of *The Ohio Journal of Science,* the official organ of the Ohio Academy of Science.

CHAPIN, ASSOCIATE PROFESSOR WILLIAM H.

Graham's Law of Gaseous Diffusion. (*School Science and Mathematics,* June, 1917.)

COLE, DEAN CHARLES N.

Discussion of paper by Dr. C. H. French, on ''The Efficient College'' (Bulletin of the Association of American Colleges, March, 1917.)

Report of the Committee on Educational Policy. (Report of the Ohio College Association for 1917.)

The Secret Fraternity Cases: Committee Report. (*Alumni Magazine,* Oct., 1916.)

The Lowest-Third Rule. (*Alumni Magazine,* Feb., 1917.)

FISKE, PROFESSOR G. WALTER

The Development of Rural Leadership. (*The American Sociological Society Publications,* Vol. XI, March, 1917.)

FULLERTON, PROFESSOR KEMPER

Studies in Isaiah. (*Journal of Biblical Literature,* March-June.)

Isaiah's Earliest Prophecy against Ephraim. (*American Journal of Semitic Languages and Literatures,* Oct., 1916.)

GEISER, PROFESSOR KARL F.

The Merits and Defects of the American Political System. (*The Chinese Students Monthly*, Dec., 1916.)

Book Reviews.

HANNAH, PROFESSOR IAN C.

Quaker-Born. (G. Arnold Shaw, New York.)

The Mediaeval Cathedrals of Ireland. (*The Archaeological Journal*, London, Second Series, Vol. XXIII.)

HOLMES, PROFESSOR HARRY N.

The Colloidal Phosphates and Arsenates of Iron. (*Journal of the American Chemical Society*, Oct., 1916.) (Co-authorship with R. E. Rindfusz.)

HUBBARD, PROFESSOR GEORGE D.

What Has the Future for Geologists? (*Ohio Journal of Science*, Jan., 1917.)

Geography of the Columbus, Ohio, Quadrangle. (*Ibid*, March, 1917.)

HUTCHINS, PROFESSOR WILLIAM J.

The Preacher's Ideals and Inspirations. (Fleming H. Revell Co.)

JONES, ASSOCIATE PROFESSOR LYNDS

Edited the *Wilson Bulletin*.

LUTZ, PROFESSOR HARLEY L.

The Study of Taxation in Colleges and Universities. (Proceedings of the Tenth Annual Conference of the National Tax Association.)

MILLER, PROFESSOR EDWARD A.

Discussion of "The Efficient College." (Bulletin of the Association of American Colleges, Vol. III, No. 2, March, 1917.)

Associate Editor of the *School Review*.

MILLER, PROFESSOR HERBERT A.

Nationality in Modern History. (Review) (*American Journal of Sociology*.)

The Russian-Germans. (Review) (*Ibid.*)

With the Peasants of Moravia. (*Oberlin Literary Magazine,* June, 1917.)

Articles from time to time in local papers, relative to the Oberlin Federation.

MOSHER, PROFESSOR WILLIAM E.

The Scholar and the Nation. (*Chinese Students Monthly,* Jan., 1917.)

SHERMAN, ASSOCIATE PROFESSOR PHILIP D.

A Working Model of the Fortune Theatre. (Illustrated.) *(The College Magazine.)*

An Oberlin Student in the French Ambulance Corps. (New York *Globe,* New York *Sun,* Cincinnati *Post,* Dayton *Journal,* Boston *Monitor,* Sandusky *Register,* Lorain *Times-Herald,* and eleven smaller local papers.)

An Annotated List of Holiday Books. (The Burrows Brothers Co., Cleveland.)

The Cosmopolitanism of Oberlin College (Illustrated.) (New York, Boston, and local Ohio papers.)

Nineteen special articles, many illustrated, presenting various aspects of Oberlin College life, history, etc., printed in New York, Boston, Cleveland, and local Ohio papers.

Oberlin Students in France. *(The College Magazine.)*

Oberlin and Student Federation. *(The Toledo Blade.)*

UPTON, PROFESSOR WILLIAM T.

Music Critic for the *Alumni Magazine.*

WAGER, PROFESSOR CHARLES H. A.

Two reviews in *The Dial.*

WELLS, ASSOCIATE PROFESSOR GEORGE R.

Some Experiments in Motor Reproduction of Visually Perceived Forms. (*The Psychological Review,* July, 1917.)

WILLIAMS, PROFESSOR SAMUEL R.

An Achromatoscope. (*American Journal of Science,* Jan., 1916.)

The Principle of Bernoulli and Its Relation to the Heating and Ventilating of a Building. (*The Heating and Ventilating Magazine,* Feb., 1916.)

The Determination of the Constant of a Solenoid. (*Journal of the Franklin Institute*, Sept., 1916.)

Some Relations between the Magnetic and the Mechanical Properties of Steel and Nickel. (*Journal of The Cleevland Engineering Society*, Jan., 1917.)

A Study of the Joule and Wiedemann Magnetostrictive Effects in Same Specimens of Nickel. (*The Physical Review*, Aug., 1917.)

The list of Faculty publications shows as usual a considerable number of scientific and educational papers. The editorial connection of Professor Budington with the Ohio Journal of Science, of Professor Lynds Jones with the Wilson Bulletin, and of Professor E. A. Miller with the School Review, may be noted. Attention may well be directed to Professor Sherman's widespread representation of the College in many special articles on Oberlin in high class journals all over the country. Professor Bosworth's little book "Thirty Studies about Jesus," whose value is not to be measured by its size, was written at the request of the International Committee of the Y. M. C. A. with special reference to its use in the cantonments, and is rendering large service in this way. Professor Hutchins' stimulating and inspiring book on "The Preacher's Ideals and Inspirations" has called out most favorable comment from the reviewers.

V

ALUMNI

The final strength and influence of a college are pretty accurately measured, probably, in the long run, by the faith and enthusiasm of its Alumni. If its Alumni believe in it with all their hearts, are enthusiastic concerning its ideals, and bring to it corresponding support, it is practically certain steadily and continuously to count in the life of the nation and the world. In the judgment of many men of other colleges, repeatedly expressed to the President of Oberlin, Oberlin College has been notable for such enthusiastic support on the part of its Alumni. Yet there have naturally been differences of opinion concerning various historic policies of the College. And when, last year, a few of the Alumni, under the stress of disappointment growing out of the disciplining of the sub-rosa fraternities and the resulting disastrous athletic season, indulged in considerable rather drastic criticism, as though the Oberlin Alumnus must feel generally on the defensive, the President naturally began to think of some of the many reasons, why the graduate of Oberlin not only need not feel that he had to be on the defensive concerning his Alma Mater, but might rather take the sincerest pride in her history and in her present position. And it may be worth while to remind the Alumni of some of those facts about the College that furnish solid grounds for loyalty, as they were briefly expressed, for example, at the request of the editor of the last college Annual:

Some Facts About Oberlin

A college with a history of honor:
>The first college to give a Bachelor's degree to women on the same conditions as those holding in the best men's colleges of the time.
>The first coeducational college.
>With a notable anti-slavery record.
>Most democratic in its form of government.
>As a part of its heritage, rarely combining intellectual freedom and modern viewpoint with moral and religious idealism.
>Associated with the origin of the Anti-Saloon movement.
>A charter member of the asociated colleges of the Carnegie Foun. dation for the Advancement of Teaching.

A college of wide influence with other colleges, and with world-wide recognition.

Oberlin's elaborate study of the tests of college efficiency, and its own resulting careful self-survey, have constituted an important educational contribution.

Counted one of the only four colleges of the first rank in Ohio.

The only college or university in the State of Ohio with a nation-wide constituency, bringing more than one-half of its students steadily from outside the State of Ohio, with every state and territory represented.

Of thirty-one colleges and universities in the North Central States, including state universities and leading colleges, Oberlin has the smallest percentage of loss of men between entrance and graduation.

Both Oberlin's endowment and total assets have more than doubled in fifteen years, exclusive of the Hall bequest.

Oberlin has the eleventh library in size of all the college and university libraries in the country, and the largest *college* library, and is spending more on new books than any other college.

As a single illustration of the spirit of the student body, Oberlin has probably been sending more men and women into foreign missionary service than any other institution in the country. And quite aside from foreign mission work, there has been notable testimony from a most competent source, that ''nowhere have I found such a general desire among the student body to do worth while things.''

Any one of these facts might be illustrated at length, and many other similar facts could easily be added.

The Living Endowment Union

As has been already noted the Living Endowment Union made an excellent record for the year under review. Its report, submitted by the Secretary, Mr. Irving W. Metcalf, is published once more with the supplementary reports in this volume. The Secretary notes that gains have been made during the year in the number of new subscriptions as compared to other years, the aggregate amount represented by these subscriptions, and also in holding the subscriptions already on record. The College is particularly grateful for the funds which so come to it. It counts no equal amount of money from any other source as of quite the same significance as this money, representing the interest and belief of so many individual Alumni. The President emphasizes once more the fact that the entire income from the Union, where it is not designated, is used to supplement the all too meagre funds available for scholarship and beneficiary aid.

Alumni Day in commencement week is growing steadily in interest and importance, and many children of Alumni are getting a most pleasant introduction to the College in connection with that day, with its campus illumination and evening celebration.

The College believes that great importance attaches to the regular meetings of the Oberlin Associations throughout the country, and rejoices, therefore, in the way in which these Associations have been kept up in the year just past. The College is glad regularly to send some representative of the Faculty to the meetings of these Associations.

Necrology

The necrological report of the Alumni for the year under review, as submitted by the Secretary of the College, brings the record to date of October 1, 1917, and is printed in full with the supplementary reports in this volume.

Forty Alumni (7 less than the previous year) died during the year under review,—22 men and 18 women. The average age of the men at the time of death was 62.1 years; the average age of the women 65.6; the total average age of the 40 Alumni was 63.2 years. The corresponding figure for the year 1915-16 was 66.1; for the year 1914-15 it was 65.6; for the year 1913-14 it was 64.8; for the year 1912-13 it was 68.6.

Of the total number reported, 8—an unusual number— graduated after 1900. The classes represented in the list ranged from 1857 to 1916, and the ages at death from 89 to 22. 27 of those reported reached the age of 60 years or over, 18 the age of 70 or over, and 8 the age of 80 or over.

Mr. Edmund A. West of Chicago, a graduate of the classical course in 1843, remains still the *earliest graduate* now living. Mr. West was 94 years of age April 28, 1917.

The oldest surviving graduate in point of years also, as last year, is Mr. Lester B. Kinney of Chemung, Illinois, of the class of 1847. Mr. Kinney was 98 years of age February 4, 1917.

At date of October 1, 1917, there were four other living graduates of the College who completed their courses before 1850; Mrs. Antoinette Brown-Blackwell, of the class of 1847; Mrs. Hester Van Wagner-Burhans, of the class of 1847; Mrs. Celestia Holbrook-Beach, of the class of 1848; and Mrs. America Strong-Jones, of the class of 1849.

The report as usual gives individual sketches of each of the Alumni, and these sketches cannot be reviewed without a fresh sense of the vital service that is constantly being rendered by the Oberlin graduates. The President has introduced the custom of making one Chapel service, soon after the annual meeting of the Board of Trustees, a memorial service for the Alumni who have died during the year. It seems worth while thus to remind the present students of the way in which they are linked up with the graduates of the years past, and it is only a fitting recognition of the lives whose earthly service has closed.

The name that naturally stands out in the entire list is that of Dr. Charles Jackson Ryder, of the class of 1875 and a member of the Board of Trustees, whose distinguished service has already been recorded. Those who had lived to 80 years or more, make a notable list, including such names as General Philip C. Hayes of the class of 1860, with his long record of public service; Samuel A. Cravath of the class of 1858, an honored example of the constructive citizen; Miss Esther Tapping Maltbie of the class of 1862, with her remarkable missionary record; Mrs. Elizabeth Storrs Mead, wife of Professor Hiram Mead, and for ten years President of Mount Holyoke College; and Mrs. Mary J. Andrews-Millikan, sharing most fruitfully in the long ministerial service of her husband. One is sorry to have to record so unusual a number of deaths among the younger Alumni. It is most rare to have so large a proportion of the deaths fall in classes after 1900. But here, too, the record is one of noteworthy service: the service of an able physician, winning recognition for expert investigation, like Dr. Hubbard North Bradley of the class of 1901; the service of an honored representative of the United States Government in a difficult place abroad, Mr. Charles Frederick Brissell of the class of 1906, American Consul in Bagdad; devoted missionary service like that of Mrs. Mabel D. Woodside-Stokey of the class of 1907; and the successful work of a field geologist performed by so recent a graduate as Mr. Philip H. Cary, of the class of 1913. The record includes also the names of able lawyers, like Judge Artemus B. Johnson of the class of 1864; outstanding physicians, like Dr. Frank S. Clark of Cleveland, of the class of 1887; and devoted and successful ministers like Dr. William Lawrence Tenney of the class of 1885, and Rev. Albert Louis Grein of the class of 1891. The name of Miss Calista Andrews, of the class of 1875, stands, for many, as the name of a most loyal and devoted friend of the College and of all good causes.

In connection with these deaths of Alumni, there may be appropriately mentioned that of Dr. Delavan L. Leonard, who, though not an Alumnus of the College, was the author of the history of the College which covers the larger part of its existence: "The Story of Oberlin, the Institution, the Community, the Idea, the Movement." Dr. Leonard's volume supplemented, in a most desirable way, President Fairchild's history of Oberlin's first half-century. And as a citizen of Oberlin for many years, Dr. Leonard had often made manifest his interest in the College and his loyal support of its policies.

The College once more acknowledges with deep gratitude the honor which comes to it steadily in the worthy lives and honorable service of its Alumni. For the College must live, as nowhere else, in the lives of its children.

VI

STUDENTS

Attendance

The statistics concerning the enrolment of students have already been discussed in connection with the regular report of the Secretary of the College. A word may be added concerning the *limitation of numbers,* decided upon by the Trustees four years ago, upon the recommendation of the Faculty. With the current year the five years' experiment, contemplated by the action of the Trustees, will have been completed. The question of the continuance of the policy of limitation will therefore have to be faced by the Trustees during the present year. The Faculty are recommending that the policy of limitation be continued for at least two years, on the general ground, that the ends sought by the original adoption of the policy of limitation have not yet been attained. There will still be so large an expenditure of money required to bring the quality of our present work to the point desired, that it would seem a mistake to try to increase the numbers, to which the College attempts to minister, until that better quality of work has been attained.

Foreign Students

The College has continued the special help to foreign students which for many years it has been attempting. The aim is to aid these students in adjustment to American conditions, and in getting the utmost from their present opportunities. Professor H. A. Miller, as last year, has been the special adviser appointed by the Faculty, and the same committee have been associated with him: Professors Lyman, Sherman, and Williams. A large amount of most devoted service has gone into this work. It is well to remember, as Professor Miller says, that there are two distinct types of foreign students to whom Oberlin should minister: those who come here for educational purposes only, and return to their native countries as soon as they have finished; and those who have come to America for permanent residence, either as children with their parents, or as adults on their own initiative. And the service to be rendered to these two groups is quite different, as the report of the Adviser points out. For the first group, as he says, it is desirable to furnish good educational facilities, and the best interpretation of American conditions and ideals possible. For the second group, perhaps the greatest emphasis should be laid on the latter purpose, with the expectation that they will appropriate it, while the first group may only evaluate it. Professor Miller is undoubtedly right in his judgment that the second group ought naturally to be much larger in our student body, and nothing would help to this so much as increased scholarship aid.

Health

As President of the Oberlin Hospital Association, Dr. Leonard submits his usual hospital record, which shows that during the year ending September 30, 1917, 30 students in Oberlin College received 182 days of treatment in the Oberlin hospital, valued at $429.20. The figures for 1915-16 were 40 students, 517 days, and $1,315.07. This was 25.90 per cent of the total number of patients (154), 13.6 per cent of the total days of service rendered (1,338), and 10.94 per cent of the total earnings of the hospital ($3,920.72). There were no deaths. The bills of 10 students, who had received 88 days of treatment, were remitted under the terms of the Trustee gift of $750. The service thus charged off was valued at $199.75 ($449.60 in 1915-16). These figures mean, that there has been considerably less serious illness in the year under review than in the year previous, and that the direct contribution from the Trustee appropriation to the hospital for the year amounted to more than $550.

Only one death among the students of the College occurred during the year under review—that of Miss Luther
VanDoren Avery, a student in the Conservatory of Music,
who died in Oberlin, December 6, 1916.

An unsuccessful attempt was made during the year to
persuade the members of the Village Council to unite with
the Village Board of Health, the Board of Public Works, the
Township Trustees, and the College to employ a thoroughly
trained *public health officer*. This would be so real a gain
that it is still hoped that the plan may later be carried
through. The epidemic of mild scarlet fever cases last year
and the year before, as Dr. Leonard says, "furnishes a strik-
ing illustration of the need of some public officer trained in
modern methods of detecting the presence, tracing the causes,
and preventing the appearance and spread of contagious diseases among us. And this would be only a part of the service which such a man would render to the community and
the College."

The gains in the care of the health of the students, especially the women students, through the infirmary at the Browning house, and the effective work of the visiting nurse, made
possible by the Dudley P. Allen fund, have already been recorded. Provision like that made for the women very much
needs also to be made for the men. So that the College is
anticipating with special eagerness the building of the Allen
Memorial Hospital, and the knitting up of adequate nurse
service with that hospital. When that hospital is built it is
hoped that the "positive physical efficiency program" set
forth last year, including the care of serious illness, the care
of minor illness and convalescence, dispensary service, and
the work of visiting nurses for both men and women, may be
completely carried through; though more endowment and
larger equipment will be required than are quite yet in sight.

The *scholarship* and *conduct* of students, and the need of
further *beneficiary aid* for them have already been discussed

in previous sections of this report. One of the most valuable supplements of such beneficiary aid, as the College has been able to give to needy but deserving students, has been the aid which it has afforded in securing *employment* for such students. A part of this work has been done by the Young Men's and the Young Women's Christian Associations, as will be recorded in the reports of their work for the year; but the Assistant Secretary of the College has borne primary responsibility for securing student employment for the men, especially during the summer months. His report for the year shows that 54 men have been placed through his effort in 61 positions, with possible earnings amounting to more than $6,300. These positions were assigned to 33 new men and to 21 men who had been previously enrolled. The time required for this work makes a heavy draft upon the Secretary's office, and the Assistant Secretary hopes that some more effective way of handling this very important aspect of the work of the College may be devised. He suggests that the work might possibly be connected with the work of the Bureau of Appointments or with the office of the Dean of College men.

Outside Activities

The most signal change in the outside activities of the students, for the year under review, was naturally in those activities that reflected the war. As already indicated, many men took up military training in the latter part of the college year, and many women Red Cross work. In addition, a number of both men and women were excused, the latter weeks of the college year, for various forms of agricultural work. A campaign for relief in the prison camps was pressed through under student auspices, and netted $3,761.59. The Women's League, which initiated in December a movement for raising money for the much needed Women's Building, decided in the spring, at the entrance of the United

States into the war, to turn their efforts to war relief, and
$228.00 was thus raised for war purposes. In addition to
this, French orphans were adopted by several boarding
houses, and the League is extending its war work for the current year both in raising money and in coöperation with the
Red Cross and other agencies.

Other outside activities of the students included the
work of the Men's Senate, of the Women's League, of the
Conservatory Boards, of the Honor Courts, and of the Christian Associations. These are all important agencies in securing intelligent coöperation between Faculty and students,
in enlarging and bettering the service of the College to its
students. It should be mentioned in this connection that
student women are included in the committee dealing with
the discipline of women, and student men in the committee
dealing with the discipline of men. It may be doubted if
there has ever been a better spirit of coöperation on the part
of the student body than at present.

Besides these activities, there are also those of the various class organizations in the different departments; of the
literary societies; of the Union Literary Association, and the
publications issued under its auspices; of the "Hi-O-Hi,"
the regular annual of the Junior class; of the Student Missionary Volunteer Band; of the Union of the Graduate School
of Theology; of the College Glee Club, Men's Mandolin Club,
Women's Mandolin Club; of the College Athletic Association; of the Women's Gymnasium and Field Association and
its subordinate clubs; and of the Cosmopolitan Club.

The other organizations which have a joint Faculty and
student membership are the Shansi Memorial Association,
the Musical Union, the Conservatory Orchestra, the various
church choirs, the Dramatic Association, and the Press Club.

The mere mention of this range of outside activities suggests both the very genuine enrichment of the life of the
College, which comes through these organizations, and also

the wisdom of the policy of the College, in restricting the number of hours to be given to such work lying outside the curriculum.

The College *Glee Club* continued under the able direction of Mr. J. E. Wirkler, Assistant Secretary of the College. It appeared in 27 concerts outside of Oberlin, and three concerts at home. The club found it possible also to serve during its trips abroad the Presbyterian and Methodist Churches at Iron Mountain, Michigan, the Plymouth Church at Minneapolis, Minnesota, and the Congregational Church at Cuyahoga Falls, Ohio. The club had part, too, in the Washington Birthday celebration at Oberlin, and in one of the Oberlin Union Lenten services. The absence of the club from actual college work was only three and a half days. Of the 27 concerts given, 13 were in Ohio and 14 outside the state as follows: Michigan, 8; Wisconsin, 3; Illinois, 2; Minnesota, 1. The work of the club is kept up to a high standard, and yet effort is made not to have the rehearsals encroach unduly on the regular work of the College. The College takes pride in the fine representation given it by the Glee Club.

The Christian Associations

For the year under review the Young Men's Christian Association was in charge of Mr. Carl C. Compton, of the Theological class of 1917, and the Young Women's Christian Association was under the direction of Miss Helen Hutchcraft, of Wellesley College. Both Secretaries rendered excellent service. For the year just beginning the work for the men is in charge of Mr. J. M. Groves, a Harvard graduate, who comes to Oberlin after varied and rich experience as Secretary of the Christian Association at the Phillips Brooks House, Cambridge, and in Association work at Manilla, Philippine Islands. Mr. Grove's coming marks an advance in Oberlin's Association work, in that he will give his full

time to this interest, and because he brings a degree of ma-
turity and experience to the office not possible to obtain,
heretofore, on the part-time arrangement for a student secretary. The College this year recognizes the importance of
the work under the new plan by meeting part of the salary
of the Secretary. The work of the Young Women's Christian Association will be continued by Miss Hutchcraft, who
enters upon a second year of successful and satisfactory service. The Associations both during the year just past and for
the current year are meeting heavy emergency responsibilities in connection with the war, coöperating in the raising of
funds for the relief of prisoners-of-war and for the other
important Association work being carried on at home and
abroad and for the American soldiers and sailors and the
other forces under arms.

The budget of the Association was provided as usual by
a joint compaign early in the year, $1,376.23 being provided
for the Y. M. C. A. and $1,899.46 for the young women's
work. These sums do not take account of the large special
amounts raised under the auspices of the Associations for
war relief.

The Secretary of the Young Men's Christian Association
says concerning the work of that Association: "Every activity is planned to be of some definite service to Oberlin or the
community and furthermore to interest college men in Christian services. The Association's chief responsibility is the
development of Christian leaders. It furnishes a practical
and very necessary outlet for the Christian spirit of the men
of Oberlin." The spirit of this purpose is carried out in
manifold ways, and it would be hard to over-emphasize the
value of the work which the Association does with the student
body and the community, making sure that the new students
start the year's work in the right fashion, and that the year
brings to all of the men rewarding opportunities for service.
The public meetings for men naturally dealt with the vital

questions raised by the war, in addition to the important subjects which are necessarily considered relating to student problems and college life. The average attendance at these meetings was 225 men.

The work of the Young Women's Christian Association was somewhat reorganized during the year under review, with two points in mind: to secure a more efficient grouping and coördination of its activities, and to bring into the active work of the Association a larger number of college women. Under the new plan the work of the Association is divided into four main sections: campus service, community service, religious education (including mission study and Bible study, religious meetings, church relationships, etc.), and a publicity department. The results attained have fully justified this new plan of organization.

The President wishes to express his appreciation of the great value of the Associations' work in developing and conserving student interest for all special occasions, including the Day of Prayer, Shansi Day, and the Community Lenten services. The college was privileged this year to have Mr. John R. Mott for the principal addresses connected with the Day of Prayer.

While the work of the Associations is planned primarily to meet local needs, both the Y. M. C. A. and the Y. W. C. A. keep in close relations to the National and International Association work, and were represented at the usual State and National Conferences. From time to time representatives of both the State and International Committees have been present in Oberlin, and have given valuable coöperation.

The Associations have been helpful, as heretofore, in relieving the College to a considerable extent of the problem of finding employment for self-supporting students.

In addition to the work of the Christian Associations, mention should be made of the valuable service given by members of the Faculty who serve on the Committee on Religious Interests, and who in a variety of ways serve the local churches and the community. Special notice may well be called to the large amount of field work done by the men of the Graduate School of Theology.

Oberlin-Shansi Memorial Association

It is fitting that there should appear each year in the Annual Reports special mention of the work which the Oberlin-Shansi Memorial Association is doing in the Province of Shansi, China, a work made possible by the generous gifts of students, Faculty, and friends of the College.

The Association has been compelled to face a particularly difficult financial problem during the year under review, in that the annual budget amounting to $5,000 was of necessity expanded to $6,250, on account of the cost of exchange in China, a peculiar situation produced by the world war. Toward this budget there was subscribed on Shansi Day $3,300. Additional subscriptions have been secured for this purpose, but unless generous help is received before the close of the fiscal year, December 31st, the Association will be compelled to close its year with a deficit. The officers of the Association realize that the war is making very unusual demands in every direction. Nevertheless they are of the opinion that there never has been a time when it was more important that the moral and religious and educational institutions of the world should be kept at their fullest efficiency than in the present crisis. They have, therefore, no hesitancy in urging the claims of Oberlin's educational work in Shansi and in asking for adequate support that the splendid beginning already made in laying educational and religious foundations in that important province of China shall not fail to come to maturity and full fruition in the days of stress and change which are just ahead for that country and for all the world.

Although the staff in charge of the work at Taiku and Fenchow has been much smaller than the work calls for, a very satisfactory year's work was reported at the annual meeting of the Shansi District, April 1st. From this meeting there came to the Executive Committee a very carefully prepared report, prepared by Rev. Paul L. Corbin and approved by the Mission, entitled ''An Appeal for the Establishment of the Hall Foundation.'' It was the purpose of this report to outline comprehensively a program for an educational system, centering in a college enterprise which should be established on the foundation of a prospective gift from the Hall estate. In brief the plan calls for elementary schools for both boys and girls with adequate supervision, academies for boys and girls at both Fenchow and Taiku, a men's college, and a women's normal school, and in connection with these two, an extension department to carry on much needed educational work of a general character throughout the province. The plan has been very thoughtfully worked out and is worthy of careful consideration, although it is probable that only a small part of the entire scheme can be undertaken in the near future. It is hoped that from the funds designated by Mr. Hall's will for educational work in the Far East a sum may be assigned for the use of the Shansi Memorial Association which will make possible in the very near future an appreciable expansion of the work Oberlin is now trying to do.

The constituency of the Shansi Association is necessarily limited and the Association must naturally look to the alumni for its main support outside of the student body. It is hoped therefore that an increasing number of the alumni may include the work of the Shansi Association in the list of those objects toward which annual contributions are made by them. This work is essentially an Oberlin enterprise and a memorial to the Oberlin men and women whose lives were sacrificed in the Boxer outbreak in 1900. It would be difficult to overemphasize the strategic importance of educational work in China at the present time.

In accordance with the usual custom the annual meeting of the Shansi Memorial Association was held on Sunday evening of Commencement week.

Lectures, Concerts, Recitals, and Dramatic Performances

The lectures, concerts, and other entertainments brought to Oberlin chiefly through the College constitute no small factor in the broadening and enriching of the life of the students, and the list for the year 1916-17 is therefore here given. The bare list shows how much of value has been offered to the students in this way during the year under review:

September 13—President Henry Churchill King. ''The Double Challenge of College Life.'' Opening Chapel Address.

September 14—Professor Ian C. Hannah. ''America's New Place in the World.'' Opening Address of the Graduate School of Theology.

September 27—Mr. Matthew Liston. ''Mormonism.'' Lecture.

September 29—Dr. Harry F. Ward. ''Some Aspects of the Revolutionary Nature of Christianity.'' Lecture.

October 1—Dr. Paul W. Harrison. ''Needs of Arabia.'' Address.

October 10—Mr. Percy Grainger. Piano Recital.

October 11—Mr. Hamilton Holt. ''The Great War and Peace.'' Lecture.

October 13—Professor Scott Nearing. ''Earning and Owning a Living.'' Lecture.

October 17—Professor Edward Dickinson. ''The Present Social Movement in American Music and Drama.'' Lecture.

October 18—Professor T. Wingate Todd. ''The Significance of the Egyptian Mummy.'' Lecture.

October 24—Mrs. Edward MacDowell. ''The Works of Edward MacDowell.'' Lecture and Recital.

October 26—Mr. Lincoln Steffens. ''What is Doing in Mexico.'' Lecture.

November 7—Mrs. Charlotte D. Williams, Mr. Frederick Goerner, Mr. Maurice Koessler, Mr. William K. Breckenridge. Recital of Music for Strings and Piano.

November 10—Mr. Henry Turner Bailey. ''The Enjoyment of Pictures.'' Illustrated Lecture.

November 11—Latin Play in English. ''Menaechmi,'' Plautus.

November 17.—Mr. Nathan C. Kingsbury. Transcontinental Telephone Demonstration and Lecture.

November 20—Professor R. D. V. Macgoffin. ''On Foot in Italy's Alban Hills.'' Lecture.

November 21—Dr. Charles F. Aked. ''America and the World State.'' Lecture.

November 23—Dr. Mitchel Carrol. ''Arts and Crafts in Prehistoric Ages.'' Lecture.

November 24—Rev. Leyton Richards. ''The Heroisms of Peace.'' Address.

November 29—The Philadelphia Symphony Orchestra. Mr. Leopold Stokowski, Conductor. Mme. Olga Samaroff, Pianist. Orchestra Concert.

December 1—Mr. William M. Salter. ''Nietzsche and the War.'' Lecture.

December 5—Mme. Margarete Matzenauer. Song Recital.

December 7—Dr. Frederick R. Green. ''The Social Mission of Modern Medicine.'' Lecture.

December 14—The Oberlin Musical Union. Choral Concert.

December 18—Sir Rabindranath Tagore. ''The Cult of Nationalism.'' Lecture.

January 6—The Oberlin Musical Union. Choral Concert.

January 9—Mr. Samuel S. McClure. ''Editing as an Art, or the Making of a Magazine.'' Lecture.

January 11—Dr. Edward H. Griggs. ''The World War and Ethics.'' Lecture.

January 11—The Portmanteau Theatre Company. ''The Birthday of the Infanta.'' ''The Very Naked Boy.'' ''The Gods of the Mountains.'' ''Voices.''

January 13—The New York Symphony Orchestra. Mr. Walter Damrosch, Conductor. Mr. Maurice Koessler, Violinist. Orchestra Concert.

January 20—The German Club and the Dramatic Association. ''Hänsel and Gretel.''

February 4—Mr. Cnarles D. Hurrey. ''Christian Nationalism Among College Students.'' Address.

February 5—M. Joseph Bonnet. Organ Recital.

February 6—Dr. Bliss Perry. ''The Youth of Napoleon.'' Lecture.

February 7—Members of the Conservatory Faculty and Students. Concert.

February 10—The Oberlin College Glee Club. Concert.

February 11, 18, 25, March 4, 11—Lenten Services. Sermons by President Henry C. King, Bishop Thomas Nicholson, President Clarence A. Barbour, Professor Hugh Black, Professor William J. Hutchins.

February 13—M. Jacques Thibaud. Violin Recital.

February 14—Mr. Granville Barker. ''New Ideas in the Theatre.'' Lecture.

February 16—Professor Henry A. Saunders. ''Miniatures and Bible Text of an Early Commentary on Revelation.'' Lecture.

February 19—Professor Clarence Ward. ''The Cathedral of Reims.'' Lecture.

February 20—Mr. John Kendrick Bangs. ''More Salubrities.'' Lecture.

February 22—Professor Ian C. Hannah. ''If Washington Were Living Today.'' Address.

February 24—The Oberlin College Glee Club. Matinee Concert for Children.

February 28—Dr. John R. Mott. ''Impressions and Experiences in the War Zone.'' Lecture.

February 28-March 2—Dr. John R. Mott, Miss Margaret Burton, and Dr. Dan F. Bradley. A series of addresses.

March 3—Miss Irene Eastman. Lecture-Recital.

March 7—The Cincinnati Symphony Orchestra. Dr. Ernst Kunwald, Conductor. Mr. Emil Heermann, Violinist. Orchestra Concert.

March 13-16—Professor H. H. Powers. ''The Deeper Causes of the War.'' A series of lectures.

March 17—The Oberlin College Men's Mandolin Club. Concert.

March 19—Mrs. Frances A. Ballard. ''The Legal Status of Women in Ohio.'' Lecture.

March 20—The Flonzaley Quartet. Concert.

March 22—Dr. Edgar L. Banks. ''A Thousand Miles Down the Tigris.'' Illustrated lecture.

March 22-23—Conference on Vocations for Women: Miss Mildred Chadsey, ''State and City Positions open to Women.'' Miss Mabel Robinson, ''How to Decide upon a Vocation.'' Mrs. Helen Thompson Woolley, ''New Fields for College Women.'' Miss Helen Martin, ''Opportunities for College Women in Library Work.'' Miss Rachel S. Gallagher, ''State and Local Plans for Vocational Bureaus.''

April 4—Patriotic Mass Meeting. Speeches by Mr. W. H. Phillips, Professor G. W. Fiske, Mr. Wilford H. Evans, and President Henry C. King.

April 10—Rev. John Kelman. ''Life in the Trenches.'' Address.

April 10-12—Professor Frank Chamberlain Porter. "The New Testament and the Religion of the Spirit." Three lectures.

April 11—Mr. James Schermerhorn. "The Soul of a City." Lecture.

April 12—Miss Florence Scofield. "French War Orphans." Lecture.

April 13—Professor Gustave Lanson. "The Essential Traits and Characteristics of the French People." Lecture.

April 14—Professor and Mrs. A. M. Charles. Puppet Plays.

April 16, 17—Miss Ellen Gates Starr. "William Morris." "Bookmaking." Two lectures.

April 21—The French Club and the Dramatic Association. "Le Monde ou l'on s'ennuie."

April 25—Mr. W. R. Rose and Mr. J. H. Donahey. "A Few Remarks and a Little Art." Illustrated lecture.

April 27—Professor John A. Scott. "Homer." Lecture.

May 1—Mr. Ossip Gabrilowitsch. Piano Recital.

May 4—Mr. Sidney Dickinson. "Petrograd and the Picture Gallery of the Hermitage Palace." Illustrated lecture.

May 13—President Henry Churchill King. "Good Thoughts in Bad Times." Baccalaureate Sermon of the Graduate School of Theology.

May 17—Dr. Robert E. Speer. "The Greatest Unsolved Problem in the World." Commencement Address of the Graduate School of Theology.

May 21—The Oberlin Musical Union and the Chicago Symphony Orchestra. "The New Life," Wolf-Ferrari.

May 22—The Chicago Symphony Orchestra. Mr. Frederick Stock, Conductor. Orchestra Concert.

May 22—The Oberlin Musical Union and the Chicago Symphony Orchestra. "Parsival," Wagner.

May 24—Dean E. A. Birge. "The Ends of Scholarship." Phi Beta Kappa Address.

May 28—The Oberlin College Dramatic Association. "The Lost Silk Hat," Lord Dunsany. "The Gift of Time," Miss Marion M. Heusner. "The Work House War," Lady Gregory.

June 10—President Henry Churchill King. "Grounds of Hope in the Changing World-Order." Baccalaureate Sermon.

June 10—Rev. James L. Barton. "The Service of Missionaries in the Present World Crisis." Address.

June 12—President Henry Churchill King. Review of the Year 1916-17. Alumni Address.

June 12—Dedication of the Dudley Peter Allen Memorial Art Building. Addresses by Mr. Cass Gilbert, Professor Clarence Ward, Mr. Frederic Allen Whiting and President Henry C. King.

June 13—Professor Hugh Black. Commencement Address.

June 13—Reunion Glee Clubs. Concert.

June 15—Professor Clarence Ward. ''The Bible of the Middle Ages in Stone and Glass.'' Illustrated lecture.

June 22—Members of the Conservatory Faculty. Concert.

June 29—Professor R. A. Jelliffe. ''The Rubaiyat and Rabba Ben Ezra.'' Lecture.

July 6—Professor R. P. Jameson. ''France under Louis XIV.'' Lecture.

July 13—Professor H. L. King. ''Some Phases of Study in the Foreign Archives.'' Lecture.

July 20—Professor D. R. Moore. ''Foreign Influence in South America.'' Lecture.

July 27—Professor P. D. Sherman. ''An Evening with Sir Walter Scott.'' Illustrated lecture.

VII

RELATION TO OTHER EDUCATIONAL INSTITUTIONS

Educational and Civic Meetings

The College has continued its participation, through its Trustees, officers, teachers, and other representatives, in the various educational and civic associations with which it is most naturally connected.

Of *associations of general and national scope,* the College has been represented during the year at the Carnegie Foundation for the Advancement of Teaching, the National Collegiate Athletic Association, the American Association for the Advancement of Science, the American Association for Collegiate Registrars, the Association of American Colleges, the National Conference of Charities and Corrections, and the Association of Collegiate Alumnae.

Of *general educational associations not national in their range,* the College was represented at the annual meetings of the North Central Association of Colleges and Secondary Schools, the Ohio College Association, the Ohio Academy of Science, the Ohio Athletic Conference, and the Rhodes Scholarship Selection Committee for Ohio.

Of the *associations more distinctly departmental in their character*, the College was represented by the members of its faculties at the meetings of the American Chemical Society, the American Economics Association, the Association of American Geographers, the Association of American Geologists, the Geological Society of America, the American Historical Association, the American Hospital Association, the American Mathematical Society, the Mathematical Association of America, the American Oriental Society, the Congress of the American Ornithologists' Union, the American Philological Association, the American Political Science Association, the American Physical Society, the American Sociological Society, the Society of Biblical Literature and Exegesis, the conference of the Classical Association of the Middle West and South, the Conference of Deans of Women in connection with the Association of Collegiate Alumnae, the Conference of the Deans of Women in connection with the National Education Association, the conference of College and University Executives at Washington, the Association of Modern Language Teachers of the Central West and South, the Society of the Directors of Physical Education in Colleges and Universities, the Athletic Research Society, the Association of Directors of Physical Education for Women, the Association of Ohio Teachers of Mathematics and Science, the Ohio Music Teachers Association, and the Josselyn Botanical Society of Maine.

Colleges and Universities

The College was also represented at various university and college functions of note, including the presidential inaugurations at Tabor College, Dartmouth College, Wilson Col.

lege, Alma College, Westminster College, the University of
Texas, Atlantic Christian College, Northeastern College of
the Boston Y. M. C. A., the State University of Iowa, and
Northwestern College; the installations of the President of
Mills College, and of the Professor of Biblical Theology and
Biblical Archaeology at Xenia Theological Seminary; the
one hundred and fiftieth anniversary of Rutgers College; the
fiftieth anniversaries of Pacific Theological Seminary, Carleton College, and Howard University; and the memorial service for·President Francis Brown of Union Theological Seminary.

Secondary Schools

The relations of the College to the secondary schools were
so fully outlined in the report of last year that they need
not be reviewed again. The College is trying to do everything
possible to make these relations mutually cordial and helpful. The chief responsibility for maintaining these relations
naturally rests upon the office of the Secretary of the College,
but many other members of the Faculty share in various
forms of service to the high schools.

VIII

The Relations of the College to its Vicinage

The relations of the College to its vicinage were discussed so fully in last year's report, that it is hardly necessary to dwell upon them in the present review of the year.
Some progress has been made, we may hope, in the direction
of the many-sided coöperation which was urged last year.
The inevitable work together in much common war-service,
in the recent months, has certainly helped to that end.

IX

Gains

It remains to bring together in summary form the gains of the year and the needs still felt.

The great gains of the year have come through the gifts previously recorded, which for the first time bring the total assets of the College to more than five million dollars, exclusive of income from the Hall estate; through the completion of the beautiful Art Building; and for the current year, through the income from the Hall bequest. This income from the Hall bequest has made possible three things for the year 1917-18: provision for the deficit in the current budget, the greatly needed increase in salaries, and needed enlargement of the staff of teachers at a number of points.

The year has included also further enlargement of the grounds of the College, in line with Mr. Gilbert's general plan, and considerable improvements in buildings and equipment. The President particularly prizes genuine gains in the quality of the work of the College,—a better approximation to ideals long cherished.

X

Needs

The greatest immediate need of the College is the clearing up of all accumulated deficits and of its whole "Advances" account. The greatest single need of the College of Arts and Sciences is probably the new recitation building, which Dean Cole so earnestly urges; the greatest need of the Graduate School of Theology is also for new buildings; and the greatest need of the Conservatory of Music is probably endowment for scholarship and loan funds. Other needs are endowment for buildings, increased equipment and library appropriations, a general lectureship, the completing of the science quadrangle as soon as possible, especially the Physics laboratory, more halls of residence both for men and for women, a women's building and a women's gymnasium, the completion of the athletic field, and the meeting of the recreation needs set forth in the recommendations of the Women's Board, already recorded.

I may perhaps fittingly close this annual report and this statement of gains and needs, with the less academic forecast of the future of the College, as it lies in my hopes, which was prepared for the students' Annual of the year under review:

> First of all, I hope that Oberlin may be as good a college as can be made; needing to apologize for no element in its life or work; emphasizing quality rather than quantity, in harmony with its limitation of numbers; putting first things first, as illustrated in its limitation of outside activities; maintaining a high standard in all parts of its work, so that its degree may be one in which all its graduates may take pride.
>
> I hope that Oberlin College may continue to be a college of marked individuality, not a copy or imitation of any other, but with that genuine self-respect that a true man ought to have.
>
> As a part of this individuality, I hope Oberlin may continue to stand for some thing worth while; for courage, for convictions, for ideals, for a training that gives world-vision and prepares for world-living, for citizenship in the new civilization which we may trust is dawning. I hope its life may be a life of self-discipline, permeated by the convictions of the social consciousness, democratic through and through, and free from all cynicism and stand-pattism.
>
> I hope that in even larger degree than hitherto Oberlin's training may look to the whole man, giving an education deserving to be called "hastened living," because it helps the individual to more accurate and broader and prompter results than he could find for himself.
>
> I hope that Oberlin may soon be able fully to carry out its positive physical efficiency program, and its plan providing staff and equipment for careful and repeated

scientific studies of all the individual students to insure to them the best possible guidance in their choice of studies and later choice of vocation.

I hope that in all these ways it may be able largely and increasingly to help in providing that unselfish leadership peculiarly demanded by a democracy, and a deep-going self-control, and large-visioned ideals which may help to that mastery of the prodigious resources of power and wealth and knowledge demanded above all by the present world.

I hope that in its architecture and in all plans for future growth it may find a fit embodiment for the best in its spirit.

And I hope that whatever larger tasks may open before it, the College may face and master them, with steadily deepening faith in the highest Christian ideals for personal, national, and international life.

HENRY CHURCHILL KING.

REPORTS OF GENERAL OFFICERS AND
HEADS OF DEPARTMENTS

REPORT OF THE SECRETARY

To the President:

SIR—I have the honor to present herewith my annual report as Secretary of Oberlin College, covering the year 1916-17.

That part of the work of the Secretary's Office that has to do with the admission of students to the College of Arts and Sciences is printed under the title ''Report of the Chairman of the Committee on Admission'' (see pages 191-207).

The material in this report is grouped under two main heads, as follows:

I. PUBLICATIONS

II. OFFICE WORK, RECORDS, AND STATISTICS

I. PUBLICATIONS

THE BULLETIN OF OBERLIN COLLEGE

The Bulletin of Oberlin College included the following numbers during the college year 1916-17.

No. 124. Student Directory for 1916-17. Edition 600. October 10, 1916.

No. 125. Annual Reports for 1915-16. Edition 4,000. November 30, 1916.

No. 126. Announcement of the Course in Public School Music. Edition 500. January 10, 1917.

No. 127. Annual Catalogue for 1916-17. Edition 8,000. January 31, 1917.

No. 128. Catalogue of the Summer Session of 1917. Edition 2,500. February 15, 1917.

No. 129. Catalogue of the Graduate School of Theology. Edition 1,700. March 1, 1917.

No. 130. Announcement of Courses, College of Arts and Sciences. Edition 5,000. April 2, 1917.

No. 131. Announcement of Commencement Program. Edition 6,400. April 16, 1917.

No. 132. Catalogue of the Conservatory of Music. Edition 2,250. July 10, 1917.

The Student Directory

The Student Directory is published each fall. It contains the addresses of students and members of the faculty, together with in. formation concerning student organizations and their officers, the office hours of the Deans and other college officers, and a directory of the dormitories and rooming houses.

The Student Directories are sold at ten cents per copy and the sales pay for a large part of the expense of the publication.

The Annual Reports

The distribution of the Annual Reports for the year 1915-16 was in general similar to that of the preceding year. Approximately 2,000 copies were sent to alumni, 600 to colleges and high schools, 600 to friends of the College upon lists of names furnished by President King and Mr. Bohn, 200 to members of the faculty and citizens of Oberlin; the remaining 600 copies were mailed in response to miscellaneous requests or retained in the office for future needs.

The plan of distribution of Annual Reports to alumni expects that every alumnus who indicates his wish to receive a report each year will have a place on the mailing list; the remaining alumni are divided into three groups and the Reports are sent to the alumni in each group once every three years. Approximately one-third of the living alumni are now on the permanent list to receive the Reports annually.

That section of the Annual Reports containing the special report of the Librarian was reprinted and distributed by Professor Root for library exchange purposes.

The cost of printing the Annual Reports for 1915-16 was $1,612. This amount was $600 more than the budget estimate, the extra expense being accounted for by the great increase in the cost of both labor and paper stock. For the coming year it is proposed to reduce the size of the edition to 3,200 copies, with a saving of $400.

The Annual Catalogue

We were again unfortunate in being delayed in the publication of the Annual Catalogue, owing chiefly to the fact that the Annual Catalogue of the College and the Annual Reports were in the same printing office at the same time. The catalogue appeared as of date of January 31, 1917, but the first copies were not received from the printer until the end of February.

To meet its most important use, that of advertising the College in the high schools of the country, the catalogue, or at least certain important sections of it, should appear not later than December oi January and be distributed promptly, and it is the hope of the office that during the coming year a gain may be made in the time of the distribution of catalogue information. The plan for the coming year involves the preparation of a Special Bulletin of Information, con-taining such information as a prospective student may require. Prob-ably a bulletin of 100 to 120 pages, accompanied by the customary book of views of college buildings and grounds, will suffice for the initial effective presentation of the attractions of the College. During the coming year requests for information concerning Oberlin College will be met by the mailing of these bulletins of special information and books of views. The saving in printing involved in the substitu-tion of a small bulletin of 120 pages in the place of the general cata-logue containing 450 pages is very considerable, and a real gain is probably made in the effectiveness of the presentation to the indi-vidual student.

The college mailing list at present includes approximately 2,500 high schools, and it is the plan of the College to send copies of the catalogue or bulletin of information to each high school of importance. Books of views accompany the catalogues and personal letters are written to the principals of high schools.

The new plan for the printing and distribution of a pamphlet containing special information in the place of the large general cata-logue is already in operation in a number of colleges and universities, and it was the favorable impression made by some of these publica-tions of other colleges that has led us to decide to try the new plan.

The Commencement Program

For several years a detailed announcement of the program and of the arrangements for the Commencement Exercises has been issued as a college bulletin and mailed to all alumni. The announcement of the Program for the Commencement Exercises of June, 1917, was is-sued under date of April 16, 1917. The size of the edition issued permitted the distribution to Seniors and miscellaneous friends of the College, as well as to the alumni.

Other Publications.

The other publications listed as college bulletins during the year include the Announcement of the Course in Public School Music, the

Catalogue of the Summer Session of 1917, the Catalogue of the Gradu. ate School of Theology, the Announcement of Courses in the College of Arts and Sciences, and the Catalogue of the Conservatory of Music. These publications followed the lines of similar publications in prev. ious years and there were no changes in them requiring special mention.

Publicity

The Oberlin College Calendar and the News Letters issued from the office of the News Bureau constitute the most important items of special advertising. It is the judgment of the Committee on Adver. tising that the small amount of money available for advertising pur. poses can be more wisely expended in postage and clerical assistance for direct communications than for general advertising in monthly or weekly publications or in the daily papers. Last year the advertise. ments of the College included a page in the Oberlin Alumni Magazine, a page in the College Annual (the ''Hi-O-Hi''), a half-page in the monthly publication issued by the students of Oberlin High School, and a half-page in the ''Ohio Congregational News,'' issued in Cleve. land.

The College Calendar

The College Calendar for 1917 was issued at the first of December, 1916, in an edition of 6,500. Approximately 2,000 of the calenders were distributed to high schools for wall advertising and an equal number were mailed to friends of the College on lists furnished chiefly by President King and Mr. Bohn. Students and members of the faculty purchased the remaining copies. The profit from the sale of the calendars meets a part of the expense of the publication. The net cost to the College was $847.28, of which amount $160 was for postage. The Calendar for 1918 is now in the hands of the printer and will be ready for distribution December 8, 1917.

The News Bureau

There has been no change during the year in the method of conducting the publicity work of the College. It has been carried forward under the general direction of the News Bureau Committee of the general faculty and under the special direction of Professors P. D. Sherman and F. B. Stiven. The methods of the committee were fully presented to the Trustees at the Annual Meeting three years ago in a special report. A stenographer, Mrs. Charlotte Ormsby, gives a large part of her time to the news letters issued under the direction of Mr. Sherman and Mr. Stiven. The expense involved during the year 1916-17, amounting to $719.52, included the stenographer's salary, the necessary stationery and postage, and subscriptions to some of the publications especially needed for the News Bureau files.

Other Advertising

Copies of the college paper, ''The Oberlin Review,'' published twice each week, were mailed at the expense of the College to thirty-three important high schools. The schools selected were those which year after year send considerable numbers of Freshmen to the College.

PRINTING NEEDED

It did not prove possible to undertake the printing of any of the three bulletins mentioned in my report of last year as constituting the new items of printing most needed by the College. These were (1) a bulletin giving information concerning the Men's Gymnasium and the facilities in Oberlin for both indoor training and out-of-door athletics and play; (2) a special bulletin giving information concerning the Men's Building; and (3) a book of college legislation, to contain a careful codification of the votes of the Trustees and Faculty. I hope that it may prove possible to issue these publications during the coming year. The Men's Gymnasium bulletin and the Men's Building bulletin should be issued in editions of 5,000 each, at a cost of approximately $400 for each bulletin. The hand-book of legislation for the guidance of members of the faculty would probably require an edition of 1,000 and would cost $200.

II. OFFICE WORK, RECORDS, AND STATISTICS

The Secretary of the College is the custodian of the official records of the Board of Trustees and of the Prudential Committee, and an important part of his work consists in the preparation of the minutes of these two bodies and in issuing notifications of official actions taken at these meetings.

For a number of years the Secretary has also served as Clerk of the General Faculty, of the College Faculty, of the General Council, and of the College Council.

OFFICE EQUIPMENT

In my last report I called attention to the need of an addresso-graph machine to care for the college mailing lists. It is a great pleasure to report that during the year a complete addressograph equipment has been installed and is now in use. When Mr. J. D. Cox assumed certain items of extra expense connected with the erection of the Administration Building, amounting to a total of $12,866, the Prudential Committee voted (February 15, 1917) that $2,500 of the old Chapel Insurance Fund might be used for an addressograph equipment for the Secretary's Office, for additional filing cases needed in several of the offices, and for storage cases and shelving for the storage rooms on the third floor of the Administration Building. The total amount expended under this vote was $2,545.85, divided as follows: $1,057.43 for the addressograph equipment, including the most recent addressograph machine and attachments, a graphotype for the making of the plates, and a complete equipment of frames, plates, cards, and the necessary filing cases; $690 for additional filing cases for various offices, the greater part of this item of expense being for cases in the Secretary's Office; $788.42 for shelving, transfer boxes, and other storage equipment for the various storage rooms on the third floor of this building. I wish to express my feeling of personal gratitude to Mr. Cox for the gifts that made possible these important additions to the work of the Secretary's Office.

Mr. Cox's promise, reported to the Prudential Committee February 15th, that he would provide for the finishing of the third floor of this building for storage purposes, including the division of the third floor space into storage rooms of convenient size, will also mean much for the orderly and effective conduct of the business of all the offices in the building. Under the authority of the Prudential Committee vote, Mr. George Feick has divided the storage space on the third floor of this building into convenient storage rooms, the partitions being of fireproof construction, and the new rooms are now ready for occupancy. A very large amount of material in the shape of catalogues, reports, pamphlets, and correspondence, some of it of very considerable historic value, can now be sorted out, stored, and indexed.

VOTE FOR ALUMNI TRUSTEE

Preliminary Ballot, 1917

The term of office of Dr. E. Dana Durand will expire January 1, 1918. In the nominating ballot for the nomination of a successor, conducted in the spring and summer of 1917, the following alumni received the largest number of nominations:

Rev. Ernest Bourner Allen, of the class of 1903
Dr. E. Dana Durand, of the class of 1893
Mr. Clayton K. Fauver, of the class of 1897
Dr. Robert A. Millikan, of the class of 1891
Mr. George B. Siddall, of the class of 1891

In the preliminary ballot of 1917 there were 114 alumni who received nominating votes. The highest number of nominations received by any one candidate (apart from the retiring Trustee) was 15. There were 73 candidates who received one vote each. The total number of nominating votes cast was 1,063. There were 498 alumni who returned their ballot cards marked ''no nomination.'' We ask the alumni to return their cards in order to verify the addresses in the mailing lists.

The following table shows the participation of alumni in the preliminary ballots for the last nine years.

Preliminary Ballot	A	B	C	D	E	F	Others	Total
1909...............	1003	21	17	13	9	..	89	1152
1910...............	1203	14	9	6	6	..	86	1324
1911...............	766	31	22	17	10	..	155	1001
1912...............	1410	6	6	5	5	..	51	1483
1913...............	814	22	19	11	11	..	125	1002
1914...............	1010	40	25	20	20	..	189	1304
1915...............	....	60	46	41	38	21	412	618
1916...............	1071	19	12	11	9	..	158	1281
1917...............	830	15	15	11	11	..	181	1063

Note. For an explanation of the letters ''A,'' ''B,'' ''C,'' etc. in the preceding table, reference should be made to the explanatory paragraph following the presentation of the results of the final ballots (see page 126).

Final Ballot, 1917

In the final ballot that closed November 1, 1917, Dr. Robert A. Millikan, of the class of 1891, received the largest number of votes and was declared elected to represent the alumni for the full term of six years beginning January 1, 1918. No previous alumni trustee election has resulted in such a close grouping of the five candidates. As will be seen by reference to the details of the ballot, the candidate ranking fifth received only fifty-two ballots less than the candidate ranking second. The following table shows the participation of the alumni in the final ballot for alumni trustees for the last nine years:

Final Ballot	A	B	C	D	E	F	Total
1909..........	1098	235	237	122	229	...	1921
1910..........	1144	192	341	165	128	...	1970
1911..........	359	273	426	703	339	...	2100
1912..........	1521	104	157	594	108	...	2284
1913··········	461	228	353	528	586	...	2156
1914..........	984	494	246	279	215	...	2218
1915..........	....	640	543	332	355	544	2414
1916··········	1215	244	634	256	746	...	2595
1917..........	440	456	436	404	693	...	2429

In explanation of the preceding tables it should be said that either five or six names have been printed upon the final ballots,—five if there was but one vacancy to be filled upon the Board, six if there were two vacancies. The votes for the various candidates are tabulated under the letters "A," "B," "C," "D," "E," and "F," candidate "A" in each case being the retiring trustee, candidate "B" being the nominee receiving the next highest number of votes on the preliminary ballot, and so on.

A comparison of the preliminary and final ballots shows that approximately half as many alumni participate in the preliminary ballot as in the final ballot; it will also be seen that the retiring trustee usually receives a very large number of nominating votes, thus practically insuring a place for the retiring trustee upon the final ballot.

In the final ballot of 1917 there were 46 defective or unsigned cards, 64 cards received with no vote indicated, and 28 cards received after the close of the balloting; the total number of all cards submitted was 2,567. If the number of living alumni shown on page 134 is correct it will easily be seen that exactly 50 per cent of the living alumni of Oberlin College actively participated in the choice of the alumni representative on the Board. This is a much larger percentage of participation than is reported by some other colleges having plans for the election of trustees by alumni.

GENERAL ENROLMENT, 1916-17

The following table shows the number of students in each department during the year 1916-17, with the corresponding figures for the two years preceding added for reference:

	1914–15			1915–16			1916–17		
	Men	Women	Total	Men	Women	Total	Men	Women	Total
The College of Arts and Sciences	395	607	1002	415	614	1029	433	644	1077
The Graduate School of Theology	50	4	54	60	4	64	50	2	52
The Conservatory of Music	48	334	382	45	372	417	47	374	421
The Academy	102	90	192	92	75	167	....	....	....
The Summer Session....	64	76	140	91	100	191	78	102	180
The Slavic Course.......	12	0	12	8	0	8	7	0	7
	671	1111	1782	711	1165	1876	615	1122	1737
Deduct for duplicates in the Summer Session..	45	50	95	65	57	122	43	62	105
Deduct for duplicates in the Slavic Course.....	8	0	8	5	0	5	1	0	1
Net Totals	618	1061	1679	641	1108	1749	571	1060	1631

There was a net loss of 118 in the total attendance in all departments. This loss was caused by the dropping of the Academy Department. There was a gain of 48 students in the College of Arts and Sciences and a gain of 4 in the Conservatory of Music; there was a loss of 12 students in the Graduate School of Theology and of one student in the Slavic Course; the total enrolment in the Summer Session showed a loss of 11, but after making deductions for Summer Session duplicates, the net figures for the Summer Session showed a gain of 7.

The above totals do not include 72 "unclassified students" who were not of college rank, who were enrolled for one subject in the Conservatory of Music. These unclassified students are students whose homes are in Oberlin or in towns near Oberlin, and almost all of them are children in the public schools of Oberlin.

States Furnishing Largest Numbers of Students

Of the 1,631 students enrolled last year, 1,550 came from 47 states and territories of the United States; 81 came from 18 foreign countries. The state of Ohio furnished 724 students. The states that sent the largest numbers of students were as follows:

Ohio	724
Pennsylvania	142
New York	93
Illinois	88
Michigan	78
Iowa	48
Indiana	48
Wisconsin	30
Minnesota	30
Massachusetts	26
Nebraska	20

There is no change in the relative order of the first ten states appearing in the above list. The large increase in the number of students from Pennsylvania is worth noting. Two years ago (in 1914-15) Pennsylvania ranked fifth with a total representation of 102.

Students from Ohio

For many years prior to 1907 the number of Oberlin students enrolled from the state of Ohio was 50 per cent of the total; during some of the years the percentage was slightly below 50, during other years it rose slightly above that mark. Between 1907 and 1910 the Ohio percentage dropped from 50 to 45. For eight years, beginning with the year 1909-10 the percentage of Ohio students has not varied much from the 45 per cent mark. These variations will be seen in the following table:

	Total	Total from Ohio	Per cent from Ohio
1906-07	1848	935	50.60
1907-08	1881	912	48.48
1908-09	1945	907	46.63
1909-10	1993	910	45.66
1910-11	2043	930	45.52
1911-12	1789	817	45.67
1912-13	1809	791	43.73
1913-14	1809	775	42.84
1914-15	1679	752	44.79
1915-16	1749	773	44.19
1916-17	1631	724	44.39

Number of Men in Oberlin

There was a decrease both in the total enrolment of men and in the percentage of men in the entire institution, fully accounted for by the discontinuance of the Academy Department. The following table gives information concerning the enrolment of men in the entire institution in recent years.

Entire Institution	Number of Men	Total Enrolment	Percentage
1904-05	652	1715	38.02
1906-07	662	1848	35.82
1908-09	690	1945	35.47
1910-11	765	2043	37.44
1912-13	693	1809	38.31
1914-15	618	1679	36.80
1915-16	641	1749	36.65
1916-17	571	1631	35.01

The percentage of men shown above is the smallest in the history of the College. No marked improvement in the percentage can reasonably be expected until the Trustees establish in Oberlin a department of work appealing primarily to men. The establishment of a strong technical school that would bring to Oberlin three or four hundred men would, in my judgment, be the most effective means of securing that approximate equality of numbers that is needed for the most perfect type of coeducation of the sexes.

Number of Men in the College of Arts and Sciences

The following table gives facts concerning the percentage of men in the College of Arts and Sciences in recent years:

The College	Number of Men	Total Enrolment	Percentage
1910-11	411	1004	40.94
1911-12	428	998	42.88
1912-13	408	1017	40.12
1913-14	426	1029	41.40
1914-15	395	1002	39.42
1915-16	415	1029	40.33
1916-17	433	1077	40.20

There is a net gain of 18 in the number of men enrolled in the College of Arts and Sciences for the year 1916-17, as compared to the preceding year. The total attendance of college men, 433, is the largest in the history of the College.

During the last seven years there has been a surprising steadiness in the percentage of men in the College of Arts and Sciences.

REPORT OF THE SECRETARY

ENROLMENT FOR TWENTY-SIX YEARS

The following chart shows the variations in enrolment during the last twenty-six years, beginning with 1891-92, the year in which the count was first made by the College year instead of the *Calendar* year:

'91 -92	'92 -93	'93 -94	'94 -95	'95 -96	'96 -97	'97 -98	'98 -99	'99 -00	'00 -01	'01 -02	'02 -03	'03 -04	'04 -05
Other Departments 1057	1098	1001	1056	975	855	877	789	906	929	883	931	985	1045
College 405	394	396	371	439	428	433	419	417	428	499	578	633	670

ENROLMENT FOR TWENTY-SIX YEARS

(Continued)

'04 -05	'05 -06	'06 -07	'07 -08	'08 -09	'09 -10	'10 -11	'11 -12	'12 -13	'13 -14	'14 -15	'15 -16	'16 -17	
													2000
Other Departments 1045	1057	1046	1063	1070	1011	1089	791	792	780	677	720	554	
													1500
													1000
College 670	714	802	818	875	982	1004	998	1017	1029	1002	1029	1077	
													500

DEGREES AND DIPLOMAS, 1916-17

The following degrees were conferred during the year 1916-17 :

Honorary—	Men	Women	Total
Doctor of Laws (LL.D.)	3	0	3
Doctor of Letters (Litt.D.)	1	0	1
Master of Arts (A.M.)	0	1	1
	4	1	5 .

In Course—			
Master of Arts (A.M.)	3	7	10
Bachelor of Arts (A.B.)	70	115	185
Bachelor of Divinity (D.B.)	12	1	13
Bachelor of Music (Mus.B.)	5	17	22
	90	140	230

In addition to the above there were fourteen diplomas issued for the completion of the work in the Teachers' Course in Physical Education; three of these were for the course for men and eleven for the course for women. All of the graduates of the Teachers' Course during the year were also graduates from the College of Arts and Sciences with a single exception; this exception was for a man who left Oberlin at the end of his Senior year without having met the technical requirements for graduation, but having completed all the special requirements for the diploma of the Teachers' Course in Physical Education, and the bestowing of the diploma of the Teachers' Course in Physical Education followed a further year of study at Cornell University.

The aggregate of degrees and diplomas issued during the year 1916-17 was 249. The figures for the last ten years are shown below:

1907-08	208
1908-09	165
1909-10	235
1910-11	251
1911-12	275
1912-13	273
1913-14	261
1914-15	278
1915-16	269
1916-17	249

Of the 249 new degrees issued there were 25 duplicate names; that is, 25 were issued to men and women who were already on the college rolls. Making this deduction the net addition during the year to the total number of individual graduates was 224.

Summary of Degrees and Diplomas

The following table shows the total number of degrees and diplomas that have been issued since the founding of the College, also the number of individual graduates, corrected to date of October 1, 1917:

	Men	Women	Total	Men	Women	Total
The College of Arts and Sciences:						
Bachelor of Arts (A.B.)	2396	1856	4252			
Bachelor of Philosophy (Ph.B.)	108	201	309			
Bachelor of Science (S.B.)	25	6	31			
Bachelor of Letters (L.B.)	1	196	197			
Other Graduates of the Literary Course (Lit.)	3	766	769			
Certificate of Teachers' Course	1	0	1			
Certificate of Teachers' Course in Physical Education	84	212	296			
				2618	3237	5855
The Graduate School of Theology:						
Bachelor of Divinity (D. B.)	462	2	464			
Diploma of Classical Course	322	2	324			
Diploma of English Course	68	2	70			
Master of Divinity (S.T.M.)	2	0	2			
				854	6	860
The Conservatory of Music:						
Bachelor of Music (Mus.B.)	74	198	272			
Diploma of Graduation	13	60	73			
				87	258	345
Masters' Degrees:						
Master of Arts (A.M.)	568	177	745			
Master of Science (S.M.)	2	0	2			
				570	177	747
Honorary Degrees:						
Master of Arts (A.M.)	67	50	117			
Master of Music (Mus.M.)	0	1	1			
Doctor of Divinity (D.D.)	50	1	51			
Doctor of Music (Mus.D.)	1	0	1			
Doctor of Laws (LL.D.)	32	1	33			
Doctor of Letters (Litt.D.)	4	2	6			
Doctor of Science (Sc.D.)	5	0	5			
				159	55	214
The Slavic Course:						
Diploma of Graduation				25	0	25
				4313	3733	8046
Names Counted Twice				1043	406	1449
Net Total of Individual Graduates				3270	3327	6597

SUMMARY OF ALL STUDENTS: EIGHTY-FOUR YEARS

When the Seventy-fifth Anniversary Catalogue was published in 1908 a complete list was printed giving the names of all the students who had been in attendance in any department of Oberlin College at any time during the seventy-five years of Oberlin history. The total was found to be 35,682. The following table shows the additional new students enrolled year by year since 1908:

Students enrolled prior to 1908..................	35,682
In the year 1908-09...........................	805
" 1909-10...........................	822
" 1910-11...........................	824
" 1911-12...........................	638
" 1912-13...........................	768
" 1913-14...........................	742
" 1914-15...........................	669
" 1915-16...........................	659
" 1916-17...........................	722
	42,331

Adding to the 1908 total the additional names of students enrolled during the last nine years, we have an aggregate of 42,331. This is the total number of students who have been in regular attendance in some department of the College, correct to date of June 30, 1917.

The above total of 42,331 is divided as follows: graduates, 6,597; non-graduates, 35,734.

SUMMARY OF LIVING ALUMNI

	Men	Women	Total
Graduates of the College of Arts and Sciences..	1961	2651	4612
Graduates of the Graduate School of Theology..	525	6	531
Graduates of the Conservatory of Music........	86	239	325
Recipients of Masters' Degrees	310	138	448
Recipients of Honorary Degrees...............	97	35	132
Graduates of the Slavic Course...............	22	0	22
	3001	3069	6070
Names counted twice.........................	586	348	934
Net total of Living Alumni..................	2415	2721	5136

OFFICERS AND TEACHERS

The officers of instruction and administration for the college year of 1916-17 were as follows:

	Men	Women	Total	Men	Women	Total
TRUSTEES	...	...	...	23	1	24
TEACHING STAFF:						
Emeritus Professors	5	1	6			
Professors	50	2	52			
Associate Professors	14	6	20			
Assistant Professors	3	0	3			
Instructors	9	20	29			
Other Teachers and Assistants in Instruction	1	3	4			
				82	32	114
ADMINISTRATIVE OFFICERS AND ASSISTANTS	...	...	...	10	13	23
LIBRARIAN AND LIBRARY ASSISTANTS	...	...	...	2	13	15
				117	59	176

Grouped by departments, the table of officers and teachers may be shown as follows:

	College of Arts and Sciences	Graduate School of Theology	Conservatory of Music	General	Total
Trustees	....	....	....	24	24
Emeritus Professors	1	3	1	1	6
Professors	26	7	19	....	52
Associate Professors	17	....	3	....	20
Assistant Professors	3	....	....	....	3
Instructors	20	....	8	1	29
Other Teachers and Assistants in Instruction	4	....	....	....	4
Administrative Officers and Assistants	5	....	3	15	23
Librarian and Library Assistants	....	....	1	14	15
	76	10	35	55	176

With reference to the preceding table it should be noted that two of the teachers classed "general" offer instruction in some department of the institution, as follows: President King in the College and in the School of Theology; Professor Root in the College. It should also be noted that Professor Hutchins of the School of Theology offers courses in the College and that Professor Dickinson of the Conservatory offers courses designed especially for college students.

While this report is supposed to cover the college year of 1916-17, it seems proper to present also a statement of the enrolment for the fall term of the present year, corrected to the date of preparation of this report (October 22, 1917). To the figures for this year have been prefixed the corresponding statistics for the preceding seven years:

The College—	1910	1911	1912	1913	1914	1915	1916	1917
Graduate Students	8	13	25	28	31	20	17	9
Seniors	.178	203	219	184	187	186	209	173
Juniors	195	220	180	188	197	215	222	181
Sophomores	278	216	214	243	247	250	235	240
Freshmen	294	278	299	309	305	312	332	306
Special Students	45	41	61	47	16	17	8	16
	998	971	998	999	983	1000	1023	925
The Graduate School of Theology	61	52	57	63	52	60	49	38
The Conservatory of Music.	406	326	351	369	390	382	407	330
The Academy	315	274	264	219	177	153	...	...
Drawing and Painting	42	42	...	...	...	...	...	...
Slavic Students	10	7	13	14	13	8	7	7
"Sub-Freshmen"	...	...	...	...	...	...	11	...
	1832	1672	1683	1664	1615	1603	1497	1300
Deductions for Slavic students classed in other departments	6	6	12	13	8	5	1	3
Net totals	1826	1666	1671	1651	1607	1598	1496	1297

In the above table no figures are shown during the last six years for the department of Drawing and Painting; the students in Drawing and Painting are now included in the totals of the College of Arts and Sciences.

During the year 1916-17 eleven students were enrolled with the classification of "Sub-Freshmen." At the time of the discontinuance of the Academy these students lacked only a few units of meeting the requirements for admission as Freshmen and they were allowed to register during the year 1916-17 for the completion of their preparatory work.

Respectfully submitted,

GEORGE M. JONES.

REPORT OF THE ASSISTANT TO THE PRESIDENT

To the President:

SIR—This report of the Assistant to the President concerns the third full year of the present appointment and affords an opportunity to summarize the work of the year and plans for the immediate future.

FINANCIAL

It is a pleasure to supplement the report appearing elsewhere concerning the gifts of the year by a somewhat more detailed comment on the growth of the particular funds to which this office has given special attention. For some time an effort has been made to increase the *loan funds* at the disposal of the College in the aid of deserving students, supplementing the help which is given in the form of outright gifts. For this purpose there will soon become available a fund of $20,000, the gift of Mr. Andrew H. Noah of Akron, Ohio, a fund made up of his former gift of $10,000 for student aid and a new fund of like amount recently promised, part of which is already in the hands of the College Treasurer. This fund when completed will make available an income of approximately $1,000, which may be loaned each year. As these loans are repaid from time to time there will gradually be built up a steadily increasing amount available for this worthy purpose. The College is exceedingly grateful to Mr. Noah for his help at this point, as the number of self-supporting men in the student body continues and the College hopes that this class of students may steadily be encouraged to secure their education here.

For *current aid of self-supporting students,* both men and women, a number of alumni and friends have contributed during the past three years small amounts to meet emergency needs not provided for by our regular scholarship and loan funds. These contributions aggregated for 1914-15, $2,010; for 1915-16, $1,750; for 1916-17, $2,121.50; a total of $5,881.50. It is highly desirable that ultimately sufficient endowment be provided that it may become unnecessary to appeal annually to these loyal alumni for current needs. Steady progress has been made in recent years, however, in building up the *endowment funds.* The principal funds in the hands of the Treasurer for scholarship and loan purposes have increased $37,473.41 in the last three years.

The *Student Employment Fund* in the theological department should have special attention called to it. For some ten years or more this department has had in operation a plan by which needy theo. logical students were given the opportunity to *earn* $125 per year by doing practical work,—preaching, acting as pastors' assistants, as superintendents of religious education, as teachers of foreigners, as directors of boys' clubs, Y. M. C. A. work, etc. The theological fac. ulty has asked that for the immediate future the raising of an addi. tional endowment of $50,000 for this purpose be made a preferred interest. Until this is accomplished it will be necessary to secure current funds to carry on this work without at all entering upon the greatly needed expansion of the plan which it is hoped may come as the student body in the School of Theology grows in numbers.

For the work of the *Shansi Memorial Association* the Assistant has been able to secure for the current year's budget $1,250, to supplement the Shansi Day subscriptions. The attention of the alumni is called to the extended reference made to the work of this Association in the President's report.

It is appropriate to make special mention also of the *gift from Mr. J. D. Cox* of Cleveland, amounting to $12,500, in addition to the generous sum previously given for the erection of the Administration Building. This fund replaces an advance made by the College in the construction of the building, and makes possible, also, the purchase of additional much needed equipment for the administrative offices. Mr. Cox very generously agreed to take on, in addition, the completion of the third floor of the building for storage purposes, the decoration of the interior walls, and the erection of handsome candelabra lighting columns at the entrance of the building.

By vote of the faculty and Prudential Committee $10,000 of the fund given by Mr. Cox was designated for the use of the permanent camp for the department of Physical Education for Women on the shore of Lake Erie, thus making possible the carrying out of a plan long hoped for by Dr. Hanna and her associates. An exceptionally fortunate site has been secured on the lake shore one-half mile west of Ceylon Junction, known as the James Black farm. This piece of property affords ample grounds for the enterprise; a creek navigable by canoes and row boats; over half a mile of very satisfactory beach, etc., giving opportunity for the development of the various kinds of work to be carried on in a summer camp. It is planned to develop this property not only for the use of the department of Physical Education for Women (the summer session of this department will be held there), but also as a general recreation place for the College. It is anticipated that the project will be increasingly significant as the scope of the plan is enlarged under the direction of Dr. Hanna and the deans of women.

One of the interesting events of the year was the raising of $1,144.81 by the Oberlin Association of New York, with the assistance of a few friends in the New England Association in Boston, to meet the expenses incurred by the College in the work of *military training and Red Cross* instruction following the entrance of the United States into the war. This timely help relieved the College in splendid fashion of what would otherwise have been an addition to a budget already over-burdened. It is planned to invite during the coming year other associations of alumni to share in a similar service in providing funds for the use of Oberlin men under arms and particularly for Oberlin men overseas.

A full report of the work of the *Living Endowment Union* appears elsewhere. It may be sufficient to note at this point that the following gains were made during the year: in the number of new subscriptions as compared to other years; in the aggregate amount represented by these subscriptions; and also in holding the subscriptions already on record, i. e. the number of cancellations and decreased subscriptions is noticeably less than in the year 1915-16, and this in spite of all the multitude of appeals being made in every direction. The total net income of the Living Endowment Fund for the year ending August 31st was $3,732.01. The total amount, exclusive of endowment, which has been received since the beginning of the Union in current funds is $44,317.89. The total endowment funds of all sorts in the hands of the Living Endowment Union are $4,175.66.

ALUMNI RELATIONS

The Assistant was privileged to attend gatherings of the alumni during the year at Toledo, Detroit, Chicago, and Cincinnati. The extensive trip planned by the President and the Assistant to the Pacific Coast had to be postponed on account of the war situation. There were, however, in addition to the alumni gatherings mentioned, numerous conferences with smaller groups at various points on matters of College interest. So far as it may be feasible it is hoped that this office may be used as a clearing house by the alumni on matters of mutual concern, and the Assistant to the President is ready at all times to render any possible help in arranging for alumni meetings, answering inquiries, etc. The usual *news letter* to the alumni was sent out in the fall and the plan will be continued this year.

NEEDS

In addition to the $50,000 needed for the endowment of the Student Employment Fund in the theological department already noted, there should be kept in mind the very urgent need for additional funds to provide adequate housing for the Graduate School of Theology. How serious the situation is at the present time may be indicated by a recent recommendation by the State Building Inspector:

> Considering the fact that this building was built in about the year 1870, also that it contains some 41 bedrooms, besides class and assembly rooms, that it is 4 stories high, of composite construction, is not equipped with proper ventilating system, lighting arrangements bad, fire hazard is great, would respectfully recommend that you discontinue the use of this building for school or college purposes as soon as possible.

This statement alone would seem fully to justify an attempt at the earliest possible date to secure funds to erect suitable buildings for this department which has meant so much to the life of Oberlin. It should be remembered in this connection that the Graduate School of Theology does not share in the benefits of the Hall bequest.

The College of Arts and Sciences also stands in need of greatly enlarged facilities for recitation purposes. Suitable buildings to meet this need should not be long delayed. To provide at all adequately for this central department of the work there should be erected a Physics Building (releasing space in Peters Hall) and at least one large centrally located building for the general use of the College.

The Assistant continues as heretofore to give such help as he may in connection with the President's teaching, in caring for the general administrative responsibilities of the office, and in the work of maintaining close relations to the constituency of the College by personal conferences, correspondence, and attendance on representative religious and educational gatherings from time to time.

Respectfully submitted,

W. F. BOHN.

THE COLLEGE OF ARTS AND SCIENCES

CONTENTS OF THE REPORT OF THE DEAN

REPORT OF THE DEAN

To the President:

Sɪʀ—I have the honor to present the following report of the work of the College of Arts and Sciences for the year 1916-17.

I. The Faculty

The *active membership* of the College faculty for the year was seventy-four. Four of this number—the Secretary, the Assistant to the President, the Assistant Secretary, and the Registrar—were officers who gave no regular instruction. The list of seventy teachers on duty for the year comprised thirty Professors, fifteen Associate Professors, three Assistant Professors, eighteen Instructors, and four Assistants. Instruction was also given in the College by nine teachers—seven Professors, one Associate Professor, and one Instructor—whose principal work lay in other departments of the institution. The nominal ratio of regular teachers to students was one to 15.3, again a slight improvement over the ratio of the preceding year. It still remains true that this ratio indicates one of the greatest weaknesses of the College. In most schools of the class to which Oberlin College belongs this ratio is not more than one to 12.

The *personnel* of the faculty showed about the usual amount of variation from the preceding year. The members absent on leave for the year were Professor Root, Associate Professor Cairns, Miss Doerschuk, and Miss Belden. Dr. Hanna was on leave for the second half-year. Withdrawals from the faculty by resignation or termination of appointment were those of Acting Assistant Professors Scott and Bryan, Dr. Miriam T. Davis, Mr. Aldrich, Miss Shirley Smith, Mr. Spore, Miss Butterfield, Mr. Coffin, Mrs. Rogers, and Mrs. Geiser. The teachers returning after leave of absence were Professor Hall, and Associate Professors Sinclair, Jelliffe, and Cochran. The new appointments for the year were those of Professor Keyes D. Metcalf, Associate Professor Shaw, Assistant Professor Domroese, Miss Brownback, Mrs. Harroun, Mr. Maclure, Miss Stephen, Miss Rodenbaeck, and at the middle of the year, Mr. Brosius.

Important Faculty Actions

Important actions by the faculty of the College of Arts and Sciences were not numerous, but they were fully up to the average in significance.

A few questions of rather large importance occupied the attention of the faculty to so great an extent that somewhat fewer decisions than usual were reached.

One of the problems that took a great deal of time was that of reorganization of the schedule of classes. The congestion of classes at certain hours, especially eight, nine, and ten o'clock on Tuesday, Thursday, and Saturday, had become so great as to make an almost unendurable condition. The faculty and various committees had been struggling with the problem for two or three years without reaching satisfactory results, but the critical situation brought the question up again at the beginning of the year under review with an insistence that would not be denied. Some other pressing problems had linked themselves up with it. The difficulty of finding sufficient daylight time for the laboratories, for athletics, both intercollegiate and intramural, and for individual and group recreation had brought a growing demand for such a rearrangement of class appointments as would give relief at this point. The apparent necessity of excusing a large number of the men from attendance at Chapel in order to give them sufficient time to attend to their preliminary duties as table waiters at the various boarding houses had long been irksome, and was becoming increasingly so from year to year. The problem as a whole was, therefore, to secure more class periods and a longer time before the mid-day Chapel without encroaching further upon the afternoon hours, or indeed, if possible, in conjunction with an actual lessening of the time required by afternoon appointments. The difficulties seemed insuperable, but a plan was finally worked out that promises to go a long way toward the desired solution. On the 28th of November the first step was taken by the adoption of Eastern standard time instead of Central time, the change beginning with the opening of the spring term. This met the demand for an extra hour of daylight in the afternoon. On the 5th of December it was voted to have all classes and the Chapel service begin on the hour instead of seven minutes after the hour, the new plan to go into effect at the opening of the year 1917-18. This change, made primarily in the hope that it would contribute to a general improvement in the punctuality of the college community, caused the Chapel service to begin and end seven minutes earlier than before, and so gave just that much additional time between the service and the noon meal. The addition has made it possible to require all table waiters, as well as all other college men, to be in regular attendance at the Chapel service.

To reduce the pressure on the most heavily congested days the faculty authorized a larger use of Monday forenoon, allowing the scheduling of more classes on Monday, Wednesday, and Friday than had been permitted before. The eight o'clock hour on Monday must still be kept free, however, and only such classes may be held at nine as require no preparation in advance on the part of students. As several such classes have been found, principally in the case of courses devoted largely to lectures or to floor work, it has proved possible to transfer a considerable amount of work in the aggregate to these other days, and to reduce somewhat the pressure at the most heavily congested points without adding to the number of afternoon classes. The afternoon situation was further improved by the arrangement that all elementary science classes shall have laboratory periods of not more than two hours. On this plan all these classes have two two-hour periods of laboratory work each week in place of the one three-hour period that was formerly more common.

The combined effect of these changes, as far as the brief experience of the new year shows it, goes to prove that we are on the right track. Further transfers of classes to the Monday, Wednesday, Friday groups will be necessary, however, and it may be found advisable to reduce further the restrictions on the eight and nine o'clock hours on Monday.

A change in routine administration was made on the 20th of February, when authority to grant permission to students to take more than the maximum of thirty-six hours in one department was delegated to the Committee on Substitutions. This action is a further step in the direction of relieving the faculty of all routine administration.

On the same date the faculty took up again the evil, often discussed, of students absenting themselves from regular tests and examinations and putting the teacher to the trouble of providing a new paper at some later time. Fees had long been imposed for such delayed tests and examinations, but excuses from these fees on the ground of sickness or other disability had always been rather freely granted. There is no question that in many cases the privilege of release on these grounds was being abused. The faculty finally came to the point of prescribing that the fees should be charged for a delayed test or examination in all cases, though it was recognized that some hardship would result when there was real illness or other reason for unavoidable absence. The hardship is comparable, however, to one's obligation in case of illness to pay for the physician's services and medicine, and it is true that, however good the reason for the absence, extra work on the teacher's part results. The new legislation brought about an immediate, decided reduction in the number of absences from regular tests and examinations.

On the 6th of March another step in the development of the aesthetic side of the college curriculum was taken. It came naturally at this time, in connection with the completion of the beautiful new Art Museum, and the establishment of the new professorship of History and Appreciation of Art. The action was the establishment of four majors in Fine Arts, a department in which there had been no major courses up to that time. The first of the four new majors is in the History of Art; the second is in Architecture; the third in Painting and Sculpture; the fourth in the Practice of Art, with larger attention than in the other majors to studio work. The establishment of major work in this subject on the same plane as in Music makes a very satisfactory recognition of Fine Arts as a suitable part of a college course.

On the same date the faculty voted to release from the final examinations in the second semester Seniors whose work up to the beginning of the examination period was of ''B'' quality or better. Whether the custom is to be regarded as permanently established was not determined; that question will need to be brought up in the course of the coming year.

Several questions relating to military training in the College and the release of students for military, naval, and agricultural work grew out of the entrance of the nation into the war. The question of military training had been taken up even earlier, with the result that a committee of the general faculty recommended to that body on the 27th of March that a Reserve Officers' Training Corps be established, that an instructor be employed for the remainder of the year to train the corps, that men who completed the course be allowed one hour of credit for it, and that permission be given, in any cases where it seemed necessary, to drop any one course with part credit, in order to make room for the new work. This recommendation was adopted, an instructor was employed, and the work was started in the spring term, with an initial enrolment of over three hundred men. This number was rapidly reduced by the later withdrawal of almost two hundred men from College for different forms of national service and for farm work, but the number finally completing the course and receiving the certificate for it was one hundred and thirty-seven. The practical results reached by the training seemed clearly to be thoroughly good, and reflected decided credit upon the instructor, Mr. H. F. Loomis, of the class of 1918 of the Graduate School of Theology, and his assistants. Among the latter were the instructors in the department of Physical Education and several upper class students who had had previous training of this kind.

With reference to future military training, it seems to be the general opinion that it is absolutely necessary for the advanced training of those who took the work last year and highly desirable for the new students coming into college this year to have an instructor of wider training, and if possible, of some direct experience with more modern phases of warfare. The search for such a man has been diligently prosecuted all through the summer, but up to the time of writing this report no candidate who seemed fully qualified to meet the new demands of the place has been found, principally because the government has swept into active service in training new recruits practically every man in the country of the type we should like to have. The search has even been extended to Canada, but there, too, the one wholly acceptable candidate who has been found was ordered abroad just as the negotiations for his coming here were on the point of being completed. The Committee on Military Affairs is still at work on the problem.

Closely parallel to the arrangements for the military training of the men has been the recognition of the Red Cross activities of the women. Three sorts of classes in this work were formed, one in First Aid, one in Surgical Dressings, and one in Dietetics, all under the auspices and direction of the local Red Cross organization. When it became evident that many college women wished to take the work, arrangements were made whereby college credit for one hour was allowed to every student completing one course successfully, and permission was granted, when necessary, to drop one college course, with part credit, to make room for this work. No additional credit was given for more than one course. As the fees charged made these courses much more expensive for the women than the military training was for the men, the College assumed half the expense for each student who carried a course through to completion. The necessary funds for this purpose and for the expense of the military training were supplied from the amount generously contributed by the New York and Boston alumni for the support of ''war work'' in the College. The number of college women completing one or more courses was four hundred and seventy-two.

The legislation by the faculty with reference to the credits of men who left college altogether for military service is also of interest. In general, the arrangement has been that men enlisting in any form of federal service have been released from their college work and given full semester credit for all the unfinished courses in which they were doing satisfactory work at the time of withdrawal. All courses in which such a student was below the passing grade or behind the class in the amount of work, were reported as conditioned or incomplete. The student has the same opportunity to bring the mark up to a satisfactory standard on the part courses that he would have had on full courses if he had withdrawn at the end of the whole semester, and secures the same credit by doing so.

The demand of the nation and the state for all possible assistance in developing the food resources of the country led to an early arrangement for the release of men who would undertake farm work. The terms of the release were the same as in the case of those going into federal service, with the further condition that the student should keep up the farm work from the date of withdrawal at least to the end of the college year. Most of the men who withdrew on that arrangement went to their own home farms, or to the farms of persons well known to them, and kept at the work through the summer. More than a hundred men working in this way undoubtedly made a very real contribution to the needs of the nation and the world. If the call should be repeated in the coming spring, as it seems likely it may be, it will probably be advisable to bind all men so released to remain at the work until the end of the summer.

In addition to releasing the men—117 is the exact number—for agricultural work, the faculty authorized releasing women on the same terms, either to help in their homes so that more men could be employed on the farm, or to contribute directly to the farm work, especially in the way of gardening. Twenty-two women were thus released. Yet another form of contribution to agricultural production was the gardening carried on in Oberlin under the general direction of Professor Chapin, who gave a course of five lectures on the principles of good gardening and supervised the practical work of the participants in the activity. A credit of one hour was allowed, as in the Red Cross courses, for the satisfactory completion of a sufficient amount of this work.

On the 8th of May, the faculty authorized an increase in the fee charged for voluntary changes of study after the schedule for the year has been filed. For some five years past a fee of fifty cents has been exacted for each change asked for by the student. It had become quite clear that this fee was not a sufficient deterrent to a large amount of purely capricious change, and the increase was made for the double purpose of bringing about more care in the original choice of studies, and of reducing the amount of arbitrary, often unreasonable, change. Experience so far seems to justify making the increase.

A good deal of attention was devoted in the year to the old question of giving or withholding credit for ''Practice Teaching.'' The question had been a subject of controversy for a number of years, and at the last long discussion of it had been laid over for two years, with a definite direction to have it taken up again in the second semester of the year 1916-17. Under the arrangement in force in the intervening time, students preparing for certification as teachers in the state of Ohio without examination were obliged to do the practice teaching required, whether in the regular year or in the summer session, as an addition to the work credited toward graduation. It had always seemed to a majority of the faculty that this kind of work was so technical and professional in character as to make it highly undesirable as part of a student's course for the A. B. degree. To the students themselves, however, and to a strong minority of the faculty, it seemed a not unreasonable view that practice teaching should be regarded as a laboratory course for the practical illustration of the principles to be put into use in their later professional work, and as such should stand upon the same basis as laboratory work of any other sort. The long contest, into the details of which it would be unprofitable to go here, was finally ended, so far as this particular question is concerned, by an almost unanimous vote of the faculty on the 1st of June, permitting this work to be credited to the extent of not more than two semester hours. This result, which came as a surprise to almost every one participating in the discussion, seems to have been due not so much to a revision of anybody's judgment on the whole matter, as to a feeling that it was not desirable to prolong a controversy which seemed bound to continue in one form or another until some allowance of credit should be made. There was also some feeling that even if the technical character of the work be fully granted, the fact that several other departments have a larger amount of such work in their curriculum than was here involved made it decidedly unfair to the department of Education to refuse the addition asked. That the general feeling of the faculty had not greatly changed, however, was indicated by the unanimous vote directing the Committee on Course to study in the coming year the whole question of the amount of vocational training in the college curriculum, with a view of reducing inequalities in the amounts allowed to the several departments.

On the 6th of June, the faculty voted to refuse final honors to any student whose work in the latter half of the senior year is not kept up to a satisfactory standard, even though his previous work fully entitled him to the honors. This is to provide for the rare case of a student who, having attained his end by fine work through the major part of his course, is willing to drop back to very ordinary work at the end.

The outstanding points in the work of the faculty as a whole are, then, the radical changes in the time of classes; revision of the scale of fees for special tests and examinations and for changes of studies; establishment of majors in Fine Arts; management of the difficult questions relating to military and agricultural activities; and settlement of the controversy over practice teaching.

The reports of the faculty for the year under review afford the usual survey of the work done and the conditions under which it is carried on. Many reports also offer general suggestions relating to the welfare of the whole institution. These general discussions are brought together as usual after the strictly departmental reports.

Bibliography, Language, Literature, and Art

For the *Department of English* Professor Wager comments upon the noticeably good effect of the institution of sub-Freshman sections in English Composition upon the writing of our students. He believes also that certain high schools have been led by the establishment of this course to put more stress upon the formal aspects of composition. "I hope," he adds, "that the new Introductory Course in Literature may have similar results in the range and accuracy of our students' reading. In fact, I trust that before long we may see our way to requiring one serious course in Literature of all our students. I am aware that it is not desirable to increase the number of requirements; at the same time, so long as we insist upon their knowing something of Economics and History and Fine Arts and Philosophy and Social and Political Science, there is a certain absurdity in allowing them to remain, as many of our men do remain, totally ignorant of Literature, in which, after all, the profoundest mental and moral achievements of our race have been expressed. I cannot but believe that the need for such literary training will be greater during the next few years than ever before, not wholly for aesthetic reasons, but chiefly for moral ones."

Professor Sherman notes particularly the interest manifested by students in the smaller advanced classes, in which some original investigation had been carried on in conference with the instructor. In the course of the year Mr. Sherman was able to add sets of stereopticon slides illustrating various aspects of the courses in literature, and secured also much original unpublished material from descendants of Sir Walter Scott, Thackery, and Dickens, shedding light on various phases of the Victorian novel. From the officials of the British Museum and the Bibliotheque Nationale, at Paris, valuable transcripts and facsimiles of sixteenth and seventeenth century books were secured. From Mr. A. H. Bullen, director of the Shakespeare Head Press, Stratford-on-Avon, the foremost authority on matters of Elizabethan and early Stuart literature, have come many copies of his publications of rare and unedited texts. All these are of special value in several of Mr. Sherman's courses.

Professor Wightman, of the *Department of French*, comments upon the increase in the number of students in the beginning course, by which the formation of a sixth section of that class was made necessary. The class in first-year Spanish also showed a notable increase in numbers, and much interest in the work as well. As a consequence Spanish is hereafter to be taught each year, instead of alternating as heretofore with Italian. Mr. Wightman feels that we shall probably be obliged also to have more than one division in beginning Spanish, and to offer a second-year course in the language. Many high schools are now teaching the subject, and several colleges are putting it on the same footing as French and German for admission. The time may have come, it is suggested, for us to take the same step. The growth of the study of French in the high schools should have the effect of lessening the pressure for beginning French in the college. An increased library allowance has enabled the department to secure the best reviews in French, Spanish, and Italian, as well as to purchase more books in these languages. The French Club was carried on with the usual success, and gave one of the best modern French comedies in a very satisfactory way. A special piece of good fortune in the year was that of securing a lecture in French by M. Lanson, one of the best known and most learned of living French savants. The hope is once more expressed that an adequate fund may be secured for the department to obtain such lectures more frequently. Another need, one of the most pressing, in fact, is that of sufficient satisfactory class rooms.

Professor Jameson notes the withdrawal, on account of the small number of students electing it, of the course in French Literary Criticism that he has given for a number of years, and the substitution of a new course in French Drama for it. The new course supplies a gap in the departmental offerings, and has been more popular than the older one, although given almost entirely in French. Mr. Jameson was again director of the French Club, and prepared, in connection with that work, some original material that he hopes to be able to get into print this year. The play given by the Club was the most ambitious yet attempted, but was entirely successful. Mr. Jameson repeats the wish, often expressed before, that the department may have an equipment fund for a phonograph, records, and other illustrative material. The need of more class rooms, to be regarded as the special property of the department of Romance Languages and to be given distinctive character by their furnishings, is also emphasized.

For the *Department of German* Professor Mosher reports that the work of the department was conducted without noteworthy change through the year. There was some falling off in the number of students after the Christmas vacation, but the effect of war conditions was not serious. The German Club was carried along on the custom-ary lines, and the annual play was presented before very good houses and was favorably received. With reference to the decrease in the registration for the coming year, Mr. Mosher expects that the study of German will suffer for two or three years to come, or even, if our troops engage in large numbers with the German troops, for a longer period. This result is to be deplored, but must be regarded as entirely natural.

Professor Lord, of the *Department of Latin,* finds the new courses in third-year and fourth-year Latin, taught by Professor Shaw, of special advantage to the department. This arrangement, with the new course in first-year and second-year Latin, introduced for the coming year, enables any student to continue his Latin from the point he reached in the high school. The enrolment in the department of Latin, as a whole, ''was gratifyingly large, and is justified by the continued call for Latin teachers. All of the students who did major work in the Latin department were enabled to find good teaching positions, and it was necessary for me to recommend for Latin positions in high schools students who had had only a year or at most two years of college Latin. It seems probable that the effect of the war and the increased interest in Romance languages may react favorably upon the teaching of Latin in the secondary school, though this is of course problematical.'' A Latin play, the ''Menaechmi'' of Plautus, was produced under the direction of Dr. Alexander, more successfully than the one of the year before. A chapter of the Archaeological Institute of America was or-ganized, with the coöperation of the Oberlin Art Association. The chief needs of the department are more periodicals in the Library and complete files of those already represented there, and a supporting mem-bership in the American School of Classical Studies at Rome. For the latter purpose an annual contribution of two hundred and fifty dollars a year by the College would be required.

Professor Alexander feels that the change in Greek 1-2, by which the number of recitations per week is increased to five, in order to correspond with the new Latin course, will make a decided improvement in the work of the class. The Latin play was very well worth while, he believes, although it required a great deal of work. The text used was the metrical translation by B. B. Rogers. Among the needs of the de-partment emphasized by Mr. Alexander are a lantern, with which repro-ductions from books as well as from slides could be presented, and an apparatus fund of ten or fifteen dollars a year to provide mimeograph outlines, summaries, lists of questions, etc. It is suggested that each of the language departments in the College might well have such a fund regularly at its disposal.

Professor Caskey devotes his entire report for the *Department of Oratory* to the discussion of intercollegiate Debate and Oratory. In the field of Debate Mr. Caskey notes a gratifying growth and improvement in the work of the league in which Oberlin is associated with Western Reserve and Ohio Wesleyan. The attainment of this league compares favorably, in Mr. Caskey's judgment, with that of other leagues in Ohio and nearby states. The loss of the home debate this year, for the only time in the past nineteen years, is ascribed to a defective system of choosing our teams, by which two inferior men were selected, and to the fact that the debates were held in the midst of the examination period, so that there was practically no audience. The debate held with Wooster, not a member of the league, was an exceptionally good one. On the oratorical side, a new system of judging the contest was put into operation in the Northern Oratorical League, by which a two-year trial of faculty judgment was inaugurated. ''Each faculty judge is to grade and rank all the contestants save his own, so that the final ranking will be the judgment of six men (all of whom are expected to be at the contest because of personal interest), men whose presence will entail no expense upon the Association. Time alone will reveal the success of this system. This year the judgment was about as diverse as it ever was under the old method.'' The action of the U. L. A. in dropping financial responsibility for the oratorical contest makes it necessary to find some new way of financing these interests. The suggestion is made that we shall probably soon find it impossible to continue attempting to meet the expense by charging an admission fee; the alternative would naturally be financing by the institution, as is done in the Universities of Illinois and Michigan.

Professor Clarence Ward, for the *Department of Fine Arts,* reports a complete revision of the courses offered in the History of Art, made to provide for the four majors that have been established in the department. The completion of the Art Building affords splendid housing for the department, which was transferred to it in the latter part of the year. Between one hundred and fifty and two hundred students are making use of the building and its equipment. There was transferred to the library of the Museum a large number of books from the main Library, and additional purchases have brought the working library up to something like a thousand well selected volumes. The photographs belonging to the department, to the number of more than eight thousand, and about eleven thousand lantern slides, have also been installed in the library of the Art Building and are now being carefully catalogued and made available for convenient use. An assistant in the department was appointed for the coming year, to work for the most part in the library on these collections. The most pressing need of the department is endowment, to permit bringing exhibitions and lectures to Oberlin and to assist in carrying the expense of the building.

Professor Oakes reports large and growing interest in the elementary course in the Theory and Practice of Art. Ninety-one students were enrolled in the department during the year, so many of them in the first semester as to necessitate the formation of two sections that semester. The Teachers' Course in Art Education was completed by four students, who received the certificate of the department in June. The removal of Society Hall from the Campus caused the transfer of the studio courses to the studio wing of the new building in May, but the inconvenience and interruption of the change did not prevent completion of the year's work in a fairly satisfactory way. The preparation of the studio for exhibition at the dedication of the building entailed a great deal of work on Miss Oakes and Miss Stephen, who themselves, for example, put the temporary covering on the walls of all these rooms. The arrangement and decoration of the rooms, the selection of furniture, and the designing of the lockers and cases were all the subject of careful attention by Miss Oakes. The placing of lockers in a separate room is different from the usual plan, but contributes greatly to the general effect of the rooms.

Mathematics and the Sciences

For the *Department of Mathematics* Professor Anderegg reports the omission for the year of the courses in Surveying, in Mechanical Drawing, and Descriptive Geometry, and in the Teaching of Mathematics on account of the absence of Mr. Cairns on leave for the year. The staff was smaller than usual for the year, and the large enrolment in some of the elementary classes made additional assistance necessary. Professor Anderegg records his profound appreciation of the fidelity, loyalty, and efficiency with which teachers in the department have always met emergencies of this sort. It may be added to his report that additional classes which were needed in Solid Geometry and Advanced Algebra were very adequately taught by Mrs. Harroun, who was called upon short notice, when the emergency arose, to assist at this point. The needs of the department are adequate equipment and furniture for the Seminar room, and an office for use in conference with students.

Professor Cairns reports spending his year of leave at the University of Chicago, where he attended lectures and worked in the library of the University, besides caring for the interests of the Mathematical Association of America, of which he is secretary-treasurer. The value of the year in providing an opportunity to come into touch with current movements in mathematical development under expert guidance, and to gain inspiration in the methods and aims of teaching, are spoken of with hearty appreciation. With reference to the Mathematical Association, Mr. Cairns records a present membership of eighty-one institutions and 1,135 individual members, a large increase having been secured in the past year. The Association has decided to give to the *Annals of Mathematics* an annual subvention for the next three years, to enable it to reduce its price and increase its scope, and has appointed a committee to investigate, with representatives of smaller associations in other parts of the country, the status of Mathematics in this country, to examine the validity of current objections to the study of Mathematics in colleges and public schools, and to propose any needed reforms.

Professor Sinclair reports a satisfactory year's work except, perhaps, in the spring, when the disturbance due to withdrawals for war and agricultural service diminished the classes. The great need in the department is better class-room facilities. Miss Sinclair also recommends division of the class in College Algebra so that the beginners and advanced students may be taught in separate sections.

Professor Grover, for the *Department of Botany*, reports a normal year, with a registration of somewhat over two hundred students, and very satisfactory work on their part. One A. M. degree was given at the end of the year, and one student graduated with final honors with a *cum laude* degree. The herbarium made a good growth, more than thirteen hundred sheets of plants being added during the year. The need most felt by the department is that of a suitable recitation room, in or near the Botany building, for its large classes. The room in Spear Laboratory hitherto used, while very suitable in itself, has been inconvenient on account of its distance, and has now become unavailable because of changes in the schedule of classes. The recitation room in the Geological Laboratory, to which Botany 1, 2 has been transferred, is so small as to cramp even the reduced class registered for the course the coming year. A new building for Botany is urgently needed.

In a supplement to his report, submitted in view of reaching his twentieth year as head of the department of Botany, Mr. Grover calls attention to the fact that since 1886 ''twenty-two graduates of Oberlin have gone into college and university positions as teachers of Botany or Agriculture or are in graduate schools in training for such work, while numerous others have entered government service in Botany or Forestry, become landscape architects, florists, agricultural experts, fruit growers and farmers, or are teaching Botany in large high schools.'' The fact that 1886 marks the entry of Oberlin graduates into the field of college teaching of Botany is due to the inspiration and teaching of Albert A. Wright, Professor of Botany, as well as of Geology and Natural History, from 1878 to 1891. He ''laid the foundations for the teaching of Botany and Zoölogy in Oberlin, . . . introduced the compound microscope into Oberlin laboratories, greatly broadening the scope of the biological teaching, and opening the whole field of the finer anatomy of plants and animals to undergraduate study, . . . and established a standard of biological teaching in Oberlin which has been difficult to maintain.'' Mr. Grover's list of twenty-two college teachers and graduate students of Botany begins with R. A. Harper, '86, Professor and Head of the Department of Botany, Columbia University, and ends with two members of the class of 1917, graduate students and assistants in Botany for 1917-18 in prominent universities.

Professor Nichols feels that, on account of the addition of a number of new microscopes, the year's work in Botany 1 and 2 was more effective than in former years, as well as easier and pleasanter for every one connected with the work. She fully agrees with Mr. Grover that the greatest need of the department is a good recitation room for the courses in Botany. Spear Laboratory is too far away to permit the use of living material for demonstration and lectures, and the room in the Geological Laboratory, though it is much nearer, and has the necessary equipment of a lantern, of a blackboard, and of space for charts, is too small to accommodate the classes comfortably. It is, however, a better arrangement than any other at present possible.

For the *Department of Chemistry* Professor Holmes comments upon a gratifying gain in the Chemistry department. More students were registered in the department than ever before, the increase being especially marked in the advanced classes. Twelve students in all completed either a major course in Chemistry or a major course in combination with some other department. The department has been very successful in getting its graduates into the best universities for advanced work, and several have been placed in attractive positions in the industrial field. Mr. Holmes urges the need of larger salaries for teaching assistants, and of more provision for research in teaching time. The new wiring of the building will make its lighting much more effective and really safe for the first time. The cost of some kinds of imported material makes it necessary to delay provision for some other needed improvements. Mr. Holmes's Laboratory Manual of General Chemistry was revised and published privately in book form. It is used in two or three other colleges also.

Professor Chapin inaugurated a new plan of teaching second-year Chemistry for the year, using a new text and manual on which he has been at work for several years. The results were highly satisfactory, both to himself and to Professor Holmes. Mr. Chapin says of the method, ''From the time I was a student in college I have felt that the work in Chemistry, well begun in the first year, was not very much extended during the second, particularly when the time was occupied with Quali. tative Analysis. My teaching during the last six or seven years has confirmed that belief, notwithstanding the fact that I have always tried to include in the course all the proper applications of Physical Chemis. try. I have felt that the student was not getting well grounded in the principles or in technique, that the work was too narrow and technical to serve as a basis for any future work, whether analytical or otherwise. . . . The course as I now give it is quantitative, not qualitative, in nature, and is based almost entirely on Physical Chemistry. The latter fact tends to bring back that most useful tool (Physical Chem. istry) into the earlier part of the student's chemical training, so that he has it to use in all of his subsequent work. . . . The method reacts most favorably on the courses in Quantitative Analysis and Organic Chemistry, which follow immediately, and on the course in formal Physical Chemistry, which comes at the end of the major work. Indeed I find that the same students in Quantitative are able to accomplish one-third more in the same time and to do it more intelligently. Professors McCullough and Cox report similar gains in the Physical and Organic, respectively, as a result of this special second-year training.'' Mr. Chapin hopes to get out a revised edition of the course next year, if possible, in book form. Some new lines of work have been opened up in preparation of the book, so that Mr. Chapin has new articles published and in preparation as a result of that work. He speaks enthusiastically of the value of such research work as this in its reaction on the department, and strongly commends the present policy of his department in making it possible for all teachers, instead of simply the head. Some needs of the department are further electrical equipment in the second-year laboratory and a large constant-temperature electric oven for the use of advanced students.

Professor McCullough believes that there have not been so many really capable and earnest advanced students in the department in the last ten years as now. He finds this due partly to present industrial conditions, which stimulate interest in all sciences, but more to the teaching and personal inspiration of the present head of the department and the departmental policy of emphasizing the individual student's needs. Increased help in the routine work contributes to the possibility of assistance in this emphasis by all the teachers in the department. The particular need emphasized by Mr. McCullough is that of a departmental library and the means to subscribe to more chemical journals. A great deal of new material in Chemistry is appearing all the time, and the amount will be increased after the war, when new discoveries now kept secret for strategic reasons are released for publication. New storage batteries and a motor-generator are also needed, but the purchase will be postponed, if possible, until prices come down from the war level. The results of rewiring the building are spoken of as exceedingly satisfactory.

In the *Department of Geology* Professor Hubbard notes that the classes were somewhat smaller than usual, continuing the decline noted the year before. The registration for the coming year, however, is considerably increased, in spite of the reduction in the number of college men, from whom the enrolment in Geology is usually more heavily drawn. Students doing major work in Chemistry are electing Economic Geology to a considerably larger extent. The Seminar was largely devoted to the preparation of students for teaching Geography in the secondary school; five students gave their attention to this phase of the work, two to Geology proper. The value of such an advanced class, in which a certain amount of research is carried on, is strongly emphasized by Mr. Hubbard. Noting the fact that within the past year not less than five leading institutions have definitely asked for graduate students of Geology from this College, and that others have written asking for advanced students who might become teachers, Mr. Hubbard feels that it would be advisable to make more effort in the direction of graduate and research work. There is need also of preparing prospective teachers in the fundamentals of several fields as well as very thoroughly in one major field. This results from the practice of requiring a teacher in the high school to give instruction in more than one science in the course of the year, and even more to the introduction of a general science course in many secondary schools. The best way to meet the difficulty, in Mr. Hubbard's view, is to make a larger use of the composite major, even though research would then in most cases have to be deferred to a graduate year. Such a year would be very desirable, however, as it would allow both some professional preparation and some experience in research before the business of teaching was actually taken up. Mr. Hubbard calls attention again to the fact that the building used by the department is inadequate in size, and is not fireproof. An addition is greatly needed if the present building must continue to be used, but replacement with a fire-proof building is much to be desired.

The work of Dr. Leonard, *Professor of Hygiene and Physical Education*, was seriously interrupted by his own illness from the end of February to the close of the spring recess. Much loss was prevented, however, by the assignment of additional reading and other work in the several courses. The department was able to assist considerably in the military training of students, both in the regular work and in the hospital corps, where Dr. Leonard gave a series of six lectures and demonstrations of first aid to the members. Dr. Leonard was also a regular instructor of the classes in First Aid under the American Red Cross organization. There were only three graduates who completed the major in Physical Education for men, all of whom are now engaged in government service of some sort. The demand for graduates of the course continues to be much greater than the supply of candidates for positions.

Professor Williams submits for the *Department of Physics* a special report on the needs of the department, with particular reference to the development that will be possible with the coming enlargement of the resources of the College. "We hope," he says, "that the material resources will be greatly augmented, the teaching staff increased, and proper housing conditions secured." His list of apparatus immediately needed would cost in excess of three thousand dollars, but would, if it were all provided, merely supply the tools needed in the shop and necessary precision apparatus for the advanced laboratory course. This is the one course now offered by the department in which real connection is made with technical, professional, and graduate work. A study of the offerings of eighteen other colleges of good standing with enrolments exceeding four hundred shows that ten of these schools have two such connecting courses, two have three such courses; only six stand with Oberlin in having but one. The addition of one or two more courses, to bring the department up to the prevailing standard, would require an increase of the teaching staff. Unless it is held that such courses lie outside the proper college scope, the increased staff should be provided, not merely to meet the needs of today, but also with an eye to the future, in which Oberlin will be found in the midst of great centers of industry lying along the southern edge of the lake shore, where land and water, coal and iron ore, all meet. In such a time it may even be found advisable to establish, with other great gifts to follow in the wake of the Hall bequest, an engineering school here. Greatly increased demands upon the college department of Physics would follow, and would intensify the need, not only of larger material equipment and increased teaching staff, but of more adequate housing as well. The situation in this respect is already difficult, partly because there is no place for advanced students to make the special apparatus needed in their research without disturbing classes in Peters Hall, partly because, from motives of economy, no attempt has been made to fit up the present quarters, destined, it is to be hoped, to be only temporary, with adequate wiring, pipe, and other fundamental requirements. A new building for Physics is the only solution. Mr. Williams also points out the advisability of having, as soon as possible, such an appropriation for each department as will make unnecesary the laboratory fees now charged.

Professor Moore notes as the outstanding fact of the year's work in Physics and Astronomy an increase in interest in the advanced courses. Some original investigation was carried on in these courses, with results that will eventually be published. This sort of work proved very advantageous to the students who were looking forward to graduate work. An informal seminar was held through the year, instructors and advanced students meeting regularly to discuss the fundamental experiments of the science and the lives of men engaged in it. Mr. Moore feels that the number of students doing major work in the sciences, in view of the fundamental importance of scientific study, is smaller than it should be. The needs of the work in Astronomy are urged once more. An expenditure of twenty-five thousand dollars would provide a suitable building, if we could be content with one in brick, and also sufficient equipment to carry on the work satisfactorily for a very long period.

For the *Department of Zoölogy* Professor Budington reports that the enrolment in the class in General Zoölogy was the largest in ten years. An extra laboratory section was required, which could be supervised, fortunately, by two very capable graduate students in the department, Messrs. E. C. and W. D. Andrus. Problem work was carried on by these two graduates, who were working on research of a physiological nature, and by three undergraduates, with good results. The laboratory directions for the course in General Zoölogy have been revised, enlarged and printed as a loose-leaf manual of fifty-eight pages. Some exceptionally successful dissections made by students were effectively displayed in a set of museum cases fitted up for the purpose by Professor Lynds Jones. The provision of a college mechanician, and of a new instructor in the department for the coming year, are noted as great advances. Among the needs of the department are new microscopes, ten of which will be required when the registration in advanced courses returns to the normal level, a new microtome, illustrative skeletal material, and a container for the material used in the course in Vertebrates. Smaller needs are new locks on the lockers, aluminum dissection pans, duplicating apparatus, and a number of lantern slides. The need of a fund for departmental lectures is urged once more. A gift of fifty dollars by Mr. J. C. Lincoln, of Cleveland, for two half-scholarships to Oberlin students taking work at the Marine Biological Laboratory at Woods Hole, Massachusetts, is grate. fully acknowledged. This gift, made through the office of the Treas. urer, places Oberlin on the list of some forty ''Coöperating Institu. tions and Societies.'' Permanent endowment of the entire scholar. ships is much to be desired. Mr. Budington records the names and present positions of ten students who in the last seven years have engaged in teaching in various colleges and medical schools, or hold research fellowships and scholarships in the universities.

Professor Rogers also comments enthusiastically upon the success of the graduate work of the Messrs. Andrus, and of the summer work of the holders of the fellowships in the Marine Biological Laboratory. The usefulness of Mr. Lincoln's gift, which is a memorial of Mrs. Meride Mackenzie Lincoln, who was for a number of years a teacher of Biology in one of the Ohio colleges, is also emphasized. The chief need mentioned by Mr. Rogers is that of the physiological dark room, which could be used for work in optics and for certain studies in animal behaviour. The room could now be provided in the basement of Spear Laboratory, at a cost of about fifty dollars. An appropriation of one hundred dollars by the College toward the support of the Woods Hole Laboratory is also suggested.

Professor Jones found the year's work unusually pleasant and profitable, until the beginning of the unrest caused by withdrawals of men for war service. Continuance in the reduction in the number of men will make it difficult to find assistants for the field work in the coming year. Some more room for laboratory purposes has been se- cured through the utilization of space in the third story formerly used for storage. The rooms are not satisfactory, and should be replaced by more adequate accommodations at the earliest possible moment. The provision thus made would be available especially for work in Economic Entomology, which is unusually full of promise of valuable results, both cultural and economic.

History and the Social Sciences

For the *Department of Medieval and Modern European History* Professor Moore reports a pleasant, satisfactory year. The addition of a capable instructor on part time made some real advances possible. One of these was the division of the large elementary course into sections, an advantage to be continued in the coming year. Some useful information about source material and other equipment was obtained in a visit in the summer to the libraries and teachers of the University of Chicago.

Professor Lutz, of the *Department of Economics*, devotes his report to an outline of his plans for the development of the department with the expected increase in its teaching staff for 1918-19 and thereafter. These plans include: first, arrangement of a coördination or sequence of courses in the department, to bring into each of the several courses a group of students of more nearly uniform qualifications for the work; second, a series of conferences with students, to discover difficulties, to assist in overcoming them, and to suggest additional reading along the line of the student's particular interest; and third, to link up the courses in the department more definitely with the economic and social environment in which the student must live after college, by coördinating the work with some of the best graduate schools of training for business and public and social service. Necessary to the carrying out of this program are: first, an adequate office for the department—neither the ordinary class room, nor room 31 in Peters, nor the seminar room in the Library is suitable and sufficiently available; second, a room in which to display charts and other illustrative material of several sorts; and third, an increased departmental appropriation for apparatus.

In reporting for the *Department of Political Science* Professor Geiser urges again the general importance of this department for the whole institution, and particularly the increased value given to it by the problems thrust upon us by the war. "It may be pointed out that whereas Oberlin has made provision for expansion in certain other departments many of the leading educational institutions of the country have, owing to the new problems thrust upon us by the war, regarded the department of politics as the one which should be, at all events, given full support; and in many cases, where expansion has been made, it was this department which has been strengthened. And surely when the world is talking of democracy and governmental reforms at home and abroad, when our whole educational system has been criticized for failure to properly educate in citizenship and politics, when in fact the government is now improvising temporary machinery to teach citizenship and the meaning of our system of government, the support and encouragement of this department should need no argument. How can we hope to inspire belief in the sincerity of our talk about democracy and our attempt to make the world better through its extension to other peoples without a serious attempt to study forms of government, political systems, and international relations?'' Plans were made for a slight expansion in the coming year, but their failure has left the department with but one teacher, whereas Western Reserve, for example, has four, two of them Oberlin graduates. The immediate needs are another teacher on full time, and an increased appropriation for the department to the Library. Greater emphasis should be placed in the Library upon permanent collections in all of the social sciences. These would include, especially, reports of the United States Supreme Court to date, the codes of the more important states, and works giving at least a general outline of the political and legal systems of various states. A number of important periodicals should also be added.

For the *Department of Sociology* Professor H. A. Miller reports an increasing popular interest in the problems of society. When the normal college enrolment is again reached, an additional teacher in the department will probably be needed. Rural Sociology is suggested as a field upon which emphasis should next be laid, in view of the growing demand for such courses and the development of a technic of instruction and field work.

Philosophy, Psychology, Education, and Bible.

Professor MacLennan, for the *Department of Philosophy*, reports that the organization and the problems of the department were the same as those reported in the preceding year. The work went forward with as much interest as in any previous year. The addition of Mr. Nicol to the regular staff on part time was a very satisfactory arrangement.

Professor Kitch made a special effort to create enthusiasm and interest in philosophical problems and to indicate their practical bearing. The success of the effort was indicated by lively discussions in the class room and frequent evidence that the problems were being carried into discussion outside the class room. The increased numbers in the advanced classes for the coming year are possibly also an indication of the success of the effort. It is hoped that the method and its success may be carried over into the coming year. A new course has been worked out under the title of "The Evolution of Social Forms, or the History of Etiquette", which it is hoped may give the fundamental problems and the logical formation of such an evolution and may furnish the solution for some of the immediate and practical problems of our social life. Out of the study has come a feeling that such research results in greater inspiration for all one's work, and an appreciation of the smallness of the time that it is possible under our present schedules to devote to such work. The need of new illustrative equipment, in the form of lantern slides and possibly a "movie" as well, was also suggested by the preparation for this course.

For the *Department of Psychology*, Professor Stetson reports as the matter of chief interest the formation of plans to enlarge the teaching staff. The plans included the appointment, as an assistant professor, of a man of special experience in vocational tests and guidance, and an arrangement by which the Bureau of Appointments was put under the charge of this assistant professor. An additional instructor was also provided in the department, to lighten the work and to make it possible to add some elementary laboratory work for students in the required course. The appointments were made as planned, but final carrying out of the plans has had to be deferred, on account of complications arising out of the war.

Professor E. A. Miller, of the *Department of Education*, regards the recognition of Practice Teaching as entitled to college credit as the most important single thing affecting the department. It is not to be expected that the action will affect the number of students in the department to any great degree, as only a few students are doing Practice Teaching, but it is worth while to afford opportunity for those who expect to teach for a considerable period to obtain some first-hand knowledge of the conditions they are likely to meet when they begin their work. Securing a certificate from the state without examination is an additional advantage. Mr. Miller sends with his report a chart showing the growth of interest in the work of the department, and also the effect of certain changes in college policy upon elective studies. The chart shows a fairly consistent and rapid increase in numbers in the department up to the end of 1910-11, when the major system was adopted. The department has never emphasized its major work, hold.

ing that students who intend to teach in high schools should preferably
do their major work in other departments. In accordance with this
policy, the graph shows a decrease for the years 1911-14. After a
further drop in 1914-15, due primarily to the absence of the professor
in charge on sabbatical leave, the upward course is resumed in 1915-16,
when some new courses were added, and continued through the following year. Mr. Miller raises the question whether it would not be good
policy to rearrange the work so as to allow the introductory course to
be taken by Sophomores. The present arrangement, by which the work
is restricted to Juniors and Seniors, makes it very difficult sometimes
for students who wish to qualify for the state certificate to secure the
courses necessary for that purpose.

General Suggestions

Several teachers offer suggestions relating to the general welfare,
some of which are most interesting and valuable.

Professor Martin urges the desirability of having more classes in
the afternoon, to relieve the congestion which still exists in the morning hours. "While it is to be feared that the majority of students
elect principally with reference to the time, and admitted that the
afternoon hours are unpopular both with students and with instructors,
there can hardly be any doubt that the interests of the College would
be better served by the introduction of more classes at both the two
and the three o'clock periods. The latter period might be used largely
by classes that recite in divisions." The suggestion, it may be noted,
is directly opposed to the whole trend of the changes made last year.

Professor E. A. Miller suggests that "in the effort made to advance the work of the College some attention be given to the possibility
of supervised study for some of the Freshman and Sophomore work,
with well prepared study coaches to assist. I am not sure that this
suggestion is practical. However, it has been found very valuable to
have something of the sort in high schools, where it has been well done.
We might be pioneers here in college work and discover that we could
be of great aid to our younger students."

Professor Mosher suggests that there would be profit in an open
discussion in the Committee of Advisers as to the function and technique
of the adviser. "That sharp lines cannot be drawn, I am well aware,
but an exchange of views might conceivably lead to a general agreement as to what extent the revised schedule should correspond to the
personal preferences of the adviser as to both courses and teachers,

and to what extent it should incorporate the desires and reasonable leanings of the advisee.'' A further suggestion is that there might well be a renewed study of the purpose and policy of the College, in view of the fact that certain alumni have graduated without assimilating college ideals to any great extent, and some members of the faculty rather clearly do not agree with the policy upon which we are now proceeding. ''It seems to me to be an entirely reasonable proposition that our policy should be so adapted to the educational ideas of the critics of the present policy and the desires of not a few of our students for more practical training that important changes in the educational process would develop. . . . It is far from my purpose to hold that the earlier academic ideal is to be reaffirmed, but I do feel that we might profitably examine student and faculty opinion with reference to it and to the tendency of the times, as well as to the wishes of our constituency. An investigation of this sort might possibly lead to a closer coöperation between faculty and student body.'' It is also urged that the general revaluing that is going on in consequence of the world war makes this a peculiarly appropriate time for such an investigation.

Professor Hubbard emphasizes the need of encouraging more research by faculty and students. More Oberlin alumni are capable of graduate work than now take it, and they should be stimulated to a desire to search out new truth. Another thing to be desired is a larger number of departmental lectures by men from other institutions. It might be possible with a comparatively small sum to do something worth while in the way of bringing in such lecturers. Mr. Hubbard also hopes to have steps taken as soon as possible to collect all the anthropologic and ethnographic material we have and start a museum for its display. A general course in Anthropology would also be a rich asset to the institution.

Professor Budington feels that we get less from the chapel organ than we should. ''The prelude is short and much subdued in nature; the hymn is an item in the devotional service. The breaking up of chapel always seems to me of the same nature as the dismissal of a large class, the customary shuffle of feet and conversational chorus being commonplace indeed. It would distinctly add to my cheerfulness (I think to that of everyone) if, when large meetings of classes, etc., are not held, the organ could send us out into the air with some splendid volume of music, joyful, awakening, inspiring. It would be one of those items on account of which I would always want to be piesent.'' Mr. Budington also suggests the gradual introduction of a custom of the Dean's, and, as far as his time would permit, the President's, visiting frequently all classes and laboratory exercises. ''I believe,'' he says, ''that their first-hand knowledge of the work of the institution thus gained would work out to the great mutual good of all concerned.''

In somewhat similar spirit Professor D. R. Moore wonders whether ''there would not be a real advantage were the Dean to do *more* in some way or other toward letting the teacher most concerned know some of the comments or criticisms made by students concerning the content or presentation of the courses given. Personally I would like very much to know what faults are found with my courses. All of us have enough and to spare. I am aware that student gossip should not be overrated, but student criticism and complaint is sometimes only too well founded. . . . It would help us all to 'see ourselves as others see us'.''

Mr. Moore would also have it an unwritten law that in faculty meetings members should speak loudly and clearly enough to be heard by those behind them, and would have notices given in chapel posted afterward on the bulletin board, on account of the difficulty in hearing them from certain parts of the hall.

Professor Lutz suggests that steps be taken toward standardization of our so-called ''seminar courses''. ''The faculty conception of such a course'', he says, ''is that it be given on Wednesday evening at 7:00. This appears to be the only particular in which the different departments are agreed, for I have observed that ordinary recitation classes, popular lectures, and research courses, are all called 'seminars.' It would surely be more in keeping with the general practice to confine the designation 'seminar' to a certain type of course; and if we followed the general practice, such a course would be one in which the student did more or less independent work of an advanced type, meeting with other students and the instructor for conference and criticism, and the presentation of results. I recommend that the Committee on Course suggest some such definition of a seminar course, and that the name be applied only to courses that meet the definition. I have no objection to other classes being held on Wednesday evening, but I do think that it is only fair to the student to understand the situation.''

Professor Holmes offers this suggestion: ''I wish to urge that the College act as an organization in town affairs. At present, through fear of antagonizing the town, we act as individuals and count as a small minority. What manufacturing company employing two thousand men in a town of five thousand would fail to see that the water works, the lighting and heating of the town, the policing, the drainage and all vital matters were managed on the same efficient plane as the company itself? In a sense, I feel that our local situation is a reflection on the College.''

Professor Lynds Jones sends the following: ''My experiences during the summer clearly indicate that something must be done to lessen the expense of preparation of gardens and other lands which ought to be planted to war gardens if people are to be expected to engage in this patriotic work. Last spring the cost of preparing an average sized town lot was seven dollars. This is a space of a little more than 13,000 square feet. From this space it is practically impossible for the ordinary citizen to harvest anywhere near seven dollars worth of food products. I found the local help extremely expensive and inefficient. I feel so certain that an ordinary Oberlin garden can be profitably fitted for crops at a cost not to exceed three dollars (not including manure or fertilizer) that I am almost willing to guarantee it. This price will yield a profit if the work is done efficiently. . . . With an outlay of some $1,500 for a tractor and plows, one that will work in the small space of a small garden, and the employment of one efficient person as the operator, it would be possible to prepare more gardens in much less time, and prepare them better.''

Professor Sherman revives the question of reorganizing the school year on a four-term basis, supporting the argument by pointing out that the Commissioner of Education has in an official bulletin strongly urged the secondary school to take this step; that the University of the State of Washington and Leland Stanford University have recently adopted the plan; that President Hopkins, of Dartmouth, has gone on record as favoring the idea; and that the State Normal School at Terre Haute, Indiana, and the George Peabody School for Teachers, at Nashville, are so organized. Mr. Sherman concludes with the following quotation from an unnamed writer in Washington, D. C.: ''One of the best results of the adoption of the four-quarter system will be the effect upon the summer schools of the land. They will have a more organic relation to the institution and will be attended by students with a more serious attention. There will be less optional taking of examinations and more enforced study. Professional vacations and sabbatical years or half-years will be adjusted on a somewhat more flexible basis. In addition the teacher and principal or president of the school and college of tomorrow will be a public character more steadily on his professional job than in the past; and the college or university through full use of its assets will be a form of institutional organization less open to attack as rusting rather than wearing out.''

Mr. Sherman also believes that the opening of the summer session should be put at a later date, declaring that his correspondence shows that between fifty and sixty foreign students were lost to us last summer because the session overlapped the regular year of the schools the students were attending, in some instances by as much as two weeks. The difficulty will be lessened for the coming year, however, by the fact that all our dates have already been made one week later. Whether the summer session should be still further deferred would seem to be worth considering.

Further suggestions by Mr. Sherman are that the President's reception at Commencement be kept on the terrace of the Art Building; that the experiment of inviting Sophomores and Freshmen to remain for Commencement be tried; and that more emphasis be put upon the need of a College Theater. On this last topic he says: ''The Dramatic Association has reached a point beyond which it cannot hope to make a larger contribution to community life, under existing conditions. We have on hand a working equipment including scenery, curtains, electrical apparatus, and general properties valued according to invoices on file at between four and five thousand dollars. Storage and handling facilities are very inadequate. We do the best that we can, but under the circumstances, whenever part of the equipment is used a certain amount of deterioration, which might be avoided were we better equipped, is inevitable. Until we have a suitable home of our own it would seem inadvisable to make further additions to what is now in storage. The extent of what we are able to do as it is may be suggested from our Treasurer's statement that last year the money turned over by the various clubs, associations, etc., making use of our equipment amounted to $3,600. It was possible for the first time for the Latin, French, and German plays to be really adequately produced. In addition to the departmental activities which the Association was able to forward, demands were made upon us during the whole year for the use of such apparatus as curtains, hangings, spot lights, foot lights, etc., which contributed materially to the interest and success of many varied activities.''

III. INSTRUCTION

The material for this report on the subject of instruction in the College has been furnished by the Secretary. As has been the custom in previous reports, the facts have been condensed into tables showing, first, the range of instruction offered, and second, the amount of work actually done in the several departments by teachers and students during the year. The first table is based upon the announcement of courses offered for the year, as printed in the bulletin of the College of Arts and Sciences of the year immediately preceding; the second is an epitome of the detailed information in regard to courses given and students taught which is printed in the back of this volume.

Range of Courses Offered

The first table shows the number of hours offered in the preliminary announcement of courses of the several departments, without regard to divisions of classes or to number of students. It is thus a simple showing of how much work students had the opportunity to elect in the given subjects. The amount of work offered is given in semester hours, a course with two, three, or four recitations a week for one semester being counted as two, three, or four hours respectively, whether the work is done in one or in more than one division of the class. The range of instruction offered in the year is fairly indicated by the number of semester hours so counted.

This table makes comparison easy, both with the offerings of the same department in previous years, and between different departments in the same year. It shows that in many subjects the range of work offered has been practically uniform for the past five years. The advances for the year 1916-17 were largely in English Composition, Fine Arts (historical courses), German, History, and Psychology.

Thirteen courses announced in the bulletin were not given, because they were not elected by a sufficient number of students. They were: Botany 9; Chemistry 10H; English Literature 21H-22H; Fine Arts 6, 16, 23, 24; German 25H, 26H; History 87, 88; Philosophy 27, 28; Physics 5; Psychology 9H, 21; Zoölogy 26H. Five of these, it will be observed, were Honors courses. A section of Economics 2 was dropped, and one course, Zoölogy 20H, was transferred from the second semester to the first.

Four courses not announced in the bulletin were organized and given. These were: an additional course in Advanced Analytical Chemistry (Chemistry 12) in the first semester; a special course in Advanced Organic Chemistry; a course in Caesar, for students deficient in the entrance requirement in Latin; and Mathematics 33, 34, the seminar in the department. Additional sections were required in the following courses: English Composition 2, 2A; French 1, 2; History 95, 96; Mathematics 1A, 1G (two), 2G, 6A (two).

Semester Hours Offered

	1916- 17	1915- 16	1914- 15	1913- 14	1912- 13
Astronomy	6	8	6	6	6
Bible and Christian Religion......	12	12	10	12	12
Bibliography	6	6	6	6	6
Botany	40	43	40	40	40
Chemistry	57	57	70	70	67
Economics	32	32	31 }	46	40
Sociology	20	20	12 }		
Education	26	26	*6	18	18
English Composition	28	20	22	16	12
English Literature	72	76	72	76	82
Fine Arts, Historical Courses......	20	12	8	8	8
Fine Arts, Studio Courses.........	34	34	34	32	30
French	46	44	44	44	42
Geology	34	39	34	34	32
German	66	54	52	58	66
Greek	22	26	22	26	26
History	60	*44	58	58	72
Italian	0	8	0	8	8
Latin	44	44	44	32	32
Mathematics	51	66	68	*50	67
Musical History and Appreciation..	16	*12	16	16	16
Oratory	18	18	18	18	18
Philosophy	47	44	44	35	32
Physical Education (for credit)...	4	4	4	4	4
Physical Education, Teachers' Course	34	34	34	34	*26
Physics	37	34	37	40	34
Physiology and Hygiene	6	6	6	6	* 0
Political Science.................	20	20	22	22	22
Psychology	46	38	39	33	24
Spanish	8	0	8	8	8
Zoölogy	83	83	61	57	45
	995	964	928	913	895

* Professor absent on Sabbatical leave.

Amount of Work Done

The next table presents the amount of work done by students in the several departments, stated in terms of ''instruction units.'' Here no account is taken of the range of instruction offered in the several courses; the total number of hours of work for credit undertaken by students in all the classes and sections in the department is the subject here studied. On this basis there is certain to be a large number of instruction units in those departments in which some courses are required, larger, usually, than in departments in which instruction is wholly elective. The number is often considerably affected by the absence of teachers in the several departments on Sabbatical leave.

As used in the following table, an ''instruction unit'' means the instruction furnished to one student in recitations which are held once a week for one semester; in other words, an ''instruction unit'' represents one student in a one-hour course for one semester. To illustrate: a three-hour course in Trigonometry enrolling twenty-five students is here counted as representing seventy-five instruction units; a two-hour course in Latin enrolling fifteen students represents thirty instruction units. The table which follows shows the instruction, so measured, furnished during the year 1916-17, with the corresponding figures for the three years preceding added for comparison:

Instruction Units

Departments	Total Classes and Sections	Hours of Teachers' Time	Students Men	Students Women	Students Total	Instruction Units 1916-17	Instruction Units 1915-16	Instruction Units 1914-15	Instrction Units 1913-14
Astronomy................	2	8	16	8	24	72	157	107	54
Bible and Christian Religion.....	8	16	369	465	834	1668	1538	1454	1600
Bibliography.............	3	6	32	19	51	102	132	88	146
Botany....................	10	105	62	143	205	710	760	789	464
Chemistry................	17	202	295	182	477	1939	1714	1646	1418
Economics................	27	64	266	244	510	1495	1740	1414	1758
Sociology.................	8	20	100	252	352	981	570	624	
Education..... ...	10	29	85	215	300	797	665	192	361
English Composition .. .	46	92	384	479	863	1711	1592	1580	2196
English Literature .	26	56	283	895	1178	2935	3053	2732	2415
Fine Arts, Historical Courses.....	7	16	49	111	160	343	374	236	378
Fine Arts, Studio Courses... ..	12	70	30	124	154	299	269	287	154
French....................	40	110	222	537	759	2324	2272	1985	1694
Geology..................	8	54	32	28	60	205	280	364	419
German...................	48	133	311	479	790	2612	2771	2790	3133
Greek....................	6	20	19	52	71	295	370	347	405
History...................	28	67	367	360	727	2030	1541	2029	1597
Italian...................	0	0	0	0	0	0	60	0	24
Latin....................	24	61	85	356	441	1244	1144	1281	954
Mathematics	36	101	348	299	647	1899	1808	1805	1851
Musical History and Appreciation	7	24	54	106	160	332	27	350	309
Oratory..................	8	24	69	45	114	342	282	258	309
Philosophy....... .	16	46	95	144	239	713	854	670	871
Physical Education (for credit)..	24	84	380	534	914	914	821	814	945
Physical Education, Teachers' Course...................	22	62	67	244	311	547	468	762	1078
Physics..................	8	84	96	48	144	570	581	553	369
Physiology and Hygiene	2	6	29	57	86	258	324	282	591
Political Science	8	20	179	82	261	714	815	758	766
Psychology...............	21	87	118	176	294	852	756	761	757
Spanish	2	8	10	34	44	176	0	60	16
Zoology	22	161	133	197	330	1039	978	925	845
Totals........	506	1831	4585	6915	11500	30118	28716	27943	27967

The column marked ''Hours of Teachers' Time'' includes all time spent by teachers and assistants in class-room recitations and in laboratory instruction.

The enrolment for 1916-17 was forty-eight more than in the preceding year. The increase in the entire amount of instruction furnished corresponds almost exactly to the gain in number of students.

The largest gains in instruction units furnished, exclusive of variation due chiefly to the return of teachers on leave for the preceding year, are these: History, 489; Sociology, 411; Chemistry, 225; Education, 132; Latin, 100. There were considerable losses in the following: Economics, 245; German, 159; Philosophy, 141; English Literature, 118; Political Science, 105.

The department of English Literature furnished the largest number of instruction units, with German second, French third, History fourth, Chemistry fifth, Mathematics sixth, English Composition seventh, Bible eighth, and Economics ninth. In 1915-16 the order of the first seven was: English Literature, German, French, Mathematics, Economics, Chemistry, English Composition.

In the two semesters of 1916-17 there were 506 classes and sections. The figures for the two years preceding were 472 and 480. The average enrolment in these 506 classes was 22.7, corresponding to 23 in 1915-16 and 23.10 in 1914-15. Last year there were seven departments in which the average size of classes and sections exceeded thirty. In the year under review there were six, as follows:

Bible and Christian Religion	104
English Literature	45
Sociology	44
Physiology and Hygiene	43
Physical Education (for credit)	38
Political Science	33

The average size of classes is not so significant as it may seem, for in some cases it is obtained by averaging several very large classes with an equal number of very small elective courses. The real question is: How many recitation courses number more than thirty? It is not practicable to obtain statistics on this point, because in many courses a combination of the lecture and recitation methods is used. Few sections, however, are now so large as to make the instruction in them difficult.

Changes in Instruction

There were several additions to the staff of instruction in 1916-17. In the department of Fine Arts an entire professorship of the History and Appreciation of Art was made possible by the bequest of Dr. Dudley Peter Allen for that purpose; in the department of Physical Education for Women the return of Dr. Cochran from her three-years' leave of absence added one teacher to the staff, but the addition was partly offset by Dr. Hanna's leave of absence in the second semester; between the departments of Psychology and Philosophy one-half of the time of an assistant professor was divided, the other half going into the administrative work of the Assistant Dean of Men; in the department of Romance Languages an instructorship in French on half time was added, increased after the beginning of the year to three-fourths time; an instructorship was divided between the departments of History and Economics; an instructorship was added in the department of German, but was offset in part by the withdrawal of an instructor on half time who had been Assistant Dean of Women; and an instructorship in English Composition was added at the middle of the year. Most of these changes were made necessary by the growth of the departments concerned. Some further advances were made to take effect in the coming year, but there still remain several points at which additions should be made as soon as financial conditions permit.

iv. Students

The material here presented in regard to the number and work of the student body has been drawn in large part from the reports of the Registrar and the Chairman of the Committee on Admission. These reports, which are printed in full in a later part of the report of the College of Arts and Sciences, may perhaps best be discussed, as far as discussion is necessary, in this connection.

Enrolment

The total number of students registered in the two semesters of the regular year was 1,077, of whom 679 had previously been enrolled in the College of Arts and Sciences, and 398 were new students. Of the latter number 60 were admitted to advanced standing, 56 of whom came from 42 other colleges.

The facts in regard to the total registration and the registration of men and of women in the regular year for the past sixteen years may be seen in the following table:

	Men	Women	Total
1901-02	242	257	499
1902-03	267	311	578
1903-04	279	354	633
1904-05	294	376	670
1905-06	297	417	714
1906-07	317	485	802
1907-08	307	511	818
1908-09	360	515	875
1909-10	395	587	982
1910-11	411	593	1004
1911-12	428	570	998
1912-13	408	609	1017
1913-14	426	603	1029
1914-15	395	607	1002
1915-16	415	614	1029
1916-17	433	644	1077

Scholarship

The Freshman Honor List, containing the names of the Freshmen who ranked highest in scholarship in the first semester, and of the schools from which they came, is regularly published in this place. The students whose names appear on it all took at least eleven hours of regular Freshman studies. Any who did not take the full schedule of fifteen or sixteen hours usually filled out the remainder with studies in the Conservatory or in Fine Arts. The names of the highest tenth of the class are published in alphabetical order, but as a further distinction the names of the first *ten* are printed in italics within that list. The list for 1916-17 is as follows:

Isabel Allen, E. Northfield, Mass., Northfield Seminary
Wallace Robert Bostwick, Montclair, N. J., High School
Mildred Josephine Brigham, Toledo, Ohio, Scott High School
Helen Laura Carter, Bryan, Ohio, High School
William Clark Child, Ravenna, Ohio, High School
Jane Elizabeth Conrath, Johnstown, Pa., High School
Elizabeth Emma Crofts, Toledo, Ohio, Waite High School
John Percy Dalzell, Omaha, Nebr., High School
Karl William Dittmer, Napoleon, Ohio, High School
Anna Elizabeth Earl, Norwalk, Ohio, High School
Florence Jenkins Gerhan, Cleveland, Ohio, Lincoln High School
Howard Lewis Hall, Amherst, Ohio, High School
Luther Grant Hector, Warren, Pa., High School

Deborah Langston Henderson, Detroit, Mich., Central High School
Raymond Guthrie Hengst, Logan, Ohio, High School
James Frederick Hollister, North Stonington, Conn., Wheeler School
Ruth Clawson Ice, Logansport, Ind., High School
Alice Mary Johnson, St. Joseph, Mo., Central High School
Carroll Pollock Lahman, Franklin Grove, Ill., High School
Marian Julia Lawrence, Norwalk, Ohio, High School
Frank Edward Morse, Troy, Pa., High School
Elizabeth Pape, Kidder, Mo., Kidder Institute
Esther LaVerne Parks, Oberlin, Ohio, High School
Leonard Clough Peabody, Chicago, Ill., Wendell Phillips High School
Ruth Elizabeth Reder, Logansport, Ind., High School
Corinne Burnette Schlegel, Millersburg, Ohio, High School
Martha Schlingman, Eaton, Ohio, High School
Bobbie Beatrix Scott, Tougaloo, Miss., Tougaloo Academy
Dean Page Sunderlund, Omaha, Nebr., High School
Martha Rose Terborgh, Oberlin, Ohio, Academy
Mildred Marian Tollefson, Mabel, Minn., High School
Marguerite Walters, Nova, Ohio., Troy Twp. High School
Murray Edwards Wilcox, Parkville, Mo., Park Academy

The highest average grade was secured by Miss Earl.

The second highest average grade was secured by Miss Gerhan.

Honorable mention is made of the following student who carried fourteen hours instead of fifteen, but whose average grades would otherwise entitle her to rank in the Honor Ten:

Mary Etta Spencer, E. Northfield, Mass., Northfield Seminary.

The preparation of the Freshman Honor List offers the opportunity to average the grades of all Freshmen, and to report back to the schools from which they came the result of their first semester's work. This practice has been of the greatest value, the Secretary reports, in our relations with contributing secondary schools.

The annual election to membership in the *Phi Beta Kappa* society provides a recognition of high scholarship maintained throughout the course. This honor was won by the following members of the class of 1917:

Harold Devere Allen, Wilton, Conn.
Dorothy Ellsworth Birkmayr, Toledo, O.
Eda Henrietta Bredehoft, Danbury, O.
Katherine Bentley Bushnell, Mansfield, O.
Nina Ruth Clay, Oberlin, O.
Laura Dasef, Barberton, O.
Uarda Evans, Cassville, N. Y.

Richard Reid Fauver, Lorain, O.
Florence Adelia Hiatt, Peoria, Ill.
Elizabeth Josephine Hill, Milford, O.
Donna Letitia Mallory, Toledo, O.
Frances Bertha Nobis, Amelia, O.
Harlan Riter Parker, Cleveland, O.
Beatrice Elizabeth Paton, Chardon, O.
John Wesley Pence, Hamilton, Ill.
Amy Louise Pendleton, Corbin, Va.
Esther Dodge Porter, East Jordan, Mich.
Marion Metcalf Root, Oberlin, O.
Willis Howard Scott, Chicago, Ill.
Elbert Minor Shelton, Wakeman, O.
Mary Thompson Sherwood, Oberlin, O.
Walter Buckingham Smith, Ashley, O.
John Ervin Stone, Salem, O.
Mary Frances Tenney, Ada, Minn.
Margaret Monahan Wilson, New York, N. Y.

Honors at graduation were awarded to eight students. This distinction is given for work in a particular field, in which the student not only completes the major work of the department, but does in addition at least the equivalent of ten semester hours without credit. His mastery of the subject is tested by a rigid oral examination, and the honors awarded are in one of three grades, *summa cum laude, magna cum laude,* or *cum laude,* according to the quality of the examination. The distinction is thus a mark of special attainment rather than of all-round excellence, differing in that respect from membership in Phi Beta Kappa. The students who earned Final Honors were the following:

Summa cum laude

Walter Buckingham Smith, with honors in Political Science

Magna cum laude

John Fitch King, with honors in Chemistry
John Wesley Pence, with honors in Political Science

Cum laude

Harold Devere Allen, with honors in Sociology
Katherine Bentley Bushnell, with honors in History
Harold Haydn Clum, with honors in Botany
Nelle Marie Frederick, with honors in Zoölogy
Ida Stone, with honors in Latin

The amount of failure in scholarship is shown in the table below, in which the corresponding figures for the three years preceding are added for comparison. In the column marked ''Courses Incomplete'' is given only the number of courses left unfinished by students who also incurred one or more conditions or failures.

	Students Involved	Failures and Conditions	Courses Incomplete
1913-14			
First semester	205	255	28
Second semester	163	213	14
1914-15			
First semester	174	226	29
Second semester	157	212	25
1915-16			
First semester	214	292	64
Second semester	111	140	11
1916-17			
First semester	158	213	39
Second semester	127	162	18

In the first semester 106 students who incurred no failures or conditions left the work of one or more courses incomplete, making a total of 166 courses left unfinished by such students. In the second semester 46 students who had no conditions or failures left one or more courses incomplete, making a total of 54 courses left unfinished by such students. Such incomplete courses are usually finished in the following semester, or at most in the following year.

At the close of the first semester 7 men had scholarship records so unsatisfactory that they were required to discontinue their work either for a semester or, in the worst cases, permanently; at the end of the year 8 men and 7 women were suspended or dismissed for the same reason. The number thus sent away was a little smaller than for the preceding year. Several more, just what number it would be difficult to say, withdrew voluntarily in the year or at its end because of unsatisfactory results in their work.

v. NEEDS

Of the two great needs that have been emphasized in these reports for several years past one, that of an increase in the salaries of the staff sufficient to enable its members to cope in some measure with the rapidly mounting cost of living, has been met, most opportunely, by devoting to it a large part of the expected income from the Hall bequest. While the new salary scale is not yet up to the plane reached by the best colleges of the country, it is so far in advance of the old one as to seem, for the time being, very satisfactory. It is to be hoped that further progress may become possible before the pressure again becomes as intense as before.

The other need, that of new recitation and laboratory halls, is, on the contrary, more deeply felt than ever. In spite of all the work put upon the rearrangement of the schedule of classes last year, the congestion at the time of this writing is more severe than in any previous year. Peters Hall and French Hall are used to their full capacity from eight o'clock in the morning to three o'clock in the afternoon all through the week, and Sturges is used all through the morning hours. Yet it is necessary at some hours to press into service not only the recitation rooms in the several laboratories, but even laboratories themselves, for classes in other departments, often to the disadvantage of the department to which the building belongs; to send classes in other subjects than Fine Arts to the distant Art Building; to borrow a room in Council Hall from the School of Theology; and even to resort to the Library not merely for the seminar rooms, but for the Faculty room and the children's room as well. The inadequate size of some of these rooms and their lack of wall space for sufficient blackboard, the poor light and ventilation of others, the distance of others from the centers of college life, and the interference in some cases with the uses for which the room was intended—all these difficulties make the present situation all but intolerable. We need, as I believe we need nothing else in the whole institution at this moment, a new recitation hall for the College of Arts and Sciences.

Other needs must be passed with a word. Three new laboratory buildings should be provided as soon as possible, for Physics, Botany, and Geology. Much apparatus is needed by several scientific departments. Increase of the library equipment is urgently required by almost all departments. A general lectureship for the institution and funds for departmental lectureships would be a most helpful addition to our equipment. And additional housing accommodations for students, especially for men, is a need that is bound to become more keen as time goes on. But all else can wait much better than can the new recitation hall.

Respectfully submitted,

CHARLES NELSON COLE.

REPORT OF THE ACTING DEAN OF COLLEGE MEN

To the President:

SIR—I have the honor to submit my third and last report as Acting Dean of College Men, covering the events of the year 1916-17.

The number of men enrolled in the College of Arts and Sciences was 433, a gain of eighteen over the preceding year. The gain in the Senior class was six, in the Sophomore class one, and in the Freshman class twenty-eight. There was a loss of two in graduate students, of nine in the Junior class, and of six in special students. The enrolment in the several classes was as follows:

Graduates	6
Seniors	83
Juniors	79
Sophomores	105
Freshmen	158
Special Students	2
Total	433

The work of the office was carried on, as in the two years preceding, in conjunction with the deanship of the College. The difficulties of this arrangement, referred to more than once in preceding reports, were greatly relieved by the effective help of the Assistant Dean of College Men, Dr. Carl C. W. Nicol, who carried on the routine work in the office and assisted in the management of several disciplinary cases that came up in the course of the year. In the effectiveness of his work and in the strength of the hold he secured upon the regard and respect of the men Dean Nicol showed such ability and promise that he was unhesitatingly advanced at the end of the year to the position of Acting Dean, with entire responsibility for the office in the coming year.

In spite of the unpromising opening of the year, due to the aftermath of discontent and unrest that naturally followed the secret fraternity upheaval discussed in the report of last year, there were comparatively few disciplinary cases in the year, none of a serious character. The prevailing dissatisfaction was the subject of serious attention throughout the year, and proved, fortunately, capable of very decided amelioration even in that time. The efforts made toward that end, and some items of the work still to be done, should be described briefly in this report.

The direct impetus for what was done came from student agitation. A memorial from a self-constituted committee of nine students was presented to the faculty on the 24th of October, setting forth various grievances, some real, some fancied, that were given by the men as grounds for dissatisfaction with existing conditions. A committee appointed by the faculty, after careful consideration of the memorial, arranged for a conference between a sub-committee, with the President at its head, and the signers of the memorial. This conference did much to clear away misconceptions and to revive confidence in the faculty's real interest in the problems of the life of the men, and brought about the beginning of a decided improvement in the temper of the men generally.

On the 10th of January a mass meeting of the men of the College was held, at which the subjects of discussion were the rooming-house situation, the coaching of the athletic teams, the formation of a Men's League, and the college rule prohibiting smoking by students. A report to the faculty and the Men's Senate grew out of this meeting, to consider which a second faculty committee was appointed. This committee invited the coöperation of the Men's Senate, which appointed a group of students to act with the faculty men as a joint committee. This joint committee held many meetings during the rest of the year, with results that may be summarized as follows:

1. To improve the rooming-house situation, it was recommended:

a. That the College establish two new rooming houses for men, each house to accommodate a group of about twenty men and to be under the house-government plan. This recommendation was adopted and the two groups were formed and accepted, but the whole plan was finally given up for the coming year because so many men from the groups went into federal service as to cause the disbanding of the rest, and the prospect of renting the houses, in view of the general falling off of attendance of men, was too remote to warrant trial of the plan until war conditions change.

b. That the dormitory section of the Men's Building be divided by permanent walls into four parts, each to accommodate from eighteen to twenty-two men; one section to be primarily for Seniors, one primarily for Freshmen, one primarily for officers of student organizations, and one to be undesignated; each section to be under the house-government plan, and the whole dormitory to be under a committee representing the several sections. This recommendation was accepted and has been carried out.

2. To improve the coaching of athletic teams, it was recommended:

a. That a new assistant professorship be established in place of one of the instructorships in the department of Physical Education, the incumbent of which should be head coach of all teams.

b. That the College assume the part salary of two instructors, ordinarily amounting to $800 or $850, hitherto carried by the Athletic Association, leaving that amount free for the Association to use for supplementary coaching.

These two recommendations were adopted and have been put into effect for the coming year. .

3. The question of forming a Men's League was left for consideration and action by the Men's Senate.

4. It was recommended, and voted, that the question of modifying the rule prohibiting the use of tobacco be laid over for two years, and then be considered on its merits; that meantime every effort be made to enlist student coöperation in securing adequate observance of the regulation.

It is not supposed that the necessary work on these problems has been completed, or that it will be done when the deferred recommendations have been carried out. A good beginning has been made, and the way to better conditions has probably been found. There will be no cessation of the effort until much more nearly complete success is reached.

I have asked Dean Nicol to speak of his experience in supervising the class attendance of the men. His response is as follows:

"The serious problem which the excusing officer has constantly to face is the problem of dealing fairly yet adequately with the various forms of delinquency in connection with class attendance. This delinquency is accentuated and the problem made more difficult by the fact that the employment of self-supporting students is in many cases responsible, and also by the fact that there is a growing tendency on the part of such students not to take any wholehearted responsibility either for their college work or for their "outside work." The one is played off against the other and the student feels himself singularly free from blame. In his effort to make his case perfectly clear either to his employer or to the excusing officer there is a slight tendency to exaggerate the dilemma. This to my mind constitutes a situation which is demoralizing in the extreme and one that is wholly artificial. The student ought to accept squarely the responsibility for using his time and should make sure that he does not take on obligations which are in direct conflict.

Already enough data has been collected to warrant recommendations which look towards a solution of this problem. These recommendations will come through an appropriate committee."

Respectfully submitted,

C. N. COLE.

REPORT OF THE DEAN OF COLLEGE WOMEN

To the President:

SIR—The enrolment of women in the College of Arts and Sciences for the academic year 1916-17 was 644, compared with the preceding year and distributed as follows:

	1915-16	1916-17
Holders of Fellowships	2	1
Graduates	9	14
Seniors	109	124
Juniors	118	137
Sophomores	159	149
Freshmen	197	203
Special Students	20	16
Total	614	644

During the year there were 36 withdrawals, 11 of these being students who were spending their first year in Oberlin; 18 were occasioned by illness, 7 by illness or death at home; 3 left for financial reasons, 2 to attend other schools, 4 to be married, and 2 for travel. In addition there were 16 who left the latter part of the spring term in response to the call for help in farming communities.

A careful record of all illnesses involving absence from classes has been kept and tabulated. This shows an average of ten absences occasioned by illness for each woman. Ten per cent of the classes missed were due to serious illnesses such as appendicitis and scarlet fever, six per cent to accidents, and over fifty per cent to colds, tonsilitis, indigestion, headaches, and other causes which are largely matters of hygiene. This is the place where effort for improved health must be chiefly expended. It seems particularly important, in this connection, to call attention to the gas situation in Oberlin as responsible in no small measure for the difficulty with eyes and the attending headaches, and to a certain extent also, for the frequent colds. Nothing is more urgently needed from the point of view of health than improved lighting and heating. Most encouraging is the fact that only one case of scarlet fever, one of diphtheria, and two each of mumps and measles have occurred among college women; there have been a few similar illnesses in the Conservatory but no epidemic. This indicates the efficiency with which our college nurse and matrons have cared for these matters.

Miss Vera E. Dye, as secretary to the Dean of College Women, brought to her work office training, whole-hearted loyalty, and personal interest in the women and rendered valuable assistance both in the routine of the office and in correcting the papers of the large class in Freshman Bible. She resigned at the close of the year to accept a business position in Torrington, Conn.

It is impossible to tabulate all the work of this office. Conference with various groups and organizations of students, as well as with individuals, calls for much thought and time. The usual groups of students have been entertained. The Dean has also met the women for General Exercises each month, the upper classmen and Freshmen separately, has given a series of five talks for Freshman Women in the fall and has spoken before the Y. M. C. A., the Y. W. C. A., and the Women's League, as well as at smaller Oberlin gatherings. There have also been several addresses outside of Oberlin. Other phases of the work are given in the report of the Chairman of the Women's Board.

Respectfully submitted,

FLORENCE M. FITCH.

REPORT OF THE REGISTRAR

To the President:

SIR—As Registrar of the College, I have the honor to present herewith my annual report, covering the year 1916-17.

Enrolment

The enrolment in the College for the year 1916-17 was as follows:

	Men	Women	Total
Holders of Fellowships............	0	1	1
Graduate Students	6	14	20
Seniors	83	124	207
Juniors	79	137	216
Sophomores	105	149	254
Freshmen	158	203	361
Special Students	2	16	18
Total	433	644	1077

These students represent a very wide geographical area, as shown
by the map below.

Degrees

The number of students completing the work required for the degrees given below during the year 1916-17 is as follows:

	Men	Women	Total
Master of Arts	3	8	11
Bachelor of Arts	75	115	190

Any discrepancy between the above figures and corresponding data given in the Secretary's report is accounted for by the difference in the basis of computation. This table shows the completion of requirements in academic work for the degree, while the Secretary's figures show the actual issuing of the degree, taking into account both academic work and financial or other obligations. In the above numbers eleven students, four men and seven women, really belong to other classes and are so enrolled in our alumni lists. For various reasons, the work required for the degree was not completed until last year. They are not considered in the following statistics.

The Class of 1917: Losses and Gains—Year by Year

	Men	Women	Total
*Admitted as Freshmen, September, 1913	145	167	312
Accounted for as follows:			
Completed work for degree, 1917	56	68	124
Classed Senior, failed to complete work required for degree	2	4	6
Graduated, 1916	2	0	2
Now in College, in class of 1918	4	12	16
Now in College, in class of 1919	1	1	2
Left College during or at the end of the Freshman year	45	47	92
Left College during or at the end of the Sophomore year	16	33	49
Left College during or at the end of the Junior year	15	2	17
Entered the class of 1918—withdrew for Military Service	4	0	4
Totals	145	167	312

*These totals do not include nineteen students, nine men and ten women, belonging to other classes, but classed Freshman for technical reasons, and so listed in the Catalogue of 1913-14.

	Men	Women	Total
Admitted as Sophomores, September, 1914	15	29	44
Accounted for as follows:			
Completed work for degree, 1917....	5	18	23
Classed Senior, failed to complete work required for degree.......	3	4	7
Now in College, in class of 1918....	0	1	1
Withdrawn from College	7	6	13
Totals	15	29	44
Admitted as Juniors, September, 1915	11	21	32
Accounted for as follows:			
Completed work for degree, 1917...	7	12	19
Classed Senior, failed to complete work required for degree......	2	1	3
Now in College, in class of 1918....	0	3	3
Withdrawn from College..........	2	5	7
Totals	11	21	32
Admitted as Seniors, September, 1916	7	10	17
Accounted for as follows:			
Completed work for degree, 1917...	4	10	14
Failed to complete work required for degree	3	0	3
(Two of these are now in College, in class of 1918)			
Totals	7	10	17

The table above shows that during the four years in college there were four hundred and five students enrolled as members of 1917 at one time or another for longer or shorter periods, varying from one semester to four years. Twenty-one of those dropping from the class roll are now in college, members of 1918, with every prospect of completing the work required for the Bachelor of Arts degree. The percentage of graduation from the original membership of the class is slightly lower than that for 1916. The comparative percentages for the last seven years are as follows: for the class of 1911, 45.6; for 1912, 49.0; for 1913, 42.8; for 1914, 41.1; for 1915, 35.4; for 1916, 41.7; for 1917, 39.7. The percentage of loss at the end of the Freshman year is slightly larger than that of the preceding year. Comparative statistics for the last seven classes are as follows: 1911, 22; 1912, 24; 1913, 21; 1914, 28; 1915, 30; 1916, 28; 1917, 29. The higher standards adopted in scholarship undoubtedly account in part for this increased percentage of loss in later years, but with the fuller understanding of these standards and the methods now in use by the Committee on Admission, I anticipate that succeeding reports will show a decrease in this respect.

The following table accounts for the 178 students, at some time members of 1917, who withdrew from College before graduation. It is quite possible that a few who transferred to the Conservatory of Music and other schools should be noted as withdrawing because of poor scholarship, or an initial mistake in choosing their line of work.

Entered as—	Freshmen September, 1913									Sopho-mores Sept. '14			Jun-iors Sept. '15			Sen-iors Sept. '16			
	Left during or at end of									Left before gradua-tion			Left before gradua-tion			Did not gradu-ate			
	Freshm'n year			Soph're year			Junior year												
Reasons for Withdrawal	Men	Women	Total	Men	Women	Total	Men	Women	Total	Men	Women	Total	Men	Women	Total	Men	Women	Total	Grand Total
To enter other Colleges or Normal Schools	24	16	40	11	13	24	2	1	3	2	5	7	1	0	1	0	0	0	75
Poor health or illness at home	1	2	3				0	1	1										4
Poor scholarship, not allowed or not encouraged to return	9	8	17	3	2	5	1	0	1	3	0	3	0	1	1				27
Financial reasons or to enter business or teaching	2	2	4	1	1	2	1	0	1	1	0	1	0	1	1				9
To enter Oberlin Conservatory of Music	0	3	3	1	2	3							1	0	1				7
To enter Oberlin Kindergarten Training School	0	1	1																1
Dismissed	1	0	1	0	1	1	10	0	10										12
To carry out previous plan				0	2	2							0	1	1				3
Dissatisfied or discouraged	2	1	3																3
To be married	0	1	1	0	2	2							0	1	1	0	1	1	5
Reasons unknown	6	13	19	0	10	10	1	0	1	1	0	1	0	1	1				32
Total	45	47	92	16	33	49	15	2	17	7	6	13	2	5	7				178

Of the students who withdrew or were dismissed for a semester during or at the end of the Freshman year because of poor scholarship, three men and four women entered other schools. The large number of men dismissed at the end of the Junior year was due to the fraternity trouble which developed and came to a climax at that time. The usual reasons, desire to be nearer home, or to begin technical or professional study, account for many of the transfers to other colleges or universities. Schools of Civics and Philanthropy, Home Economics, Business Administration, and Engineering present strong appeals to many students, especially during the last few years.

The table below shows the choice of majors of the last five classes, 1913 being the first to graduate under that system.

Department	Class				
	1913	1914	1915	1916	1917
English	32	30	36	32	45
French	5	4	7	4	8
German	21	16	8	12	10
Greek	0	0	0	1	0
Latin	21	11	14	15	14
History	9	6	14	17	16
Economics	13	8	5	14	9
Political Science	12	13	15	12	13
Sociology	10	15	9	11	9
Mathematics	11	4	3	7	8
Physical Education	30	27	27	22	12
Animal Ecology	0	1	5	1	2
Botany	4	4	5	2	5
Chemistry	6	7	5	6	9
Geology	3	4	5	4	4
Physics	5	0	1	4	3
Zoölogy	4	6	3	11	4
Philosophy	7	5	4	4	2
Psychology	2	6	1	4	1
Education	0	0	1	0	1
Bible	0	1	0	0	0
Theology	0	1	0	0	0
Music	4	6	5	3	0
Pre-Medical	..	..	..	..	4

Honors

Twenty-five students were elected to the Zeta Chapter of Phi Beta Kappa. Four of these and four others were graduated with special honors, the departments of Chemistry, Sociology, History, Botany, Zoölogy, and Latin being represented by one student each, and Political Science by two.

Freshman Electives

The table below gives a basis of comparison in the choice of Freshman electives during the last six years. It indicates also the enlarged range of electives offered to Freshmen with the alternative choice of Mathematics or Ancient Language. A few students enter college with some entrance requirements to meet, so that the final choice of all Freshman electives cannot be shown at this date.

	1911	1912	1913	Fall 1914	1915	1916
No. of Freshmen entering college	283	302	309	307	327	332
No. of Freshmen electing—						
Freshman Latin	71	70	84	82	86	87
Academy Latin	17	20	21			
3rd-4th yr. Latin (taught in college)	..	..	..	35	36	34
Beginning Greek	14	7	16	9	12	6
Advanced Greek	5	3	5	2	0	0
Mathematics	140	153	177	162	160	181
Beginning German	57	55	71	64	46	55
Advanced German	120	154	158	137	141	134
Beginning French	60	54	56	72	76	118
Advanced French	23	26	29	29	35	26
Science—						
Astronomy	..	1	0	1	1	1
Botany	6	4	4	9	7	4
Chemistry	57	62	56	60	51	64
Geology	7	6	6	5	2	1
Physics	0	6	8	11	10	10
Zoölogy	5	4	6	6	7	5
History	83	63	77	78	66	90
English Literature	36	49	64	70	82	92
Theory of Music	13	25	14	15	11	9

Last year, in Oberlin, as in most colleges and universities, there were many withdrawals for various forms of service to the country. One hundred and seventy-nine men shared in such work: thirty in the U. S. Naval Reserve; five in the U. S. Navy; four in the U. S. Army; one in the British Army; eight in the American Ambulance Service abroad; two in the Officers' Reserve Corps; seven in the Lakeside Hospital Unit; one in a Youngstown Hospital Unit; one in a Chicago Hospital Unit; two in the Medical Reserve Corps; one in industrial service; and one hundred and seventeen in agriculture. Twenty-two women also withdrew for agricultural work, making a total of two hundred and one. At the close of the year and during the summer forty-five Oberlin men, mostly from last year's student body, enlisted in an ambulance unit, known as U. S. A. A. C., Section 587.

The beginning of the present year marks another withdrawal from my office force. Mrs. Agnes G. Nicol was with me most of last year, on part time, and proved herself a most valuable assistant from every point of view, in the excellence of her work, her willingness to undertake any task, and her rare personality. I had also the help of two others, one a student, both of whom rendered excellent service. These two, both on part time, are helping me at present. But as I said in my last report, these frequent changes, in work involving so many details and absolute accuracy, are very expensive in time and energy, both to myself and to those learning the work, and make it far more difficult to keep up the standard of efficiency, and to render the service that I am most anxious the Registrar's office should give.

In April I again enjoyed the great privilege of attending the annual meeting of the American Association of Collegiate Registrars. It was held at the State University, in Lexington, Kentucky. All preliminary arrangements for the meeting and for our comfort and pleasure were so perfectly made by Mr. Gillis and his associates that the very full program for the three days was carried through with great success. In addition to this the rare hospitality of that lovely southern city contributed greatly to make our stay there one never to be forgotten. The membership of the Association is approaching one hundred, representing the strongest institutions of the country. War conditions prevented quite as large an attendance as usual, but the country, from ocean to ocean, and from the Gulf of Mexico to Toronto, Canada, was represented. One session was added to the already full program for the consideration of problems in connection with the war and the national emergency. The program was very valuable, and a certain definiteness ran through it that was helpful and illuminating. Papers and discussions brought out many suggestions and ideas which we hope may bear fruit in the schools in which we work. I am sure no finer fellowship can exist than prevails in this Association, and each year witnesses its growth in numbers, its genuine helpfulness to its members, and, we trust, its real value to our colleges and universities.

Respectfully submitted,

FLORA ISABEL WOLCOTT.

REPORT OF THE CHAIRMAN OF THE COMMITTEE ON ADMISSION

To the President:

SIR—This report includes only those matters directly connected with my work as Chairman of the Committee on Admission to the College of Arts and Sciences. For the other work of the Secretary's office, reference is made to pages 119-136.

ANALYSIS OF THE COLLEGE ENROLMENT

The following table shows:

(1) The students who returned during the year 1916-17 after previous enrolment in the College of Arts and Sciences;

(2) The new students for whom the year 1916-17 was the first year in the College :

	Men	Women	Total	Per cent of whole No.
(1) Students who returned after previous enrolment in the College of Arts and Sciences—				
Enrolled preceding year (1915-16)	255	390	645	59.88
Enrolled prior to 1915-16...	9	25	34	3.16
	264	415	679	63.04
(2) New students—				
Never before enrolled in any department	156	220	376	34.91
Enrolled previously in Oberlin Academy	13	9	22	2.05
	169	229	398	36.96
Complete Totals	433	644	1077	100.00

From this table it will be seen that 679 students, representing 63.04 per cent of the total, had been in previous attendance in the College of Arts and Sciences, and that 398 students, representing 36.96 per cent of the total, were new students in this department. These percentages are almost exactly the same as for the preceding year. For the last seven years, during which time the enrolment in the College of Arts and Sciences has been maintained at approximately the same point, namely, 1,000 students, there has been only a slight variation in the percentages of returning students and new students; the percentage of returning students in 1910-11 was 63.45; in 1911-12, the percentage was 65.60; in 1912-13, the percentage was 61.40; in 1913-14, the percentage was 61.00; in 1914-15, the percentage was 62.78; in 1915-16, the percentage was 62.78.

The number of men who entered as new students in the College of Arts and Sciences showed a gain of 22 as compared to the number who entered in 1915-16. This number has been exceeded only once in the history of the College, the total number of new men enrolled in the year 1913-14 being 174.

CLASSIFICATION OF NEW STUDENTS

The 398 new students admitted to the College of Arts and Sciences were classed as follows:

	Men	Women	Total
Admitted as Graduate Students	0	1	1
Admitted as Seniors	4	3	7
Admitted as Juniors	8	11	19
Admitted as Sophomores	9	16	25
Admitted as Freshmen	147	187	334
Admitted as Special Students	1	11	12
	169	229	398

In addition to the 334 Freshmen shown above, there were 27 others whose names were listed in the catalogue as members of the Freshman class who were Freshmen during the preceding year and failed to advance to a higher classification. The total number of all Freshmen as shown in the final edition of the catalogue for 1916-17 was 361.

An increasing number of students complete high school work at the middle of the year and enter the Freshman class at the opening of the second semester.

New Students: Comparison for Nine Years

A comparison showing the classification of new students for nine years is added at this point:

	'08 -09	'09 -10	'10 -11	'11 -12	'12 -13	'13 -14	'14 -15	'15 -16	'16 -17
Admitted as Graduate Students	6	5	3	3	2	9	2	2	1
Admitted as Seniors	6	7	12	6	7	9	6	9	7
Admitted as Juniors	17	18	18	12	24	17	16	19	19
Admitted as Sophomores	18	35	30	25	28	25	28	25	25
	47	65	63	46	61	60	52	55	52
Admitted as Freshmen	257	319	267	270	284	311	307	305	334
Admitted as Special Students	43	37	37	27	47	30	14	23	12
Totals	347	421	367	343	392	401	373	383	398

The table shows that in 1916-17 there was only a slight variation from the corresponding figures of the preceding year.

In administering the rule limiting the total attendance to 1,000, it has seemed wise to continue to accept students planning for regular college work in preference to those desiring classification as Special Students and planning for only one or two years of study in Oberlin.

Students Admitted to Advanced Standing

The preceding table shows that 52 new students were admitted to higher rank than Freshman. In addition to this number there were eight students classed as Freshmen who came from other schools or colleges presenting credits that entitled them to rank with advanced standing. The aggregate number of students admitted with advanced standing should therefore be considered as 60 rather than the number shown in the table.

Of this total of 60 students who were admitted with advanced standing, 56 came to Oberlin College from 42 institutions as shown in the following table:

Alabama Polytechnic Institute, Alabama	1
Allegheny College, Pennsylvania	1
Baldwin-Wallace College, Ohio	1
Bethel College, Kansas	1
Cedarville College, Ohio	1
Chicago Normal School of Physical Education, Illinois	1
College of Puget Sound, Washington	1
Colorado Agricultural College, Colorado	1

Concordia College, New York...................... 1
Cornell College, Iowa............................. 2
Dartmouth College, New Hampshire................. 1
Denison University, Ohio.......................... 1
Findlay College, Ohio............................ 1
Fredonia State Normal School, New York........... 1
Goshen College, Indiana 1
Houghton Wesleyan Seminary, New York............. 8
Hunter College, New York......................... 1
Illinois Woman's College, Illinois................ 1
Keystone State Normal School, Pennsylvania........ 1
McCormick Theological Seminary, Illinois.......... 1
Margaret Morrison Carnegie School, Pennsylvania..... 1
Morningside College, Iowa........................ 3
Mount Holyoke College, Massachusetts............. 1
Muhlenburg College, Pennsylvania................. 1
Northern Normal and Industrial School, South Dakota 1
Northland College, Wisconsin..................... 1
Oberlin Kindergarten Training School, Ohio......... 1
Ohio State University, Ohio...................... 2
Ohio Wesleyan University, Ohio................... 3
Olivet College, Michigan 1
Peking University, China......................... 1
Rollins College, Florida......................... 1
Royal Frederick's University, Norway.............. 1
San Jose State Normal School, California.......... 1
Teachers College, Columbia University, New York.... 2
Toledo University, Ohio.......................... 1
University of California, California.............. 1
University of Michigan, Michigan................. 1
University of Minnesota, Minnesota............... 1
University of Nebraska, Nebraska................. 1
Ursinus College, Pennsylvania.................... 1
Wilson College, Pennsylvania..................... 1
                                                   ──
                                                   56

One student, who graduated from one of the good high schools of the state of Illinois, took entrance examinations for advanced credit in college for extra subjects completed by her throughout her high school course and received sufficient advanced credits in this way to secure rank as a Sophomore.

Three students who had been classed in the Conservatory of Music for two or more years and had taken some college work in connection with their Conservatory studies, transferred their enrolment to the College of Arts and Sciences and were found to have sufficient college credits to secure classification as Sophomores.

Students Admitted as Freshmen and as Special Students of Freshman Rank

It is of interest to note where the Freshmen and the College Special Students of Freshman rank received their preparation. As stated on page 193 of this report, there were 346 new students admitted to the College of Arts and Sciences with classification either as Freshmen or as College Specials (334 Freshmen, 12 Special Students). Deducting the 8 students referred to at the beginning of the preceding section, who, while classed as Freshmen, came from other colleges and should fairly be considered as students with advanced standing, and deducting one Armenian student who was allowed to register without any adjustment of credits, we have remaining a total of 337 students. These 337 students came to Oberlin from 218 different high schools, academies, and other preparatory schools. Oberlin Academy was represented by 22 students and Oberlin High School by 19. Of the outside schools, Lincoln High School of Cleveland (Ohio) ranked first with 9, followed by Elyria (Ohio) High School with 7. Four schools were represented by 4 students each; eight by 3 students each; 38 by 2 students each, and 164 by one each.

The 218 schools that furnished new students of Freshman rank for Oberlin College were as follows:

Ada, Minn., High School	1
Afton, N. Y., High School	1
Akron, O., Central High School	1
Albert Lea, Minn., High School	2
Albion, Ill., Southern Collegiate Institute	1
Albion, N. Y., High School	1
Albion, Pa., High School	1
Amherst, O., High School	2
Angola, Ind., Tri-State College High School	1
Arlington Heights, Ill., High School	1
Ashley, O., High School	1
Avalon, Pa., High School	1
Beaver, Pa., High School	1
Belleville, Kans., High School	1
Bellingham, Minn., High School	1
Ben Avon, Pa., High School	3
Benzonia, Mich., Academy	1
Berlin Heights, O., High School	1
Big Rapids, Mich., High School	1
Birmingham, Ala., Central High School	1
Blue Earth, Minn., High School	2
Bridgeport, O., High School	1
Bridgeton, N. J., High School	1
Brockport, N. Y., High School Dept., State Normal School	1

Bryan, O., High School............................ 2
Bucyrus, O., High School.......................... 3
Buffalo, N. Y., Lafayette High School............. 2
Caldwell, Ida., Academic Dept., College of Idaho... 1
Caldwell, Ida., High School....................... 1
Calumet, Mich., High School....................... 1
Canton, China, Christian College.................. 2
Centerville, O., Washington Township High School.. 1
Chagrin Falls, O., High School.................... 1
Chardon, O., High School.......................... 3
Chicago, Ill., Austin High School................. 2
Chicago, Ill., Hyde Park High School.............. 3
Chicago, Ill., Wendell Phillips High School....... 2
Chicago Junction, O., High School................. 1
Cincinnati, O., H. Thane Miller School............ 1
Clear Lake, Iowa, High School..................... 1
Cleveland, O., Central High School................ 1
Cleveland, O., East High School................... 1
Cleveland, O., Lincoln High School................ 9
Cleveland, O., South High School.................. 2
Cleveland, O., West High School................... 4
Cleveland, O., West Technical High School......... 1
Cochranton, Pa., High School...................... 1
Conneautville, Pa., High School................... 1
Crafton, Pa., High School......................... 1
Culver, Ind., Military Academy.................... 1
Cuyahoga Falls, O., High School................... 1
Dayton, O., Steele High School.................... 3
Daytona, Fla., High School........................ 1
Deer Park, Wash., High School..................... 1
Denmark, Iowa, Academy............................ 1
Detroit, Mich., Central High School............... 1
Detroit, Mich., Detroit Seminary.................. 1
Douglas, Wyo., Converse County High School........ 1
Dover, O., High School............................ 1
Downers Grove, Ill., High School.................. 1
Duluth, Minn., Central High School................ 1
Dunkirk, N. Y., High School....................... 1
East Cleveland, O., Shaw High School.............. 1
East Liverpool, O., High School................... 1
East Northfield, Mass., Northfield Seminary....... 2
East Palestine, O., High School................... 1
Eaton, O., High School............................ 1
Elliottville, N. Y., High School.................. 1
Elyria, O., High School........................... 7
Erie, Pa., High School............................ 2
Fayette, O., High School.......................... 1
Forestville, N. Y., Free Academy.................. 1
Fort Atkinson, Wis., High School.................. 1
Fort Madison, Iowa, High School................... 2
Franklin, N. Y., Delaware Literary Inst. and Union
    Free School 1

Franklin Grove, Ill., High School	1
Fulton, N. Y., High School	1
Geneva, O., High School	2
Gettysburg, Pa., Academy	1
Grand Rapids, Mich., Union High School	1
Grandview, Tenn., Normal School	1
Greenfield, O., High School	2
Greenville, O., High School	2
Guilford, Conn., High School	1
Gustavus, O., Centralized High School	2
Hamilton, Ill., High School	1
Hastings, Nebr., High School	1
Hightstown, N. J., Peddie Institute	1
Houston, Tex., Central High School	1
Houston, Tex., Colored High School	1
Huron, O., High School	1
Ionia, Mich., High School	3
Irwin, Pa., High School	1
Jamestown, N. Y., High School	1
Jefferson, O., High School	1
Johnstown, Pa., High School	1
Joshu, Japan, Fomioka High School	1
Kane, Pa., High School	1
Kankakee, Ill., High School	1
Kansas City, Kans., High School	1
Kansas City, Mo., Westport High School	1
Kennett Square, Pa., High School	1
Kenton, O., High School	1
Kidder, Mo., Institute	1
Kingsley, Iowa, High School	1
Lake Forest, Ill., Academy	1
Lakewood, N. J., High School	1
Lakewood, O., High School	1
La Salle, Ill., La Salle-Peru Township High School	2
Lebanon, Ind., High School	3
Leonia, N. J., High School	1
Lexington, Ky., Chandler Normal School	1
Linden, Mich., High School	2
Linesville, Pa., High School	1
Logan, O., High School	1
Logansport, Ind., High School	2
Lorain, O., High School	1
Lynchburg, Va., Theological Seminary and College	1
Mabel, Minn., High School	1
McBain, Mich., High School	1
McConnelsville, O., McConnelsville-Malta High School	2
Madison, Nebr., High School	1
Manchester, Mass., High School	1
Manistee, Mich., High School	1
Mansfield, O., High School	1
Marengo, Iowa, High School	1
Marinette, Wis., High School	1

Medina, O., High School.............................. 1
Mendota, Ill., High School........................ 1
Mercer, Pa., High School........................... 1
Middletown, N. Y., High School.................... 1
Millersburg, O., High School....................... 1
Minonk, Ill., High School.......................... 1
Missoula, Mont., County High School.............. 1
Mitchell, S. Dak., Academy Department, Dakota Wes-
    leyan University 1
Mobile, Ala., High School.......................... 1
Monroe, Mich., St. Mary's Academy............... 1
Montclair, N. J., High School...................... 2
Monticello, Ill., High School...................... 1
Mount Clemens, Mich., High School............... 1
Mount Hermon, Mass., Mount Hermon School........ 2
Mount Pleasant, Utah, Wasatch Academy........... 1
Napoleon, O., High School.......................... 1
Newark, O., High School............................ 1
New Castle, Pa., High School...................... 4
New London, O., High School....................... 1
Newton, Mass., High School........................ 1
Niles, O., High School............................. 2
Northfield, Mass., High School.................... 1
North Stonington, Conn., Wheeler School........... 1
North Tonawanda, N. Y., High School.............. 1
Norwalk, O., High School........................... 2
Nova, O., Troy Township High School.............. 1
Oak Harbor, O., High School....................... 1
Oak Park, Ill., Oak Park and River Forest Township
    High School 2
Oberlin, O., Academy............................... 22
Oberlin, O., High School........................... 19
Oelwein, Iowa, High School......................... 1
Oil City, Pa., High School......................... 2
Omaha, Nebr., High School.......................... 3
Orwell, O., High School............................ 1
Painesville, O., High School....................... 1
Parkville, Mo., Park College Academy.............. 1
Petersburg, O., High School........................ 1
Philadelphia, Pa., Friends Central School.......... 1
Pioneer, O., High School........................... 4
Pittsburgh, Pa., Allegheny High School............ 2
Pittsburgh, Pa., Peabody High School.............. 1
Pittsburgh, Pa., South High School................ 1
Punxsutawney, Pa., High School.................... 1
Putnam, Conn., High School......................... 2
Quincy, Ill., High School.......................... 1
Ravenna, O., High School........................... 2
St. Joseph, Mo., Central High School.............. 1
St. Marys, O., High School......................... 1
Salem, O., High School............................. 1
Sandusky, O., High School.......................... 2

Santiago, Chile, Santiago College.................... 2
Sharon, Pa., High School......................... 2
Sharpsville, Pa., High School..................... 1
Shelby, O., High School.......................... 1
Shelton, Conn., High School....................... 1
Somerset, O., High School........................ 1
South Bend, Ind., High School.................... 2
South Dayton, N. Y., High School................. 1
Stillman Valley, Ill., High School................. 1
Suffolk, Va., Jefferson High School............... 1
Tabor, Iowa, Academy............................ 1
Tacoma, Wash., Stadium High School............. 1
Tiffin, O., Ursula Academy........................ 1
Toledo, O., Scott High School...................... 2
Toledo, O., Waite High School.................... 4
Toronto, O., High School......................... 1
Tougaloo, Miss., Tougaloo College Academy......... 2
Trenton, N. J., High School...................... 1
Troy, Pa., High School.. 2
Twinsburg, O., High School....................... 1
University Place, Nebr., High School.............. 1
Vermilion, O., High School........................ 1
Victor, N. Y., High School........................ 1
Walpole, Mass., High School...................... 1
Warren, O., High School.......................... 1
Warren, Pa., High School......................... 1
Washington, D. C., Central High School........... 1
Watervliet, Mich., High School.................... 1
Welch, W. Va., High School....................... 1
Wellesley, Mass., Dana Hall...................... 1
Wellington, O., High School...................... 2
West Lafayette, O., High School.................. 2
West Philadelphia, Pa., High School............... 1
Westtown, Pa., Westtown School................... 1
West Winfield, N. Y., High School................ 1
Wheaton, Ill., High School........................ 1
Winnipeg, Can., Luxton Collegiate Institute.......... 1
Woodsfield, O., High School...................... 1
Yonkers, N. Y., High School...................... 1
Youngstown, O., Rayen School..................... 1
Zanesville, O., High School....................... 1

STUDENTS ADMITTED FROM OBERLIN ACADEMY

For many years Oberlin Academy stood at the head of the list of schools furnishing new students for the College of Arts and Sciences. In 1916-17 there were 22 students admitted to the Freshman class in the College after previous enrolment in the Academy. These 22 students represent 5.6 per cent of the total number of new students admitted. In the fall of 1895 the Academy furnished 94 students out of a total of 140, being 67.1 per cent. The decreasing percentages of recent years will be seen from the following table:

Year	From Oberlin Academy	Total New Students	Per cent
1895-96	94	140	67.1
1900-01	76	170	44.6
1901-02	64	207	30.9
1903-04	69	287	24.0
1905-06	44	272	16.2
1907-08	40	323	12.4
1909-10	53	421	12.6
1911-12	36	343	10.5
1913-14	28	401	7.0
1914-15	24	373	6.4
1915-16	22	383	5.7
1916-17	22	398	5.6

STUDENTS ADMITTED FROM OBERLIN HIGH SCHOOL

The importance of Oberlin High School as a fitting school for Oberlin College, and the details of enrolment of Oberlin High School students in the College during the thirteen years since the High School course was extended to include the fourth year of preparation for college, are shown in the following table:

Year	From Oberlin High School	Total New Students	Per cent
1904-05	20	261	7.7
1905-06	14	272	5.1
1906-07	19	321	5.9
1907-08	14	323	4.3
1908-09	40	347	12.2
1909-10	29	421	6.9
1910-11	22	367	6.0
1911-12	31	343	9.0
1912-13	20	392	5.1
1913-14	19	401	4.7
1914-15	21	373	5.6
1915-16	22	383	5.7
1916-17	19	398	4.7

GEOGRAPHICAL DISTRIBUTION OF NEW FRESHMEN AND OF NEW COLLEGE
SPECIALS OF FRESHMAN RANK

The number of new students of Freshman rank who received preparation for college in the state of Ohio, exclusive of Oberlin Academy
and Oberlin High School, was 116. Pennsylvania ranked second with
38, Illinois third with 24, followed by New York with 17, Michigan
with 16, and Indiana and Massachusetts with 9. The table which
follows gives detailed information for each state:

Alabama	2	New Jersey	7
Connecticut	5	New York	17
District of Columbia	1	Ohio	155
Florida	1	Pennsylvania	38
Idaho	2	South Dakota	1
Illinois	24	Tennessee	1
Indiana	9	Texas	2
Iowa	8	Utah	1
Kansas	2	Virginia	2
Kentucky	1	Washington	2
Massachusetts	9	West Virginia	1
Michigan	16	Wisconsin	2
Minnesota	8	Wyoming	1
Mississippi	2		
Missouri	4	Foreign	6
Montana	1		
Nebraska	6		337

AMOUNT OF ENTRANCE CREDITS

No student is classed as a Freshman who presents less than fourteen
units of entrance credit, as defined in the catalogue. For full rank
as a Freshman the student presents fifteen entrance units. Ordinarily
the preparation received in a good high school ought to include sixteen
entrance units, but the College allows college credit for the extra unit
of preparation only upon an examination to be taken on the first
Monday after the opening of the college year. Our experience with
the operation of this restrictive arrangement has been entirely satisfactory.

The ''unit'' of work for entrance is defined as ''a course covering
an academic year that shall include in the aggregate not less than 120
sixty-minute periods of class-room work, two hours of laboratory work
being equivalent to one hour of class-room work.'' The work usually
done in a subject in a high school during a year of thirty-six weeks
with recitations five times a week, each recitation nominally forty-five
minutes in length, but actually about forty minutes in length, exactly
meets this definition.

The two tables that follow give information concerning the entrance credits of the 337 students admitted as Freshmen and as Special Students of Freshman rank:

Table No. 1	Men	Women	Total
14 units	12	8	20
Between 14 and 15 units	6	14	20
15 units	31	42	73
More than 15 units	97	127	224
	146	191	337

Table No. 2	No. of Students	Per cent 1916-17	Per cent 1914-15	Per cent 1909-10	Per cent 1903-04
14 units	20	5.9	5.9	7.3	12.3
Between 14 and 15 units	20	5.9	7.3	9.0	23.2
15 units	73	20.7	23.8	15.4	18.0
More than 15 units	224	66.5	63.0	68.3	45.5
	337	100.0	100.0	100.0	100.0

From the above tables it will be seen that 18 men and 22 women, a total of 40 students, were admitted with less than the full requirement of fifteen units. The percentage of students thus admitted with less than the full requirement of fifteen units is steadily decreasing, as will be seen by reference to table No. 2 above. An inspection of the records of the 40 students admitted to college with less than fifteen units of preparatory credit reveals the fact that these students usually do poor work in college. Four of the number did excellent work, ranking in the highest third of the Freshman class; three made fair records, ranking in the middle third; at least twenty-six of the number ranked in the lowest third, more than half of them ranking in the lower half of the lowest third.

The tables show that a total of 297 students presented fifteen or more units of entrance credit. Fully half of this number presented sixteen or more acceptable high school credits.

For a number of years an arrangement has been in force by which students who present sixteen units of entrance credit may receive college credit for the extra unit of high school work not needed for admission to college. Not more than two or three per cent of the students who presented extra units cared to face the special examinations necessary in order to secure college credit. In general the Committee on Admission recommends that students should not attempt these examinations, urging that the students content themselves with the assignment of full Freshman classification.

The arrangement in force governing the assignment of college credit for a postgraduate year of high school preparation provides that four semester hours of college credit may be granted for each unit of excess entrance credit earned during the postgraduate year of work. Under this arrangement a small number of students each year receive allowances of college credit for extra preparation secured during a fifth year of high school enrolment. In 1916-17 there were two men and seven women who received allowances of college credit for extra high school units under the above arrangement.

Entrance Credits Presented by Freshmen

The customary study of details of entrance credits has been omitted this year because of my feeling that there have been such slight variations from facts presented in other years that it is not necessary to present this detailed study this year. It is worth while, however, to note the following points: (1) The requirement of a half-unit in Advanced Algebra and the requirement of a half-unit of Solid Geometry cause more technical deficiencies at entrance than all the other requirements combined; probably one-eighth of all the students who enter college have not taken Solid Geometry in their high school courses; (2) the number of students entering without preparation in Latin is increasing, and the number of students who drop Latin in the high schools after two years of study is also showing a very decided increase; the requirement of a minimum of two units of preparation in either Latin or Greek ranks next to the Mathematics requirements in causing entrance deficiencies; (3) the number of Freshmen who present some high school work in the subject of French is increasing very rapidly, due to the war conditions that have led to the choice of French rather than German in the high school. A large election of French by Freshmen in preference to German also indicates the sympathies of the students in the war conditions.

Registration of Freshmen for 1917-18

The registration of Freshmen and other new students for the year 1917-18 began July 1, 1917. At that time there were on hand the registration cards of 583 students who had been in attendance during the preceding year and had signed registration cards for the coming year, a loss of 120 over the preliminary registration figures of the previous year. This loss was due to the withdrawals of men and women for war service of one character or another. The withdrawals from college during the spring of 1917 numbered approximately 180, about one-half of this number withdrawing for farm work and the other half for army, navy, aviation, hospital, and other war services. During the summer 97 registration cards were received from students who were absent at the time of the preliminary registration in May; this number, added to the 583 above referred to, makes a total of 680 registration cards received from students who were in attendance during the year 1916-17.

With the departure of the ambulance unit soon after Commencement and the summoning by draft of a considerable number of other Oberlin students for army service, the spring registration figures suffered a large shrinkage. It became evident early in the summer that there would be a decided loss in the total enrolment of students for the new year, and the special efforts of this office were directed toward the task of making the net loss as small as possible. At the time of the trustee meeting we hoped that we might enroll 900 students in the College of Arts and Sciences, and this hope was realized, as will be seen by the final attendance figures presented elsewhere in this report, the final attendance total in the College of Arts and Sciences for the first semester of the present year being 925.

On October 3, 1916, the faculty adopted three recommendations from the Committee on Admission, as follows: (1) that the preliminary registration of Freshmen for 1917-18 shall begin at once; (2) that the total number of Freshmen to be admitted shall be 330 (155 men and 175 women); (3) that the Secretary of the College shall issue written promises for the admission of students in September, 1917, these promises to be issued with the coöperation of the Deans. The Secretary's Office began at once the issuing of promises in accordance with this authorization, the conditions attached to the promises reading as follows:

> 1. That as soon as possible after graduation from high school (or other secondary school) the applicant shall have his credentials sent to the Secretary of the College, in any event not later than July 1, 1917.
> 2. That the certificate record of preparatory work shall show actual graduation from the secondary school, with grades sufficiently high to merit the recommendation of the Principal.

3. That in no case shall the College be bound by this agreement to accept a student whose rank in his graduating class was in the ''lowest third.''

4. That the registration card with the applicant's choice of studies for the year 1917-18 shall be filled out and returned to the Secretary of the College with reasonable promptness after the final adjustment of credits is reported to him, the approximate date for the mailing of registration cards being July 1, 1917.

5. That the applicant shall be under obligation to report immediately to the College Secretary any change in plans that will prevent him from coming to Oberlin in accordance with this arrangement.

By the middle of April the limit of 175 promises issued to women was reached and a waiting list was begun. At one time the names of as many as fifty women were on this list, waiting for admission to the Freshman class. At a special meeting of the Committee on Admission, held August 30, the registration facts were considered and it was voted that in view of the decrease in the number of men making application for admission to the Freshman class the College would receive thirty additional women in the Freshman class, bringing the total of women to 205. The total number of Freshman cards received during the entire summer was as follows: 110 men, 211 women, total 321. Some of those who registered failed to claim their cards and the final attendance figures for the present semester show 101 men and 205 women, a total of 306.

At date of July 1 the number of registration cards on hand, as above reported, was 583. By August 1 this number had increased to 783; by September 1, to 976; by September 17, to 1,025; a large number of additional registration cards came in during the two days of registration; by the end of September the number of registration cards on hand had been increased to 1,079; the final number of registration cards was 1,087.

In putting into effect the rule limiting the actual attendance to 1,000 students in the College of Arts and Sciences, there is presented to the Committee on Admission an interesting problem in estimating the possible shrinkage in registrations received. In May of each year the old students register for the succeeding year, and the number of cards received from old students has varied from 593 in 1912 to 703 in 1916, dropping to 583 in 1917. During the summer enough additional registration cards are accepted to bring the total to the desired point. The problem set before the Committee is to estimate how many probable shrinkages there will be, both in the number of registration cards received in the spring from old students, and in the number of registration cards accepted from new students. The following table gives the experiences of the last six years:

	Number of Registration Cards Accepted	Number of Students Enrolled First Semester	Shrinkage
1912	1075	998	77
1913	1087	1005	82
1914	1089	983	106
1915	1116	1000	116
1916	1164	1023	141
1917	1087	925	162

The unusual percentage of shrinkage for the year 1917 is of course accounted for by the withdrawals of men for government service. It is becoming more and more customary for all the old students to go through the process of registration even though at the time there is little probability of return to Oberlin in the succeeding year. The shrinkage is largely in the cards received from old students; there is a very small shrinkage in the registrations of new students. The experience of the six years has shown that a 10 per cent shrinkage may be expected in the registration of old students; in the registration of new students the shrinkage is between 4 and 5 per cent.

ENROLMENT FOR THE SECOND SEMESTER OF 1917-18

For several years the College has made special effort to bring to Oberlin for enrolment in the second semester a sufficient numbr of new students to take the place of those who withdraw during the first semester or at its end. For the first time in the history of the College it has been possible to make the attendance during the two semesters practically equal. The experience of the College during the last seven years is shown in the following table:

	Actual Attendance First Semester	Actual Attendance Second Semester	Net Shrinkage
1910-11	998	957	41
1911-12	971	940	31
1912-13	998	948	50
1913-14	999	982	17
1914-15	983	948	35
1915-16	1000	966	34
1916-17	1023	1015	8

It has been found that it is safe to accept forty new students at the opening of the second semester to balance the withdrawals during the first semester or at its end. For the second semester of the present year we have already issued fourteen promises, and unless the operation of the war draft interferes we shall expect that the attendance during the second semester will be above the 900 mark.

REGISTRATION OF FRESHMEN FOR 1918-19

We shall again issue promises of admission for men and women for the Freshman class. At the time of the preparation of this report 63 of these promises have already been issued. I do not anticipate that there will be any trouble in securing the attendance of 200 Freshman women, but there is no reason to think that we shall be able to enroll more than 100 or 110 men in next year's Freshman class.

Respectfully submitted,

GEORGE M. JONES.

REPORT OF THE SECRETARY OF THE BUREAU
OF APPOINTMENTS

To the President:

SIR—During the first part of the last academic year the Bureau of Appointments was conducted along the regular lines established in the last few years. With the entry of the United States into the war, entirely new conditions arose, so that the work of the Bureau has been greatly changed and considerably increased. We have had many more calls for teachers than ever before, and many new lines of activity for our graduates have been opened.

During the early part of the year I endeavored to secure openings for men with a number of business houses. These efforts were, in general, very successful, and I am more than ever convinced that the college man can easily achieve a business career. The American Telephone and Telegraph Company sent representatives here from Cleveland, Chicago, and New York to confer with our men. Several men were offered positions with this Company, and one of them accepted a position in the Chicago office. I received also a very interesting letter from the United Motors' Corporation, inquiring for graduates with three to five years' successful business experience, at salaries ranging from two to ten thousand dollars. I was able to refer them to several of our graduates who have made conspicuous successes in business. Among the other business houses who either applied to us for men or who said they would be glad to employ our graduates, were the large packing houses in Chicago, a branch of the Glidden Varnish Company in Detroit, several of the large automobile concerns, and the Western Electric Company of Erie, Pa.

Another interesting feature of the year's work was the correspondence with the Chicago office of the U. S. Department of Labor. An employment bureau has been established by this Department in Chicago, which expects to coöperate with the different colleges in finding occupations for graduates. I recommended a number of our graduates to this Department and filed their credentials there.

There has been an unusual call during the latter part of the year and during the summer for women to replace men who have enlisted in government service. A typical call of this kind came from The Ironton Engine Company of Pittsburgh. This Company wished to employ a young woman, at an initial salary of $100 a month. The only technical requirement was Mechanical Drawing. We had no one to suggest for the position, but any young woman who had had the course in Mechanical Drawing offered by the College would have been eligible for this position. Another such call came from the Western Electric Company of Erie, Pa. During the coming year there will undoubtedly be many more calls of a similar nature, and one service which I hope the Bureau may render during the year is to direct the women of the graduating class to positions of this type.

The call for teachers was never so great. So far as I know, not a single graduate registered with us is without employment. Many positions which were open only to men last year were this year filled by women. Of course this situation is only temporary, and after the close of the war we must expect the normal number of men in the teaching profession. Meanwhile, I hope that the occupations for women will increase in number, so that women with the ''I may have to teach'' attitude will no longer need to burden that profession.

Next year there will be an even greater call for teachers of Spanish than there was this summer, and I hope that the College may prepare for this by offering a second year of work in this language. There undoubtedly will also be some opportunity for teachers of Italian and Portuguese.

We were asked to make recommendations this year for thirty-four college positions, and many more positions of this kind could be secured if we had more graduates with the Master's degree to recommend. Most of the small colleges desire teachers with the Master's degree in order to keep up their rating with the North Central Association of Colleges and Secondary Schools. I wish that more of our students might attain this advanced degree, so that more of these attractive positions could be open to them. More opportunities in social work are open this year than ever before, and an increasing number of young women are preparing to take these positions.

As in previous years, most of the people who registered with the Bureau belonged to the graduating class. This is especially true in

the present year because it was so easy for graduates to find situa.
tions that many who have formerly registered with us did not renew
their registration. A great number of former graduates who were not
registered with the Bureau have, however, asked us to send their cre.
dentials to prospective positions, or to recommend them for places.
In all such cases the Bureau has complied with the request, even though
the fifty cent fee had not been paid. One hundred and twenty-nine
of last year's class registered with the Bureau; 123 during the pre.
ceding year. The entire 129 people have been placed; and the Bureau
has recommended for positions many of the graduating class who did
not register with us.

The following table contains a list of the positions for which
the Bureau was requested by the employer to make recommendations. It
does not include positions for which we made recommendations at the
request of persons registered with the Bureau:

Business (including newspaper work)..........   16
Secretary (including Pastor's Assistant)......   21
Social Service   12
Y. M. C. A. and Y. W. C. A.................   16
Executive teaching positions   25
Teaching   336
Miscellaneous   11

A number of very interesting positions are included in the miscellaneous list. Among them was a request for a translator to work with
a publishing house, a request for a draftswoman, and for a man to
conduct psychological experiments for business efficiency. I was very
sorry that we were able to find no suitable person to recommend as an
assistant to Mr. Walter Dill Scott, who is doing very interesting work in
Pittsburgh in psychological experiments in business efficiency. This
field and the field of vocational guidance seem to me to offer unusual
openings for young men and young women at the present time.

The following table shows the distribution of the 336 teaching
positions referred to in the preceding table:

Subject	Teaching this Subject	
	Alone	With other subjects
Agriculture	0	2
Art	2	2
Athletics	1	9
Biology	5	2
Botany	0	2
Chemistry	3	6
Commercial	3	0
Domestic Science	0	4
Economics	0	1
Education	2	0
English	18	22
French	0	10
German	8	9
Grades	7	1
History	6	6
Latin	8	21
Manual Training	1	2
Mathematics	9	15
Music	22	8
Philosophy	0	1
Physical Training	62	5
Physics	0	8
Public Speaking	0	2
Rural Schools	3	0
Science	11	8
Sociology	0	1
Spanish	3	11
Tutor	3	0
Zoölogy	1	0

The number of calls which the Bureau received this year is almost twice the number for last year, 437 instead of 243. The Bureau was able to secure positions for graduates for less than half of these 437 requests. This was due to the fact that during the last month the Bureau has had very few candidates to recommend for any sort of position. This has been especially true in the field of Physical Training. The call for occupations in connection with the war, and the new laws in New York and New Jersey requiring every high school to have a physical director, opened so many places to young men that practically all the men who could be recommended for Physical Training positions were placed before the close of school. In this respect I think the conditions will be even worse during the coming year. The table below shows the distribution by month of the calls received:

September 31	March 37
October 17	April 49
November 14	May 41
December 17	June 51
January 31	July 62
February 21	August 66

The following tables show the occupational distribution of the last graduating classes:

	1916	1917
Regular Teaching	60	57
Physical Training	14	11
Business	26	17
Social Service or Y. M. C. A. or Y. W. C. A........	9	10
Church work (not including Theological Students)..	0	1
Library work	0	4
Secretarial work................................	5	4
Newspaper work.................................	4	2
Government Service.............................	0	26
Postgraduate study 31	31	22

Botany	1
Business	2
Law	1
Library	2
Medicine	3
Music	1
Nursing	3
Philosophy	1
Physics	1
Social Service.........................	1
Theology	4
Y. W. C. A.	1
Zoölogy	1

At Home...	23	12
Indeterminate	7	0
	179	166

	Per cent 1916	Per cent 1917
Teaching (including Physical Training)............	41.34	40.96
Business (including newspaper work)..............	16.79	11.44
Social Service or Y. M. C. A. or Y. W. C. A.........	5.04	6.02
Library work	0.00	2.41
Secretarial work................................	2.80	2.41
Church work (not including Theological Students)..	0.00	.60
Students	17.34	13.25
Government Service..............................	0.00	15.69
At Home..	12.86	7.22
Indeterminate	3.83	0.00

During the coming year the Bureau will be engaged in collecting and tabulating material to show what preparation is necessary for entrance to the various professions and occupations. I hope that it may be possible to publish as one of the bulletins of the College a list of occupations open to men and women, with the preparation necessary in each case. I expect to be able during the year to visit a number of men employing large numbers of college people, to ascertain just what type of college course best fits graduates for their needs. It seems to me that such a list could be made quite definite and useful. If such a pamphlet is published it could be put into the hands of the students during their first and second years, so that elections might be made with greater intelligence.

Respectfully submitted,

LOUIS E. LORD.

REPORT OF THE DIRECTOR OF THE SUMMER SESSION

To the President:

SIR—The attendance of students at Oberlin College during the summer of 1917 was 111. This number was 68 less than the attendance of last year. In my opinion it was due in the main to the fact that many of our young men undertook some form of war service which called them away from the school.

Of the students enrolled, 28 were men and 83 were women; 15 were graduates and 96 were undergraduates; of the graduate students, 5 were men and 10 were women. The undergraduate students were distributed as follows: 9 men and 35 women were incoming or actual Seniors; 1 man and 15 women were incoming Juniors; 3 men and 8 women were incoming Sophomores; 10 men and 15 women were special students; a total of 23 men and 73 women. Of the above undergraduates, 8 were Chinese students.

The attendance of students in the various classes was as follows:

Course	Men	Women
Economics 1	1	3
Economics 2	4	5
Education 1	3	19
Education 2	3	6
Education 3	3	4
English Composition 1	1	7
English Composition 2	1	2
English Literature 1	1	7
English Literature 2	1	10
English Literature 3	0	8
English Literature 4	2	16
English Literature 5	0	16
English Literature 6	1	2
Fine Arts 1	4	9
Fine Arts 2	0	2
French 1 and 2	7	6
Geology 2	3	5
Greek Literature 1	0	2
History 1	2	4
History 2	5	6
History 3	2	0
History 4	5	0
History 5	4	6
History 6	2	3

Course	Men	Women
Latin 1	0	3
Latin 2	0	4
Mathematics 1	0	2
Mathematics 2	2	2
Philosophy 1	3	14
Philosophy 2	1	11
Political Science 1	1	3
Political Science 2	2	3
Psychology 1	5	14
Psychology 2	2	8

The total number of instructors engaged in the Summer Session was 14; the total number of hours offered was 165.

In reviewing the financial situation of the Summer Session the report will be presented in two parts:

A. Receipts
    (1) From the general collegiate work offered on the grounds................$2,428.00
    (2) Surplus from past years............. 1,019.61
    (3) From the Carnegie Peace Foundation.. 250.00
    (4) Appropriation for Practice Teaching.. 118.50

        Total $3,816.11

Expenses (salaries, administration).............$3,979.03

        Net deficit ....$ 162.92

B. Receipts from professional teachers' training courses ....$ 127.50
Expenses (salaries and guarantee).............. 246.00

        Net deficit ....$ 118.50

This deficit in the teachers' courses was covered by the vote of the Prudential Committee guaranteeing $300 toward the expense of carrying them.

The Summer Session is deeply indebted to members of the faculty, to the Conservatory of Music, and to Talcott household for the various lectures and entertainments which added so markedly to the instruction and pleasure of the members of the school.

       Respectfully submitted,

            S. F. MACLENNAN.

THE GRADUATE SCHOOL OF THEOLOGY

REPORT OF THE DEAN

To the President:

SIR—The attendance in the Graduate School of Theology has been seriously affected by war conditions. Most of those whose earlier correspondence indicated that they were planning to enter Oberlin this fall were, as time went on, called into army work either as soldiers or Y. M. C. A. secretaries. A number of those who were here last year are in various forms of army work. This has reduced the attendance at the present time to thirty-eight, five of whom are women. This figure may be increased by two or three at the beginning of next semester. The final figure last year was fifty-two, of whom two were women. The number of men therefore this year is about two-thirds that of last year. Only three who were members of the Junior and Middle classes last year have gone to other theological schools for the present year.

Of the fifteen men who received degrees at the last commencement five have gone to foreign missionary work, two into work of the Young Men's and Young Women's Christian Associations, one is a member of a hospital unit in France, one is doing further graduate study, and six are pastors.

Professor Hutchins and Professor MacLennan represent the faculty in war work. Professor Hutchins was asked to assist the Young Men's Christian Association in the organization of religious work in Camp Sheridan, Montgomery, Alabama, during September and October. The troops have been assembled so slowly there that it has just now seemed necessary for him to decide to continue until near the end of the first semester. He is doing a very important piece of work and through him the Theological School is making a large contribution to the efficiency and welfare of many soldiers. Professor MacLennan, a third of whose time has hitherto been given to the Theological School, is doing education work in army camps.

Professor Fiske is taking his sabbatical year after ten years of hard and effective service. At present he is working in the libraries in and about Cambridge, Massachusetts.

We are being helped from the outside this year by Professor Walter Rauschenbusch, of Rochester Theological Seminary, who comes to Oberlin two days a week this fall to give two courses; and by Professor Frank H. Foster, Professor of Church History here from 1882 to 1892, who gives a ten weeks course in Homiletics. His return to Oberlin as a place of residence this fall has made it possible to secure his valuable services in this emergency. Professor Fullerton has taken on for ten weeks the course in Biblical Homiletics which Professor Hutchins would have given. The students are adjusting themselves finely to unusual conditions and the work of the School has never been carried with better spirit than so far this year.

The attendance though smaller is as cosmopolitan as ever. Thirty universities, colleges, and theological schools are represented; and the home addresses of the students are in eighteen States—between New Hampshire and California—and two foreign countries.

Now that the absolute necessity of an increase of salaries has been met, the outstanding needs are suitable buildings and an enlargement of the Student Employment Fund. The very generous gift of $100,000 from the D. Willis James estate, which had been preceded by more than $140,000 from the same source, has been set aside as a part of what is necessary for the erection of new buildings, although the gift was not restricted by the donors to this use. Mr. Cass Gilbert has completed plans for a beautiful though not extravagant or elaborate plant. The State Building Inspector has recommended the discontinuance of the use of Council Hall in the near future. We hope therefore that the rest of the amount necessary for a new building may soon be secured.

Enlargement of our Student Employment Fund would enable us to put students into the church and missionary work of Cleveland to a larger extent than has been possible in the past. To make this work effective on the larger scale we need not only to give the student a chance to earn what he needs but to provide for transportation and living expenses while in the city. We have funds enough to do this for only a few students. Since we have usually had a good many students to provide for we have been obliged to develop opportunities for their work nearer Oberlin where the incidental expenses are slight. We must push on much further along this line and really utilize for ourselves the advantages of work in the large city which might be ours as well as the advantage to scholarship incident to location in a small town. We have tried out the Student Employment system for nearly fifteen years and no one among either students or faculty would think for a moment of returning to the earlier ''Beneficiary Aid'' method.

Respectfully submitted,

EDWARD I. B

THE CONSERVATORY OF MUSIC

REPORT OF THE DIRECTOR

To the President:

SIR—In these depressing times, one is glad to turn at once to the point of view that gives most courage and hope for the future. In reviewing the year just passed, the high light of success shines most clearly on the financial standing as shown in the Treasurer's report. After meeting all the expenses of the year, we have been able to turn over more than $11,000 on the advances made on Rice Memorial Hall. The director, who urged the erection of Rice Hall and the money for its equipment, so trustfully provided by our Trustees, has always had an ambition to see this debt entirely cancelled before his retiring years overtook him. It is therefore a little startling to find that at the present rate of payment less than two years would be required to do this. However, with the world war interfering with all things financial and artistic we shall probably not attain this desired end for some time to come. Though the number of our students has decreased and all supplies have increased in price owing to the war, we hope by strict economy to operate within our budget for the present year.

The Faculty

There was only one new appointment made in our faculty the past year, that of Mr. Maurice Koessler, Professor of Violin. After a most successful year as teacher and player he now enters on the new year with a full professorship with the best prospects for a long and useful career in the violin and ensemble department.

Miss Margaret H. Whipple, Instructor in the Children's Department, was given a year's leave of absence for study. She decided to offer her services to the Red Cross and is serving in some capacity in that work in New York City.

Miss Lelah E. Harris, who graduated in 1916 and who has been employed in the Children's Department, has been appointed to take Miss Whipple's place for one year.

Mr. Harold D. Smith, who for the past two years has been teaching in the theory department and who expected to continue with us this year, entered the Field Hospital of the regular army service and is at Gettysburg, Pa.

The outside activities of the faculty members remain about the same from year to year. Four churches in Oberlin depend entirely upon the Conservatory for their organists and choir leaders. Other churches in Elyria and Lorain and three important churches in Cleveland employ organists from our faculty.

The string department was unusually active last year in public work. One of the most successful concerts in the Artist Recital course was given by Mrs. Williams, violin, Mr. Koessler, viola, Mr. Goerner, 'cello, and Mr. Breckenridge, piano, in an evening of music for Piano and Strings. They have been invited to give a similar concert in this year's course. They also had engagements in Cleveland and appeared at the State Teachers' Association· beside furnishing most exquisite music on numerous public occasions in Oberlin.

Dr. Andrews, Professor Alderfer, and Professor Stiven continued the series of free organ recitals on the great organ in the Chapel before increasingly interested audiences. Dr. Andrews has given many recitals in various parts of the country and Professor Stiven was invited to play at the University of Toronto.

The Artist Recital Course

The concerts in the Artist Recital Course are becoming a feature of college and town life and are drawing increasingly from surrounding towns. Oberlin has the reputation among artists and managers of offering one of the most select series of concerts to be found in the country, and artists of the highest class covet the honor of an appearance here. It furnishes to our students the best models to be found in the world in all lines of solo performances and the orchestra concerts appeal to all classes who respond to music in its highest form.

The following Musical Organizations and Artists have appeared under Conservatory management during the year:

Mr. Percy Grainger, Piano recital
Mrs. Charlotte Demuth Williams, Violinist
Mr. Maurice Koessler, Violinist
Mr. Friedrich Goerner, 'Cellist
Mr. William K. Breckenridge, Pianist
The Philadelphia Symphony Orchestra and
Mrs. Olga Samaroff, Pianist
Mme. Margarete Matzenauer, Vocal recital

The New York Symphony Orchestra
Mr. Joseph Bonnet, Organ recital
Mr. Jacques Thibaud, Violin recital
The Cincinnati Symphony Orchestra
The Flonzaley Quartet
Mr. Ossip Gabrilowitsch, Piano recital
The Chicago Symphony Orchestra and
Miss Marcella Craft, Vocal Soloist

Statistics

The following statistics will show the number of students enrolled in the various subjects during the year 1916-17:

	First Semester	Second Semester
Pianoforte	374	378
Organ	133	123
Singing	243	242
Violin	43	41
'Cello	12	12
Wind	3	3
Harp	6	7
Instrumentation	6	10
Counterpoint, Form, Composition.	50	57
Harmony	230	205
Ear Training	196	155
History of Music	110	113
History of Music, advanced	9	9
Public School Music	91	. . .
Normal Course in Piano Teaching	34	54
Special Sight Singing	29	. . .
Terminology	. . .	. . .
Kindergarten Class	46	51
Violin Class	. . .	18
Dramatic Expression	32	34
Children's Classes	61	61
Appreciation of Music	79	68

Respectfully submitted,

CHARLES W. MORRISON.

REPORT OF THE DEAN OF CONSERVATORY WOMEN

To the President:

SIR—I have the honor to submit to you the following report of the year 1916-17:

There is at present more unity in the accommodations offered and in the general social conditions in the dormitories and boarding houses than in any previous year. However, the fact that our late registration often leaves new Conservatory students no possibilities in the choice of residence makes the situation unsatisfactory.

For some time I have felt that the housing of our first year Conservatory women in College halls might help to solve some of our problems. We are making the experiment this year, by putting groups of first year Conservatory women in Allencroft, Ellis Cottage, and the home of Mrs. C. H. Dudley next to Allencroft,—the entire number, forty-five in all, boarding at Allencroft.

Having so many of the incoming class together will make it easier to carry out plans for the social life of the young women, as well as to assist them in adjusting themselves to the standards of Oberlin. This has been made difficult because in the past years they have been scattered in small groups throughout the town. Then, too, we are hoping that the present arrangement will aid us in discovering qualities of leadership and cultivating initiative in Conservatory women.

There is no doubt that it is mutually beneficial for Conservatory and College women to live together. But we believe that they can gain more from the remaining years of their college experience and contribute more to it, after a year's residence in a college hall, where the life can be adapted to their particular needs. The plan is already working admirably and if it results as well as it promises, I hope in the future we may be able to house all our first year Conservatory women in College halls.

One of the most interesting things I have to report is the development of the plans for the opening of a special dormitory and social center for Conservatory students. Although we have been unable to build the addition to Barrows House as we had hoped, the house with its small family has more than justified its purchase. Our aim in directing the activities of the house has been to carry on those traditions of courtesy and hospitality that were established in the days of President and Mrs. Barrows. The beauty and dignity of the house and grounds, I am sure, have had an influence upon the lives of the students residing there. We are anxious that both College and Conservatory students should feel that Barrows House is theirs at all times for all kinds of functions and festivities. And last year the students availed themselves of this opportunity. During the year the house was opened for many social affairs. Both faculty and students appreciated the change from the basement of Rice Hall to Barrows House for the Fall reception and the Thanksgiving party. The Seniors held one of their ''soirées'' in the spacious parlors. The ladies of the Y. W. C. A. board gave a supper on the lawn to the young women of the cabinet. Many a committee and board meeting seemed a little less prosaic when held in the hospitable library, and even ''General Ex.'' took on a different aspect when Barrows House was thrown open and a cup of hot coffee was served. On Tuesday evening of Commencement week the Conservatory faculty entertained the Seniors and their out-of-town guests with a garden party. Perhaps there was no social affair of the whole year more appreciated than this.

We deeply regret the loss of Mrs. Maud Taylor as matron of Barrows House. Her efficient management and gracious personality contributed much to the success of our first year. Mrs. Harper, who won the love and confidence of all the young women at Fairchild House last year, has now been transferred to Barrows House.

Excellent work was done last year in the care of our young women who were ill. Eighty-nine girls were cared for at Browning House during the year. Miss Swayze, the visiting nurse, made over 1,400 calls upon sick girls and gave bed-side care to 467. I wish to take this opportunity to express our appreciation of the superior work done by Miss Swayze during her stay in Oberlin. She has left many friends among students and faculty.

I take great pleasure in reporting the growth in our facilities for taking care of the sick the coming year. As Mrs. Browning's home was no longer available, the old house at 268 Forest Street has been renovated and made fresh and attractive for our use. We are happy to report that Mrs. Andrus is in charge of the house. The second floor has two large sunny rooms attractively furnished where five patients may be cared for. A pleasant room for the nurse, besides bath and kitchenette, make this a particularly desirable arrangement. Miss Thorpe, a graduate nurse of Lakeside Hospital, is in charge. For some time the matrons have reported the need of a room where young women who are tired and nervously worn out might go for rest and solitude. Such a room has been provided in the new infirmary. Here a girl may have complete rest and isolation and such care as she desires.

The year was entirely free from any serious cases of discipline. The Conservatory women took a more active part in all legislative and administrative matters in the Women's League, and consequently came to a better understanding of the purpose and wisdom of the rules affecting the women, and coöperated more cordially in their support and administration.

Respectfully submitted,

FRANCES G. NASH.

REPORT OF THE LIBRARIAN

To the President:

SIR—I submit herewith the report of the library for the year 1916-17.

Growth of the Library

Of the total number of pieces during the year by purchase, gift, or exchange, the following proved to be additions: 10,997 bound books; 6,047 pamphlets and unbound books; 12,035 numbers of magazines; 9,910 numbers of newspapers; 250 maps and charts; 7 file cases of manuscript; and 100 prints, photographs, and other miscellaneous articles; a total of 39,356 pieces. The number is larger as to bound volumes than in any previous year with a single exception. This is due largely to the addition of the Callender Library. It still remains true that almost nothing can be had from Germany, although we were fortunate in getting two books through just before the declaration of war by the United States.

The additions for the last five years are shown in the following table:

	Bound	Unbound	Total
1912-13	10,602	8,300	18,902
1913-14	8,192	4,546	12,738
1914-15	10,054	6,357	16,411
1915-16	10,090	6,167	16,257
1916-17	10,997	6,047	17,044

The library on September 1, 1917, contained the following:

Bound volumes	175,625
Unbound volumes and pamphlets	147,555
Unbound volumes of newspapers (estimated)	5,950
Magazines (incomplete and unbound volumes)	25,000
Maps and charts (estimated)	5,000
Miscellaneous manuscripts (number of file cases filled)	164
Coins, prints, photographs, etc. (estimated)	1,800
Total	361,094

In addition the library possesses about 90,000 duplicates, making the total number of pieces under the immediate charge of the librarian 451,094. In the above enumeration everything bound is called a book

and everything unbound, with the exception of magazines and newspapers, etc., a pamphlet. If one were to count pamphlets containing
more than 80 pages as a book, after the custom of some libraries, it is
probable that the aggregate of ''books'' on this basis would exceed
265,000 volumes.

Additions of the Year

The 10,997 bound volumes added during the year were received
from the following sources: through purchase, 5,431; through gifts,
5,227; through exchange, 339.

In my last year's report I gave a table showing the period of
origin of the books added to the library during that year. A similar
table follows for the additions of the present year:

Published in the	Number
16th century	1
17th century	0
18th century	44
19th century	3,010
20th century	7,198

These figures correspond very closely to those of the previous
report, emphasizing again, as I have before said, that we are adding
pretty largely books of current origin. Obviously, a library which is
to be for research workers must include as well the literature of earlier
centuries. Every early printed book, every 16th century pamphlet, every
book which marks an epoch in the scholarship of any given field adds
to the ability of the library to help trace the development of knowledge.
It seems to me that we ought to purchase more of this older material,
but our main dependence must be upon those who have these older books,
which are becoming too expensive to be bought with the funds available for purchases. There must be among our graduates and among
friends of the College many collectors of these books of earlier generations. It is to them that the library must look for its valuable additions. Correspondence in regard to such collections is always welcomed
by the librarian.

Purchases

The purchases of the year have been of the usual wide range of
interest. The most expensive have naturally been in connection with the
Art library of the new Art Museum. I give below some of the more
important additions of the year

Amundsen, R. E. G. South pole. 2 volumes.

Bagwell, Richard. Ireland under the Stuarts and during the interregnum. 2 volumes.

Bailey, L. H. Standard encyclopedia of horticulture. Volumes 5 and 6.

Baring-Gould, Sabine. Lives of the saints. 16 volumes.

Baudot, Anatole and Perrault-Dabot, A. Les cathédrales de France, 2 volumes.

Baum, Julius. Romanesque architecture in France.

[Beilby, Ralph.] General history of quadrupeds, 1792. Illustrations by Bewick.

Bibliothèque de l'enseignement des beaux-arts. 43 volumes.

Blomfield, R. T. History of French architecture from the reign of Charles VIII till the death of Mazarin. 2 volumes.

Blomfield, R. T. History of Renaissance architecture in England. 2 volumes.

Blondel, J. F. Réimpression de l'architecture française. 4 volumes.

Bond, Francis. Gothic architecture in England.

Bond, Francis. Introduction to English church architecture from the eleventh to the sixteenth century. 2 volumes.

Bradford, T. L. Bibliographer's manual of American history. 5 volumes.

Briggs, M. S. Baroque architecture.

British museum. Department of Greek and Roman antiquities. Catalogue of Greek and Etruscan vases in British museum. 4 volumes.

Bruce, Herbert. Age of schism. 7 volumes.

Butler, Alfred J. Ancient Coptic churches of Egypt. 2 volumes.

Butler, H. C. Architecture and other arts.

Byne, Arthur. Spanish architecture of the 16th century.

Cambridge songs, a goliard's song book of the XIth century.

Cejador y Frauca, Julio. Historia de la lengua y literatura castellana. 3 volumes.

Choisy, Auguste. L'art debâtir chez les Byzantins.

Choisy, A. Histoire de l'architecture. 2 volumes.

Cichorius, Conrad. Die reliefs der Traianssäule.

Circolo matematico di Palermo. Rendiconti. 40 volumes.

Collezione di monographie illustrate. Series 1a Italia artistica, diretta da Corrado Ricci. 7 volumes.

Complete index to Avery's History of the U. S.

Cory, G. E. Rise of South Africa. 2 volumes.

Cummings, Charles A. History of architecture in Italy from the time of Constantine to the dawn of the Renaissance. 2 volumes.

Dalton, O. M. Byzantine art and archaeology.

Dehio, G. G. and Bezold, G. von. Die kirchliche baukunst des abendlandes. 9 volumes.

Durand, Georges. Monographie de l'église Notre-Dame cathédrale d'Amiens. 2 volumes.

Durm, Josef. Die baustile.

Eliot, George. Works. Boston, Jefferson Press. 24 volumes.

English catalog of books. Volume 9.

Espouy, Hector d'. Fragments d'architecture antique d'après les relevés et restaurations des anciens pensionnaires de l'académie de France à Rome. 2 volumes.

Federal council of the churches of Christ in America. Library of Christian coöperation. 6 volumes.

Fletcher, B and Fletcher, B. F. History of architecture. ed. 5.

France. Commission des monuments historiques. Archives. 5 volumes.

Friedlaender, Max. Das deutsche lied im 18 jahrhundert. 3 volumes.

Gauckler, Paul. Basiliques chrétiennes de Tunisie.

"The Georgian period," being measured drawings of Colonial work. 12 volumes.

Guadet, Julian. Éléments et théorie de l'architecture. 4th ed. 4 volumes.

Gurlitt, Cornelius. Die baukunst Frankreichs. 2 volumes.

Hartmann, K. O. Die baukunst in ihrer entwicklung von der urzeit bis zur gegenwart. 3 volumes.

Hartung, Hugo., ed. Motive der mittelalterlichen baukunst in Deutschland in photographischen originalaufnahmen. 3 volumes.

Hastings, James, ed. Dictionary of the Apostolic church.

Hawley, W. A. Oriental rugs, antique and modern.

Helbig, Wolfgang. Führer durch die öffentlichen sammlungen klassischer altertümer in Rom. ed. 3. 2 volumes.

Herbert, J. A. Illuminated manuscripts.

Hoare, A. Italian dictionary.

Hodgson, S. H. Philosophy of reflection.

Hoskier, H. C. Codex B and its allies. 2 volumes.

International standard Bible encyclopaedia. 5 volumes.

Jackson, T. G. Byzantine and Romanesque architecture. 2 volumes.

Jackson, T. G. Gothic architecture in France, England, and Italy. 2 volumes.

Jastrow, Morris. Civilization of Babylonia and Assyria.

Kober, G. M. and Hanson, W. C. Diseases of occupation and vocational hygiene.

Lasteyrie du Saillant, R. C. comte de. L'architecture religieuse en France à l'époque romane.

Lefèvre-Pontalis, Eugène. L'architecture religieuse dans l'ancien diocèse de Soissons au XIe et XIIe siècle. 2 volumes.

Legge, Francis. Forerunners and rivals of Christianity. 2 volumes.

Legros, L. A. Typographical printing-surfaces.

Lenoir, A. A. Architecture, monastique. 2 volumes.

Lucanus, Marcus Annaeus. Pharsalia, edited by C. M. Francken. 2 volumes.

Lucilius, Gaius. Carminum reliquiae, edited by F. Marx. 2 volumes.

Lübke, Wilhelm. Grundriss der kunstgeschichte. 3 volumes.

Lunge, George. Coal-tar and ammonia. Fifth and enlarged ed. 3 volumes.

Mach, E. R. O. von, ed. Official diplomatic documents relating to the outbreak of the European war.

Macler, Frédéric. Miniatures arméniennes.
Male, Émile. L'art religieux de la fin du Moyen age en France.
Male, Émile. Religious art in France. XIII century.
Manuel d'art Musulman. 2 volumes.
Martin, Camille. L'art gothique en France.
Martin, Camille. L'art roman en France. 3 volumes.
Martin, Camille. L'art roman en Italie.
Maskell, A. O. Ivories.
Mély, Fernand de. Les primitifs et leurs signatures.
Michel, André. Histoire de l'art. 10 volumes.
Mythology of all races. Volumes, 1, 6, 9-10.
Napoleon I, emperor of the French. Unpublished correspondence of Napoleon I, preserved in the War archives. 3 volumes.
Ovidius Naso, Publius. Metamorphoseon libri XV. Edited by Hugo Magnus.
Palestine exploration fund. Survey of western Palestine. 11 volumes.
Paris. Musée de sculpture comparée. Album...pub. sous la direction de P. Frantz Marcou. 5 volumes.
Perrot, Georges and Chipiez, Charles. Histoire de l'art. Volumes 9-10.
Petites monographies des grands édifices de la France. 21 volumes.
Petrie, W. M. F. Pyramids and temples of Gizeh.
Plekhanov, G. V. History of Russian social ideas. 2 volumes.
Porter, A. K. Lombard architecture. Volumes 1-3. Also atlas.
Porter, A. K. Medieval architecture. 2 volumes.
Prentice, A. N. Renaissance architecture and ornament in Spain.
Prior, E. S. and Gardner, Arthur. An account of medieval figure-sculpture in England.
Redesdale, A. B. F.-M., baron. Memories.
Reference handbook of the medical sciences. Volume 7.
Reymond, Marcel. La sculpture Florentine. 4 volumes.
Ricci, Corrado. Baroque architecture and sculpture in Italy.
Sanford, A. H. Sanford's American history maps. ed. 2.
Satow, Sir E. M. Guide to diplomatic practice. 2 volumes.
Schütz, Alexander. Die renaissance in Italien. 4 volumes.
Science abstracts. 7 volumes.
Scott, W. W. Standard methods of chemical analysis.
Shakespeare's England; an account of life and manners of his age. 2 volumes.
Smith, G. A. Atlas of the historical geography of the Holy Land.
Standard dictionary. 1916.
Statuen deutscher kultur, ed. by Will Vesper. 16 volumes.
Stevenson, B. E., comp. Home book of verse, American and English. 8 volumes.
Supino, I. B. Le sculture delle porte di San Petronio in Bologna.
Talmud. New edition of the Babylonian Talmud. English translation. Ed. by M. L. Rodkinson. 10 volumes.
Thorpe, Sir Thomas E. Dictionary of applied chemistry. 5 volumes.
Treitschke, H. G. von. Politics. 2 volumes.

Thompson, David. David Thompson's narrative of his explorations in western America, 1784-1812.

Uhde, Constantin. Baudenkmaeler in Grossbritannien. 2 volumes.

Uhde, Constantin. Baudenkmaeler in Spanien und Portugal. 2 volumes.

Vitry, Paul. La cathédrale de Reims. 5 volumes.

Vogüé, C. J. M., Marquis de. Syrie centrale. Architecture civile et religieuse du Ier au VIIe siècle. 2 volumes.

Walpole, Sir Spencer. History of England. 6 volumes.

Walters, H. B. Classical dictionary. 1916.

Ward, W. H. Architecture of the renaissance in France.

Ward, W. H. French châteaux and gardens in the XVIth century.

Ware, W. R. American Vignola. 2 volumes.

Watson, W. C. Portuguese architecture.

Wilson, H. W., firm, publishers. Children's catalogue of thirty-five hundred books.

Wilson, Woodrow. History of the American people. 5 volumes.

Yerkes, C. T. Yerkes collection of Oriental carpets.

Gifts of the Year

Ex-Senator Theodore E. Burton, upon his removal to New York, presented to the library large numbers of volumes and pamphlets from his private library. Among these was a large and extremely interesting collection of books and pamphlets gathered by him during his recent trip to South America. This collection contained some very interesting historical, statistical, and economical material upon the various South American republics, which will prove of very great value to students of these countries.

In addition, ex-Senator Burton gave us many pamphlets accumulated by him during his years in Washington and many valuable governmental publications. He also presented the library of the late Giles W. Shurtleff, Professor and Treasurer of Oberlin College for many years. Professor Shurtleff occupied for many years the chair in Latin and developed his private library as a supplement to the material possessed by the college. His library, therefore, contains much classical material which was not in the library and will add many of the standard editions of the classical writers.

Another important gift came to us from Mr. E. Snell Hall of Jamestown, N. Y., who presented the library of his father, the Rev. Elliott Hall of the same place. The father had been a friend of the library for many years, making frequent gifts of books and periodicals. It seems exceedingly appropriate, therefore, that his library should come to us. The collection numbered over 500 volumes.

Professor Albert H. Currier sent us more than 250 volumes besides many magazines from his overflowing book shelves. Other Professors generously remembering the library are C. G. Rogers, G. F. Wright,

George W. Andrews, Louis E. Lord, J. A. Demuth, C. W. Barry, and Philip D. Sherman.

Dr. Nellie M. Caulkins of Manito, Illinois, presented us with 150 volumes. Mr. J. E. Everett of Remsen, N. Y., presented us with 40 volumes of periodicals published in the Welsh language. Mrs. J. K. Greene sent us a large number of valuable books and pamphlets from Dr. Greene's library. Mr. C. L. Williams, having in previous years given valuable books and magazines, also presented a number of periodicals this year. Miss Kate B. Leonard sent a large number of valuable books from the library of her father, the Rev. D. L. Leonard, D. D. Dr. Leonard had been for many years one of our most diligent users and had added very greatly to our collection of books and magazines relating to foreign missions. C. J. Clark sent us a collection of 100 volumes or more. Among these were many early Ohio imprints which we are glad to add to our growing collection of books which illustrate Ohio history.

To all these donors and to innumerable other givers of one or two or more books whose names cannot here be mentioned for lack of space, the thanks of the library are hereby recorded. Every year we are astonished at the number and great value of these gifts and wonder if the stream will continue to flow. Without such gifts the library would be of much less value. We hope that the generosity of our friends both in Oberlin and elsewhere will continue to manifest itself through such additions.

Exchanges

The number added by exchange is 339, which is decidedly smaller than in recent years. The chief endeavor during the year has been to dispose of duplicates. On the first of each month a list of 200 duplicate titles has been selected from our duplicate catalogue, mimeographed and sent to other libraries. A very considerable number has been taken by some one of the libraries to which the lists were sent. The total number of duplicates disposed of by exchange was 593 bound volumes and 2,725 unbound books, pamphlets, and magazines. In addition 97 volumes and 324 magazines were sold. Among libraries with which exchanges were carried on are the following: Library of Congress, University of Chicago, Western Reserve Historical Society, Garrett Biblical Institute, University of Minnesota, New York Public Library, and Missionary Research Library.

While there is perhaps less of distinctly notable worth in the additions this year than usual, the books were quite worth adding to our collection and would have cost some hundreds of dollars if purchased.

Work of the Cataloguing Department

The following table shows the extent to which the library is now catalogued:

	Completely Catalogued	Temporarily Catalogued	Uncat- alogued	Total
Bound volumes	168,950		6,675	175,625
Unbound volumes and pamphlets	97,624		49,931	147,555
Unbound volumes of newspapers (estimated)		5,950		5,950
Magazines (incomplete and unbound volumes)		25,000		25,000
Maps and charts (estimated).			5,000	5,000
Miscellaneous manuscripts (boxes)			164	164
Miscellaneous (coins, photographs, prints, etc.), estimated			1,800	1,800
	266,574	30,950	63,570	361,094

During the year 10,890 bound volumes were catalogued and 6,357 pamphlets and unbound volumes were catalogued. This involved the preparation of 46,942 new cards for the catalogue and the alteration, chiefly by the incorporation of additional information of 18,382 cards previously written. 9,150 cards were withdrawn from the catalogue. These were largely written cards, mostly 2x5 size, which were replaced by the printed cards of the Library of Congress. Our card catalogue is now estimated to contain 519,161 cards.

The work of revision, which never ends, required the alteration of 1,939 cards previously written. 732 volumes and 93 pamphlets required changes in the book number. 638 volumes and 138 pamphlets were withdrawn from the library as duplicates.

While the work of the Cataloguing department is larger in amount than ever before it was not able to keep pace with the growing number of additions, so that the number of books in arrears has somewhat increased.

Work of the Reference and Circulating Departments

During the year the library was open 305 days; the total number of readers was 213,674, as compared with 201,130 the previous year. The distribution of this attendance among the different rooms was as follows: Reference Room, 142,928; Open Shelf Room, 57,868; Children's Room, 12,878. No record of those using only the Seminar rooms is kept. A person using two or more rooms during the same visit to the library would be counted at least twice. It is not probable that there is a great number of such cases.

The largest attendance in any one day was: in the Reference Room, 1,010 (Jan. 18); in the Open Shelf Room, 385 (Jan. 26); in the Children's Room, 144 (Nov. 3). The smallest attendance in any one day was: in the Reference Room, 30 (Aug. 23); in the Open Shelf Room, 28 (June 12); in the Children's Room, 10 (Sept. 15). The average daily attendance during the nine months from September 1st to May 30th was 852; during the three months, June 1st to August 31st, 227; the average daily attendance for the entire year, including the summer and all other vacations, 700.

The following table shows the attendance by months for the year:

	Morning	Afternoon	Evening	Total
1916—				
September	4,563	4,701	3,143	12,407
October	8,642	8,163	6,055	22,860
November	9,290	10,373	7,056	26,719
December	7,113	8,167	4,073	19,353
1917—				
January	8,552	9,593	6,786	24,931
February	8,865	10,205	7,011	25,081
March	9,407	9,376	6,256	25,039
April	7,012	8,347	5,298	20,657
May	6,202	6,810	4,898	17,910
June	3,291	4,631	1,026	8,948
July	1,815	3,289		5,104
August	991	2,674		3,665
	75,743	86,329	51,602	213,674

A comparison with a similar table in last year's report shows a slight loss in the morning, a considerable gain in the afternoon, and a large gain in the evening.

The number of books drawn for use outside of the building during the year was 63,841 as compared with 63,184 drawn during the previous year. Books were drawn from the various rooms as follows, the figures for the preceding year following in parenthesis: Reference Room, 24,007 (27,126); Open Shelf Room, 29,156 (27,635); Children's Room, 10,678 (8,423). These volumes were drawn by 5,093 persons as compared with 5,073 persons drawing in the previous year. Of these, 1,832 obtained their books from the Reference Room; 2,400 from the Open Shelf Room; 861 from the Children's Room. The 1,832 drawn from the Reference Room were classified as follows: faculty, 160; students, 411 (81 counted as residents of the town); citizens, 711 (81 of these were also students); out of town and other libraries, 50. Of the 2,400 drawn from the Open Shelf Room, 157 were faculty; students 856 (113 counted as citizens); citizens, 1,374 (113 were also students); out of town and other libraries, 13. If we count the 861 drawing from the Children's Room as citizens, we have an aggregate of 2,946 citizens drawing from the library during the year. To this total should be added the members of the faculty who are also citizens. While there are doubtless in these numbers many who are counted twice because they draw from both the Reference Room and the Open Shelf Room yet, notwithstanding this fact, the showing of the circulation among the town people is notably high. If we include with the students the local students, we have, drawing from the Reference Room, 992 and from the Open Shelf Room, 969, the total being 1,961. While again there are many duplications of names, it seems reasonable to estimate that at least 1,400 of our students have drawn books from the library during the past year.

So far as loans could be granted without interference with our own work, it has been a pleasure to serve people outside of Oberlin. Loans have been made to 54 individuals and to nine other libraries. We have found it necessary to borrow from ten other libraries, 41 books.

The administration of the silence rule in the reading rooms was carried out under somewhat unusual conditions, particularly in the Reference Room when the excitement about the war was at its height. It was also enforced in the Reference Room by a new person, which always introduces a variable element in comparison with previous years. I give below the figures for the year, appending in every case the corresponding figures for the pervious year. It has been necessary to enforce the rule in 157 (186) cases. The first offense: penalty, warning only, 130 (164) cases. Classified by departments: College of Arts and Sciences: Seniors, 19; Juniors, 11; Sophomores, 30; Freshmen, 24; total, 84. Conservatory, 9; Kindergarten, 1; Public Schools, 33; other Townspeople, 3. Second offense: penalty, exclusion from the reading rooms for two weeks; 22 (19) cases. College department: Seniors, 4; Juniors, 3; Sophomores, 5; Freshmen, 2; total, 14; Public schools, 7; Town, 1. Third offense: penalty, student excluded until the librarian is satisfied that future conduct will be satisfactory; Seniors, 3; Juniors, 1; Town, 1. While we have not yet secured what we consider an ideal condition, there is a marked improvement and we hope the rule is generally supported by the students.

Special Work of the Year

The situation in our book stacks at the beginning of the year was an almost hopeless one. The shelves were so crowded that it was literally impossible to put one new book on the shelves and difficult to remove one from the shelves. Therefore, at the very beginning of the year it was decided that as far as possible, every inch of space in the Seminar rooms should be utilized, and many sets were transferred to these rooms. While every effort was made to select those sets which were less in demand, the inevitable result of the transfer was an increase of page work in bringing books to and from these rooms. In this way the shelves were relieved enough to permit the addition of the new books until about the first of July. Since that date it has been practically impossible to find places for the new books, and we have been forced to pile sets upon floors, against the side walls of the stack, and on the window-shelves. In view of this urgent situation and the vacating of the space intended for the two additional floors of the stack room, which, until Commencement time had housed the Olney Art Collection, the Prudential Committee decided, in spite of prevailing high prices, to install two additional floors of the stack in the space, now, for the first time, available. A contract was entered into with the Art Metal Construction Company of New York, which furnished the four lower floors, to install two upper floors at a cost slightly exceeding $10,000. The new floors will contain room for about 70,000 volumes and may meet our immediate needs for three or four years. If, however, adequate space is left for future growth in redistributing our books, and if the books now stored in closets, in the attic of the Men's Building, in the Seminar rooms and other places, are restored to their proper places in the stack, we shall have to face within a year or two the necessity of an addition to the present library building. I have spoken quite at length in earlier reports as to what should be provided in such an addition and need not repeat those suggestions at the present time. In view of the prevailing high prices, which seem to bid fair to continue for a considerable period, I doubt whether we can build what we shall need in order to make adequate provision for the future for less than $150,000. It would be highly desirable, if authority were given to begin the preliminary work of planning such an addition at once, in order that plans and details of specifications may be at hand when needed.

Absence of the Librarian

From the 15th of September to the 1st of August the librarian was absent from the library on leave of absence, acting as Principal of the Library School connected with the New York Public Library. The year spent in New York was a most delightful one and the opportunity given to see from the inside the working of the largest library system in the world a very exceptional one. The librarian is very grateful to the College for releasing him to gain this added experience and feels that the benefit which he derived from it ought to prove of service in the development of the College Library.

Through the courtesy of the New York Public Library, which is hereby gratefully acknowledged, Mr. Keyes DeWitt Metcalf, of the Class of 1911, was released from his services at that library in order that he might fill the librarian's place during the year. Mr. Metcalf had given much service to the library during his college course and had been directly connected with the library during the librarian's absence in 1912. He was, therefore, much the most desirable person to take charge of the work in the librarian's absence. The expressions of satisfaction which I have heard since my return indicate that his work was, in every respect, acceptable. In addition to the library work, Mr. Metcalf also carried the courses in bibliography, taught by the librarian. It is my duty and very great pleasure to record my personal gratitude to Mr. Metcalf for being willing to undertake this special service, and to express my entire satisfaction with the work which was done by him during my absence.

The needs of the New York Public Library compelled Mr. Metcalf to return to that institution July 1st, after which date the work was again in charge of the librarian. During the month of July, Miss Eoline Spaulding, head of the cataloguing department, was the responsible person on the ground and I take this opportunity to express my appreciation of her kindness in assuming this extra responsibility. May I also add my word of appreciation of the work of all members of the library staff. Under conditions of increasing difficulty, the members of the staff have worked most faithfully and to them is due in large measure the success which has attended the work.

Respectfully submitted,

AZARIAH S. ROOT.

REPORT OF THE CHAIRMAN OF THE WOMEN'S BOARD

To the President:

SIR—The enrolment of women in the departments of the College for the year 1916-17 was 1,060, compared with the preceding year and divided as follows:

	1915-16	1916-17
College	614	644
Conservatory	372	374
Academy	75	
Graduate School of Theology	4	2
Summer Session	43	40
	1,108	1,060

The loss occasioned by this first year of the discontinuance of the Academy is made good in part by the increase in the enrolment of college women.

The year 1916-17 has marked the passing of the first generation of students connected with the work of the Women's League. Its significance in the life of the women has become so apparent that there is no uncertainty as to its continuance and increasing influence. Miss Katherine B. Bushnell, as president, continued the record for fine scholarship and efficiency in leadership so well established by her predecessors. All the usual lines of work in connection with new students and the coöperation of the various houses were continued.

The Vocational Conference was held March 22-23, with the assistance of Miss Hazel Kyrk, vocational secretary for the year. The program was as follows:

Thursday

3:00 p. m.—''State and City Positions Open to Women,'' Miss Mildred Chadsey, Instructor in Social Science, Western University, formerly Chief of Bureau of Sanitation, Cleveland, Ohio.

4:00 p. m.—''How to Decide Upon a Vocation,'' Miss Mabel Robinson, Work Investigator, Carnegie Foundation.

8:00 p. m.—''New Fields for College Women,'' Mrs. Helen Thompson Woolley, Director Vocation Bureau, Cincinnati Public Schools, Ohio.

Friday

3:00 p. m.—''Opportunities for College Women in Library Work,'' Miss Helen Martin, Head of Children's and Extension Public Library, New London, Ohio.

4:00 p. m.—''State and Local Plans for Vocational Bureaus,'' Miss Rachael S. Gallagher, Director Girls' and Women's Bureau, State-City Labor Exchange, Cleveland, Ohio.

In December the Women's League initiated a movement to raise money for the much needed women's building. Various committees undertook different methods of securing funds with the result that $477.47 was turned into the treasury. Early in the spring, after the United States entered the war, the young women felt that their efforts should be given to war relief. They therefore voted to discontinue work for the women's building; similar lines of committee activity were continued and $228 was raised for war purposes. In addition to this French orphans were adopted by several of the boarding houses. The League is planning to extend its work for war relief during the present year, both in raising money and in coöperation with the Red Cross and other local agencies.

Under the enthusiastic leadership of Miss Dye, secretary to the Dean of College Women, the Home Girls' Association was organized and has been officially recognized as a department of the League. It includes all girls whose homes are in Oberlin and others who are living in private families, and aims to give them a larger share in the life of the college. This meets most hopefully one of the perplexing social questions connected with college life.

The Joint Council of the Women's League has had several meetings. Disciplinary action has been taken in the case of one College and three Conservatory women, who have been placed on probation for short periods because of disregard of the social regulations, and one College woman suspended for one semester on recommendation of the Honor Court. It is a satisfaction to record again the frankness and loyalty and high standards which the young women of this Council bring to the consideration of all such questions. No important changes have been made in the regulations, but it has been decided that a careful study of the whole situation shall be made during the year 1917-18. It is important to consider how successful the League has been and what further gains can be made, either in organization, administration, or in the individual enactments. It is also right, if student government is to be more than a name, that each college generation should have the opportunity to consider carefully the regulations under which it lives and to express its judgment.

The Women's Advisory Committee has continued its work through five sub-committees. The Committee on Curriculum has made a study of the present resources, bringing to the attention of the women students such courses as seem adapted to their peculiar interests. It also has taken great pleasure in recommending to the College Committee on Course, the course on ''The Evolution of Social Forms and Customs— A History of Etiquette,'' to be taught by Miss Ethel Kitch in the second semester. The first suggestion of this course originated in the Advisory Committee several years ago. At its request Miss Kitch has given much thought to the question during her years of graduate study and of teaching. We believe that this subject is to be studied in a thoroughly scientific way for the first time in any American college and that it should be of significance for the more perfect understanding of social ideals and the adjustment of our standards of social conduct to the rapidly changing conditions of society.

The Social Committee has had as its aim ''to add opportunity for social training without multiplying social events.'' It has made a careful study of the elements in our social life which need correction and has made valuable suggestions. It has also arranged with the members of the faculty that they are to be at home to students on the first Saturday evening of each month. It is believed that in this way the friendly contact between instructors and students, so characteristic of Oberlin life, may be made even more helpful and personal.

The Committee on Recreation has worked along the same lines as last year, utilizing as fully as possible the resources at hand in providing recreation for the students, both men and women. The Committee on Self-Supporting Students finds much to occupy its thought, although there are no new lines of undertaking to report. The Committee on Health worked out plans for a more careful study of the nature of illnesses.

Miss Frances Hosford, acting as assistant in this office, has taken charge of the work connected with both of these last two committees. Reports have been received each day from the matron of each boarding house, giving account of any illness in her house. These are tabulated monthly by classes and by the nature of the illness and should give very valuable data for the study of health conditions when we have the records of a few successive years. Miss Hosford has also done most valuable work in personal conference with the matrons. The aim has been three-fold, to secure an accurate report of the number of students in each house and of its capacity and accommodations, especially as to light and plumbing, to consult about individual students who are in need of special care along any line, and to give the matrons such encouragement and suggestions as may make their service more efficient. For many years the Deans have wished to be able to do more of this work and it has been a great satisfaction to have Miss Hosford available for it.

The report of Browning House, the infirmary for women students, is given by Miss Nash, as chairman of the committee in charge.

Last year attention was called to the recommendations of Mrs. Foulk in regard to the management of the college halls. The unusually difficult financial situation has made it seem impossible to prepare definite budgets and unwise to introduce some of the other changes which she recommended. The matrons are working out a uniform accounting system, and it is hoped that it may be possible soon to unify still further the business management of the halls. At the beginning of the winter term an increase of fifty cents per week in the price of board was made in private boarding houses and in all of the college halls except Lord and Churchill Cottages, where the increase was twenty-five cents. An addition of from twelve to fifteen per cent on the price of board seemed the least that could be made when food prices and labor had increased from twenty-five to thirty per cent.

A year ago Barrows House and Fairchild House were opened, the first houses entirely for Conservatory women. In the spring it was decided that Fairchild House should be used for College men and therefore the Women's Board voted to use Allencroft and Ellis Cottage for Conservatory women. Fairchild House finally reverted to the women but the plan to have Allencroft and Ellis as the center for Conservatory first-year women has been carried out. It is too early to speak definitely of the success of this segregating of first-year women, but it has undoubtedly many advantages in increasing acquaintance and class spirit.

Among the private boarding houses, the most important changes have been the completion of their work as matrons of women's houses by Mrs. J. C. Andrus, Mrs. A. R. Holton, Mrs. L. M. Jenney, Mrs. J. S. Klinefelter, and Mrs. Frederick Webster, all of whom have given faithful service for several years, Mrs. Webster having completed more than fifteen years of service for the college. This fall we welcome Mrs. H. T. Hill, Mrs. Effie Hillbrant, and Mrs. Nellie Smith to our list of matrons to supply the loss created by the dropping of other places. Arrangements have been made for more women to room outside and board at the larger halls and houses. This is considered a much less satisfactory arrangement but seemed the best expedient in view of present war conditions.

The report a year ago stated that arrangements had been made for housing a larger number of college Freshmen in the residence halls, decreasing the number of upper classmen that could be accommodated.

The result was that eighty-two Freshmen women were in the college
halls as compared with seventy the preceding year. There was also
some increase in the number of Sophomores. Last spring when the
places for the year 1917-18 were assigned, it was found impossible to
accommodate a considerable number of Seniors who had as yet had no
residence in the halls. The faculty therefore voted to increase the fifty
per cent allowed to Seniors so as to accommodate all who desired admission. At present, therefore, about sixty per cent of the places in the
larger halls are occupied by Seniors. The number of Sophomores was
reduced accordingly but no decrease made in the Freshmen received.
The problem of suitable distribution becomes increasingly perplexing.
It seems certain that no final solution can be reached until there are
more halls under the control of the college. One of the most serious
defects of the present arrangement is the fact that there is a very small
number of any class, with the exception of Seniors, in any hall or
boarding house. Another problem connected with the halls is that of
the method which should be used in assigning places. No applications
are received before April first of the year preceding admission to college, but even so, the method of waiting lists is increasingly unsatisfactory; too many names are registered on a single day.

At the request of the president who asked the various departments
to make recommendations as to desirable advances, the Women's Board
made a careful study of the needs of the women and of the social life
of the College. It seems wise to quote here from the report submitted
at that time:

> The chief social problems are two—housing and recre-
> ation.
> It is the judgment of the Board that as rapidly as pos-
> sible college residence halls should be supplied for all
> women who wish to live in them. If the enrolment of the
> women continues stationary at about 1,000, there would be
> needed accommodations for approximately 750 to 800, the
> remainder being young women whose homes are in town
> or who work in private families or for other reasons
> prefer to live in more quiet homes. There should there-
> fore be added to our present equipment the enlarge-
> ment of Barrows House and, if possible, of Shurtleff Cot-
> tage and the addition of six other buildings, accommoda-
> ting an average of fifty to sixty. It would not be de-
> sirable, even if it were possible, to make so large a pro-
> vision suddenly but probably one building could be added
> every two or three years without embarrassing the sit-
> uation of the town matrons.
> The question of recreation seems naturally to devolve
> upon women for study, although it concerns men as well as
> women. The need of the men is perhaps even greater

than that of the women because women have more of the home-making instinct and therefore utilize resources at hand. The nation-wide interest in recreation and the recognition of its educational value make it suitable that the college should plan for this means of enriching the life of its students.

In Oberlin the social life of the students centers largely in the boarding houses. On the whole, this has been desirable and furnishes much of the distinctive charm of the Oberlin life, but it has its perils and limitations and needs to be supplemented, especially when the group is small and not congenial and where one or two upper classmen are isolated among younger students. There is danger of too great freedom and lack of dignity because of the very intimacy of the life. It is also difficult to combine the good times of the household with suitable conditions for receiving calls. Furthermore the natural desire ''to get out in the free hour after dinner and do something'' tends to make people restless. On the physical side, especially to relieve nervous strain, there is need for exercise in the form of play, for an opportunity to relax and lose self-consciousness; here lies the value of real amusements as contrasted with lectures and formal social engagements. For ''the socially available'' men and women there should be something more wholesome than picture-shows and evening strolls. For the student who is isolated or timid or abnormal there should be opportunity to be with other men or women in informal companionship, to meet and know the other sex in a natural, spontaneous, and yet impersonal way, and to carry a certain amount of responsibility for others' enjoyment and so to learn to forget one's self.

These recreational needs must be met by plans for the life of the men themselves, for the life of the women, and for men and women together both formally and informally. In this study we include merely informal social life. Formal occasions are not essentially recreational and do not call for any equipment other than that which is under the recreational needs, to be listed later. The requirements for the men are being considered by other committees. For the women there should be provided in all the larger halls a recreation room for women alone, distinct from the parlors which are open to men. There should be also a center open every evening to all women with some simple entertainment planned and a different committee as hostesses each evening. This would make possible the further development of class fellowship, of the organization of the town girls, general sings and other forms of social comradeship. Further athletic development would be of help here. There should be gatherings for organized play for miscellaneous groups and places for classes, societies, and other congenial groups to meet under influ-

enees which guard against crudeness and undue familiarity. For couples and groups of couples there should be
quiet places to talk other than the street and a chance
to do things together, which is the ''best safeguard against
unwholesome sentimentality.'' Rooms for games and
reading, and small entertaining in groups would provide
this opportunity.

The needs in the way of equipment are therefore:

1. A Director of Recreation to study the situation, to
supervise, to utilize faculty coöperation, and to direct committees of students. She would also be able to enlist those
students who especially need such experience. It would
be desirable to have such a woman at once for part time
at least. She might be able to combine with this some
assistance in the gymnasium or teaching eurhythmic dancing in the Conservatory. Even our present resources could
be utilized much more fully than they are if someone
had time to give to it; it is not right to ask much help
from the gymnasium teachers who already have full schedules. Ultimately this director should have all her time
for the recreational work.

2. More adequate lighting of the campus and providing the campus with seats. It should be possible to make
the campus a social center during the fall and spring where
informal concerts by the band and mandolin clubs, class
sings, story telling hours, and informal talks would provide entertainment. Country group dancing might also be
introduced as an attractive feature, under proper supervision.

3. Lighting the tennis courts would increase their usefulness.

4. The Women's Building seems the most important
addition to equipment. It should not be utilized as a dormitory and therefore would probably need some endowment. It should provide a center for the various activities
and interests of the women and for the social life of
couples and small groups of men and women. It might
also serve temporarily for the mixed social life of the
college.

5. Ultimately there should be a large social center
open every afternoon and evening with an auditorium,
equipped for moving pictures, for amateur dramatics and
for entertaining lectures and readings. There should be
rooms for organized games, bowling alleys, et cetera, and a
floor for roller skating.

6. Swimming pools would contribute to wholesome recreation as well as to gymnasium work.

7. An artificial ice rink would be a most valuable
asset in providing out of door recreation during the
winter months. It has been suggested that if placed
near the ice plant, perhaps on the farm land of the

Academy property, its maintenance would not be a heavy expense.

In submitting these recommendations the Women's Board would express its conviction that it is as important that the students be supplied with opportunities for thoroughly wholesome and uplifting recreation as that other needs, which we think of as more distinctly the responsibility of the college, should be met.

Respectfully submitted,

FLORENCE M. FITCH.

REPORT OF THE DIRECTOR OF THE MEN'S GYMNASIUM

To the President:

SIR—Harold Church Spore resigned as Instructor in Physical Train-ing at the close of the college year 1915-16, after two years of very satisfactory service in that position, and in the fall of 1916 went to Min-neapolis to become director of physical training in the North High School. Louis Finley Keller, Jr., and Howard Cone Curtis were reap-pointed instructors in June of 1916, and one new man was added to the department—David Paul Maclure, who studied for one year in the physical training department of the International Young Men's Chris-tian Association College at Springfield, Mass., and had completed the work of our Teachers' Course in Physical Education, although he did not graduate from the College till June of 1917. During the past sum-mer he was a student in the courses in physical education at the Har-vard University Summer School. The men of the teaching and coach-ing staff continued our practice of meeting at regular intervals for a departmental luncheon, at which problems of policy and management are taken up and discussed informally. There were twelve such gath-erings during the year.

A reflector to give uniform illumination to the charts used in eye examinations was purchased in September. The largest single item of expense about the building was incurred in connection with repairs on the skylight over the main gymnasium. A number of the lights had been broken during a severe wind storm, and faulty construction which had led to troublesome leaking necessitated extensive alterations during the winter and spring. In March of 1910 a piano was moved from the Conservatory of Music to the gymnasium and has been rented ever since for use with classes. At the end of the last college year a total of $342.50 had been paid in rental, and by arrangement with the Director of the Conservatory the piano has now become the property of the gymnasium. Class parties and other social gatherings in the building which wished to use the piano have been regularly charged four dollars an evening. The income from this source has met the greater part of the annual rental, but hereafter no such charge need be made. During the summer months the janitor did some necessary painting and car-penter work and made miscellaneous repairs. The walls and ceilings of the Director's suite of offices were repainted and new and more modern lighting fixtures were substituted for the old combination gas and electric ones, in order to secure more adequate illumination, especially needed in the examining room. Another steel filing case was purchased, and a table for use in medical examination of the heart and other organs was added to the equipment of the examining room, together with several pieces of improved apparatus.

The plan of furnishing regular assistance to the janitor by renting a room on the top floor at the north end of the building to two students, who gave in return a certain amount of service per day, was followed as in 1915-16. The net cost for their services, charging them one dollar a week apiece for rental and crediting them twenty cents an hour for work actually done (370 hours), and including the laundry charges for sheets and pillow-cases, was only $13.25 for the year. To this should be added the cost of electric current for lights in their room, and of gas used for fuel when heat from the central plant was insufficient or not available.

Prompt registration for use of the gymnasium was secured at the very opening of the college year by means of the plan mentioned in my last report. Seventy-seven per cent of the total number of men entered on the gymnasium roll for the entire year were secured within the first week,—a better showing even than in 1915-16, when the corresponding figure was 73.5 per cent. Improved office arrangements also made possible a more rapid handling of the line of men on registration days.

The men who made use of the gymnasium in 1916-17 were distributed as follows:

	Listed in Catalogue	Enrolled at Gymnasium	In Credit Courses
The College—			
Graduates	6	3	0
Seniors ....,....	83	82	5
Juniors	79	78	26
Sophomores	105	98	34
Freshmen	158	157	143
Specials	2	1	0
Total College	433	419	208
Graduate School of Theology.....	56	25	0
Conservatory of Music...........	47	23	2
Total, all departments......	536	467	210
Members of Faculty..............	...	14	0
High School Students............	...	26	0
Business College Students........	...	12	0
Not Classified (Citizens)..........	...	18	0
Grand totals	...	537	210

It appears from this table that 87.13 per cent of the men in all departments made some use of the gymnasium, and 97.42 per cent of College undergraduates. The corresponding percentages for 1915-16 were 87.42 and 96. The per cent of College undergraduates enrolled in credit classes was 48.71 (46.44 in 1915-16). Thirty-five of the total number (208) attended for one semester only. The enrolment of persons outside the college family was very nearly the same as in the previous year. Beginning November 4th, each of four boys' clubs had the use of the smaller gymnasium from 6:30 till 7:30 on four evenings of the week throughout the winter. Basket ball and occasional evening class parties and dances by the young women were provided for in the usual manner, and a beginning was made in the way of accommodating boarding-house groups for "play nights," as part of the movement for more wholesome recreation of our young men and women.

A total of 207 physical examinations was made, including 34 reëxaminations; 163 of this number were completed within the first five weeks, and 195 before the Christmas holidays. With the assistance of Mr. Keller, who was made familiar with the necessary procedure, it was possible for the first time to introduce a routine test of vision as part of the examination given to every entering student.

Work in the gymnasium went on along the lines indicated in my last report. The military training of the spring term, and the departure of so many men for various forms of government service, inevitably interfered with our usual activities toward the close of the year. On the other hand the adoption by the Trustees, in June, of the faculty recommendation that an assistant professorship in physical education be substituted for one of the three instructorships in the department, was most encouraging. The present Director of the Men's Gymnasium comes to the end of twenty-five years of service in that position with a feeling of profound gratitude for the support and coöperation of colleagues on the faculty and of members of the Board of Trustees which have rendered possible whatever progress has been made since the department of physical education for men was organized on a permanent basis. Much remains to be done, but a review of the past gives ground for hope that the years just ahead may see even larger gains in the way of service to the entire student body.

Respectfully submitted,

FRED EUGENE LEONARD.

REPORT OF THE DIRECTOR OF ATHLETICS

To the President:

SIR—The athletic history of the year 1916-17, both intramural and intercollegiate, is unique. The unusual conditions occasioned by the world war, the loss of our regular foot ball coach through illness, and the disciplining of sub-rosa fraternities, combined to give Oberlin the poorest record she has ever made in intercollegiate sports and reacted unfavorably upon the interest taken in intramural activities.

The foot ball team was particularly hard hit by the disciplinary measures. To this misfortune was added the loss of Coach Howard C. Curtis, '15, through illness, after only two days of active coaching. It was found necessary to remove Mr. Curtis to the Oberlin Hospital where he had to undergo an operation which incapacitated him for coaching until after the foot ball season had closed.

Mr. Paul R. Des Jardien, a graduate of the University of Chicago, and a player of national reputation, was secured to take the place of Mr. Curtis for the foot ball season. It was an impossible task for Mr. Des Jardien to develop a team out of the inferior material at hand and our foot ball team went through the season without a victory. The spirit of the team under such conditions and the loyalty of the student body, in spite of the consistently unsuccessful work of the team, deserve especial mention and commendation. The experience of the season, though unpleasant, resulted in a more complete recognition of the good sportsmanship which has become characteristic of Oberlin's teams, and of the more fundamental truth that Oberlin College is conducting athletics not simply for the winning of intercollegiate contests.

The cross country team, without a coach, but under the leadership of Captain Edwin H. Fall, '17, was unusually strong and well-balanced. It won second place in the Ohio Conference Meet at Columbus, November 4th, Ohio State winning first place. Captain Fall was the first runner to cross the finish line.

The basket ball team was coached by Mr. D. P. Maclure, '16. Though three of the members of the team of 1916 were still in college, the team never reached first-class form. Captain Harry R. McPhee, a player of highest calibre, was unable to play during the first part of the season and he never attained his customary form because of an injury received in foot ball. Two victories and nine defeats show a season far below the usual standard of Oberlin basket ball teams.

Spring athletics were seriously handicapped by the declaration of war, the consequent rush to enlistment in the various branches of the service open to college men, and the release of men to farm and shop work. In addition, the practice of the teams as developed was greatly interfered with by the military training of practically all of the men three afternoons per week. At one time, it appeared almost necessary to discontinue athletic sports of every form, but believing that physical activity is a strong and important factor in making young men capable of military service, Oberlin held steadily to her athletic activities and, although at a very great financial loss, played out her intercollegiate schedules.

The base ball team, again coached by Mr. Louis F. Keller, '15, won two games and lost four of a schedule that was shortened by cancellations by other teams. Our base ball teams are usually much more successful.

The track team, coached by Mr. Curtis, won the Triangular Meet with Case and Wooster; defeated Case in an impromptu dual meet hurriedly arranged to take the place of the meet cancelled by Ohio Wesleyan, and easily won second place in the meet of the Ohio Intercollegiate Athletic Association at Columbus. In this meet, Captain Edwin H. Fall won the mile run, setting a new Ohio record at 4:20-3/5; and the Oberlin relay team won the beautiful one-mile relay cup. At the Western Conference Meet in Chicago, Captain Fall, single-handed, won fourth place for Oberlin by winning the one-mile run in the remarkable time of 4:16-4/5, a new Western Conference record; and by shortly afterward returning to the track and winning the two-mile run in 9:41. The track season alone may be considered unusually successful.

At the beginning of the tennis season, interest seemed unusually strong and a good season was anticipated. However, the unfavorable weather and the cancellation of matches by Chicago, Syracuse, and Ohio Wesleyan, leaving only Kenyon and Ohio State on the schedule, made the season far from satisfactory. Oberlin won the Kenyon match and lost to Ohio State University. At the ''Big Six'' tennis meet in Columbus, the State meet, our team was runner-up in both singles and doubles, losing the State championship to Ohio State University.

Effort was again made to establish association foot ball as an intramural sport, without success. It was with 'difficulty that enough men were gotten out to form a college team and this team could not be organized until the incentive of an intercollegiate contest with Ohio Wesleyan University and a trip to Delaware was offered. This one contest resulted in a 4-1 defeat by Ohio Wesleyan.

Intercollegiate schedules and scores were as follows:

Foot Ball 1916

September	30	Oberlin 3, Heidelberg 33; at Oberlin
October	7	Oberlin 0, Hiram 61; at Oberlin
October	14	Oberlin 0, Ohio State 128; at Columbus
October	21	Oberlin 7, Ohio University 13; at Oberlin
November	4	Oberlin 3, Western Reserve 53; at Cleveland
November	11	Oberlin 0, Case 41; at Oberlin
November	18	Oberlin 0, Mt. Union 49; at Oberlin

Association Foot Ball (Soccer) 1916

October	28	Oberlin 1, Ohio Wesleyan 4; at Delaware

Basket Ball 1917

January	6	Oberlin 43, Baldwin-Wallace 1; at Oberlin
January	13	Oberlin 14, Ohio State 37; at Columbus
January	27	Oberlin 12, Case 28; at Oberlin
January	29	Oberlin 19, Denison 33; at Granville
February	3	Oberlin 33, Ohio University 17; at Oberlin
February	9	Oberlin 23, University of Buffalo 28; at Buffalo
February	10	Oberlin 19, Cornell 42; at Ithaca
February	17	Oberlin 18, Western Reserve 21; at Oberlin
February	24	Oberlin 26, Denison 31; at Oberlin
March	3	Oberlin 23, Case 39; at Cleveland
March	10	Oberlin 10, Ohio State 28; at Oberlin

Base Ball 1917

April	21	Oberlin 2, Western Reserve 9; at Oberlin
May	2	Oberlin 13, Baldwin-Wallace 8; at Berea
May	12	Oberlin 8, Case 2; at Oberlin
May	19	Oberlin 11, Western Reserve 12; at Cleveland
May	26	Oberlin 10, Case 16; at Cleveland
June	3	Oberlin 0, Ohio State 11; at Oberlin

Track 1917

March 17—Indoor Meet at Delaware; Oberlin 28½, Ohio Wesleyan 71½

April 28—Triangular Meet at Oberlin; Oberlin 71½, Case 49, Wooster 41½

May 12—Dual Meet at Columbus; Oberlin 56, Ohio State 61

May 19—Dual Meet at Oberlin; Oberlin 80 1-3, Case 49 2-3

May 26—"Big Six" Meet at Columbus; Oberlin 63½, Ohio State 76½, Case 10, Denison 7, Wooster 6, Kenyon 1

Cross Country 1916

November 4—Ohio Intercollegiate Cross Country Run at Columbus; Oberlin 31, Ohio State 16, Cincinnati 56, Wooster 64, Ohio Wesleyan 76.

Tennis 1917

May 12—Oberlin 3, Kenyon 0; at Gambier

May 17-19—"Big Six" at Columbus; Oberlin runner-up in singles and doubles.

May 30—Oberlin 1, Ohio State 5; at Columbus

Intramural activities in the fall seemed about normal. The inter-class foot ball series was played out, a tennis tournament held, and a number of Freshmen and ineligibles took cross country training with the varsity squad.

In basket ball, in addition to the interclass games, two Boarding House Leagues, Class A and Class B, comprising together twenty teams, played out a long schedule. Greater interest was shown in this branch of intramural activity than ever before. This was the real advance of the year in intramural sports.

The usual indoor Sophomore-Freshman and interclass track meets were held and the interclass track meet at the beginning of the spring season was also fairly successful.

Because of the wet season and the demands upon the men's time made by military drill, intramural base ball was entirely abandoned.

A hand ball tournament was arranged and played through for the first time. The lack of courts prevented any large competition.

For the first time, also, an interclass bowling league was organized. Four teams played through a short schedule.

The Athletic Efficiency competition brought out only fifteen men. Of these, twelve men qualified, two of whom won silver medals, one in the pole vault, the other in the javelin throw.

The total number of college men participating in the various branches of intramural sports was as follows:

Sport	No. of Teams	Individuals
Foot ball	4	65
Basket ball	24	192
Base ball	0	00
Indoor track	4	57
Outdoor track	4	50
Tennis		44
Athletic efficiency		15
Hand ball		26
Soccer foot ball		15
Bowling		25
Outdoor relay		20
Total		509

	Men in Class	Participants	Percentage 1916-17	1915-16
Seniors	83	55	66.27	72.60
Juniors	79	57	72.16	69.13
Sophomores	105	82	78.09	79.12
Freshmen	158	112	70.88	78.81
Total	425	306	72.	75.47

In spite of the fact that intramural base ball was abandoned and that a large number of men left college before the spring athletics were begun, the above table shows 72 per cent of our men participating in some form of athletic activity as compared with 75.47 per cent in 1915-16, a falling off of only 3½ per cent.

The Graduate Treasurer, Mr. George M. Jones, submits the following summary of the financial condition of the Athletic Association at the close of the year:

New Athletic Field Construction Account

Total expenses of new field, paid by the Treasurer of Oberlin College	$ 24,819.17
Total expenses of new field paid by the Athletic Association	5,230.40
	$ 30,049.57
Payments made upon new field	15,964.33
Unpaid balance being carried in the College Treasurer's Office	$ 14,085.24

Athletic Association Account

Borrowed by the Athletic Association at the State Savings Bank	$ 5,135.00
Due to Oberlin College for interest on advances and payment of part salary of athletic coaches	2,054.88
Debt, August 31, 1917	$ 7,189.88

The New Field Account shows an advance of $14,085.24 still being carried by the Athletic Association, because the Alumni Athletic Fund failed to reach its $50,000 goal. The interest load occasioned by this advance is largely responsible for the present debt of the Association, now amounting to $7,189.88.

Last year, because of our weakened and unsuccessful intercollegiate teams, our income suffered a very marked decrease. The unfortunate day which was mentioned in my last report as probable, when it would become necessary to abandon all forms of intercollegiate sport not financially profitable, such as tennis, track, soccer, cross country, and base ball, together with all intramural activities, seems to have arrived. Unless relief is found, athletic activities for the year 1917-18 must be limited to foot ball and basket ball.

In this connection, it should be said that the load of the Athletic Association has been made easier for the future by the vote of the faculty and Trustees last spring that the College budget should assume hereafter the entire salaries of the staff in the men's department of Physical Education. This will relieve the Association of practically the entire cost of coaching. This, however, is not relief enough, for surely the cost of equipment and care of fields for intramural sports ought to be assumed by the College. Either Oberlin must find and set aside an endowment for this phase of her work or we ought to adopt a student athletic fee to be paid with the tuition, as is the ease today in most of our Ohio colleges.

Another notable advance of the year was the decision of the faculty and Trustees to appoint a man with the salary and rank of an assistant professor in the department of Physical Education, who should act as foot ball coach and thus bring greater experience and longer tenure of office into that important work.

The completion of the athletic field remains as the paramount need after the indebtedness of the Association has been cleared away. It is, of course, true that the work which was estimated to cost $45,000 two years ago will now require at least $60,000, possibly $75,000, because of increased costs of material and labor. The need for the completion of the field, for added opportunities for sports, seems to me to be greater than ever before. My fondest hope is that the completed field with endowment or athletic fee sufficient to maintain it, may soon be realized.

Your Director of Athletics was retained on the American Intercollegiate Foot Ball Rules Committee by the National Collegiate Association, and again taught in the Chautauqua School of Physical Education during the summer of 1917. While representing the College at the National Collegiate Athletic Association in New York during the holidays, he also attended the annual meetings of the Society of the Directors of Physical Education in Colleges and Universities and of The Athletic Research Society.

Your Director was asked to represent the College and the Ohio Conference Colleges at a special meeting of the National Collegiate Association at Washington on August 2nd. The meeting was to decide the question of the continuance of intercollegiate sports during the period of the war. After a most interesting discussion and after listening to a most admirable address by the Secretary of War, Newton D. Baker, the following resolutions were adopted:

> ''Whereas, college athletics, as stated by Secretary Baker in his address to this Conference, are of great use in developing the qualities of a good soldier,
>
> Therefore, be it Resolved, that we recommend to the colleges:

First, That athletic sports be continued during the coming year, with an increased effort to develop athletics for all students rather than a chosen few.

Second, That the schedule for intercollegiate sports be carried out so far as local conditions allow, care being taken not to interfere with the military training of the students or to conflict with the military interests of the nation.

Third, That there be no pre-season coaching during the coming academic year.

Fourth, That training tables be given up.

Fifth, That professional coaching and the expenses incidental thereto be reduced to a minimum.

Sixth, That the number of officials at intercollegiate games and their fees be kept as low as possible.

And further, be it Resolved, that the Association reiterates its belief in the eligibility rules which it has already endorsed, including the Freshman rule, and recommends to the colleges that there be no lowering of eligibility standards because of present conditions.

This conference and the resultant resolutions cannot fail to have a most salutary effect upon intercollegiate sport throughout the United States. Athletics for all instead of for the few, no pre-season coaching, no training tables, professional coaching minimized, expenses reduced, and eligibility maintained,--how familiar all these things are. to us. But what a pity that at just this time, when President Wilson and Secretary Baker and the National Collegiate Association advise greater extension of athletic sports as a war efficiency measure, Oberlin finds herself face to face with the necessity of curtailment.

The athletic review of the year would be far from complete if mention were not made of the endeavor of a small group of alumni to influence the policy of the President and faculty with regard to intercollegiate athletics. These alumni, several of them former athletes, unable to stand the lack of success of our athletic teams, wrote letters of censure to members of the faculty, sent delegates to interview the President and Dean of the College, participated in a protracted forum conducted by the Alumni Magazine, and even started the circulation of a petition among alumni designed to bring about a more indulgent attitude on the part of the faculty toward the athlete, both the men in college and the prospective student. This agitation served to clear the atmosphere considerably, bringing out abundant support for the College administration. The whole matter is indicative of the great interest of the alumni in the achievements of their College upon the athletic field.

Respectfully submitted,

C. W. SAVAGE.

REPORT OF THE DIRECTOR OF THE WOMEN'S GYMNASIUM

To the President:

Sir—Dr. Cochran's return, making a second physician in the department, relieved the Director of a greater part of the physical examinations. This gave the Director more leisure to consider the work as a whole. As soon as the physical examinations were completed, in accord with a request from the President, the Director and Dr. Cochran used part of this leisure time in drawing up plans for a new gymnasium.

There has been great rejoicing in the department over the purchase of the Black farm on Lake Erie, which is to mean so much in the development of the Teachers' Course in Physical Education and the recreation of the college women as a whole. We are eager to begin drawing up plans for the camp buildings and the laying out of the grounds, but they may be somewhat delayed by the work in connection with the proposed course for "Medical Aides." Before we begin to build, we ought to have, in addition to money already available, about $5,000. We hope that some good friend of the College may be found who will be willing to give us this amount.

The course for "Medical Aides" has been undertaken by vote of the College in response to a request from the War Department that the Department of Physical Education give a three months' course to train women as Medical Aides. These Aides will assist in the Reconstruction Hospitals of the Army in the after-treatment of wounded soldiers. The course will include instruction in anatomy, physiology, personal hygiene, massage, movements, bandaging, hydrotherapy, and electrotherapy. The War Department also requests that we interest our graduates in this war work, as the more experienced women are needed as well in the Army Hospitals.

The women who made use of the gymnasium during the year 1916-17 were as follows:

The College—	No. in Catalogue	No. using Gymnasium	In Credit Courses	In other Courses	Not taking Class Work
Graduates	14	2	2	..	..
Seniors	124	31	17	8	6
Juniors	137	46	32	9	5
Sophomores	149	74	61	11	2
Freshmen	203	182	165	13	4
Specials	16	3	2	1	..
Total College..	643	338	279	42	17

The Conservatory of Music	374	175	131	34	10
Unclassified Students	50	...	...	...	...
Sub-Freshmen	...	2	2	...	...
Others	...	5	2	2	1
Total, all departments ..	1067	520	414	78	28
Public Schools	...	1		1	
Kindergarten	...	1	...	1	
Private pupils	...	4	...	4	...
Grand totals...	1067	526	414	84	28

In addition to the 526 who took regular work in the gymnasium, 138 members of the Gymnasium and Field Association, who were not doing gymnasium work, were supervised in their sports.

Three hundred and fifty-seven new students received physical examinations, and 200 were reëxamined. The figures for the previous year were 366 and 240.

Special Report of Freshman Required Work

Number of Freshmen Women

Enrolled in College.. 203
Completing the required work in physical education.......... 158
Previously completed the work............................ 9
Entering the second semester............................. 10
Postponing gymnasium for health reasons.................. 10
Postponing gymnasium for other reasons.................. 3
Leaving college on account of health..................... 7
Leaving college for other reasons......................... 4
Permanently excused from the required work.............. 2

The work of the four Freshman sections and the two first year Conservatory sections in the regular gymnasium work progressed as usual. There was an increase in the number enrolled in one of the two advanced sections, due to a change of hour.

Following the general recreational plan outlined last year, the different houses were invited, once a week, for play hours at the Women's and Men's Gymnasia. The leaders were provided from the departments of Physical Education, and the Seniors doing major work in physical education. Many houses had picnic suppers on Dickinson Field, with the privilege of building a bon-fire on the out-door skating rink. The Gymnasium and Dickinson House fields were used for volley ball and base ball games, by the different houses.

In addition to those who took work in the gymnasium, the following numbers played games under supervision:

Field Hockey 126
Basket Ball 121
Base Ball 127
Class Tennis 165
Tennis Tournaments 105

The number of women who completed their two semesters of ten mile walks was 83, covering a total distance of 7,304 miles.

Teachers' Course in Physical Education

The number of students in the Teachers' Course was distributed as follows: Graduates, 2; Seniors, 11; Juniors, 22; Sophomores, 18; Freshmen, 24; total, 77. By the end of the year one Junior, four Sophomores, and one Freshman, either from choice or from lack of fitness, dropped the course.

The total enrolment for the four preceding years was as follows: 1912-13, 106; 1913-14, 90; 1914-15, 97; 1915-16, 82.

One Junior entered the course from Allegheny College, one Sophomore from Morningside College, and one Freshman from Colorado Agricultural College.

The Gymnasium and Field Association

The membership of the Association for the year was 511.

It has been the desire of the Association for some time to open a tea room on the upper floor of Dickinson House. As Mrs. Eldred, who has been such an excellent matron for four years, was unwilling to undertake this, Mrs. Taylor, formerly matron of Barrows House, was engaged to serve as matron and to conduct the tea room. The rooms have been tastefully decorated and fitted out, and we hope they will do much toward making Dickinson House more of a recreation center for the women.

Outside Activities

The following extension lectures were given:

MISS BOWEN

"The Value and History of the Playground Movement," at Wakeman, Ohio.

"The Value of Play," before The 95 Club, Elyria, Ohio; The Parent-Teachers' Association, Kenton, Ohio; The Women's Civic Club, Akron, Ohio; The Physical Education Conference for Public School Teachers, Lorain, Ohio.

MRS. HATCH

"Physical Training in the Grades," before the Wellington Public School Teachers. "Value of Play," before the Civic Club, Rocky River, Ohio. "Playgrounds," before the Prospect School Parent-Teachers' Association, Oberlin, Ohio. "Play and Games in Elementary Schools," before the Physical Education Conference for Public School Teachers, Lorain, Ohio.

Miss Eldred studied in the Summer School of Teachers College, Columbia University. Mrs. Hatch taught and studied in the Chautauqua Summer School of Physical Education.

Dr. Cochran attended the meeting of the Association of Directors of Physical Education for Women held at Randolph-Macon Woman's College, Lynchburg, Va., April 13 and 14, at which she gave a report on enlarged thyroid gland. During the summer, Dr. Cochran was one of the Councillors at Pinewood Camp on Burt Lake, Michigan. She gave the physical examinations and had charge of the tennis.

The Director spent the half year of absence granted to her in Florida. In July, she went to New York to visit the New York American Baby Hospital, where one of our graduates, Dr. Gertrude Sturges, is doing such fine work in the after-treatment of infantile paralysis. The Director also studied this treatment at the Children's Hospital in Boston. In view of planning for our camp at the Lake, the Director visited the Sargent Camp at Peterboro, Vermont.

Respectfully submitted,

DELPHINE HANNA.

REPORT OF THE SUPERINTENDENT OF BUILDINGS AND GROUNDS

To the President:

SIR—The following properties have been acquired by the College since my last report: the sites of the Methodist Church and the Town Hall, and the Beers and Royce properties.

The Art Building was completed early in June, together with the grading and planting of the lawn and court, and the construction of brick walks and approaches, according to plans furnished by the architect. As soon as the Art Department could be moved to the studio wing from Society Hall the latter was torn down, greatly enhancing the view from the campus toward the Chapel and adjacent buildings. The removal of the Olney Art Collection from the library made possible the erection of the remaining stories of the stack room, a contract for which was placed with the Art Metal Construction Company of Jamestown, N. Y.

An order from the State Inspector of Public Buildings at Columbus for the rewiring of Peters Hall and Severance Chemical Laboratory was executed this summer by the Enterprise Electric Construction Company of Cleveland. A subsequent order for fire gongs, new exit lights, and other safety devices in all of the college buildings is being complied with as rapidly as possible. This order includes two fire escapes for Severance Chemical Laboratory and one for Warner Gymnasium.

The dormitory portion of the Men's Building on the third and fourth floors was too large to be used successfully as a single unit, and has been divided into four separate parts by placing partitions across the hallway on the third floor and erecting two additional stairways. Two bedrooms on this floor were provided with the necessary fixtures for toilet rooms for the new units.

The attic of the Administration Building has been divided by fireproof partitions into a number of storage and unpacking rooms for the use of several of the offices. The expense of this improvement, as well as that of the two candelabra on the front terrace, has been borne by the donor of the building.

That portion of the roof of the Straus Block over the hotel dining room had to be renewed this year, together with the substitution of hanging gutters in place of the worn-out standing gutters which required constant repairs. The dining room was redecorated and wired for electric lighting. The large lecture room of French Hall was also redecorated.

The infirmary and rest rooms for women, provided for by the use of a few rooms in a private house, has proven itself very useful, but had to be discontinued there this year, so the entire house owned by the College at 268 Forest street has been prepared and furnished for this purpose, rooms being provided for a matron and nurse.

Trouble having been experienced because of the crossing of the wires of the college gong system and those of the town lighting plant, a portion of the wires of the former were placed under ground by the Enterprise Electric Construction Company. The old wires had been in use a number of years and the insulation had become defective.

A contract for a large portion of the winter's supply of coal for the heating plant having been made early in the summer with the Pursglove-Maher Coal Company of Cleveland, the College has not suffered any ill effects from the coal shortage. Large temporary bins were erected outside the building and a quantity of coal stored during the latter part of the summer.

New hot water and steam boilers were erected at the Barrows House and Allencroft, and a new hot air furnace in the building occupied by the Superintendent of Buildings and Grounds and the Y. W. C. A.

Because of my enforced absence during the latter part of the summer and fall, on account of sickness, I wish to convey to Mr. Hatch, my assistant, and to Dean Cole, Professors Root and Morrison, and Treasurer Thurston my thanks for their assistance in bringing to completion much of this work, and I only regret the necessity of having added to their many duties part of mine.

Respectfully submitted,

C. P. DOOLITTLE.

SUPPLEMENTARY REPORTS

REPORT OF THE SECRETARY OF THE LIVING ENDOWMENT UNION

To the President:

SIR—This report as usual is chiefly prepared by the Assistant to the President, Mr. W. F. Bohn, who conducts the correspondence of the Union, and who gives very efficiently much valuable time to promoting the interest and contributions of the alumni. All of the money is received and paid out by Mr. H. B. Thurston, the Treasurer of the College, as directed by the Prudential Committee, and the accounts are audited annually by the Chartered Accountant employed by the Trustees of the College.

This report follows the form adopted last year for printing in the volume of Annual Reports. It is hoped by this method to make possible comparisons from year to year at various points. It is interesting to note that gains have been made in the number of new subscriptions as compared to other years, the aggregate amount represented by these subscriptions, and also in holding the subscriptions already on record, i.e. during the year just past the number of cancelations and decreased subscriptions is noticeably less than in the year 1915-16, in spite of all the multitude of appeals being made in every direction.

The number of new subscriptions received during the twelve months under review is 150. In addition, it should be noted that during the same time 20 subscribers increased the amount of their subscriptions. The total annual payments represented by the new subscriptions amount to $285.50; the total amount of increase is $36.75. The prospective annual income, therefore, of the Union has been increased, during the past year, $322.25. To this should be added the income from the special endowment of the Class of 1889, toward which $2,525.41 has already been paid in.

The following table shows the amounts contributed during the year by classes of 1851 to 1916, inclusive:

Year	Amount	Year	Amount
1851	$ 2.00	1887	$ 37.00
1857	1.00	1888	31.25
1858	12.00	1889	14.25
1859	5.00	1890	107.00
1860	10.00	1891	161.00
1861	7.00	1892	42.00
1863	10.00	1893	42.50
1864	5.00	1894	57.00
1865	13.00	1895	40.00
1866	2.00	1896	30.00

1867	10.00	1897	56.25
1868	12.00	1898	6.00
1869	2.50	1899	66.25
1870	33.00	1900	41.00
1871	25.00	1901	57.00
1872	21.00	1902	20.50
1873	25.00	1903	57.25
1874	3.00	1904	40.25
1875	11.00	1905	96.10
1876	32.50	1906	95.50
1877	3.00	1907	120.00
1878	139.50	1908	117.25
1879	32.00	1909	108.25
1880	23.75	1910	161.75
1881	20.00	1911	135.00
1882	5.00	1912	179.00
1883	20.00	1913	125.00
1884	66.00	1914	137.50
1885	59.00	1915	128.00
1886	39.75	1916	126.56

The largest contribution is to be credited to the Class of 1912, $179.

The total number paying subscriptions to the Union during the year past was 1,050. The net income during the twelve months was $3,732.01. It is worthy of note that the splendid gain in net income made last year of over $1,000 has been maintained under the very unusual conditions of the present year, a fact which would seem to indicate the members of the Living Endowment Union are loyal to a very unusual degree to the College and the particular phase of the work which the Union is trying to do.

The following table indicates the growth of the Living Endowment Union for the past seventeen years:

1900-01	$ 470.50
1901-02	650.00
1902-03	727.50
1903-04	705.50
1904-05	1,110.80
1905-06	2,214.35
1906-07	2,660.30
1907-08	2,833.68
1908-09	2,810.01
1909-10	2,549.32
1910-11	2,812.48
1911-12	2,562.28
1912-13	2,485.40
1913-14	2,526.85
1914-15	2,718.74
1915-16	3,781.72
1916-17	3,732.01
Total	$44,317.89

The paid up endowment funds of the Union amount to $1,650.25, to which should be added the Class of 1889 Fund, $2,525.41, making a total of $4,175.66 of invested funds paying annual income to the Union.

No account has been made in this report of the moneys received through the Living Endowment Union for the L. L. S. Fund, as they are included in the report of that Fund, and do not affect the accounts of this organization. The sum of $210.75 was paid into this Fund through the Union during the fiscal year.

We regret to report the deaths of the following members of the Living Endowment Union, loyal and devoted friends of the College:

1875	Andrews, Calista
1905	Auten, Esther Hall
1906	Brissel, Charles Frederick
1916	Brownell, Willard Foote
1913	Cary, Philip Hulbert
1863	*Church*, Frances Adelaide Lord
1887	Clark, Frank S.
ex-1856	Cunningham, Joseph Oscar
1905	*Fishback*, Carrie Lenore Rose
ex-1907	*McQueen*, Florence Belle Sawyer
1862	*Maltbie*, Esther Tapping
1878	Wilcox, Francis Albert

The secretary wishes to call attention to the fact that from many indications it is clear that the alumni generally approve heartily the particular designation which has been made for several years of the entire income from the Living Endowment Union for the aid of self-supporting students. There is no doubt at all that the general body of the alumni are interested in making it steadily possible for self-supporting men and women to secure their education at Oberlin and there is evident willingness that the President and the Prudential Committee should continue their policy of applying the income, now amounting to over $3,000, from the Living Endowment Fund as a supplement to our all too meager funds available for scholarship and beneficiary purposes. The College is making a definite effort to increase its endowment funds at this point and when sufficient funds are available it would be reasonable again to assign the income from the Living Endowment Fund for emergency purposes arising during the year.

The Executive Board wishes to take this opportunity to thank all the subscribers to the Living Endowment Union for their hearty support during the past year, when so many urgent demands have been made in every direction for worthy causes, both at home and abroad.

Respectfully submitted,

IRVING W. METCALF.

REPORT OF THE OBERLIN SECTION OF THE INTERCOLLEGIATE INTELLIGENCE BUREAU

To the President:

SIR—The Intercollegiate Intelligence Bureau was organized in Washington in February, 1917, with the approval of the national government. In the weeks immediately following branches were established in most of the important colleges and universities in the United States. Under date of March 20th the general faculty of Oberlin College voted to establish a section of this Bureau.

In order that Oberlin College might be able to place its resources at the service of the government it was necessary to secure as early as possible information concerning its most recent students. In April approximately 4,000 printed letters and census blanks were sent out from the Oberlin Bureau to the following groups:

(1) Present students—all men in every department and all women above Sophomore classification.

(2) All graduates—both men and women—from 1890 to 1916.

(3) Former students—both men and women—of the years 1913-14, 1914-15, and 1915-16.

(4) College officers and faculty members.

The canvass resulted in securing replies from 378 present students, 1,181 graduates, 108 former students, and 34 officers and faculty members, a total of 1,701. To have this material available for easy reference and to meet the wishes of the National Bureau, a card file was prepared which involved the writing of somewhat more than 6,000 cards. In view of the present European situation it might be wise for the Bureau now to seek information concerning all of its ex-students,—graduates and non-graduates.

Since the establishment of the Bureau in Oberlin, 68 emergency requests, calling for one or more applicants, have been received. These calls have permitted the Adjutant to bring to the attention of the National Bureau at Washington the qualifications of over 250 candidates. In preparing statements of individual fitness and training it has been necessary to write over 400 letters. There is no machinery for reporting back to the local bureau the acceptance of the candidates so it is difficult to give information as to the number of Oberlin men receiving appointments through the bureau. An exception to this, however, is the Oberlin College Ambulance Unit, now at Allentown, which brought together a group of forty-five men of the most recent generation of students for service under the government.

A recent study seems to indicate that 268 present and former students are active in some form of government service on account of the war. Those engaged in the various types of service may be classified as follows:

Table No. 1.

Branch	Number
Army	77
Navy	45
Aviation	21
Ambulance	58
Hospital	16
Y. M. C. A. and relief work	30
Special Service	13
Miscellaneous	S
	268

Table No. 2.

Group	Number
Faculty	5 (Four are duplicates)
Graduates	116
Former students	52
Present students	99
	268

Of this number probably 44 are abroad. These figures by no means can be counted upon as indicating all of the Oberlin graduates and non-graduates performing service. The Alumni Magazine and the Secretary's office are urging that the entire Oberlin family assist in furnishing news items and reports concerning the federal service of any of its members.

Respectfully submitted,

J. E. WIRKLER.

NECROLOGY

To the President:

SIR—I beg to submit the following biographical sketches of alumni whose deaths have been reported to this office to date of October 1, 1917. The list includes 40 alumni.

In this list of 40 alumni who have died during the year there were 22 men and 18 women. The average age of the men at the time of death was 62.1 years; the average age of the women at the time of death was 65.6; the total average age of the 40 alumni was 63.2. The corresponding figure for the year 1915-16 was 66.1; for the year 1914-15, it was 65.6; for the year 1913-14, it was 64.8; for the year 1912-13, it was 68.6.

Eight of the alumni whose deaths are here recorded reached the age of 80 years or more, 4 men and 4 women; 10 others reached the age of 70 or more, 4 men and 6 women; 9 others, 6 men and 3 women, reached the age of 60 or more. Reduced to percentages, 20.0 per cent of the alumni whose deaths are here recorded reached the age of 80 years; 45.0 per cent reached the age of 70 years; 67.5 per cent reached the age of 60 years.

The earliest graduate now living is Mr. Edmund A. West of Chicago, a graduate in the Classical Course in 1843. Mr. West was 94 years of age on April 28, 1917. At the present time the oldest surviving graduate in point of years is Mr. Lester B. Kinney of Chemung, Ill., of the class of 1847. Mr. Kinney was 98 years of age February 4, 1917.

At date of October 1, 1917, there were four other living graduates of the College who completed their courses before 1850, as follows: Mrs. Antoinette Brown-Blackwell, of the class of 1847; Mrs. Hester Van Wagner-Burhans, of the class of 1847; Mrs. Celestia Holbrook-Beach, of the class of 1848; and Mrs. America Strong-Jones, of the class of 1849.

Respectfully submitted,

GEORGE M. JONES.

INDEX

NECROLOGICAL RECORD OF ALUMNI
OCTOBER 1, 1916—OCTOBER 1, 1917

1857

MARY JANE ANDREWS-MILLIKAN was born in Rochester, N. Y., May 3, 1834. She entered Oberlin in 1854 as a second-year student in the Literary Course and graduated with the diploma of that course in 1857. From 1859 to 1864 she served as matron of the ladies' depart. ment of Olivet College. She was married September 13, 1864, to Rev. Silas F. Millikan, who was also a graduate of the College, in the class of 1855. Mr. Millikan's active ministry covered forty years in various towns in the states of Iowa and Kansas, including Maquoketa, Emporia, Wichita, Mason City, Kingsley, and Anamosa. Mrs. Millikan died March 20, 1917, at the home of her daughter in Marshalltown, Iowa. Following an attack of grip she gradually weakened and then quietly passed away without suffering. She is survived by three sons and three daughters, all graduates of the College.

1858

SAMUEL AUSTIN CRAVATH was born in Conneaut, Pa., September 27, 1836. From 1852 to 1854 he attended the Oberlin Preparatory Depart. ment. He entered the College in 1854 as a Freshman and graduated with the degree of Bachelor of Arts in 1858. He also received the degree of Master of Arts from Oberlin in 1865. From 1858 to 1863 he engaged in teaching, being the Superintendent of Schools of Marion, Ohio, during the years from 1861 to 1863; he then studied medicine both in Columbus and in Cincinnati, with a view to entering the army as a surgeon, and he received a degree of M. D. from the Cincinnati College of Medicine and Surgery in 1864. After the close of the War he practiced medicine in Springfield, Ohio, and later moved to Iowa. In 1872 he gave up the practice of medicine and entered newspaper work. He was editor of the Grinnell Herald, at Grinnell, Iowa, from 1872 to 1894. From 1895 to 1900 Mr. Cravath was President of the Grinnell Savings Bank, and from 1900 to 1905 he was President of the Merchants' National Bank. For a number of years he was a member of the Board of Trustees of Grinnell College and President *ad interim*. He was married July 11, 1860, to Mary Raley, a college classmate. In June, 1916, he was compelled to submit to a serious operation and never completely rallied from the shock. He died in Chicago, Ill., March 20, 1917.

PERRY RANSOM was born in Salisbury, Herkimer County, N. Y., August 11, 1827. He entered Oberlin as a preparatory student in 1853, was classed as a Freshman in 1854, and graduated with the degree of Bachelor of Arts in 1858. He engaged in teaching for one year after graduation and then opened a machine shop in Oshkosh, Wis., develop-ing a manufacturing business, in which he continued until the time of his death. He was married August 22, 1859, to Lydia F. Smith. He died October 2, 1916, at Stoneham, Mass., the cause of death being a disease of the spine. He is survived by three sons and one daughter.

1859

ELIAS TOUSSAINT JONES was one of the best known of the colored graduates of Oberlin. He was born in Raleigh, N. C., June 9, 1834. His father moved to Oberlin in 1843, the family consisting of five sons and one daughter. He was enrolled in the Oberlin Preparatory Department for two years, from 1853 to 1855, and in the College from 1855 to 1859. He graduated in 1859 with the degree of Bachelor of Arts. For a few years after graduation he engaged in teaching and then for more than twenty-five years worked as a miner in British Columbia. He returned to Oberlin in 1892 and retired from active work. He was greatly interested in the work of the National Association for the Advancement of Colored People. He was married August 12, 1893, to Mrs. Blanche Harris Brooks, by whom he is survived. He died in Oberlin May 13, 1917, the cause of death being paralysis.

1860

FANNY MARIA THOMSON-CLARKE was born in Sparta, N. Y., October 12, 1834. She entered Oberlin in 1856 as a first-year student in the Literary Course and graduated from this course in 1860. After a period of five years spent in teaching she was married on September 7, 1865, to Joseph B. Clarke, who was for many years one of the prominent citizens of the village of Oberlin. She resided continuously in Oberlin from that time until her death, making her home on West Lorain Street. She died in Oberlin May 29, 1917, the cause of death being an attack of grip followed by heart failure and other complications. She is survived by a son and a daughter.

PHILIP CORNELIUS HAYES was born in Granby, Conn., February 3, 1833. His preparatory work was taken in Farm Ridge Academy, Illinois. He entered the College as a Freshman in 1856 and graduated in 1860 with the degree of Bachelor of Arts. He was enrolled as a student in Oberlin Theological Seminary at the outbreak of the war and received his diploma of graduation from the Theological Seminary as with the class of 1863, although his enlistment in the service of the United States government interrupted his studies during the latter part of his theological course. The College bestowed upon him the degree of Master of Arts in 1863. During his college course he was the chairman of the committee that recommended the change in the name of one of the men's literary societies, from "Young Men's Lyceum," to "Phi Kappa Pi." He served in the United States army from 1862 to 1865. He was made captain of the 103rd Ohio Infantry, July 16, 1862; lieutenant colonel, November 18, 1864; he was appointed colonel, but not mustered in; he was brevetted brigadier general March 13, 1865, for gallant and meritorious service during the war. From March, 1877, to March, 1881, he served as a member of the forty-fifth and forty-sixth congresses and represented the seventh district of Illinois. He was a delegate to the Republican National Convention in 1872; a member of the Grand Army of the Republic, and for one year Commander of the Department of Illinois. From the close of the war until 1894 he was actively engaged in journalism in Morris, Ill. After 1894 he made his home in Joliet, Ill. He was the author of "Journal History of the One

Hundred and Third Ohio Volunteer Infantry Regiment;'' ''Socialism and What it Means;'' ''War Verse and Other Verse.'' He recently served as a member of the Perry Victory Centennial Committee. He was married to Amelia E. Johnson of Oberlin, January 25, 1865, and is survived by his wife and four of their six children. He died at Joliet, Ill., July 13, 1916, the cause of death being apoplexy.

LOUISE EMILIE NASH-LOOMIS was born in Picton, Ontario, Canada, December 29, 1836. She entered Oberlin in 1856 and graduated from the Literary Course in 1860. She engaged in teaching for one year after graduation and was then married to Dr. P. H. Loring, April 21, 1861. After his death she was married to A. J. Loomis, May 12, 1869. For almost forty years she made her home in Blue Rapids, Kan. She died July 9, 1916, at Long Beach, Cal., the cause of death being bronchial trouble. She is survived by her son, Guy J. Loomis.

1861

SUSAN JANE BEVIER-BROWN was born in Plymouth, Ohio, December 28, 1842. She entered Oberlin in 1859, receiving classification in the third year of the Literary Course and graduating in 1861 with the diploma of that course. In 1865 she was married to Mr. George Byron Brown and made her home in Toledo, Ohio, for the remainder of her life. For twenty years, from 1893 to 1914, she held the position of Treasurer of the Ohio Woman's Home Missionary Union. She died in Toledo, May 17, 1917, the cause of death being arterio sclerosis.

LOVEJOY JOHNSON was born in La Porte, Lorain County, Ohio, September 24, 1837. He entered Oberlin in 1859 with rank as a Junior and graduated in 1861 with the degree of Bachelor of Arts. He received the degree of Master of Arts in 1865. He engaged as a teacher in Winnebago, Ill., and then became superintendent of colored schools in Helena, Ark., a position that he held for two years. In 1864 he engaged in business in Stillman Valley, Ill., continuing in business in the same place until his death. He was married December 26, 1862, to one of his college classmates, Lucinda M. Adams. He died in Stillman Valley, January 12, 1917, death being caused by pneumonia following an attack of grip. He is survived by his wife and one daughter.

1862

HOWARD A. BURRELL was born in Sheffield Township, Lorain County, Ohio, January 4, 1838. In 1858 he began his college work and graduated from Oberlin in 1862, with the degree of Bachelor of Arts. In 1866 he became editor and publisher of the Washington County Press, Washington, Iowa, and continued in active charge of this paper until his retirement in 1903. He was married October 15, 1863, to Harriet Everson, who died in 1876, leaving three children. In 1877 he was married to Martha Jackson, who died in 1908. His public services included twelve years as Regent of the State University of Iowa, two years as councilman in his home town, as well as service for many years upon the city library board. He died in Washington, Iowa, July 15, 1916, after an illness of a year. The immediate cause of his death was heart trouble.

ESTHER TAPPING MALTBIE was born in Southington, Trumbull County, Ohio, April 30, 1836. She entered the Preparatory Department in Oberlin in 1857, was admitted to the Freshman class in 1858, and graduated in 1862 with the degree of Bachelor of Arts. The College bestowed the degree of Master of Arts in 1892. She engaged in teaching for eight years after graduation and then accepted appointment as a missionary teacher in Samokov in what was then European Turkey, now Bulgaria. She was soon made Principal of the Girls' Boarding School at Samokov, under the direction of the American Board. When the Ohio branch of the Woman's Board of Missions for the Interior was organized she was the first missionary to be adopted by it and in all the years of its existence her name headed the list of honored workers supported by the Ohio women. Later she became the special missionary of the First Church of Elyria. She gave forty-two years of her life to this work among the women of Bulgaria. In 1912 a stroke of paralysis compelled her withdrawal from the work and she returned to the United States to spend the remaining years of her life among her friends. She died at Springfield, Mo., March 11, 1917, the cause of death being paralysis and old age.

1863

FRANCES ADELAIDE LORD-CHURCH was born in Randolph, Ohio, August 9, 1840. She enrolled in the Literary Course in Oberlin in 1858, but changed to the regular Classical Course and graduated with the degree of Bachelor of Arts in 1863. She also received the degree of Master of Arts from Oberlin in 1896. After graduation she taught for two years in Janesville, Wis., in the institution for the blind. In 1865 she was married to Edward P. Church, and Mr. and Mrs. Church went to Honolulu, Hawaii, where Mr. Church served as a teacher and Mrs. Church acted as matron of the boarding department of Oahu College. After ten years in Hawaii they returned to the United States, living for thirteen years in Greenville, Mich., for four years in Cadillac, and for eight years in Lansing. Since Mr. Church's death in 1901 Mrs. Church has made her home in Oberlin. She was always active in W. C. T. U. and in general charitable and religious work and held many important positions in temperance and benevolent organizations. She died at the home of her son in Newark, Ohio, June 13, 1917, after an illness of eighteen months, the cause of her death being pulmonary tuberculosis.

1864

RACHEL ANN MARSHALL-JAMESON was born in Rochester, Ohio, May 17, 1838. She entered Oberlin in 1859 as a first-year student in the Literary Course and graduated from that course in 1864. For three years after graduation she served as a teacher and then married Robinson H. Jameson, October 29, 1867. Her husband died six years later, leaving two children. During almost all of her life Mrs. Jameson was a resident of Oberlin. She died in Brighton, Ohio, November 17, 1916, the cause of death being senile gangrene.

ARTEMAS BELL JOHNSON was born in Norwalk, Ohio, September 9, 1843. He entered Oberlin as a Senior in the Preparatory Department in 1859, was classed as a Freshman in 1860, and was graduated in 1864 with the degree of Bachelor of Arts. The College granted to him the degree of Master of Arts in 1870. After graduation he studied law and taught for two years and was then admitted to the bar. He practiced law in Kenton, Ohio, from 1866 to the time of his death with the exception of five years spent on the bench. He was prosecuting attorney of Hardin County, Ohio, from 1868 to 1872, mayor of the city of Kenton for four years, judge of the common pleas court from 1890 to 1895. He held appointment as a member of the special commission to report upon the convict labor question, serving from 1900 to 1902; he was a member of the State Board of Examiners for admission to the bar, from 1903 to 1908. He was married to Louise M. Crane July 3, 1866. After her death he was married December 12, 1893, to Mrs. Anna E. Welch, who survives him. He is also survived by six children, all of whom have been students in Oberlin. He died in Kenton, Ohio, May 10, 1917, the cause of death being nephritis.

1868

MARTHA ANN ROBINSON-CANFIELD was born in Freedom, Portage County, Ohio, September 10, 1845. After previous study at Hiram College she came to Oberlin in 1867 with advanced standing and graduated with the diploma of the Literary Course in 1868. She also received from Oberlin in 1891 the honorary degree of Master of Arts. She engaged in teaching for one year and then entered a medical course in the Homeopathic Hospital College of Cleveland, receiving the degree of M. D. in 1875. She was a pioneer among women in the profession of medicine. From 1890 to 1897 she held appointment as professor of diseases of women in the Cleveland Homeopathic College and was a member of the faculty of the Maternity Hospital, Cleveland, from 1897 to 1915. She was also President of the Women's Hospital Association. She was married September 7, 1869, to Harrison W. Canfield. Mr. Canfield and three of their children survive her. She died in Cleveland, Ohio, September 3, 1916.

1870

SIMON BYRON HERSHEY was born in Marshallville, Wayne County, Ohio, September 21, 1847. He entered Oberlin as a Junior in the College in 1868, after previous study at Otterbein University, and graduated in 1870 with the degree of Bachelor of Arts. He took the first part of his theological course in Oberlin, but completed the theological course in Yale Theological Seminary, where he graduated in 1874. He was ordained to the ministry in Danbury, Conn., October 27, 1874, and held important pastorates in Danbury, Conn., Ashtabula, Ohio, and Ashland, Ohio. In 1898 he left the active work of the ministry and spent the remainder of his life in lyceum and lecture work, serving as manager of the Central Lyceum Bureau of Cleveland, Ohio, and of the American Lyceum Union of Rochester, N. Y. Recently he delivered special lectures in connection with the world peace movement. He was married August 18, 1874, to Thirza E. Johnson of Oberlin, who survives him. He died February 10, 1917, at Ashtabula, Ohio, the cause of death being angina pectoris.

1872

JOSEPH PERRY PRESTON was born in Galena, Ohio, January 10, 1837. During the Civil War he served as a private in Company C of the 88th Ohio Volunteer Infantry. He entered Oberlin in 1869 as a student in the Theological Seminary and graduated from the Seminary in 1872. He held pastorates in Michigan, Ohio, Iowa, Illinois, Kansas, and Nebraska covering a period of forty years. He retired from the active work of the ministry in 1912, making his home in Florence, Nebr. He was married February 18, 1874, to Mary C. Raymond. He is survived by his wife, one son, and one daughter. Mr. Preston died September 18, 1915, at Florence, Nebr., death resulting from a fall complicated by an attack of grip.

1873

EMMA ANNA HOLBROOK-MEAD was born in Madison, Ohio, February 10, 1851. She spent the year 1866-67 in Oberlin as a preparatory student and returned for college work in 1870, graduating in 1873 with the diploma of the Literary Course. For three years after graduation she engaged in teaching in Cleveland, Ohio, and was then married to Homer L. Mead, December 25, 1876. Her home was in Escanaba, Mich., for twelve years, then in Centralia, Wash., and recently in Tacoma, Wash. She died in Tacoma, February 4, 1917, the cause of death being pernicious anaemia. She is survived by a son and two daughters.

JOHN MILTON MERRILL was born in Warsaw, N. Y., March 25, 1850. He entered Oberlin as a preparatory student in 1867, was classed as a Freshman in 1869, and graduated with the degree of Bachelor of Arts in 1873. He received a part of his theological preparation in Harvard and a part in Oberlin. He was ordained to the ministry at North Ridgeville, Ohio, January 13, 1876. From 1882 to 1894 he held pastorates in Brooklyn Village and in Ashland, Ohio. In the summer of 1894 ill health compelled him to drop his active work in the ministry and he never fully recovered from this illness. The family removed to Oberlin in the fall of 1894 and except for occasional supply work Mr. Merrill did not thereafter engage in much preaching. He was married December 1, 1875, to Marion L. Wood of the class of 1870. He is survived by his wife and three daughters, all graduates of the College. He died in the hospital at Mt. Airy, Philadelphia, Pa., January 10, 1917, the cause of death being heart trouble.

1874

FANNY FORESTER RICE-SMITH was born in Benson, Vt., September 27, 1849. She received her preparation for college in the academy at Barre, Vt., enrolled in Oberlin as a Freshman in 1870, and graduated in 1874 with the degree of Bachelor of Arts. She was permitted by the faculty to deliver her own oration at graduation, being the first woman to be allowed this privilege. She received the degree of Master of Arts in 1877. She engaged in teaching in Hallowell, Me., from 1875 to 1878, and then became Tutor in Latin in the preparatory department of Oberlin College, continuing in this work from 1881 to 1888. She was married October 7, 1888, to Hiram Smith, a schoolmate in

Barre Academy. In 1902, after the death of her husband, Mrs. Smith returned to Oberlin with her three children and lived in Oberlin for the next fourteen years. In October, 1916, she went to her old home in Vermont, hoping to be benefitted in health. Seeming to improve she remained in Orwell, where she died February 3, 1917, the cause of death being angina pectoris. She is survived by one daughter and two sons.

1875

CALISTA ANDREWS was born in Lovell, Maine, October 13, 1845. She enrolled in Oberlin in 1873 for special studies after considerable experience as a teacher, and was regularly graduated from the Literary Course in 1875. For many years she was permanent secretary of her class and to her efforts were due in large measure the very successful reunions of her class in the years 1908 and 1915. During the year following her graduation she was employed as a teacher of mathematics in Oberlin Academy. In 1876 she returned to her home in River Falls, Wis., and gave her attention to homemaking for relatives. She moved back to Oberlin in 1890 in order to provide educational advantages for those in her charge and resided in Oberlin until 1897. From 1897 to 1912 she made her home in Danvers, Mass. After 1912 she lived with her nephew, Dr. Walter H. Winchester, in Flint, Mich., and it was in Dr. Winchester's home that she died February 23, 1917, the cause of her death being heart disease. She was always interested in missions and gave largely of her resources and of her own personal services for the advancement of various missionary enterprises.

MARTHA JEANNETTE NICHOLS-PHILLIPS was born in Columbia, Lorain County, Ohio, January 28, 1853. She entered Oberlin in 1871 as a first-year student in the Literary Course and graduated with the diploma of that course in 1875. Twenty-five years later she returned to Oberlin for a year of further study and received the degree of Bachelor of Philosophy in 1901. She engaged in teaching for thirteen years after graduation, the last year of teaching being in Oberlin Academy in 1887-88. Ill health caused frequent interruptions in her work as a teacher. She was married May 8, 1889, to Mr. Sceva S. Phillips. Mr. and Mrs. Phillips made their home thereafter in New York, Mrs. Phillips being engaged in writing for juvenile and sunday school publications. Five years ago her health began to fail and she died in Kissimmee, Fla., May 27, 1917, the cause of death being catharal asthma. She is survived by her husband and two sisters.

CHARLES JACKSON RYDER was born in Oberlin December 25, 1848, and was connected with Oberlin College in an unusually intimate way throughout his entire life. He began a course in the preparatory department in 1863, was classed as a Freshman in 1871, graduated with the degree of Bachelor of Arts in 1875, enrolled in the Seminary in 1876 and graduated from the Seminary in 1880 with the degree of Bachelor of Divinity. He also received the degree of Master of Arts in 1887 and the honorary degree of Doctor of Divinity in 1894. Dr. Ryder served the College as a member of the Board of Trustees for seventeen years, from 1900 to the time of his death. Thirty-two years of Dr. Ryder's life were given to the service of the American Missionary Association as

Field Superintendent, Manager of the eastern district, and in recent years as Corresponding Secretary. He was married August 21, 1876, to Sarah H. Tenney, and is survived by his wife, two sons, and two daughters. His last illness began with a slight cerebral hemorrhage, and during the succeeding month other more serious hemorrhages followed. For years the strain of overwork had been reducing his vitality. He died at Stamford, Conn., September 24, 1917.

1878

JAMES HENRY LEONARD was born in Bridgewater, Mass., March 8, 1852. He entered Oberlin as a student in 1873 after previous study in Bridgewater Normal School. He was classed as a Freshman in 1874 and graduated with the degree of Bachelor of Arts in 1878. He taught in Leicester, Mass., during the year 1878-79, then studied law and was admitted to the bar in Taunton, Mass., in 1881. He located in Elyria, Ohio, in 1882, where he engaged in the practice of his profession and made his home for the remainder of his life. He was prominent in his profession and gave much time to public affairs. For the last seven years of his life he was President of the board of health of the city of Elyria. He was married January 11, 1882, to Mary C. Johnston of Elyria. He is survived by his wife and one son. He died in Elyria May 6, 1917, after a long illness, the cause of death being enlargement of the heart.

FRANCIS ALBERT WILCOX was born in Richfield, Ohio, May 17, 1852. He entered Oberlin in 1870 in the preparatory department, received classification as a Freshman in 1874, and graduated with the degree of Bachelor of Arts in 1878. He engaged in teaching in Akron, Ohio, from 1879 to 1882, and in business in Akron from 1882 to 1899. He then became manager of a manufacturing plant, locating in Erie, Pa., and later in Jeannette, Pa. He returned to Akron in 1906, engaging in the real estate loan and insurance business. He was married to Della M. Doyle, November 9, 1893. He died November 16, 1916, at Akron, Ohio, the cause of death being paralysis. He is survived by his wife, a daughter, and an adopted daughter.

1880

WILLIAM BIGLER FISHER was born in Upper Augusta, Pa., October 12, 1851. He entered Oberlin in 1879 as a Senior in the Theological Seminary and graduated from the Seminary in 1880. He was ordained to the ministry at Spring Hill, Kan., in 1880. During the years of his active ministry he served in various towns in Kansas, Missouri, and Washington. He was married June 23, 1880, to Linda L. Peirce, who, with one son, survives. He died February 1, 1917, in Seattle, Wash., the cause of death being cancer.

1882

LOIE ABRA CHILDS-GAYLORD was born in Sandusky, Ohio, January 5, 1860. She prepared for college in the Sandusky High School. She enrolled in Oberlin in 1880 as a third-year student in the Literary Course and graduated in 1882 with the diploma of that course. For seven years after graduation, from 1883 to 1890, she was a teacher in the Sandusky High School. She was married March 10, 1891, to Dr. William Gaylord and lived in Sandusky, where Dr. Gaylord practiced his profession until the time of his death in 1900. Mrs. Gaylord died at the Good Samaritan Hospital in Sandusky November 13, 1916, the cause of death being pneumonia. She is survived by a son and a daughter.

1885

WILLIAM LAWRENCE TENNEY was born in Boston, Mass., September 9, 1862. He prepared for college in the schools of Boston and for two years in the preparatory department of Oberlin College. He was classed as a Freshman in 1881 and graduated with the degree of Bachelor of Arts in 1885. He immediately entered the Theological Seminary and in 1888 graduated with the degree of Bachelor of Divinity. Knox College granted to him the degree of Doctor of Divinity in 1903 and Oberlin bestowed the same degree in 1908. The year following his graduation from the Theological Seminary he spent in New Orleans, La., as Professor of Mental and Moral Philosophy in Straight University. He then accepted the pastorate of the Madison Avenue Congregational Church of Cleveland, remaining in this position for two years. The next three years were spent in Holbrook, Mass., and during his pastorate in Holbrook Mr. Tenney pursued graduate study in Harvard University. During the year 1894-95 he was the college pastor at Olivet, Mich., and taught the subject of Logic in Olivet College. He then moved to North Adams, Mass., and after five years accepted the appointment of District Secretary of the American Missionary Association, remaining in this work until 1905. He then resumed pastoral work, holding important positions in Sioux City, Iowa, Minneapolis, Minn., and Brooklyn, N. Y. His last charge was at Lee, Mass. On November 14, 1916, an automobile in which he was riding to meet a church appointment was wrecked in a collision with a motor truck. Dr. Tenney was thrown from the machine and suffered a fracture of the skull, and died three days later. His first wife was Flora A. Calkins, a graduate of Oberlin in the class of 1884. His second wife was Elizabeth Brodie, who survives him.

1887

FRANK S. CLARK was born in Tallmadge, Ohio, May 27, 1865. He enrolled as a Freshman in Oberlin in 1883 and graduated with the degree of Bachelor of Arts in 1887. He immediately enrolled for study in the Medical Department of Western Reserve University and received his M. D. degree from that institution in 1890. He also received the degree of Master of Arts from Oberlin College in 1890. For twenty-six years Dr. Clark practiced his profession in Cleveland, and at the time of his death was chief of staff of St. Ann's Maternity Hospital. He was also a member of the faculty of the medical school of Western Reserve University and was considered one of Cleveland's leading physicians. He was married May 22, 1896, to Elizabeth A. Marvin, who survives him. He died in Cleveland November 23, 1916, the cause of death being acute intestinal infection. It was the judgment of the attending physician that he would have recovered from this illness had he not completely exhausted his vitality by years of overwork.

1890

ELIZABETH STORRS BILLINGS-MEAD was born in Conway, Mass., May 21, 1832. She completed her studies in the school of Mr. and Mrs. Cowles at Ipswich, Mass., and engaged in teaching for a number of years. In 1858 she was married to Rev. Hiram Mead and they located in South Hadley, Mass., where they remained for nine years. In 1867 Mr. Mead was called to Nashua, N. H., leaving there two years later to accept a professorship in Oberlin Theological Seminary. Before Professor Mead's death in 1881 Mrs. Mead became associated with the English department as Instructor in English Literature, and continued this work until 1883, when she moved to Andover, Mass., as an associate of Miss McKean in the management of Abbott Academy. In 1890 she accepted the presidency of Mount Holyoke College, a position that she held until 1901. At the age of sixty-nine she resigned the presidency of Mount Holyoke College, and after a year of foreign travel, moved to Oberlin, residing with her daughter, Mrs. A. T. Swing, living in Oberlin for almost all of the remainder of her life. Oberlin College granted the honorary degree of Master of Arts in 1890, and Smith College that of L. H. D. in 1900. She died in Cocoanut Grove, Fla., March 25, 1917, after an illness of one week, the cause of her death being intestinal trouble. She is survived by her daughter, Mrs. A. T. Swing, and her son, Professor George H. Mead of the University of Chicago.

1891

ALBERT LOUIS GREIN was born in Buffalo, N. Y., August 16, 1866. He entered Oberlin in the preparatory department in 1886 for the completion of his preparatory work, was classed as a Freshman in 1888, and graduated with the degree of Bachelor of Philosophy in 1891. Immediately after graduation he entered the Yale Divinity School, from which he graduated in 1894 with the degree of Bachelor of Divinity. Oberlin bestowed the degree of Master of Arts in 1894. From 1894 to 1898 he was pastor of Plymouth Congregational Church, Buffalo, N. Y. In 1898 he was called to be the pastor of the Pilgrim Congregational Church of Buffalo and continued in this pastorate until the time of his death. He died at the Homeopathic Hospital in Buffalo, September 16, 1917, the cause of death being intestinal tuberculosis. He was unmarried.

1899

ELIZABETH CHENEY-STILES was born in Emerald Grove, Wis., October 30, 1876. She entered Oberlin as an academy student in 1891, received classification as a Freshman in 1894, and graduated with the degree of Bachelor of Arts in 1899. For two years after graduation she engaged in teaching in Manchester, Iowa. She was married August 20, 1901, to Rev. Hubert W. Stiles, of the class of 1896. Mr. and Mrs. Stiles made their home in Ada, Minn., from 1901 to 1906, in Dundee Ill., from 1906 to 1916, and moved to St. Croix Falls, Wis. in 1916. It was at St. Croix Falls that Mrs. Stiles died May 22, 1917, after several years of illness, the cause of her death being a tumor. She is survived by her husband and two of their three children.

1901

HUBBARD NORTH BRADLEY was born in Cedar Rapids, Iowa, May 23, 1874. He received his preparatory education in the high school of South Haven, Mich., and in Oberlin Academy. He enrolled as a Freshman in Oberlin College in 1897 and received the degree of Bachelor of Arts in 1901. He immediately began the study of medicine at the University of Michigan and graduated from the medical department in 1905 with the degree of Doctor of Medicine. He began the practice of his profession in Bay City, Mich., in 1905, where he made his home until his death. In recent years Dr. Bradley withdrew somewhat from general practice in order to devote himself to certain special phases of his calling, particularly x-ray work. He died in Augustana Hospital, Chicago, August 30, 1917, death resulting from an operation for intestinal trouble. He was married to Harriet R. Wyman, June 25, 1906, and is survived by his wife and two children.

1905

ESTHER HALL AUTEN was born in Princeville, Ill., April 23, 1881. Her preparatory work was taken in Princeville Academy and in Bradley Polytechnic Institute, Peoria, Ill. She entered Oberlin with rank as a Freshman in 1901 and graduated from the College in June, 1905, receiving the degree of Bachelor of Arts and with it the diploma of the Teachers' Course in Physical Training. For eleven years after graduation Miss Auten served as a teacher, six years in Albion College, Albion, Mich., and shorter periods in Atlanta, Ga., and in Cleveland, Ohio. She left a position near St. Louis in December, 1915, on account of ill health, and during the remaining months of her life was at the home of her parents in Princeville, Ill. She died in Princeville, October 16, 1916, the cause of her death being acute peritonitis.

CARRIE LENORE ROSE-FISHBACK was born in Kipton, Ohio, June 6, 1883. She entered Oberlin as a senior academy student in the fall of 1900, received Freshman classification in 1901, and graduated with the degree of Bachelor of Arts in 1905. The year 1905-06 was spent in graduate study, and the degree of Master of Arts was bestowed by Oberlin in 1906. The next nine years were spent in teaching in Atlantic Mine, Michigan, Oberlin, the Needles, Cal., and Orange, Cal. She was married June 30, 1915, to Mason M. Fishback, who survives her. She died at Orange, Cal., April 19, 1917, the cause of death being tumor on the brain.

1906

CHARLES FREDERICK BRISSEL was born in Brooklyn, N. Y., September 29, 1880. He completed his preparatory course in Oberlin Academy in 1900 and entered upon his college work in September of that year. His college course was interrupted, but he graduated in June, 1906, receiving the degree of Bachelor of Arts. For three years after graduation Mr. Brissel was engaged as a teacher in Mills Institute, Honolulu, Hawaii. In 1909 he accepted a position as a teacher in Amoy, China, but after three months of service he received appointment as American Vice Consul and served in this position for four years. He returned to America for a short furlough in the early part of the year 1914 and then received appointment as American Consul in Bagdad, Turkey, a position that he held from June, 1914, until his death. The following quotation is from a letter from Mr. Brissel's successor in the consulate at Bagdad, written under date of February 9, 1917: "I am sorry to inform you that Mr. Brissel died of cholera on October 31, 1916, and was buried here in Bagdad. The funeral was attended in person by Khalil Pasha, the Governor General and Commander-in-Chief of the Sixth Army Corps. There were also present a company of Turkish soldiers and a military band. The assistant Governor General and many of the higher Turkish officials together with the leading business men of Bagdad attended the funeral. Mr. Brissel was held in the highest esteem by all classes of the population and his death was mourned by all. Yours very truly, Oscar S. Heizer, American Consul.''

THOMAS KELLY JAY was born in St. Mary's Ohio, June 6, 1883. He graduated from St. Mary's High School in 1901 and entered Oberlin as a Freshman in September, 1901. Ill health caused by a sunstroke interrupted his college course for one year and he graduated in 1906 with the degree of Bachelor of Arts. For several years after graduation he engaged in business in St. Mary's and then enlisted in the United States Navy for clerical service as yeoman, hoping to strengthen his health. Following his return six years ago from a cruise with the Atlantic battle fleet he took a cold while in Philadelphia. Treatment failed to clear the cold and he was assigned to the Naval Hospital at Las Animas, Colo., where he stayed for two years, followed by four more years of life in other parts of Colorado. He was benefitted, but not cured, and suffered a relapse during the winter of 1916-17. He died May 17, 1917, in Denver, Colo., the cause of his death being tuberculosis. He was not married.

1907

MABEL DREISBACH WOODSIDE-STOKEY was born in Chicago, Ill., January 12, 1884. She enrolled in Oberlin as a senior academy student in 1902, was classed as a Freshman in 1903, and graduated with the degree of Bachelor of Arts in 1907. Following graduation she spent a part of a year in graduate study in Oberlin, after which she enrolled as a medical student in the American Medical Missionary College at Battle Creek, Mich., where she remained until 1910. She entered upon medical missionary work in Africa in the autumn of 1910 under appointment with the American Board and remained in service until 1914, when ill health compelled her to return to the United States. In the meantime she was married to Dr. Fred E. Stokey, who was also engaged in medical mission work in Africa. She died May 6, 1917, at Chicopee Falls, Mass. the cause of death being tuberculosis. She is survived by her husband. '

1913

PHILIP HULBERT CARY was born in Elyria, Ohio, July 4, 1889. He graduated from Elyria High School in 1908 and entered Oberlin in 1909 as a member of the Freshman class. He graduated from Oberlin in June, 1913, with the degree of Bachelor of Arts, spent the following year as graduate assistant in Geology in Oberlin College, carrying on advanced study in the department of Geology, and received the degree of Master of Arts in 1914. During the year 1914-15 he continued his studies in the University of Minnesota, acting as assistant in Paleontology. He then accepted a position as Field Geologist in the employ of J. Elmer Thomas of Tulsa, Okla. He was married August 20, 1915, to Elizabeth S. Brown of Oakes, N. Dak., by whom he is survived. In the fall of 1916 he contracted typhoid fever and started toward home. At Oberlin he was taken to the hospital where his death occurred, October 27, 1916.

1916

WILLARD FOOTE BROWNELL was born in St. Charles, Ill., September 5, 1894. He graduated from the St. Charles High School in 1912 and entered Oberlin as a Freshman in September of that year. In May, 1916, one month before the time of graduation he began to suffer from the disorder that ultimately caused his death and was not able to be present in person to receive his degree on Commencement Day, but by special vote the Trustees granted his degree in absentia. He recovered sufficiently to return to his home in St. Charles and after a few weeks moved to California to live with his sister in the city of San Rafael, where he died February 7, 1917. The cause of his death was acute kidney trouble.

STATISTICS OF INSTRUCTION AND ATTENDANCE

Year of 1916-17

The schedule numbers in the following tables refer in general to the courses as described in the bulletin of the College of Arts and Sciences for the year 1916-17 (Bulletin No. 121).

In science courses, the hours of instruction spent by the teacher in Laboratory work are marked with the letter ''L''; in courses in Fine Arts and Physical Education, the hours spent in supervision are indicated by the letter ''S''; the letter ''R'' is used to denote hours in regular instruction.

Discussion of the statistics in the following sections will be found in the report of the Dean of the College of Arts and Sciences, pages 168-173.

I. THE COLLEGE OF ARTS AND SCIENCES

INSTRUCTOR AND COURSE	Semester	Teaching Hours per week	Men	Women
Astronomy				
Associate Professor E. J. MOORE		L 4, R 4		
1. Astronomy (credit: 3 hours)......	I	L 2, R 2		5
2. Astronomy (credit: 3 hours)......	II	L 2, R 2	8	3
Bible				
President KING		2		
Professor BOSWORTH		2		
Professor FITCH		8		
Professor HUTCHINS		4		
3. Freshman Bible, required (2 sec.) (credit: 2 hours).............	I	4	161	193
4. Old Testament b (2 sec.) (credit: 2 hours)	II	4	114	91
9. Introduction to the Old Testament	I	2	2	20
10. Introduction to the New Testament	II	2	3	20
11. Senior Bible, required...........	I	2	76	125
12. Senior Bible	II	2	13	16

INSTRUCTOR AND COURSE	Semester	Teaching Hours per week	Men	Women
Bibliography				
Mr. METCALF		6		
2. Use of Libraries and Elementary Bibliography	II	2	21	8
3. History of the Printed Book	I	2	1	10
4. Illustration and Decoration of Books	II	2	10	1
Botany				
Professor GROVER		L26, R11		
Associate Professor NICHOLS		L37, R 9		
Mr. CLUM		L20		
Mr. TSIANG		L 2		
1. General Botany (credit: 4 hours)	I	L20, R 3	11	45
2. General Botany (credit: 4 hours)	II	L22, R 3	9	43
3. Plant Morphology (credit: 4 hours)	I	L 8, R 2	2	3
4. Plant Morphology (credit: 4 hours)	II	L 8, R 2	2	3
8. Dendrology (credit: 2 hours)	II	L 6, R 2	15	14
10. Advanced Taxonomy of the Spermatophytes (credit: 3 hours)	II	L 2, R 1	0	3
11. Plant Cytology and Cytological Technique (credit: 3 hours)	I	L 7, R 1	1	2
13. Organic Evolution	I	3	19	28
15. Research (credit: 2 hours)	I	L 6, R 1	1	0
(credit: 5 hours)			0	1
16. Research (credit: 2 hours)	II	L 6, R 2	1	0
(credit: 3 hours)	·	· ·	1	0
(credit: 9 hours)	·	· ·	0	1
Chemistry				
Professor HOLMES		L42, R18		
Associate Professor CHAPIN		L41, R 5		
Associate Professor McCULLOUGH		L31, R 7		
Mr. FALL		L32		
Miss ARNOLD		L30		
1. General Inorganic Chemistry (2 sec.) (credit: 4 hours)	I	L32, R 6	93	82
2. General Inorganic Chemistry (2 sec.) (credit: 4 hours)	II	L36, R 6	76	63
3. Organic Chemistry (credit: 4 hours)	I	L23, R 2	24	9
4. Organic Chemistry (credit: 4 hours)	II	L17, R 2	17	3
6. Food Chemistry (credit: 4 hours)	II	L 5, R 2	6	5

INSTRUCTOR AND COURSE	Semester	Teaching Hours per week	Men	Women
7. Analytical Chemistry: Qualitative (credit: 5 hours).............	I	L15, R 2	21	8
8. Analytical Chemistry: Quantitative (credit: 5 hours).............	II	L12, R 2	18	7
9. Physical Chemistry (credit: 4 hours)	I	L 8, R 2	13	1
12. Advanced Analytical Chemistry (credit: 2 hours).............	I	L 1	0	1
12. Advanced Analytical Chemistry (credit: 3 hours).............	II	L 3	3	0
(credit: 4 hours).............	.	.	2	0
(credit: 5 hours).............	.	.	4	0
14. Theory of Industrial Chemistry...	II	2	5	0
16. Inorganic Preparations (credit: 2 hours)	II	L 7	9	0
17 H. Research (credit: 4 hours).......	I	L10	1	0
(credit: 6 hours).............	.	.	0	1
(credit: 11 hours).............	.	.	1	0
18 H. Research (credit: 4 hours).......	II	L 6	1	0
(credit: 5 hours).............	.	.	0	1
— Advanced Organic Chemistry (credit: 2 hours).................	I	L 1	1	1

Economics

INSTRUCTOR AND COURSE	Semester	Teaching Hours per week	Men	Women
Professor LUTZ		24		
Miss KYRK		28		
Mr. H. L. KING		12		
1. Elementary Principles of Economics (9 sec.) (credit: 3 hours)..	I	19	78	104
2. Elementary Principles of Economics (8 sec.) (credit: 3 hours)..	II	17	83	98
7. Public Finance and Taxation.....	I	3	13	0
8. Principles of Banking...........	II	3	20	0
10. Principles of Business Administration.....................	II	3	24	3
13. The Economic Position of Women.	I	2	1	8
14. The Economic Position of Women.	II	2	1	15
17. Railway and Trust Problems.....	I	3	6	0
19. Problems of Distribution (credit: 3 hours)	I	2	10	4
20. Poverty and the Dependent Classes (credit: 3 hours).............	II	2	21	11
21. Economic Seminar (credit: 2 hours)	I	4	5	1
22. Economic Seminar (credit: 2 hours)	II	4	4	0

INSTRUCTOR AND COURSE	Semester	Teaching Hours per week	Men	Women
Education				
Professor E. A. MILLER		29		
1. History of Education............	I	3	12	37
2. Modern Educational Theory......	II	3	12	33
3. Secondary Education	I	2	14	23
4. School Management	II	2	19	34
5. Educational Classics............	I	3	6	18
6. Principles of Education..........	II	3	9	28
7. School Administration	I	3	5	17
8. The Psychology and Method of High School Subjects..........	II	3	5	15
9. Seminar (credit: 2 hours)........	I	5	1	5
10. Seminar	II	2	2	5
English Composition				
Associate Professor JELLIFFE		12		
Associate Professor SHERMAN		8		
Miss BROWNBACK		22		
Miss WARD		18		
MR. BEATTIE		22		
MR. BROSIUS		10		
1. Freshman Composition (15 sec.) (credit: 2 hours)............	I	30	156	197
2. Freshman Composition (16 sec.) (credit: 2 hours)............	II	32	118	161
1 B. Freshman Composition (2 sec.) (credit: 2 hours)............	I	4	10	11
2 A. Freshman Composition (3 sec.) (credit: 2 hours)............	II	6	32	43
1 F. Composition for Foreign Students (credit: 1 hour).............	I	2	8	0
2 F. Composition for Foreign Students (credit: 1 hour).............	II	2	6	1
3. Argumentative Composition.......	I	2	14	4
4. Argumentative Composition.......	II	2	11	3
5. Narrative Writing	I	2	2	11
6. Narrative Writing	II	2	3	8
7. Exposition and Essay Writing....	I	2	8	13
8. Exposition and Essay Writing....	II	2	10	8
9. Literary Composition...........	I	2	4	9
10. Literary Composition...........	II	2	2	10

INSTRUCTOR AND COURSE	Semester	Teaching Hours per week	Men	Women
English Literature				
Professor WAGER		20		
Associate Professor SHERMAN		20		
Associate Professor JELLIFFE		12		
Miss WARD		4		
9. Shakespeare and the Drama of the Sixteenth and Seventeenth Centuries	I	3	8	27
10. Shakespeare and the Drama of the Sixteenth and Seventeenth Centuries	II	3	6	33
13. Burke	I	2	8	0
14. Burke	II	2	5	0
15. Victorian Prose	I	3	18	46
16. Victorian Prose	II	3	18	39
15 H. Victorian Prose (3 hours)	I	.	1	3
16 H. Victorian Prose (3 hours)	II	.	1	4
17. Early Nineteenth Century Poetry.	I	2	3	16
18. Early Nineteenth Century Poetry.	II	2	1	18
19. The English Novel	I	3	3	14
20. The English Novel	II	3	4	13
23. American Literature (credit: 3 hours)	I	2	52	136
24. American Literature (credit: 3 hours)	II	2	67	176
27. Tennyson and Browning	I	3	7	36
28. Tennyson and Browning	II	3	14	48
29. Old and Middle English	I	2	0	16
30. Old and Middle English	II	2	0	14
33. Milton and the Literature of the Seventeenth Century	I	2	0	5
34. Milton and the Literature of the Seventeenth Century	II	2	0	5
35. Teachers' Training Course	I	2	1	23
36. Teachers' Training Course	II	2	1	24
39. The Classics in Translation	I	3	35	96
40. The Classics in Translation	II	3	28	91
45. The Principles of Literary Criticism	I	1	1	6
46. The Principles of Literary Criticism	II	1	1	6

INSTRUCTOR AND COURSE	Semester	Teaching Hours per week	Men	Women
Fine Arts				
Historical Courses				
Professor WARD		6		
Professor MARTIN		10		
1. History of Ancient Art..........	I	2	8	25
2. History of Ancient Art..........	II	2	14	23
3. History of Greek Sculpture (2 sec.) (credit: 2 hours)..............	I	4	8	30
4. History of Greek Sculpture.......	II	2	9	20
8. Renaissance Painting in Italy.....	II	3	7	13
12. Medieval Architecture	II	3	3	0
Studio Courses				
Associate Professor OAKES		S41½, R6		
Miss STEPHEN		S18½, R4		
17. Theory and Practice of Art (credit: 2 hours).................	I		8	24
18. Theory and Practice of Art (Credit: 2 hours).................	II		2	15
19. Theory and Practice of Art (credit: 2 hours).................	I		–	5
20. Theory and Practice of Art (credit: 2 hours).................	II		12	23
21. Free-Hand Drawing (credit: 2 hour)	I		2	6
(credit: 2 hours).............	·		0	1
(credit: 3 hours).............	·		1	3
22. Free-Hand Drawing (credit: 1 hour)	II		1	1
(credit: 2 hours).............	·		1	3
(credit: 3 hours).............	·		0	3
25. Water Color Painting (credit: 1 hour)	I		0	2
(credit: 2 hours).............	·		0	7
26. Water Color Painting (credit: 1 hour)	II		0	4
(credit: 2 hours).............	·		0	8
27. Design in Theory and Practice (credit: 2 hours).............	I		1	5
28. Design in Theory and Practice (credit: 2 hours).............	II		–	6
29. Design in Theory and Practice: Advanced Course (credit: 2 hours)	I		0	4
30. Design in Theory and Practice: Advanced Course (credit: 2 hours)	II		0	4

INSTRUCTOR AND COURSE	Semester	Teaching Hours per week	Men	Women
French				
Professor WIGHTMAN		20		
Associate Professor COWDERY		28		
Associate Professor JAMESON		30		
Mrs. COWDERY		32		
1. Elementary French (7 sec.) (credit: 4 hours)	I	28	88	124
2. Elementary French (7 sec.) (credit: 4 hours)	II	28	66	113
3. Reading (3 sec.) (credit: 3 hours)	I	9	13	43
4. Reading (3 sec.) (credit: 3 hours)	II	9	8	39
5. Grammar and Composition (3 sec.) (credit: 1 hour)	I	3	12	42
6. Grammar and Composition (3 sec.) (credit: 1 hour)	II	3	11	38
7. Conversation	I	2	2	12
8. Conversation	II	2	2	13
9. French Prose of the Nineteenth Century	I	3	1	12
10. French Prose of the Nineteenth Century	II	3	1	11
15. French Poetry of the Seventeenth and Eighteenth Centuries	I	3	3	11
16. French Poetry of the Nineteenth Century	II	3	2	11
17. French Drama of the Eighteenth and early Nineteenth Centuries.	I	3	0	7
18. French Drama of the Eighteenth and early Nineteenth Centuries.	II	3	0	9
21. History of French Literature	I	2	2	9
22. History of French Literature	II	2	2	8
23. Advanced Grammar and Composition	I	1	4	15
24. Advanced Grammar and Composition	II	1	1	12
25. Teachers' Training Course	I	1	2	4
26. Teachers' Training Course	II	1	2	4
Geology				
Professor HUBBARD		L17½, R19		
Miss EASTON		L 7½		
Mr. ROTHROCK		L10		
1. Physiography (credit: 3 hours)	I	L 9½, R2	4	6
2 B. Geography of Europe (credit: 3 hours)	II	L 2½, R2	3	6
3. General Geology (credit: 4 hours).	I	L 8½, R3	6	5

INSTRUCTOR AND COURSE	Semester	Teaching Hours per week	Men	Women
4. General Geology (credit: 4 hours).	II	L 7½, R3	6	4
5. Economic Geology (credit: 3 hours)	I	L 1½, R2	3	0
6. Economic Geology (credit: 3 hours)	II	L 1½, R2	2	0
(credit: 4 hours)	.	.	2	0
7. Seminar (credit: 2 hours)	I	L 2, R3	2	1
(credit: 3 hours)	.	.	1	1
(credit: 5 hours)	.	.	0	1
(credit: 9 hours)	.	.	0	1
8. Seminar (credit: 2 hours)	II	L 2, R2	2	2
(credit: 3 hours)	.	.	1	0
(credit: 4 hours)	.	.	0	1

German

Professor MOSHER		27		
Professor ABBOTT		24		
Assistant Professor DOMROESE		24		
Miss BACH		26		
Miss RODENBAECK		32		
1. Elementary German (3 sec.) (credit: 4 hours)	I	12	36	40
2. Elementary German (3 sec.) (credit: 4 hours)	II	12	33	38
3. Second Year German (6 sec.) (credit: 4 hours)	I	24	75	76
4. Second Year German (6 sec.) (credit: 4 hours)	II	24	63	72
5. Third Year German (3 sec.) (credit: 3 hours)	I	9	23	43
6. Third Year German (3 sec.) (credit: 3 hours)	II	9	19	37
7. Introductory Composition (3 sec.) (credit: 1 hour)	I	3	23	25
8. Introductory Composition (3 sec.) (credit: 1 hour)	II	3	10	31
13. Recent German Drama	I	3	1	4
14. Recent German Drama	II	3	1	4
17. Goethe's Faust	I	3	3	10
18. Goethe's Faust	II	3	2	10
19. Lessing	I	3	1	15
20. Lessing	II	3	1	14
19 H. Junior Honors Course (3 hours)	I	1	0	1
20 H. Junior Honors Course (3 hours)	II	2	0	1
25. History of German Literature	I	3	3	6
26. History of German Literature	II	3	3	5
27. Advanced Composition (3 sec.) (credit: 1 hour)	I	3	4	20

INSTRUCTOR AND COURSE.	Semester	Teaching Hours per week	Men	Women
28. Advanced Composition (3 sec.) (credit: 1 hour)..............	II	3	3	21
29. Teachers' Training Course.......	I	2	4	3
30. Teachers' Training Course.......	II	2	3	3

Greek

INSTRUCTOR AND COURSE.	Semester	Teaching Hours per week	Men	Women
Professor MARTIN		12		
Assistant Professor ALEXANDER		8		
1. Elementary Greek (credit: 5 hours)	I	4	6	16
2. Elementary Greek (credit: 5 hours)	II	4	3	16
3. Freshman Greek.................	I	3	6	9
4. Freshman Greek.................	II	3	3	8
17. Aristophanes, Theocritus.........	I	3	0	2
18. Aristophanes, Theocritus.........	II	3	1	1

History

INSTRUCTOR AND COURSE.	Semester	Teaching Hours per week	Men	Women
Professor HALL		17		
Professor D. R. MOORE		22		
Professor MOSHER		4		
Assistant Professor ALEXANDER		6		
Mr. H. L. KING		18		
1. History of Greece and Rome......	I	3	13	19
2. History of Greece and Rome......	II	3	14	23
21. Introduction to Medieval and Modern European History (3 sec.) (credit: 3 hours).............	I	7	39	27
22. Introduction to Medieval and Modern European History (3 sec.) (credit: 3 hours).............	II	7	47	43
31. Medieval Civilization, Renaissance, and Reformation..............	I	2	14	15
32. Medieval Civilization, Renaissance, and Reformation..............	II	2	13	14
37. European History Since 1815.....	I	3	27	36
38. European History Since 1815.....	II	3	27	27
37 H. Honors Course in European History Since 1815 (credit: 2 hours) .... (3 hours).....................	I ·	1 ·	2 3	0 3
38 H. Honors Course in European History Since 1815 (credit: 2 hours) .... (3 hours).....................	II ·	1 ·	1 3	0 3
47. Seminar and Teachers' Training Course	I	2	7	4
48. Seminar and Teachers' Training Course	II	2	7	4

INSTRUCTOR AND COURSE	Semester	Teaching Hours per week	Men	Women
61. American History (credit: 3 hours)	I	4	32	31
62. American History (credit: 3 hours)	II	4	37	27
65. Slavery in Arms................	I	2	6	3
66. Slavery in Arms................	II	2	5	3
81 English History................	I	3	18	20
82. English History (credit: 3 hours).	IJ	4	22	35
95. History Club: Current Events (2 sec.) (credit: 2 hours)........		4	13	10
96. History Club: Current Events (2 sec.) (credit: 2 hours)........	Iı	4	12	9
97. Seminar and Teachers' Training Course	I	2	2	2
98. Seminar and Teachers' Training Course	II	2	3	2

Latin

INSTRUCTOR AND COURSE	Semester	Teaching Hours per week	Men	Women
Professor LORD		22		
Professor COLE		11		
Associate Professor SHAW		12		
Associate Professor HOSFORD		6		
Assistant Professor ALEXANDER		10		
— Cæsar	I	3	6	18
— Cæsar	II	3	6	17
1. Cicero's Orations, Vergil's Aeneid.	I	3	11	18
2. Cicero's Orations, Vergil's Aeneid.	II	3	9	20
3. Vergil's Aeneid, Horace's Odes...	I	3	5	10
4. Vergil's Aeneid, Horace's Odes...	II	3	5	12
5. Cicero, Terence, Horace (3 sec.) (credit: 3 hours).............	I	9	20	76
6. Cicero, Terence, Horace (3 sec.) (credit: 3 hours)'.............	II	9	17	77
7. Cautullus, Plautus, Cicero........	I	3	0	8
8. Catallus, Plautus, Cicero........	II	3	0	8
11. Latin Writing	I	2	0	12
12. The Private Life of the Romans...	II	2	0	18
15. Latin Literature of the Republic..	I	3	2	9
16. Latin Literature of the Republic..	II	3	2	9
21 H. Honors Course..................	I	2	0	8
22 H. Honors Course..................	II	2	0	6
23. Teachers' Training Course.......	I	2	1	13
24. Teachers' Training Course.......	II	2	1	12
23 H. Honors Course (1 hour)..........	I	.	0	3
24 H. Honors Course (2 hours).........	II	1	0	2

INSTRUCTOR AND COURSE	Semester	Teaching Hours per week	Men	Women
Mathematics				
Professor ANDEREGG		22		
Associate Professor SINCLAIR		31		
Mr. CARR		36		
Mrs. HARROUN		12		
1 A. Advanced Algebra (2 sec.) (credit: 3 hours)	I	6	17	22
2 A. Advanced Algebra	II	3	6	9
1 G. Geometry: Solid and Spherical (4 sec.) (credit: 3 hours)	I	12	34	35
2 G. Geometry: Solid and Spherical (2 sec.) (credit: 3 hours)	II	6	13	23
3. Trigonometry (6 sec.) (credit: 3 hours)	I	18	103	68
4. Trigonometry (2 sec.) (credit: 3 hours)	II	6	29	28
5. Plane Analytic Geometry	I	3	8	7
6 A. Plane Analytic Geometry (6 sec.) (credit: 3 hours)	II	18	82	54
6 B. College Algebra	II	3	16	15
11. Advanced Analytic Geometry	I	2	3	3
12. Advanced Analytic Geometry	II	2	2	3
13. Calculus	I	3	14	4
14. Calculus	II	3	11	3
15. Theory of Equations	I	3	1	4
16. Theory of Equations	II	3	1	4
25. Analytic Mechanics	I	3	4	0
26. Analytic Mechanics	II	3	3	0
32. History of Mathematics	II	2	1	4
33. Seminar	I	1	0	7
34. Seminar	I	1	0	6
Music				
Professor DICKINSON		24		
21. History and Criticism of Music (2 sec.) (credit: 3 hours)	I	8	1	3
22. History and Criticism of Music (2 sec.) (credit: 3 hours)	II	8	1	6
23. The Appreciation of Music (credit: 2 hours)	I	3	31	48
24. The Appreciation of Music (credit: 2 hours)	II	3	21	48
26. History of Music: Advanced (credit: 3 hours)	II	2	0	1

INSTRUCTOR AND COURSE	Semester	Teaching Hours per week	Men	Women
Oratory				
Professor CASKEY			24	
1. General Course (2 sec.) (credit: 3 hours)	I	6	32	15
2. Oratory (2 sec.) (credit: 3 hours)	II	6	24	10
4. General Course	II	3	8	4
5. Literary Interpretation	I	3	0	1
6. Dramatic Reading	II	3	5	12
7. Dramatic Reading	I	3	0	3
Philosophy				
Professor MacLENNAN			16	
Associate Professor KITCH			24	
Assistant Professor NICOL			6	
1. Introduction to Philosophy	I	3	7	24
2. Introduction to Philosophy	II	3	15	17
4. Logic	II	3	9	6
5. Ethics (2 sec.) (credit: 3 hours)	I	6	14	30
6. Ethics	II	3	9	21
7. History of Philosophy	I	3	8	14
8. History of Philosophy	II	3	9	14
13. General Ethics: Evolution of Morality	I	3	4	4
14. General Ethics: Evolution of Morality	II	3	4	4
15. General History of Philosophy	I	3	5	0
16. General History of Philosophy	II	3	4	0
17. Contemporary Philosophy	I	3	3	4
18. Contemporary Philosophy	II	3	2	4
23. The Evolution of Religion	I	2	1	1
24. The Evolution of Religion	II	2	1	1
Physical Education (for credit)				
Professor SAVAGE			12	
Mrs. HATCH			24	
Miss ELDRED			16	
Miss BOWEN			8	
Mr. KELLER			12	
Mr. CURTIS			6	
Mr. MACLURE			6	
1. Elementary Course (8 sec.) (credit: 1 hour)	I	28	161	216
2. Elementary Course (8 sec.) (credit: 1 hour)	II	28	160	199

INSTRUCTOR AND COURSE	Semester	Teaching Hours per week	Men	Women
3. Advanced Course (4 sec.) (credit: 1 hour)	I	14	34	64
4. Advanced Course (4 sec.) (credit: 1 hour)	II	14	25	55

Teachers' Course in Physical Education

INSTRUCTOR AND COURSE	Semester	Teaching Hours per week	Men	Women
Professor LEONARD		13		
Professor HANNA		5		
Professor SAVAGE		8		
Associate Professor COCHRAN		6		
Mrs. HATCH		12		
Miss ELDRED		s 2, R10		
Miss BOWEN		s27, R 7		
Mr. KELLER		1		
5. Theory of Play and Games	I	2	0	22
6. Organization and Administration of Play (credit: 1 hour)	II	3	0	21
7. Human Anatomy 1 (credit: 3 hours)	I	2	9	20
8. Theory of Physical Education	II	3	11	19
12. Human Anatomy 2	II	1	0	19
13. Advanced Physical Education (credit: 1 hour)	I	4	10	0
14. Advanced Physical Education (credit: 1 hour)	II	4	12	0
15. Junior Practical Work (credit: 1 hour)	I	3	0	22
16. Junior Practical Work (credit: 1 hour)	II	3	0	21
17. History and Literature of Physical Education	I	2	4	11
18. History and Literature of Physical Education (credit: 2 hours)	II	1	3	11
19. Theory of Games	I	1	3	0
20. Theory of Games	II	1	3	0
22. Physical Examination and the Prescription of Exercise (credit: 1 hour)	II	2	3	0
23. Medical Gymnastics 1 (credit: 3 hours)	I	2	0	13
24. Medical Gymnastics 2 (credit: 1 hour)	II	4	0	12
25. Physical Examination and Diagnosis (credit: 2 hours)	I	3	0	13
26. Emergencies	II	1	0	12

INSTRUCTOR AND COURSE	Semester	Teaching Hours per week	Men	Women
27. Practical Work and Teaching (credit: 1 hour)	I	.	5	0
28. Practical Work and Teaching (credit: 1 hour)	II	.	4	0
29. Senior Practical Work and Teaching (credit: 2 hours)	I	10	0	14
30. Senior Practical Work and Teaching (credit: 2 hours)	II	10	0	14

Physics

Professor WILLIAMS		L48, R 6		
Associate Professor E. J. MOORE		L18, R12		
1. General Physics (credit: 4 hours).	I	L12, R 3	33	24
2. General Physics (credit: 4 hours).	II	L12, R 3	32	21
3. Advanced General Physics (credit: 5 hours)	I	L 6, R 3	5	2
4. Advanced General Physics (credit: 5 hours)	II	L 6, R 3	6	1
7 Advanced Laboratory Course (credit: 3 hours)	I	L 9	5	0
8. Advanced Laboratory Course (credit: 2 hours)	II	L21	1	0
(credit: 3 hours)	.	.	7	0
(credit: 4 hours)	.	.	1	0
11. Electricity and Magnetism: Molecular Physics	I	3	3	0
12. Electricity and Magnetism: Molecular Physics	II	3	3	0

Physiology and Hygiene

Professor LEONARD				
1. Physiology and Hygiene	I	3	16	31
2. Physiology and Hygiene	II	3	13	26

Political Science

Professor GEISER		20		
1. American Government	I	3	40	40
2. American Government	II	3	37	35
5. Elements of Jurisprudence	I	3	10	0
6. Municipal Government	II	3	25	5
7. International Law	I	2	28	1
8. American Diplomacy	II	2	22	1
13. Seminar	I	2	8	0
14. Seminar	II	2	9	0

INSTRUCTOR AND COURSE	Semester	Teaching Hours per week	Men	Women
Psychology				
Professor STETSON		L20, R20		
Associate Professor WELLS		L20, R18		
Assistant Professor NICOL		3		
1. Introductory Psychology (4 sec.) (credit: 3 hours)	I	12	44	65
2. Introductory Psychology (4 sec.) (credit: 3 hours)	II	12	34	61
3. Advanced General Psychology	I	3	2	0
7. Experimental Psychology (credit: 2 hours)	I	L18, R 1	2	1
(credit: 3 hours)	·	· ·	7	3
8. Experimental Psychology (credit: 2 hours)	II	L12	2	4
(credit: 3 hours)	·	·	4	1
9. Experimental Psychology of Education (credit: 2 hours)	I	L 6	0	5
(credit: 3 hours)	·	·	0	1
10. Experimental Psychology of Education (credit: 3 hours)	II	L 4	0	1
10 H. Senior Honors Course (3 hours)	II	·	1	0
11. Aesthetics: The Psychology of Art	I	2	3	3
12. Abnormal Psychology	II	3	6	8
15. Psychology of Development and Training	I	3	0	8
16. Psychology of Education	II	3	5	13
22. Seminar	II	2	5	2
21 H. Junior Honors Course (2 hours)	I	·	2	0
22 H. Junior Honors Course (2 hours)	II	·	1	0
Sociology				
Professor H. A. MILLER		20		
1. Introduction to Sociology	I	3	21	70
2. Social Problems	II	3	31	108
15. Social Organization	I	3	7	9
16. Immigration and the Immigrant	II	3	13	18
18. The History of Sociological Theory	II	2	4	7
19. The Race Problem	I	2	13	24
21. Seminar	I	2	5	9
22. Seminar	II	2	6	7
Spanish				
Professor WIGHTMAN		8		
1. Grammar, Reader	I	4	5	18
2. Spanish Prose of the Nineteenth Century	II	4	5	16

INSTRUCTOR AND COURSE	Semester	Teaching Hours per week	Men	Women
Zoology				
Professor BUDINGTON		L43, R16		
Professor ROGERS		L49, R 9		
Associate Professor JONES		L22, R13		
Miss FREDERICK		L 9		
1. General Zoölogy (credit: 4 hours)	I	L15, R 3	31	30
2. General Zoölogy (credit: 4 hours)	II	L13, R 3	30	29
3. Zoölogy of Invertebrates (credit: 5 hours)	I	L 6, R 3	4	4
4. Zoölogy of Vertebrates (credit: 5 hours)	II	L 7, R 3	7	3
9. Histology and Microscopical Technique (credit: 4 hours)	I	L 3, R 1	1	0
10. Histology and Microscopical Technique (credit: 2 hours)	II	L 2	1	0
13 H. Advanced Course (credit: 3 hours)	I	L 9	0	1
14 H. Advanced Course (credit: 3 hours)	II	L 5	0	1
16. Cytology and Embryology (credit: 5 hours)	II	L 9, R 2	3	5
19. Comparative Physiology (credit: 5 hours)	I	L12, R 2	4	3
20 H. Experimental Zoölogy (credit: 5 hours)	I	L 4, R 2	2	0
23 H. Advanced Course (credit: 5 hours)	I	L 6, R 1	2	0
24 H. Advanced Course (credit: 6 hours)	II	L10	2	1
25 H. The Classics of Zoölogy (2 hours)	I		1	0	1
27. Seminar	I		2	5	2
28. Seminar	II		2	5	2
30. Ornithology: Beginning Course (2 sec.) (credit: 2 hours)	II	L12, R 4	27	102
31. Ornithology: Advanced Course (credit: 2 hours)	I	L 2, R 2	1	3
32. Ornithology: Seminar (credit: 1 hour)	II	1	3	3
(credit: 2 hours)	.	.	1	2
35. Ecology (credit: 4 hours)	I	L 4, R 3	2	2
36. Ecology (credit: 4 hours)	II	L 4, R 3	2	3

II. THE GRADUATE SCHOOL OF THEOLOGY

Old Testament

Professor FULLERTON		18			
3. History of Israel	I		3	24	1
4. History of Israel	II		3	21	1
7. Hebrew (credit: 5 hours)	I		4	4	0
8. Hebrew (credit: 5 hours)	II		4	4	0
11a. The Psalms in English	I		2	2	1
14. Genesis	II		2	6	1

New Testament

Professor BOSWORTH		17			
1. Teaching of Jesus and Primitive Christian Theology	I		3	25	0
2. Teaching of Jesus and Primitive Christian Theology	II		3	26	0
7. Gospel of Mark (credit: 5 hours)	I		4	18	1
8. Gospel of Mark (credit: 5 hours)	II		4	15	0
10. Romans or Hebrews	I		3	2	1

Philosophy of Religion and Christian Ethics

Professor LYMAN		14			
Professor MACLENNAN		6			
1. Contemporary Philosophy	I		3	1	0
2. Contemporary Philosophy	II		3	2	0
3. Philosophy of Religion	I		3	20	0
4. Philosophy of Religion	II		3	21	0
5. Christian Ethics	I		2	17	3
6. Christian Ethics	II		2	18	5
9. Psychology of Religion	I		2	8	0
10. Present Problems of Religious Thought	II		2	14	1

Church History

Professor HANNAH		5			
2. History of the Reformation	II		3	11	0
4. Medieval Church History	II		2	10	0

INSTRUCTOR AND COURSE	Semester	Teaching Hours per week	Men	Women
Systematic Theology				
President KING		10		
Professor LYMAN		4		
1. Theological Introduction.........	I	2	16	0
2. The Work of Preaching..........	II	3	14	0
3. Systematic Theology, Critical and Constructive	I	3	17	1
4. Systematic Theology, Critical and Constructive	II	3	17	1
5. Seminar in Theology.............	I	2	10	1
6. Seminar in Theology.............	II	2	8	1
Homiletics				
Professor HUTCHINS		16		
1. The Work of Preaching..........	I	3	12	1
2. The Work of Preaching..........	I	3	14	0
3. A Year's Preaching.............	I	2	9	0
4. A Year's Preaching.............	II	2	10	0
5. Biblical Homiletics.............	I	2	17	0
6. Practical Preaching (credit: ½ hour)	II	2	7	0
7. Assembly Hour (credit: ½ hour).	I	1	47	0
8. Assembly Hour (credit: ½ hour).	II	1	47	1
Practical Theology and Religious Education				
Professor FISKE		13		
2. Church Polity..................	II	1	14	1
3. Church Administration..........	I	3	13	1
4. Church Administration..........	II	3	23	1
5. The Social Gospel (credit: 2 or 3 hours)	I	2	16	0
7. Social Evangelism. The Country Community	I	2	10	0
9. Field Work....................	I	.	42	2
10. Field Work....................	II	.	39	1
12. Religious Education (credit: 2 or 3 hours)	II	2	21	0
Comparative Religion and Christian Missions				
Professor HUTCHINS		2		
Professor MacLENNAN		6		
1. The Evolution of Religion........	I	2	3	0

INSTRUCTOR AND COURSE	Semester	Teaching Hours per week	Men	Women
. The Evolution of Religion........	II	2	3	0
. Comparative Religion............	I	2	2	0
6. Modern Missions...............	II	2	7	1

Elocution

Professor NASH		2		
1. Public Speaking (credit: ½ hour)	I	1	10	0
2. Public Speaking (credit: ½ hour)	II	1	9	0

Slavic Department

Professor MISKOVSKY		22		
Psychology	I	5	4	0
Ethics	II	5	4	0
Bohemian Bible...................	I	5	4	0
Bohemian Bible...................	II	5	4	0
English	I	2	1	0

REPORT OF THE TREASURER

CONTENTS OF TREASURER'S REPORT

TREASURER'S STATEMENT

To the Board of Trustees of Oberlin College:

The Treasurer of the College submits his annual statement for the year ending August 31, 1917, as follows:

INVESTMENT FUNDS

SPECIAL INVESTMENTS

	Principal August 31, 1917	Net Income
Springer Fund—		
Cleveland real estate....................	$ 4,438.50	$170.35
Carroll Cutler Fellowship—		
American Real Estate Co. Bond. $2,794.17		
Cash 2,785.83		
	5,580.00	120.49
Totals	$10,018.50	$290.84

GENERAL INVESTMENTS

The other funds are invested as a whole. A list in detail of all investments will be found beginning on page 341 of this report.

The net income of general investments for the year is as follows:

From investments interest.........................	$ 88,384.53
From interest, other sources........................	14,633.07
From interest Shedd Fund loans....................	330.10
From rents	14,799.24
From West Virginia oil lands.....................	341.39
	$118,488.33

Less		
Loan expense items...............	$ 155.72	
The Cleveland Trust Co., commission.	3,314.35	3,470.07
Net income		$115,018.26

The net income of general investments was distributed at the rate of 4.325% to those funds sharing in general investments.

The following table shows the income and expense for the year and the accumulated deficits, by departments:

	Income	Expense	Deficit 1916-17	Accumulated Deficit
University ....$	82,826.89	$113,049.07	$30,897.29	$ 49,357.13
College of Arts and Sciences	133,106.84	146,012.24	13,110.17	37,678.19
Graduate School of Theology	26,275.23	22,882.79	1,647.56	4,820.19
Conservatory of Music	94,318.19	94,318.19		
Academy				22,378.42
	$336,527.15	$376,262.29	$45,655.02	$114,233.93
Income unexpended...	5,919.88			
		330,607.27		
Deficit		$ 45,655.02		

The cost of operating the Central Heating Plant for the year was as follows:

Labor ....$	3,888.60
Coal	18,206.78
Supplies and repairs....................	1,084.31
Telephones	36.00
Water	167.60
Lights and power.......................	173.72
Interest on advances for construction......	4,974.00
Sundries	26.80
	$28,557.81

This expense was distributed according to radiation and heating hours and is shown in the expense accounts of buildings in the various departments.

GIFTS OF THE YEAR

GIFTS FOR CURRENT USE

From Miss Joanna M. Binford, $5.00 for current expense.

From Mrs. Joseph P. Noyes, $1.00 for current expense.

From A. Eilers, $50.00 for the department of Geology.

From William A. Bowen, $25.00 to purchase reproductions of Greek coins.

From classes in Ancient Art, $16.50 for the department of Art and Archaeology.

From The Association for International Conciliation, $250.00 to provide a course in "International Relations" in the Summer Session.

From the Oberlin Association of New York, $995.00 for military and Red Cross training expenses.

From Irving W. Metcalf, $5.25 for labels for pictures in Park Hotel.

From an anonymous donor, $35.00 for expenses of lecture on Political Science.

From John L. Severance, $10,000.00, balance of his gift for the site of the Art Building.

From Mrs. Elisabeth S. Prentiss, $62,510.16, additional for the construction of the Art Building.

From the Carnegie Foundation for the Advancement of Teaching, $7,105.04 for retiring allowances.

From J. D. Cox, $12,866.00, the amount of the cost of the Administration Building in excess of funds previously furnished by him.

From members of the class of '91, $844.59 to purchase the Guy Stevens Callender collection for the Library. In addition to this amount, $200.00 has been received from the class as a permanent fund, the income to be used for the care of the collection.

From members of the Living Endowment Union, $3,732.01. As designated by certain donors, $200.00 was added to the Class of '89 Fund, and is shown in the gifts to capital; $100.00 was credited to the Physical Laboratory, $10.00 was credited to the Library, $1.00 was credited to the Summer Camp, $10.50 was credited to the department of Physical Education for Women, and the balance, $3,410.51 was used for scholarship aid.

For the Athletic Field from—

Cleveland R. Cross	$ 25.00
E. A. Miller	10.00
J. P. Robertson	2.50
	$ 37.50

For the Summer Camp from—

Mrs. Augusta J. Street	$ 5.00
Miss Georgina B. Allison	10.00
Mrs. Maud M. Wolfe	5.00
Miss Ruth Acker	5.00
	$ 25.00

For the Student Employment Fund from—

Frank M. Wilson.................................$	25.00
Mrs. Sarah E. Woolworth.........................	5.00
Henry W. Farnam	100.00
Thomas Henderson	100.00
Charles E. Harwood	100.00
Second Congregational Church of Oberlin...........	100.00
C. W. Grupe.....................................	5.00
Mrs. Martha A. Brooks...........................	5.00

$ 440.00

For special scholarship aid from—

F. S. Cunningham ....$	45.00
Wells L. Griswold................................	25.00
N. C. Kingsbury.................................	50.00
A. F. Estabrook.................................	100.00
R. T. Miller....................................	100.00
H. H. Lauderdale................................	150.00
Mrs. J. F. Crumbie..............................	110.00
Mrs. Etta F. Miller.............................	75.00
John T. Reeder..................................	10.00
Mrs. I. F. Blackstone...........................	100.00
Mrs. E. B. Monroe...............................	60.00
Mr. and Mrs. W. Spencer Bowen..................	50.00
New England alumni.............................	87.50
Cleveland alumni	69.00
J. H. McCord...................................	100.00
W. O. Jones....................................	10.00
Estate of Sidney Shepard........................	100.00
Warren H. Wilson...............................	40.00
Mrs. W. H. Crosby..............................	50.00
Mrs. Ada C. Gates..............................	150.00
C. W. Seiberling................................	200.00

$1,681.50

The total amount of these gifts for current use is $100,424.55. This amount is distributed in the statement of income and expense among the following accounts:

University ....$	1,001.00
Library	760.00
University, special accounts..............	86,509.54
College of Arts and Sciences.............	3,410.51
College, special accounts.................	4,823.50
Graduate School of Theology, special accounts	3,920.00

$100,424.55

GIFTS TO CAPITAL

To form new funds or increase old ones

From Charles S. Brown, $50.00 for the Endowment Union Fund.

From H. H. Johnson, $150.00 for the Anderegg Loan Fund.

From A. H. Noah, $1,000.00 to be added to the A. H. Noah Loan Fund.

From the Class of '89, $210.00 for endowment.

From the Estate of Miss Laura C. Holbrook, $7,763.75, her undesignated bequest to Oberlin College.

From William A. Bowen, $200.00 for endowment of the Graduate School of Theology.

From the Class of '98, $14.00 for endowment.

From the Trustees of the Estate of Charles M. Hall, $100,000.00, part of his bequest to establish an endowment fund for the care of the campus and other grounds.

From the Class of '91, $200.00 to establish the Callender Collection Fund in the Library.

From Miss Mary J. Brown and Miss Carrie Brown, $2,000.00 to found the Anna B. Gray scholarship for women, at present carrying an annuity.

The total of these gifts to capital account is $111,587.75. This amount is distributed in the statement of receipts and payments among the following accounts:

University $111,387.75
Graduate School of Theology.............	200.00
	$111,587.75

BALANCE SHEET

August 31, 1917

ASSETS

INVESTMENT—

Notes and mortgages.............................$	394,709.42
Bonds	919,899.39
Stocks	354,317.00
Short time notes	19,050.00
Collateral loans	62,912.22
Real estate	408,549.99
University houses and lands......................	240,358.11
Bills receivable	28,001.02
Advances for purchase, construction, and repair of College properties	356,404.80
Cash in hands of Trustee for investment............	138.90

Total investment assets $2,784,340.85	
Student loan fund notes.........................	24,489.32

CURRENT—

General supplies	8,499.74
Insurance prepaid	2,133.84
Advances to various accounts.....................	182,818.29
Deposits subject to check and cash................	27,655.26

	$3,029,937.30

DEFICITS	114,233.93

Total assets except buildings and equipment.........$3,144,171.23	
BUILDINGS AND EQUIPMENT (less included in advances)....	2,039,513.32

	$5,183,684.55

The above assets are stated in detail beginning on page 341.

BALANCE SHEET

August 31, 1917

LIABILITIES

ENDOWMENT FOR CURRENT EXPENSE—
University $1,226,713.85	
Library 203,575.26	
College of Arts and Sciences............ 419,584.95	
Graduate School of Theology........... 566,344.16	
Conservatory of Music................. 41,419.50	

$2,457,637.72

SCHOLARSHIP FUNDS—
University ....$ 67,271.00	
College of Arts and Sciences............ 43,869.79	
Graduate School of Theology........... 71,541.95	
Conservatory of Music................. 2,450.00	

185,132.74

Student loan funds (income only loaned)............	13,000.00
SPECIAL FUNDS	34,640.58
ANNUITY FUNDS	93,929.81

$2,784,340.85

STUDENT LOAN FUNDS...............................	27,419.22

CURRENT ACCOUNTS—
Income unexpended	20,968.03
Sundry balances	121,443.13
Bills payable	190,000.00

$3,144,171.23

EDUCATIONAL PLANT CAPITAL ACCOUNT..................	2,039,513.32

$5,183,684.55

The above liabilities are stated in detail beginning on page 331.

COMPARATIVE STATEMENT

The following is a comparative statement of the Endowment, Scholarship and Loan Funds, and Total Assets of the College including Buildings, Grounds and Equipment:

Year	Endowment	Scholarship and Loan Funds	Total Endowment Assets	Total Assets Including Buildings, Grounds, and Equipment
1855.....	$ 84,450.58	$	$ 84,450.58	$ ....
1875.....	159,787.34	9,045.00	168,832.34	333,832.34
1895.....	680,523.15	55,345.18	735,868.33	1,612,415.86
1905.....	1,254,399.45	91,934.75	1,346,334.20	2,422,660.33
1910.....	1,729,747.26	112,825.71	1,842,572.97	3,524,272.36
1911.....	1,841,678.26	115,874.51	1,957,552.77	3,754,400.04
1912.....	2,139,657.95	164,862.55	2,304,550.50	4,161,782.62
1913.....	2,151,072.87	172,827.64	2,323,900.51	4,207,868.07
1914.....	2,156,488.91	171,944.39	2,328,433.30	4,265,898.88
1915.....	2,223,609.82	185,343.92	2,408,953.74	4,389,934.57
1916.....	2,343,148.80	193,863.80	2,537,012.60	4,787,181.03
1917.....	2,457,637.72	225,551.96	2,683,189.68	5,183,684.55

In addition to the above endowment funds having a total of $2,457,-637.72, a fund of $50,000.00 has been placed with The Cleveland Trust Company, as Trustee, the income of which is available for expenses of the College for health service. There is also a fund of $100,000.00 with The Cleveland Trust Company, as Trustee, the income of which is available for the purposes of the Adelia A. F. Johnston Professorship of Art.

LIST OF ACCOUNTS

The accounts hereinafter presented are:

First, a set of tables showing the current income and expense of each Department in detail. (See pages 315-330.)

Second, a list of all the Funds and Balances in the care of the Treasurer, showing their amounts at the beginning and at the end of the year. (See pages 331-340.)

Third, a classified list of the properties, or assets in which the Funds and Balances are invested. (See pages 341-346.)

Fourth, a list of buildings, grounds, apparatus, etc., in use for College purposes, not valued on the Treasurer's books. (See page 347.)

HIRAM B. THURSTON,

Treasurer.

Oberlin, Ohio,
November 16, 1917.

TREASURER'S ACCOUNTS

INCOME AND EXPENSE

UNIVERSITY

INCOME

From invested funds.........................$	47,711.77
From the Trustee of the Dudley P. Allen Fund	3,564.73
From the Trustee of the Johnston Professorship of Art (part)........................	625.00
From boarding halls........................	950.00
From diploma fees.........................	422.00

From Men's Gymnasium—

Term bills ....$	888.00	
Other fees and rentals..........	401.00	
Athletic Association.............	450.00	
		1,739.00

From Women's Gymnasium—

Term bills $1,791.00		
Other fees and rentals.......... 35.00		
		1,826.00

From Men's Building—

Fees $2,447.50		
Room rents 4,047.66		
		6,495.16

From Slavic Department....................	75.00
From Conservatory of Music................	1,000.00
From interest on subscriptions to endowment..	101.00
From rent of Chapel.......................	415.00
From gifts for current expense..............	1,001.00

For the Library—

From invested funds....................	8,795.98
From income Zoölogical Laboratory Fund.	173.00
From dividend G. F. Harvey Co..........	100.00
From Village of Oberlin................	1,600.00
From interest on subscriptions to endowment	6.00

From department appropriations—
College $3,751.50
Graduate School of Theology.. 204.00
Conservatory of Music........ 300.00
Slavic Department 40.00
                                          4,295.50
From Olney Art Gallery................. 175.00
From registration fees................. 213.00
From examination fees................. 258.00
From fines 271.50
From sale of books 253.25
From gifts for current expense........... 760.00

    Total income ....$ 82,826.89

EXPENSE

President's Office—
Salaries ....$ 8,399.71
Stationery, printing, and postage—
President $288.19
Assistant 285.81
                              574.00

Traveling expenses—
President $365.50
Assistant 286.88
                              652.38
                                          $ 9,626.09
Secretary's Office—
*Salaries ....$ 2,870.00
*Clerks 659.39
*Miscellaneous printing 807.92
*Postage 461.89
*Catalogue 988.72
Annual Reports 1,612.48
Alumni Trustee election..... 306.35
Advertising—
Clerks $355.00
Publicity 364.52
Calendars 847.28
                              1,566.80
                                          9,273.55
Treasurer's Office—
Salaries ....$ 4,225.80
Stationery, p r i n t i n g, and
postage 496.45
Auditing books 143.80
Bond of Treasurer 50.00
                                          4,916.05

*Part. Balance is charged in College Department.

Library—
Salaries ....$	12,760.17	
Books and periodicals.......	6,363.90	
Reprints	102.64	
Stationery, p r i n t i n g, and postage	251.15	
Library of Congress cards...	400.00	
Binding	1,324.91	
Express, freight, etc.........	261.33	
Supplies	813.82	
Special book stacks........	84.00	
		22,361.92

Men's Gymnasium—
Salaries ....$	3,458.00	
Stationery, p r i n t i n g, and postage	44.97	
Clerks	37.55	
Apparatus	27.14	
		3,567.66

Women's Gymnasium—
Salaries ....$	3,000.00	
Stationery, p r i n t i n g, and postage	48.81	
Apparatus	44.34	
Music	58.85	
		3,152.00

Art Museum—
Director ....$	625.00	
Custodian ....·...	60.00	
		685.00

Buildings and Grounds, Care and Repair—
General expense—
Salaries ....$	1,677.50	
Stationery, print- ing, and postage	19.77	
General supplies..	136.03	
Care and supplies for horse	286.16	
Carpenter shop...	920.05	
Miscellaneous	474.47	
	——$	3,513.98

Campus—
Labor and supplies$	2,561.72	
Lights	116.45	
	2,678.17	
Academy	493.49	
Arboretum	42.85	

Library—
   Janitors $1,201.00
   Heat 2,416.13
   Lights and power. 1,337.39
   Water 172.55
   Telephone 27.00
   Insurance 93.50
   Supplies a n d re-
     pairs 812.73
   Interest on advance 890.31
                 6,950.61

Men's Gymnasium—
   Janitors ....$ 545.50
   Custodians 212.05
   Heat 2,776.10
   Lights and power 438.17
   Water 194.60
   Telephone 36.00
   Insurance 57.80
   Grounds 5.00
   Supplies a n d re-
     pairs 798.47
   Interest on advances 263.17
                 5,326.86

Women's Gymnasium—
   Janitors ....$ 345.68
   Heat 752.12
   Lights 175.66
   Water 82.35
   Telephone 25.00
   Insurance 17.00
   Grounds 126.40
   Supplies a n d re-
     pairs 361.63
   Payment on ad-
     vances 193.00
   Interest on advances 18.67
                 2,097.51

Art Museum—
   Janitors ....$ 54.94
   Heat 2,491.80
   Lights and power 90.12
   Telephone 2.50
   Supplies and re-
     pairs 472.94
                 3,112.30

Administration Building—
Janitors ....$ 720.00
Heat 363.34
Lights 93.19
Water 40.50
Telephones 194.75
Insurance 3.40
Supplies and re-
pairs 112.21
Interest on site. 295.00
                            1,822.39

Superintendent's Office—
Janitors ....$ 103.00
Heat 120.84
Lights 8.71
Water 5.00
Telephones 37.50
Supplies and re-
pairs 113.30
                            388.35

Chapel--
Janitors ....$ 360.00
Heat 1,707.81
Lights and power. 512.76
Water 50.05
Insurance 76.50
Supplies and re-
pairs 439.89
Interest on ad-
vances 1,529.58
                            4,676.59

Men's Building—
Janitors $1,370.03
Custodians 1,000.00
Heat 3,096.57
Lights and power. 943.94
Water 862.50
Telephone 39.00
Insurance 73.10
Billiard tables tax 60.00
Laundry 98.38
New equipment.... 95.21
Supplies a n d re-
pairs 1,767.24
Interest on ad-
vances 827.12
Special expense... 65.20
                            10,298.29
                                        41,401.39

Outside representation		330.55
Alumni Dinner (net)....................		749.13

Olney Art Gallery—

Custodian ....$	325.00	
Janitors	28.75	
Heat and Lights.., ...	175.00	
Telephone	17.50	
Insurance	56.25	
Incidentals	11.73	
Purchases	19.57	
Moving collection	53.19	
		686.99

Sundry Expense—

Monthly lectures ....$	460.00	
Washington birthday reception	170.36	
Commencement	2,169.23	
Y. W. C. A...............	100.00	
Liability insurance	467.81	
Miscellaneous	1,036.61	
Interest on bills payable....	1,775.67	
		6,179.68

Health Service—

Oberlin Hospital ..:........$	750.00	
Detention Hospital	211.03	
Special medical service......	14.00	
Visiting nurse and infirmary..	1,342.71	
		2,317.74

Living Endowment Union—	
Stationery, printing, and postage	46.32
Special annuity payments...................	2,800.00
Special retiring allowances.................	3,960.00
Expenses military and Red Cross training	
(provided by gifts)....................	995.00

Total expense	$113,049.0'

SUMMARY-UNIVERSITY

Total income ....·.....		$ 82,826.89
Less unexpended special income—		
Library $497.10		
Olney art collection............ 178.01		
		675.11
		$ 82,151.78
Total expense		113,049.07
Deficit		$ 30,897.29

Special Accounts—University

RECEIPTS

Interest on funds for special uses—

Art Building furnishings....$	216.25	
Men's Building Reading Room	49.74	
Hannah Snow Lewis........	21.62	
Folts Tract Fund..........	21.63	
Annuity funds	4,482.77	
Scholarship funds	3,385.97	
Noah Loan Fund..........	432.50	
Alvan Drew Loan Fund......	43.25	
Parker Loan Fund	43.25	
		$ 8,696.98

Student loan funds—

Interest on loans...........$	599.77	
Loans repaid	4,705.44	
Entry of notes to establish principal	17,760.57	
		23,065.78

From boarding halls—

Talcott Hall ....$	3,041.79	
Baldwin Cottage...........	3,964.56	
Keep Cottage	2,369.61	
Dascomb Cottage	61.27	
Shurtleff Cottage	935.21	
Allencroft	1,236.18	
Keep Cottage Annex........	510.91	
Ellis Cottage	422.16	
Churchill and Tenney Cottages	162.85	
Barrows House	202.81	
Fairchild House	1,099.40	
		14,006.75

Gifts for capital account—

Endowment $108,237.75		
Loan funds	1,150.00	
Annuity	2,000.00	
		111,387.75

Gifts for current expenses—

J. D. Cox, special gift......$	12,866.00	
Art Building site...........	10,000.00	
Art Building construction....	62,510.16	
Summer Camp	26.00	
Park Hotel	5.25	
Class of '91 Fund..........	94.59	
Retiring allowances	935.04	
Political Science lecture.....	35.00	
Athletic Field	37.50	
		86,509.54

Miscellaneous—
Reserve income of general
    investments ....$ 4,871.66
Sale of tracts 16.33
                    ————————   4,887.99
                              ———————— $248,554.79

PAYMENTS

From funds for special uses—
Art Building furnishings......$ 446.98
Art Building construction..... 62,510.16
Art Building site............. 9,700.60
Men's Building Reading Room.   49.74
Hannah Snow Lewis Fund....   29.65
Foltz Tract Fund.............   35.63
Annuities 8,715.50
Scholarship aid (from income). 3,621.59
Athletic Field (advances re-
    paid) 37.50
Campus Improvement (wrecking
    Society Hall) 754.00
Vocational Secretary 5.64
J. D. Cox Gift—furnishings for
    Administration Building...   2,545.85
Retiring allowance (Carnegie
    Foundation) 935.04
                    ———————— $89,387.88

Student loan funds, loans made............   4,996.50
Boarding Halls—
To University ....$ 950.00
Repairs 7,558.03
Interest on advances.......... 3,259.41
To income of general invest-
    ments (part) 1,079.16
Advances repaid 774.81
Deficit Lord Cottage.........   546.54
                    ————————   14,167.95

Miscellaneous—
Loss and depreciation in value
    of general investments....$14,082.05
Magraugh Fund—by charge off
    advances to annuity and re-
    duction of value of prop-
    erty given to establish fund 5,333.33
Sundry small items..........   202.01
                    ————————   19,617.39
                            ———————— $128,169.72

COLLEGE OF ARTS AND SCIENCES

INCOME

From invested funds.......................	$ 17,978.37
From term bills	104,208.17
From diploma fees	991.00
From change of study fees................	247.00
From the Trustee of the Adelia A. F. Johnston Professorship of Art (part)..............	6,271.79
From Living Endowment Union for scholarship aid	3,410.51

Total income $133,106.84

EXPENSE

Instruction—
Salaries $94,807.27
Reading papers 773.56
$95,580.83

Administration—
Salaries 7,267.00
Clerks—Dean ....$ 731.75
Dean of Men.......... 28.63
Dean of Women........ 134.80
Secretary 1,679.38
Registrar 520.05
Bureau of Appointments 569.12
3,663.73

Stationery, printing, and postage—
Dean ....$ 198.97
Dean of Men.......... 88.54
Dean of Women........ 99.44
Secretary 2,650.45
Registrar 114.45
Bureau of Appointments 123.39
3,275.24

Sundry expense—
Outside representation ....$ 308.34
Diplomas 599.79
Chapel proctors 181.00
Practice teaching, Summer Session 118.50
Practice teaching, College Year. 600.00
Miscellaneous 39.50
1,847.13

Scholarships—
Trustee $6,456.48
Avery 108.00
Oberlin College 4.50
Faculty children 740.00
College teachers 130.00
Graduate 655.00
8,093.98

Buildings and grounds, care and repair—
Peters Hall—

Janitors ....$	998.26	
Heat	2,240.80	
Lights	191.31	
Water	77.65	
Telephone	72.00	
Insurance	119.00	
Supplies and repairs.	680.86	
		$4,379.88

Severance Laboratory—

Janitors ....$	600.00	
Heat	1,416.58	
Lights and power....	187.52	
Water	75.50	
Telephone	21.00	
Insurance	34.00	
Supplies and repairs.	625.00	
		2,959.60

Sturges Hall—

Janitors ....$	96.01	
Heat	530.16	
Lights	10.46	
Water	5.00	
Insurance	13.60	
Paving tax	67.45	
Supplies and repairs.	20.74	
		743.42

Botanical Laboratory—

Janitors ....$	330.00	
Heat	650.32	
Lights	59.90	
Water	18.40	
Telephone	21.00	
Insurance	32.30	
Supplies and repairs.	122.72	
Interest on advances.	51.28	
		1,285.92

Geological Laboratory—

Janitors ....$	270.00	
Heat	295.48	
Lights	9.47	
Water	5.00	
Telephone	15.00	
Insurance	11.90	
Interest on advances.	331.43	
Advances repaid (part)	872.83	
Supplies and repairs.	59.01	
		1,870.12

Spear Laboratory—
    Janitors ....$ 500.00
    Heat 693.57
    Lights 79.25
    Water 32.70
    Telephone 20.50
    Insurance 25.50
    Supplies and repairs.   317.62
    Interest on advances.   6.35
    A d v a n c e s   repaid
      (balance) ....:....   127.17
                        1,802.66

French Hall—
    Janitors ....$ 184.00
    Heat 466.55
    Lights 10.56
    Water 5.00
    Insurance 5.95
    Supplies and repairs.   132.82
                        804.88

Society Hall—
    Janitors ....$ 102.25
    Heat 141.41
    Lights 3.60
    Water 5.00
    Insurance 5.61
    Supplies and repairs.   38.01
                        295.88
                                    14,142.36

Fine Arts (from income Johnston Professorship
    of Art) 4,817.02
Special appropriations—
    Art and Archaeology—Latin....$ 23.00
    Botanical Laboratory 789.00
    Economics 45.00
    Geological Laboratory 345.00
    Geological Museum 180.00
    Greenhouse 50.00
    Herbarium 180.00
    Physical Laboratory 1,160.00
    Physical Education—Women....   28.45
    Psychological Laboratory 180.00
    Sociology 23.00
    Surveying 90.00
    Zoölogical Laboratory 300.00
    Zoölogical Museum 180.00
                        3,573.45
Library, from term bills...................   3,751.50

    Total expense $146,012.24

SUMMARY—COLLEGE

Total expense $146,012.24
Total income $133,106.84
  Less unexpended income Johns-
  ton Professorship of Art....   204.77
                                   ————————   132,902.07

    Deficit .... $ 13,110.17

Special Accounts—College of Arts and Sciences

RECEIPTS

Departmental appropriations ..$3,573.45
  (for detail see College expenses page 325.)
Special practice teaching, Summer Session 118.50
                          ———————— $ 3,691.95

Departmental fees—
  Anatomy ....$ 58.00
  Botanical Laboratory.......   431.50
  Chemical Laboratory........ 3,673.87
  Fine Arts 184.75
  Geological Laboratory.......   129.00
  Ornithology 321.00
  Physical Laboratory.........   435.33
  Summer Session 2,428.00
  Zoölogical Laboratory 603.00
                          ————————   8,264.45

Gifts for—
  Geological Laboratory ......$ 50.00
  Art and Archaeology—Greek.   41.50
  Physical Laboratory 100.00
  Summer Session 250.00
  Physical Education—Women.   10.50
  Special scholarship aid...... 1,681.50
  Retiring allowances......... 2,690.00
                          ————————   4,823.50
Income scholarship funds..............   1,634.06
Scholarship aid repaid...............   181.79
                                   ———————— $ 18,595.75

PAYMENTS

Anatomy .... $ 198.45
Art and Archaeology—Greek...........   .50
Art and Archaeology—Latin...........   53.89
Botanical Laboratory.................   1,089.39
Chemical Laboratory 4,240.84
Economics 32.85
Fine Arts............................   98.55
Geological Laboratory 534.70
Geological Museum 175.70

Physical Laboratory	1,216.10	
Physical Education—Women	28.45	
Physiological Laboratory	265.56	
Psychological Laboratory	156.60	
Greenhouse	10.25	

Summer Session—

Salaries $3,689.08		
Advertising	35.30	
Clerks	12.88	
Stationery, printing, and post-age	76.10	
Sundries	2.75	
	3,816.11	

Surveying	91.40	
Zoölogy Laboratory	948.94	
Zoölogy Museum	174.60	
Retiring allowances (Carnegie Foundation)	2,690.00	
From income of scholarship funds......	1,759.75	
Special scholarship aid (from gifts)....	1,607.80	
Purchase of Oberlin College scholarships	100.00	
		$ 19,703.09

GRADUATE SCHOOL OF THEOLOGY

INCOME

From invested funds......................	$ 24,485.73	
From incidental fees and rent of rooms......	1,724.50	
From diploma fees	65.00	
Total income		$ 26,275.23

EXPENSE

Salaries	$ 14,425.00	
Clerks	585.50	
Stationery, printing, and postage...........	497.92	
Advertising	140.10	
Outside representation and lectures.........	271.25	
Haskell lectures..........................	150.00	
Diplomas	19.35	
Sundry expense	166.20	
Appropriation to Library	204.00	

Council Hall, care and repairs—

Janitors ....$ 705.00		
Heat 1,419.41		
Lights 218.83		
Water 87.55		
Telephones 42.50		
Insurance 72.25		
Supplies and repairs.......... 540.76		
	3,086.30	

Slavic Department—
```
    Salaries .....................$2,000.00
    Student aid...................   717.00
    Term bills of students.........  137.17
    Room rent of students.........   163.00
    Travel, etc. .....:.........       5.00
    Appropriation to University....   75.00
    Appropriation to Library......    40.00
    Use of Council Hall...........   200.00
                                  ----------
                                              3,337.17
```

Total expense............ $ 22,882.79

SUMMARY—GRADUATE SCHOOL OF THEOLOGY

```
Total expense ...................        $ 22,882.79
Total income  .................$26,275.23
  Less unexpended income
  Haskell  Lectureship
     Fund ...........$ 715.00
  Ellen S. James Fund 4,325.00
                     ----------
                                5,040.00
                                          ----------
                                          21,235.23

     Deficit ......................... $  1,647.56
```

Special Accounts—Graduate School of Theology

RECEIPTS

```
Scholarship funds, interest ...............  $  3,094.19
Student Employment Fund, gifts..........        440.00
Graduate School Loan Fund—
    Loans repaid ...............$ 641.56
    By entry of notes to establish
       principal ................ 2,809.00
                                -----------
                                               3,450.56
Haskell Lectureship Fund from royalties....       1.75
Gifts to capital ........................       200.00
From the Carnegie Foundation for the Ad-
    vancement of Teaching...............       3,480.00
                                                         $ 10,666.50
```

PAYMENTS

```
To holders of scholarship orders........  $  3,732.50
Graduate School Loan Fund, loans made        690.00
Retiring allowances (Carnegie Founda-
    tion) ...............................     3,480.00
                                                         $  7,902.50
```

CONSERVATORY OF MUSIC

INCOME

From invested funds	$ 1,315.64	
From term bills	85,647.90	
From recital fees	7,074.65	
From diploma fees	110.00	
From rent Concert Hall	170.00	
Total income		$ 94,318.19

EXPENSE

Salaries	$ 55,127.32	
Musical library	740.56	
Clerks	717.75	
Stationery, printing, and postage	1,041.85	
Advertising	346.63	
Piano and organ tuning and repair	3,047.51	
Purchase of instruments	807.82	
Artist recitals	6,665.25	
Diplomas	39.90	
Sundry expense	244.45	

Building and grounds, care and repair—

Janitors	$1,365.64	
Heat	3,853.89	
Lights	305.32	
Power	982.41	
Water	129.75	
Telephones	51.00	
Insurance	315.50	
Care of grounds	36.98	
Supplies and repairs	1,391.32	
		8,431.81
Faculty children scholarships		85.00
Interest on loan for construction Rice Hall		1,585.58
University appropriation		1,000.00
Library appropriation		300.00
Publicity		50.00
Retiring allowances		2,900.00
Proctors		75.00
Net loss on dormitories		52.44
Rice Memorial Hall, advances repaid		11,059.32
Total expense		$ 94,318.19

SUMMARY—CONSERVATORY OF MUSIC

Total income	$ 94,318.19
Total expense	94,318.19

Special Accounts—Conservatory of Music

RECEIPTS

Loan Fund—
    Loans repaid ....$ 501.00
    Recital fees 84.45
    Income endowment funds.. 475.75
    By entry of loans to estab-
      lish fund 3,429.75
                       —————— $ 4,490.95
Scholarship funds, interest.....   51.90
                                 —————— $ 4,542.85

PAYMENTS

Loan fund, loans made................ $ 680.00
Scholarship aid 51.90
                                 —————— $ 731.90

SUMMARY

RECEIPTS AND PAYMENTS EXCEPT CHANGES OF INVESTMENTS

	Receipts	Payments
University, income and expense..............$	82,826.89	$113,049.07
University, special accounts.................	248,554.79	128,169.72
College of Arts and Sciences, income and expense	133,106.84	146,012.24
College of Arts and Sciences, special accounts..	18,595.75	19,703.09
School of Theology, income and expense......	26,275.23	22,882.79
School of Theology, special accounts..........	10,666.50	7,902.50
Conservatory of Music, income and expense....	94,318.19	94,318.19
Conservatory of Music, special accounts.......	4,542.85 ·	731.90
	$618,887.04	$532,769.50

Deficits—
    University $30,897.29
    College 13,110.17
    Graduate School of Theology.. 1,647.56
                            —————— 45,655.02

                                  $664,542.06
                                  532,769.50

Increase of funds and balances..... $131,772.56

FUNDS AND BALANCES

UNIVERSITY

General Endowment Funds

August 31, 1916		August 31, 1917
$175,588.86	Endowment	$175,588.86
3,000.00	Allen (Jennie) Nurse (1875)..	3,000.00
17,564.89	Alumni (1870)	17,564.89
5,000.00	Ampt (William M.) (1911)...	5,000.00
100,000.00	Anonymous (1906)	100,000.00
500.00	Anonymous (1910)	500.00
5,000.00	Anonymous (1911)	5,000.00
2,500.00	Anonymous (1911)	2,500.00
5,000.00	Anonymous (1915)	5,000.00
10,000.00	Atkinson (Sarah M.) (1908)..	10,000.00
100.00	Baker (Janette W.) (1909)...	100.00
24,475.00	Baldwin (E. I.) (1894).......	24,475.00
10,000.00	Barnes (Kora F.) (1905).....	10,000.00
275.39	Bigelow (Maria B.) (1908)...	275.39
500.00	Billings (Mrs. Frederick) (1910)	500.00
10,000.00	Bissell (Henrietta) (1879)...	10,000.00
500.00	Briggs (Dr. Charles E.) (1911)	500.00
1,505.91	Butler (1882)	1,505.91
100.00	Carrothers (Clara E.) (1909).	100.00
2,315.41	Class of 1889 (1915)..........	2,525.41
2,357.35	Class of 1898 (1905).........	2,371.35
1,000.00	Coffin (C. A.) (1911)........	1,000.00
3,028.26	Cooper (1901)	3,028.26
38,000.00	Dickinson (Julia) (1893).....	38,000.00
4,920.44	Dutton (1881)	4,674.25
1,290.00	Endowment Union (1907)....	1,650.25
37,242.19	Fairchild (James H.) Professorship (1888)	37,242.19
242.70	Finney (1882)	242.70
13,645.76	Firestone (Rose P.) (1902)...	13,645.76
2,525.00	Fowler (Kate) (1911).......	2,525.00
125,000.00	General Education Board (1911)	125,000.00
4,271.00	Gilchrist (1892)	4,271.00
709.68	Gillett (1880)	709.68
50.00	Green (Mrs. Mary Pomeroy) (1911)	50.00
10,175.00	Hall (Charles M.) (1911)....	10,175.00
100,000.00	Hall (Charles M.) (1917)....	100,000.00
2,000.00	Handy (Truman P.) (1899)..	2,000.00
31,019.63	Haskell (Caroline E.) (1905)	31,019.63
1,500.00	Haynes (Celia Morgan) (1911)	1,500.00

Amount carried forward.................. $753,240.53

	Amount brought forward..................	$753,240.53
100.00	Henderson (Thomas) (1911)	100.00
100.00	Hillyer (Appleton R.) (1911)	100.00
	Holbrook (Laura C.) (1917)..	7,763.75
854.00	Hotchkiss (Helen M.) (1902)	854.00
200.00	Hubel (F. A.) (1909)........	200.00
10,000.00	James (Ellen S.) (1911).....	10,000.00
2,000.00	Jenison (Angeline Fisher) (1907)	2,000.00
1,000.00	Jesup (Mrs. M. K.) (1911)...	1,000.00
1,000.00	Keep (Albert) (1911)........	1,000.00
2,997.97	Keith (1904)	2,997.97
48,558.45	Kennedy (John S.) (1909)...	48,558.45
3,871.25	Kimball (Edward D.) (1907).	3,871.25
1,000.00	Kirby (Martha A.) (1911)...	1,000.00
79.14	Latimer (1876)	79.14
1,000.00	Lawson (Victor F.) (1910)..	1,000.00
10,000.00	Lyon (Marcus) (1902).......	10,000.00
1,094.83	McCall (Mary Tilden) (1914)	1,094.83
800.12	McClelland (1903)	800.12
6,500.00	Magraugh (1908)	1,166.67
3,056.97	Martin (Caroline M.) (1912)	3,056.97
5,000.00	Mellon (A. W. and R. B.) (1911)	5,000.00
700.00	Miller (Amos C.) (1911).....	700.00
10,000.00	Nicholl (Lizzie) (1915)......	10,000.00
10,000.00	Olney (1904)	10,000.00
38,500.00	Osborn (William E.) (1901).	38,500.00
100.00	Perkins (Mabel H.) (1911)...	100.00
20,000.00	Plumb (Ralph) (1881).......	20,000.00
2,994.39	Prunty (Mary) (1888).......	2,994.39
47,270.85	Reunion Fund of 1900 (part)	

Class of '38........$	200.00	
Class of '42........	500.00	
Class of '43........	565.00	
Class of '45........	100.00	
Class of '46........	50.00	
Class of '47........	285.00	
Class of '48........	10.00	
Class of '50........	250.00	
Class of '51........	260.00	
Class of '54........	35.00	
Class of '55........	25.00	
Class of '56........	985.00	
Class of '57........	755.00	
Class of '59........	343.00	
Class of '60........	97.76	
Class of '61........	100.00	
Class of '62........	910.00	
Class of '63........	485.00	
Class of '64........	75.00	
Class of '65........	810.00	

mounts carried forward..........$6,840.76		$937,178.07

Amounts brought forward.........$6,840.76 $937,178.07

Class of '66........	266.50	
Class of '67........	455.00	
Class of '70........	1,480.00	
Class of '71........	450.00	
Class of '72........	561.00	
Class of '73........	1,115.00	
Class of '74........	190.00	
Class of '75........	2,698.01	
Class of '76........	858.00	
Class of '77........	562.50	
Class of '78........	9,595.00	
Class of '79........	1,288.45	
Class of '80........	459.00	
Class of '81........	525.25	
Class of '82........	1,400.00	
Class of '83........	3,191.50	
Class of '84........	1,178.20	
Class of '85........	2,650.00	
Class of '86........	624.00	
Class of '87........	464.74	
Class of '88........	380.00	
Class of '89........	2,655.00	
Class of '90........	1,991.50	
Class of '91........	727.00	
Class of '92........	500.50	
Class of '93........	1,260.50	
Class of '94........	854.00	
Class of '95........	90.00	
Class of '96........	365.00	
Class of '97........	958.34	
Class of '99........	636.10—	47,270.85

200,000.00	Rockefeller (John D.) (1902)	200,000.00
500.00	Rogers (J. R.) (1911)........	500.00
85.06	Shaw (1882)	85.06
10,000.00	Shedd (E. A. and C. B.) (1902)	10,000.00
5,000.00	Sherman (John) (1902)......	5,000.00
4,846.10	Smith (Clarissa M.) (1896)...	4,846.10
50.00	Stanley (Helen Talcott) (1911)	50.00
1,000.00	Stokes (Olivia E. P.) (1909).	1,000.00
500.00	Thompson (Mrs. W. R.) (1911)	500.00
100.00	Tracy (Mrs. F. E.) (1909)...	100.00
1,000.00	Vaile (Joel F.) (1911)........	1,000.00
16,000.00	Warner Gymnasium (1902)..	16,000.00
100.00	Webb (Rebecca) (1910).....	100.00
1,033.77	West (1902)	1,033.77
1,000.00	West (E. A.) (1910).........	1,000.00
1,000.00	Wickham (Delos O.) (1911).	1,000.00
50.00	Wrisley (Allen B.) (1911)...	50.00

                                          —————— $1,226,713.85

Amount brought forward................... $1,226,713.85

Library Book Funds

5,724.13	Alden (E. K.) (1899)........	5,724.13
1,000.00	Anonymous (1906)	1,000.00
66,632.00	Anonymous (1908)	66,632.00
100.00	Andrews (1900)	100.00
	Callender Collection (1916)..	200.00
887.00	Class of 1885 (1886).........	887.00
500.00	Cochran (1886)	500.00
1,000.00	Culver (Helen F.) (1909)....	1,000.00
2,152.50	Faculty (1902)	2,152.50
500.00	Grant (1886)	500.00
500.00	Hall (1886)	500.00
2,000.00	Hay (C. S.) (1908)..........	2,000.00
100.00	Henderson (1886)	100.00
11,176.63	Holbrook (1888)	11,176.63
500.00	Keep-Clark (1886)	500.00
42.00	Library (1889)	42.00
1,000.00	Plumb (1887)	1,000.00

Library Endowment Funds

9,980.10	Coburn (Helen G.) (1905)...	9,980.10
586.49	Davis (1882)	586.49
2,000.00	Dodge (Grace H.) (1906)....	2,000.00
9,000.00	Hall (Charles M.) (1906)....	9,000.00
1,350.00	Hall (Thomas A.) (1906)....	1,350.00
10,000.00	James (D. Willis) (1906)....	10,000.00
475.00	Kendall (Abbie R.) (1906)..	475.00
33,395.56	Lyman (C. N.) (1907).......	33,395.56
340.25	Perry (1873)	340.25
5,000.00	Severance (L. H.) (1906)....	5,000.00
5,000.00	Shedd (E. A. and C. B.)(1906)	5,000.00
4,570.00	Terrell (H. L.) (1909).......	4,570.00
2,850.00	West (E. A.) (1905)........	2,850.00
158.45	Whipple (1880)	158.45
24,855.15	Sundries	24,855.15— 203,575.26
3,028.78	Unused income book funds...	3,525.88

Annuity Funds

	Brown	2,060.00
4,985.83	Collins	4,951.47
4,676.54	Cooper	4,678.80
5,798.92	Cutler	5,719.41
5,380.61	Dascomb	5,073.32
859.42	Ellis	296.59
959.44	Fitch	940.94
1,886.29	Gilbert Memorial	1,847.87
3,175.32	Jeffers	3,192.65
1,743.85	Johnson	1,699.27
2,778.23	Pond	2,776.89
6,254.76	Ross	6,210.71

447 02 $1 433 814.99

	Amounts brought forward.................	$ 39,447.92	$1,433,814.99
46,633.30	Spear	44,950.19	
4,568.15	Springer	4,438.50	
2,199.50	Straus	1,044.63	
2,015.00	West	2,002.15	
2,057.44	Williams	2,046.42—	93,929.81

Scholarship Funds

6,500.00	Allen (Dr. Dudley) (1899)...	$ 6,500.00	
6,000.00	Avery (1862)	6,000.00	
7,278.50	Barrows (John Henry) (1906)	7,278.50	
1,000.00	Barrows (John Manning) (1902)	1,000.00	
1,000.00	Bierce (1886)	1,000.00	
1,000.00	Caroline (1881)	1,000.00	
1,000.00	Castle (Henry N.) (1900)....	1,000.00	
750.00	Churchill (Lewis Nelson) (1890)	750.00	
1,025.00	Class of 1858 (1900).........	1,025.00	
1,060.50	Class of 1869 (1900).........	1,060.50	
1,000.00	Class of 1898 (1900)..........	1,000.00	
407.00	Class of 1900 (1910)........	407.00	
1,000.00	Cowles Memorial (1884)......	1,000.00	
1,000.00	Dascomb (1879)	1,000.00	
1,000.00	Davis (Julia Clark) (1905)...	1,000.00	
500.00	Dee (Mrs. Thomas J.) (1915)	500.00	
1,000.00	Dodge (1881)	1,000.00	
1,250.00	Finney (1877)	1,250.00	
5,000.00	Goodnow (1906)	5,000.00	
1,000.00	Graves (Mary Jane Bishop) (1894)	1,000.00	
1,500.00	Hawaii (1911)	1,500.00	
1,000.00	Hayden (Ferdinand V.)(1888)	1,000.00	
1,045.00	Hinchman (1872)	1,045.00	
1,000.00	Irwin (Jean Woodward)(1902)	1,000.00	
200.00	Lincoln (Ann) (1891)........	200.00	
1,100.00	Lord (Dr. A. D.) (1882).....	1,100.00	
1,000.00	Lord (Elizabeth W. R.)(1882)	1,000.00	
1,000.00	Metcalf (1881)	1,000.00	
1,000.00	Moulton (May) (1902)......	1,000.00	
1,000.00	Newberry (Helen Handy) (1912)	1,000.00	
1,750.00	Nichols (Howard Gardner) (1902)	1,750.00	
5,000.00	Reamer (Correlia L.) (1910).	5,000.00 •	
1,000.00	Talcott (1881)	1,000.00	
2,000.00	Thompson (Lucy M.) (1905)	2,000.00	
155.00	Thompson (Rosa M.) (1913)	155.00	
1,000.00	Valentine (Howard) (1880)..	1,000.00	
1,250.00	Wardle (Mary E.) (1896)....	1,250.00	
5,000.00	Warner (Lydia Ann) (1888)..	5,000.00	
500.00	Wyett (Anna M.) (1916)....	500.00—	67,271.00

Amount carried forw

Amount brought forward............................$1,595,015.80

Loan Funds

4.58	Anderegg (1907)	$ 417.08	
1,000.00	Drew (Alvan) (1916)........	1,043.25	
62.63	Freshman Women (1907)....	584.09	
968.55	Gilchrist Banking (1906).....	12,509.47	
428.53	Jones (1859)	2,835.02	
10.00	Metcalf (Edith Ely) (1915)..	215.00	
145.39	Moulton (May) (1904)......	689.24	
10,000.00	Noah (A. H.) (1915)........	11,432.50	
1,004.58	Parker (1903)	1,132.83	
33.15	Perkins (1912)	283.92	
80.53	Scholarship (1898)	2,333.82—	33,476.22
516.66	Foltz Tract Fund (1881).....	$ 518.99	
576.43	Lewis (Hannah Snow) (1902)	568.40	
1,150.00	Y. M. C. A. Reading Room Fund (1907)	1,150.00—	2,237.39
847.34	Unused income from scholarships—		
	Dr. Dudley Allen...........	$ 50.37	
	Class of 1889	.14	
	Class of 1898..............	19.45	
	Class of 1900..............	126.54	
	Dascomb	3.25	
	Finney	360.59	
	Hawaii	51.38—	611.72
33,512.38	Balance credits, sundry accounts—		
	Art Building Fund..........	$ 7,067.77	
	Art Building site...........	299.40	
	Boarding halls	4,117.33	
	Class of 1882 Shrub Fund...	9.00	
	Class of 1891 Fund........	57.83	
	Campus Improvement Fund..	8,592.43	
	Chapel insurance...........	90.94	
	J. D. Cox Gift.............	10,320.15	
	Dormitory Fund	100.00	
	Fund for Exchange Lecturers	13.17	
	Fund for Business Training..	25.00	
	Gymnasium and Field Association	2,000.00	
	Olney Art Gallery..........	409.96	
	Summer Camp on Lake Erie..	104.00	
	Swimming Pool Fund......	699.83	
	Trustee Scholarship Fund...	130.00—	34,036.81

Amount carried forward............................$1,665,377.94

Amount brought forward..............................$1,665,377.94

COLLEGE OF ARTS AND SCIENCES

Endowment Funds

68,034.59	Endowment (1852)	$ 67,934.59
142.00	Animal Ecology Professorship (1911)	142.00
25,000.00	Avery Professorship (1867)...	25,000.00
30,000.00	Brooks Professorship (1881)..	30,000.00
25,000.00	Clark (James F.) Professorship (1883)	25,000.00
19,634.41	Dascomb Professorship (1878)	19,634.41
30,000.00	Graves Professorship (1881)...	30,000.00
55,881.37	Hull (Fredrika Bremer) Professorship (1889)	55,881.37
12,524.33	Johnston (Adelia A. F.) Professorship (1898)	12,524.33
23,748.25	Monroe Professorship (1882)..	23,748.25
20,000.00	Perkins Professorship (1888)..	20,000.00
10,720.00	Severance Laboratory (1902)..	10,720.00
45,000.00	Severance (L. H.) Professorship (1902)	45,000.00
50,000.00	Stone Professorship (1880)....	50,000.00— 415,584.95
4,000.00	Zoological Laboratory (1911)	4,000.00

Scholarship Funds

2,000.00	Andover (1900)	$ 2,000.00
5,000.00	Bartlett (Frank Dickinson) (1900)	5,000.00
1,000.00	Blackstone (Flora L.) (1892)	1,000.00
4,750.00	Gilchrist-Potter (1906)	4,750.00
7,030.39	Gilchrist-Potter Prize (1912).	7,030.39
500.00	Hall (Sarah M.) (1905)......	500.00
	Ransom (Charles A.) (1910).	3,750.00
1,000.00	Spelman (Harvey H.) (1899)	1,000.00
1,000.00	Spelman (Lucy B.) (1899)...	1,000.00
2,500.00	Starr (Comfort) (1902)......	3,339.40
500.00	Sturges (Tracy) (1881)......	500.00
1,000.00	Tracy (Mrs. F. E.) (1899)...	1,000.00
1,500.00	West (E. A.) (1897).........	1,500.00
1,500.00	Westervelt (W. A.) (1916)...	1,500.00
6,000.00	Whitcomb (Ellen M.) (1884)	6,000.00
1,000.00	Whitcomb (Janet) (1899)....	1,000.00
2,000.00	Wilder (J. C. and Elizabeth) (1902)	2,000.00
1,000.00	Williams (Jennie Morton) (1883)	1,000.00— 43,869.79

Amount carried forward..............................$2,128,832.68

Amount brought forward............................$2,128,832.68
1,130.60 Unused income from scholarships—
    Flora L. Blackstone........ $ 134.45
    Gilchrist-Potter 11.69
    Charles A. Ransom.........   66.25
    Tracy Sturges 12.12
    Jennie Morton Williams....   7.25—   231.76

7,818.53 Balance credits, sundry accounts—
    Anatomy .... $ 110.76
    Botanical Laboratory 152.93
    Chemical Laboratory 913.39
    Economics 167.13
    Economics Lecture Fund....   11.48
    English Lecture Fund......   76.73
    Fine Arts 151.99
    Geological Laboratory 77.96
    Geological Museum 4.30
    Greek Archaeology 69.11
    Greenhouse 39.75
    Johnston Professorship of Art 3,826.34
    Ornithology 144.60
    Physical Laboratory 512.73
    Physical Education, Women..   49.75
    Physiological Laboratory....   74.93
    Psychological Laboratory...   232.18
    Sociology 43.91
    Special scholarship aid......   322.62
    Surveying 20.86
    Zoölogical Museum ....   158.98—   7,162.43

GRADUATE SCHOOL OF THEOLOGY

Endowment Funds

36,767.60 Endowment (1859)............ $ 36,767.60
41,000.00 **Anonymous** (1912) 41,000.00
50,000.00 **Anonymous** (1912) 50,000.00
700.00 **Bowen** (1916) 900.00
7,494.55 **Burrell** (1882) 7,494.55
17,205.75 **Chapin (William C.)** (1904)..   17,205.75
5,016.38 **Fairfield (Edmund B.)** (1911)   5,016.38
21,371.10 **Finney** Professorship (1870)..   21,371.10
4,908.13 **Gillett** (1905) 4,908.13
20,000.00 **Haskell** Lectureship (1905)...   20,000.00
1,000.00 **Hobart (L. Smith)** (1908)....   1,000.00

Amounts carried forward................ $205,663.51 $2,136,226.87

	Amounts brought forward.................	$205,663.51	$2,136,226.87
25,000.00	Holbrook Professorship (1878)	25,000.00	
133.39	Hudson (1859)	133.39	
100,000.00	James (Ellen S.) (1915)......	100,000.00	
25,158.68	Michigan Professorship (1881)	25,158.68	
8,935.84	Morgan Professorship (1873)..	8,935.84	
4,750.00	Place (1895)	4,750.00	
40,000.00	Shansi Professorship (1907)...	40,000.00—	566,344.16
155,275.00	Walworth (1877)	155,275.00	
427.74	Warner (1891)	427.74	
1,000.00	Weston (Joshua W.) (1902)..	1,000.00	

Scholarship Funds

5,000.00	Brooks (Lemuel) (1888).....	$ 5,000.00	
1,000.00	Butler (1874)	1,000.00	
291.95	Button (Susan S.) (1900)....	291.95	
1,250.00	Cowles (Leroy H.) (1897)...	1,250.00	
1,250.00	Emerson (1892)	1,250.00	
1,000.00	Fowler (Charles E.) (1903)..	1,000.00	
1,000.00	McCord-Gibson (1884)	1,000.00	
1,000.00	Miami Conference (1879)....	1,000.00	
1,000.00	Morgan (John) (1883).......	1,000.00	
1,000.00	Oberlin First Congregational Church (1881)	1,000.00	
1,000.00	Oberlin Second Congregational Church (1878).......	1,000.00	
1,000.00	Painesville (1873)	1,000.00	
1,000.00	Phelps (Anson G.) (1890)....	1,000.00	
1,500.00	Rosseter (Jennie M.) (1881).	1,500.00	
1,000.00	Sandusky (1880)	1,000.00	
50,000.00	Student Employment (1912).	50,000.00	
1,250.00	Tracy (1890)	1,250.00	
1,000.00	Warriner (Elizabeth L.) (1909)	1,000.00—	71,541.95

1,316.59	Unused income from scholarships—		
	Lemuel Brooks	$ 221.25	
	Butler	44.25	
	Susan S. Button............	42.97	
	Leroy H. Cowles...........	55.31	
	Emerson	60.31	
	Charles E. Fowler..........	59.25	
	McCord-Gibson	49.25	
	Miami Conference	49.25	
	John Morgan	44.25	
	Oberlin First Congregational Church	49.25	
	Oberlin Second Congregational Church	44.25	

	Amounts carried forward.................	$ 719.59	$2,774,112.98

Amounts brought forward................	$	719.59	$2,774,112.98
Painesville		49.25	
Anson G. Phelps............		43.25	
Jennie M. Rosseter.........		66.38	
Sandusky		50.25	
Tracy		115.31	
Elizabeth L. Warriner		74.25—	1,118.28

85.13	Loan Fund	$ 2,845.69	
50.00	Class of 1916 Loan Fund......	50.00	
1,028.86	Haskell Lectureship income.....	1,745.61	
24.93	Balance credits, sundry accounts	24.93	
1,750.00	Special income Ellen S. James Fund	6,075.00—	10,741.23

CONSERVATORY OF MUSIC

Endowment Funds

6,000.00	**Endowment** Fund (1909).....	6,000.00	
30,419.50	**Rice (Fenelon B.)** Professorship (1901)	$ 30,419.50	
5,000.00	**Warner (Dr. and Mrs. Lucien C.) (1916)**	5,000.00—	41,419.50

Scholarship Funds

1,200.00	**Mears (Helen Grinnell)** (1914)	$ 1,200.00	
	Ransom (Charles A.) (1910).	1,250.00—	2,450.00
236.36	**Conservatory Loan** Fund (1885)		4,047.31

$2,702,116.74	Total Funds and Balances.....		$2,833,889.30
	(Increase of funds and balances, $131,772.56)		
62,000.00	Bills payable		190,000.00
38,307.33	Deposits and personal accounts		120,281.93
$2,802,424.07			$3,144,171.23

INVESTMENTS

The foregoing Funds and Balances are invested in the following properties:

NOTES AND MORTGAGES—

Akron	$ 1,000.00	
Cleveland	221,207.51	
Columbus	800.00	
Lorain	27,150.00	
Oberlin	86,434.69	
On farm lands in Ohio....	20,417.22	
Total in Ohio........	$357,009.42	
New York City..........	37,000.00	
On farm lands in Michigan	700.00	
Total Notes and Mort- gages		$ 394,709.42

BONDS—		Cost	
$15,000.00	American Agricultural Chemical Co. Conv. Deb. 5's...........$	14,737.50	
3,000.00	*American Real Estate Co. 1st 6's	2,794.17	
50,000.00	American Telephone & Tele-graph Co. 5's..............	50,390.00	
50,000.00	Anglo-French 5's	47,468.75	
25,000.00	Argentine Government Treasury 6's	25,375.00	
10,000.00	Aurora, Elgin & Chicago Ry. Co. 1st 5's	9,556.25	
20,000.00	Aurora, Elgin & Chicago Ry. Co. 1st & ref. 5's...............	18,500.00	
25,000.00	Baltimore & Ohio R. R. Co. Ref. & Gen. 5's.................	25,149.74	
6,000.00	Chicago, Milwaukee & St. Paul Ry. Co. Conv. 4½'s..........	6,000.00	
5,000.00	Chicago, Milwaukee & St. Paul Ry. Co. Series B 5's........	5,000.00	
8,000.00	Cleveland & Eastern Traction Co. 1st 5's	6,000.00	
16,000.00	Cleveland Furnace Co. 1st 6's...	16,000.00	
25,000.00	Cleveland & Southwestern Trac-tion Co. 1st Con. 5's..........	23,750.00	
Amounts carried forward.................		$250,721.41	$ 394,709.42

* Gift

Amounts brought forward.................$250,721.41 $ 394,709.42

10,000.00	Cleveland, Southwestern & Columbus Ry. Co. 1st 5's...........	9,500.00
8,000.00	Colonial Ice Co. 1st 6's........	8,000.00
10,000.00	Columbia Improvement & Realty Co. 1st 6's.................	10,000.00
13,000.00	Cuyahoga Telephone Co. 1st 5's..	10,632.95
4,599.98	Davenport Land & Improvement Co. 7's	4,599.98
47,500.00	Dominion Realty Co............	27,709.05
10,000.00	German-American Car Co. 1st Car Trust 5's	9,650.00
10,000.00	German-American Car Co. 1st Car Equipment 6's	10,000.00
1,000.00	*German-American Car Co. Series T. 6's	1,000.00
10,000.00	Glidden Varnish Co. 1st 6's.....	9,800.00
10,000.00	Green Bay Water Co. 1st 6's....	9,900.00
30,000.00	Home Riverside Coal Co. 1st 5's.	35,000.00
5,000.00	Hudson & Manhattan R. R. Co. 1st Lien 5's................	5,000.00
5,000.00	Hudson & Manhattan R. R. Co. Adj. Income 5's............	3,750.00
50,000.00	Interborough Rapid Transit Co. 1st 5's	49,662.50
15,000.00	Interlake Steamship Co. 1st 6's..	15,000.00
30,000.00	Lake Shore Electric R. R. Co. 1st 5's	25,500.00
25,000.00	Lake Superior & Ishpeming Ry. Co. 1st 6's	25,000.00
10,000.00	Lima Telephone & Telegraph Co. 1st 5's	8,101.00
15,000.00	Lorain Street Ry. Co. Con. 5's..	13,875.00
21,000.00	Luckenbach Co., Inc., 1st 6's....	21,000.00
5,000.00	Lucas Building Co. 1st 6's......	5,000.00
1,000.00	*May Department Stores 1st 6's..	1,000.00
25,000.00	Michigan Limestone & Chemical Co. Serial A 1st Mtg. 6's.....	25,000.00
20,000.00	New Orleans Great Northern R. R. Co. 1st 5's..............	18,800.00
7,500.00	New Orleans, Texas & Mexico Ry. Co. non-cumulative income 5's.	3,000.00
3,000.00	New Orleans, Texas & Mexico Ry. Co. 6's	3,000.00
20,000.00	New York Central R. R. Co. Debenture 6's	20,000.00
15,000.00	Niagara, Lockport & Ontario Power Co. 1st 5's...........	13,500.00

Amount carried forward..................$652,701.89 $ 394,709.42

---

* Gift

Amount brought forward	..................$652,701.89	$ 394,709.42
10,000.00	Northern Ohio Traction & Light Co. 1st Con. 4's	7,381.25
10,000.00	Oberlin Telephone Co. 1st 6's...	9,100.00
15,000.00	Ontario Power Co. Deb. 6's.....	14,175.00
28,000.00	Ontario Power Co. 1st 5's.......	26,740.00
22,000.00	Rogers-Brown Iron Co. 1st & Ref. 5's	21,725.00
12,500.00	St. Louis & San Francisco R. R. Co. Prior Lien 4's	10,000.00
15,000.00	St. Louis Southwestern Ry. Co. 1st Con. 4's	12,262.50
10,000.00	Sherwin-Williams Co. of Canada 1st & Ref. 6's...............	10,000.00
8,000.00	Stark Co. Ohio Telephone Co. 1st 5's	7,120.00
1,000.00	*Statler Co. 6's..............	1,000.00
10,000.00	Stephenville, North & South Texas Ry. Co. 1st 5's............	9,700.00
1,000.00	*Struthers Furnace Co. 6's......	1,000.00
20,000.00	Syracuse Rapid Transit Co. 2nd 5's	18,000.00
1,100.00	*Toledo Gas, Electric & Heating Co. 5's	1,100.00
20,000.00	United Kingdom of Great Britain & Ireland 5 yr. 5½'s......	19,700.00
10,000.00	United States Government Liberty Gold 3½'s..............	10,000.00
25,000.00	U. S. Steel Corporation Sinking Fund 5's	26,781.25
28,000.00	United States Telephone Co. 1st 5's	22,900.00
10,000.00	Western Maryland Ry. Co. 1st 4's	8,512.50
30,000.00	Wheeling Traction Co. 1st 5's..	30,000.00
	Total Bonds	919,899.39

STOCKS—

$ 600.00	*American Stove Co. stock.......$	500.00
20,000.00	Atchison, Topeka & Santa Fe R. R. Co. stock	19,637.50
24,000.00	Aurora, Elgin & Chicago Ry. Co. Pfd. stock	20,845.00
60,000.00	Baltimore & Ohio R. R. Co. stock	63,895.00
3,500.00	Brier Hill Steel Co. Pfd. stock..	3,762.50
40,000.00	Chicago, Milwaukee & St. Paul Ry. Co. stock..............	46,000.00
6,400.00	Kirby Lumber Co. stock........	2,560.00
Amounts carried forward	..................$157,200.00	$1,314,608.81

* Gift

Amounts brought forward..................$157,200.00		$1,314,608.81
7,500.00	New Orleans, Texas & Mexico Ry. stock	900.00
50,000.00	New York Central R. R. Co. stock	56,617.50
10,000.00	New York, Chicago & St. Louis R. R. Co. (Nickel Plate) 2nd Pfd. stock	8,262.50
10,000.00	New York State Railway stock..	8,937.50
66,550.00	Pennsylvania R. R. Co. stock....	80,707.50
6,200.00	St. Louis & San Francisco R. R. Co. Pfd. stock	1,364.00
8,125.00	United Coal Corporation stock...	1,055.00
6,250.00	United Coal Corporation Pfd. stock	3,750.00
17,000.00	U. S. Steel Corporation Pfd. stock	18,466.25
15,800.00	Youngstown Sheet & Tube Co. Pfd. stock	17,056.75

Total stocks	354,317.00

SHORT TIME NOTES—

$10,000.00	Central States Electric Corp'n...$	9,250.00
10,000.00	Toledo Traction, Light & Power Co.	9,800.00

Total Short Time Notes..	19,050.00
COLLATERAL LOANS	62,912.22

REAL ESTATE—

Oberlin ....$ 24,217.52		
Cleveland 227,000.00		
Elyria 136.00		
Total in Ohio	$251,353.52	
Grand Rapids ....$ 1,000.00		
Farm lands in Michigan..... 850.00		
	1,850.00	
Farm lands in Kansas.......	1,500.00	
Chicago	51,500.00	
New York City	102,346.47	
Total Real Estate.......		408,549.99

UNIVERSITY HOUSES AND LANDS..............	240,358.11
Amount carried forward...........................	$2,399,796.13

Amount brought forward.......................... $2,399,796.13

SUNDRIES—

Advances for site, construction, equipment and repairs:

Auditorium ....\$	1,000.00
Administration Building (site).......	5,900.00
Allencroft	4,704.05
Athletic Field	14,085.24
Art Building	17,332.69
Baldwin Cottage	10,881.05
Barrows House	18,737.55
Black Property, Huron County (site for Summer Camp)	23,057.70
Botanical Laboratory	1,025.53
Carnegie Library	17,806.29
Central Heating Plant	108,818.28
Churchill Cottage	2,989.77
East Side Campus development.......	81,843.48
Ellis Cottage	1,601.21
Fairchild House	5,575.45
Finney Memorial Chapel	30,591.76
Geological Laboratory	1,661.37
Keep Cottage	25,488.57
Keep Cottage Annex	2,021.36
Keep Home	563.81
Lord Cottage	2,097.43
Men's Building	17,542.49
Men's Gymnasium	5,263.41
Park project	2,722.72
Park Hotel	4,923.49
Peters Hall	1,500.00
McCall Property	415.00
Rice Memorial Hall	20,652.31
Severance Laboratory	3,506.52
Special heating equipment..........	4,599.00
Shurtleff Cottage	3,811.67
Taylor Inn	14,509.75
Warner Property, Chicago	3,883.67
Women's Gymnasium	180.30
General plan buildings and grounds.....	8,924.80
Herbarium	271.84
Coal and supplies for 1917-18..........	8,499.74
Insurance prepaid	2,133.84
Bills receivable (including Shedd Fund loans)	28,001.02

$509,124.16 $2,399,796.13

Amounts brought forward..................$509,124.16 $2,399,796.13

    Loans from Student Loan Funds—

Anderegg ....$	225.00	
Conservatory	3,429.75	
Drew	40.00	
Freshman Women	567.00	
Gilchrist Banking	11,207.75	
Graduate School...........	2,809.00	
Jones	2,593.65	
Metcalf	100.00	
Moulton	642.00	
Noah	450.00	
Parker	130.00	
Perkins	130.00	
Scholarship	2,165.17	
		24,489.32

Sundry Accounts 17,477.23

Deficits

University $49,357.13		
College 37,678.19		
Graduate School of Theology 4,820.19		
Academy 22,378.42		
		114,233.93

Depreciation in General Investments....   51,256.30

Cash in hands of The Cleveland Trust
    Co. for investment 138.90

                                               716,719.84

Deposits subject to check and cash......   27,655.26

                                             $3,144,171.23

BUILDINGS AND EQUIPMENT

The following properties in use for College purposes are not entered in the foregoing list of assets, and are not valued on the Treasurer's Books, except in so far as certain advances to construction accounts appear under the item ''Sundries'' on pages 345. The values given are reasonable estimates based on their cost and present conditions:

Academy Buildings, furniture and site.................$	25,000.00
Administration Building, furniture and site.............	85,000.00
Arboretum and other lands for Park purposes............	37,000.00
Art Building (part)	170,000.00
Art and Archæology Apparatus.........................	6,000.00
Athletic Grounds	18,000.00
Baldwin Cottage, furniture and site....................	52,500.00
Botanical Laboratory and site.........................	3,500.00
Carnegie Library, furniture and site...................	172,800.00
College Lands	230,000.00
Council Hall and site	50,000.00
Fairchild House, building and site.....................	8,000.00
Finney Memorial Chapel	134,500.00
French Hall	5,000.00
Geological Collection	9,000.00
Geological Laboratory and site.........................	6,000.00
Herbarium and Botanical Equipment....................	15,000.00
Keep Cottage, furniture and site.......................	45,500.00
Library	75,000.00
Lord Cottage, furniture and site.......................	25,000.00
Men's Building, furniture and site.....................	172,950.00
Musical Instruments and Apparatus....................	50,000.00
Musical Library	3,000.00
Olney Art Collection	114,000.00
Organ in Finney Memorial Chapel......................	25,000.00
Peters Hall	80,000.00
Physical and Chemical Apparatus......................	15,000.00
Psychological Laboratory Apparatus....................	1,500.00
Rice Memorial Hall, equipment and site................	110,000.00
Severance Chemical Laboratory........................	67,500.00
Spear Laboratory	35,000.00
Sturges Hall	15,000.00
Superintendent's Office	5,000.00
Talcott Hall and furniture	75,000.00
Warner Gymnasium and equipment......................	75,000.00
Warner Hall	175,000.00
Women's Gymnasium and equipment....................	15,000.00
Zoölogical and Anthropological Collection..............	16,000.00
	$2,222,750.00

DESCRIPTION OF FUNDS

ALDEN (E. K.) FUND   (L) $ 5,724.13
Established in May, 1899, by bequest of Dr. Edmund K. Alden, of Boston, Mass., for the benefit of the Library of the School of Theology.

ALLEN (DR. DUDLEY) SCHOLARSHIP   (U) $ 6,500.00
Established in November, 1899, by gift of property by Dr. Dudley P. Allen and Mrs. Emily Allen Severance for a fund to be known as the ''Dudley Allen Scholarship for Missionary Children,'' the income to be used in paying the tuition of the children of foreign missionaries studying in Oberlin College.

ALLEN (JENNIE) NURSE FUND   (U) $ 3,000.00
Established in July, 1875. by gift of Dr. Dudley Allen, Sr. and later increased by gift of Dr. Dudley P. Allen, the income to be used for the payment of the services of a nurse caring for students who are unable to pay for such service.

ALUMNI FUND   (U) $ 17,564.89
Established in the year 1870 by a canvass for General Endowment to which some small gifts have been added in recent years.

AMPT (WILLIAM M.) FUND   (U) $ 5,000.00
Established in January, 1911, by bequest of Mr. William M. Ampt of Cincinnati, Ohio, the income to be used for general purposes of the College.

ANDEREGG LOAN FUND   (U) $ 417.08
Established in April, 1907, by gifts of friends of Professor F. Anderegg for loans to students upon his order and under his direction.

ANDOVER SCHOLARSHIPS   (C) $ 2,000.00
Established in October, 1900, by gift of Mrs. Helen G. Coburn of Boston, Mass.; the income to be used in aid of young men from Andover, Mass., whenever there are such men in the College needing such aid and worthy of it.

ANDREWS FUND   (L) $ 100.00
Established in June, 1900, by gift of Mr. Arthur C. and Mrs. Mary H. Andrews of Minneapolis, Minn.; the income to be used for the purchase of books and apparatus for the New Testament Department of the School of Theology.

ANIMAL ECOLOGY PROFESSORSHIP   (C) $ 142.00
Gifts received in the year 1911 for the beginning of a Professorship.

ANONYMOUS FUND   (T) $ 41,000.00
    Established in January, 1912, by gift of the ''Boston Donor,'' being the balance of a gift of $200,000.00 for the construction of the Men's Building and general endowment. This fund was made a part of the funds of the School of Theology by vote of the Trustees.

ANONYMOUS FUND   (U) $100,000.00
    Established in July, 1906, by gift of an Anonymous Friend as part of the endowment fund being raised in that year. The income of this fund was designated to be used for the increase of salaries of teachers in the College and School of Theology.

ANONYMOUS FUND   (L) $ 66,632.00
    Established in May, 1908, and added to from time to time by an Anonymous Friend who designates the fund for the endowment of the Library.

ANONYMOUS FUND   (T) $ 50,000.00
    Established in July, 1912, by gift of an Anonymous Friend to endow a Chair in the School of Theology.

ANONYMOUS FUND   (L) $ 1,000.00
    Established in June, 1906, by gift of an Anonymous Friend who designates that the income be used for the benefit of the Department of New Testament Language and Literature in the School of Theology.

ANONYMOUS FUND   (U) $ 500.00
    Gift of Anonymous Friends to the Endowment Fund raised in the years from 1909 to 1911 to meet the conditional gift of The General Education Board of New York.

ANONYMOUS FUND   (U) $ 5,000.00
    Gift of an Anonymous Friend to the Endowment Fund raised in the years from 1909 to 1911 to meet the conditional gift of The General Education Board of New York.

ANONYMOUS FUND   (U) $ 2,500.00
    Gift of an Anonymous Friend to the Endowment Fund raised in the years from 1909 to 1911 to meet the conditional gift of The General Education Board of New York.

ANONYMOUS FUND   (U) $ 5,000.00
    Gift of an Anonymous Friend in April, 1915 for endowment; the income at present is assigned for use of scholarships to students.

ATKINSON (SARAH M.) FUND   (U) $ 10,000.00
    Established in May, 1908, by bequest of Mrs. Sarah M. Atkinson of Moline, Ill., unrestricted. The fund was assigned to General Endowment by vote of the Prudential Committee.

AVERY PROFESSORSHIP   (C) $ 25,000.00
    Established in February, 1867, by the executors of the estate of Rev. Charles Avery, of Pittsburgh, Pa., conditioned upon the admission of colored students to Oberlin College and free tuition for fifty of such students.

AVERY SCHOLARSHIP   (U) $ 6,000.00
    Established in December, 1862, from the proceeds of sale of land,
    the gift of Rev. Charles Avery, of Pittsburgh, Pa., for the main.
    tenance and education of needy and deserving colored people.

BAKER (JANETTE W.) FUND   (U) $ 100.00
    Established in July, 1909, by bequest of Mrs. Janette W. Baker,
    of Brooklyn, N. Y., unrestricted.

BALDWIN (E. I.) FUND   (U) $ 24,475.00
    Established in March, 1894, by bequest of Mr. E. I. Baldwin, of
    Cleveland, Ohio, designated for endowment.

BARNES (KORA F.) FUND   (U) $ 10,000.00
    Established in May, 1905, by gift of Miss Kora F. Barnes, of
    New York, for construction of an Art Building. The interest to
    be used to pay in part the cost of storing the Art Collection until
    the fund is needed for the construction of a building.

BARROWS (JOHN HENRY) SCHOLARSHIP (U) $ 7,278.50
    Established in February, 1906, by gift of Miss Grace Sherwood,
    of Chicago, Ill., as a Memorial to President John Henry Barrows.
    The original gift was $5,000.00; the income was allowed to ac-
    cumulate until September 1, 1915.

BARROWS (JOHN MANNING)
    SCHOLARSHIP   (U) $ 1,000.00
    Established in November, 1902, by bequest of President John
    Henry Barrows in memory of his son.

BARTLETT (FRANK DICKINSON)
    SCHOLARSHIP   (C) $ 5,000.00
    Established in October, 1900, by Mr. A. C. Bartlett, of Chicago,
    Ill., to be used under the direction of the President of the College.

BIERCE SCHOLARSHIP   (U) $ 1,000.00
    Established in January, 1886, by bequest of Mrs. Sophronia
    Bierce, of Akron, Ohio, and assigned to aid of self-supporting
    women.

BIGELOW (MARIA B.) FUND   (U) $ 275.39
    Established in December, 1908, by bequest of Mrs. Maria B.
    Bigelow, of Portland, N. Y., in memory of her father, Mr. Dana
    Churchill, unrestricted.

BILLINGS (MRS. FREDERICK) FUND   (U) $ 500.00
    Gift of Mrs. Frederick Billings, of New York, to the Endowment
    Fund raised in the years from 1900 to 1911 to meet the condi-
    tional gift of The General Education Board of New York.

BISSELL (HENRIETTA) FUND   (U) $ 10,000.C
    Established in November, 1879, by gift of Mr. George P. Bissell
    of Hartford, Conn., in memory of his mother, the income to be
    used for general purposes of the College.

BLACKSTONE (FLORA L.) SCHOLARSHIP   (C) $ 1,000.00
Established in June, 1892, by gift of $500.00 by William E.
Blackstone of Oak Park, Ill., and the gift of an equal amount by
the Class of 1892 of Oberlin College, to found ''The Flora L.
Blackstone Scholarship of the Class of 1892.'' The income is to
be used to aid students who shall be in preparation for work as
foreign missionaries. Any beneficiaries of the fund who fail to
enter foreign missionary work are expected to refund amounts
received with interest.

BRIGGS (DR. CHARLES E.) FUND   (U) $ 500.00
Gift of Dr. Charles E. Briggs, of Cleveland, Ohio, to the Endowment Fund raised in the years from 1909 to 1911 to meet the conditional gift of The General Education Board of New York.

BROOKS PROFESSORSHIP   (C) $ 30,000.00
Established in December, 1881, and completed in January, 1895,
by gift of Mr. Gary Brooks, of Fairport, N. Y., to a fund to be
called the Brooks Professorship of History and Political Economy.
The purpose of the gift was for the increase of the salaries of
professors.

BROOKS (LEMUEL) SCHOLARSHIP   (T) $ 5,000.00
Established in May, 1888, by gift of Miss Harriet E. Brooks of
Churchville, N. Y., in memory of her father, the income to be
used for education of students preparing for the ministry.

BURRELL FUND   (T) $ 7,494.55
Established in May, 1882, by gift of Mr. and Mrs. Jabez L. Burrell of Oberlin, for benefit of the School of Theology.

BUTLER FUND   (U) $ 1,505.91
Established in February, 1882, by gift of Mrs. Mahala Butler, of
Winchendon, Mass., unrestricted.

BUTLER SCHOLARSHIP   (T) $ 1,000.00
Established in November, 1874, by gift of the Trustees of the
estate of Mr. Ebenezer Butler, of Winchendon, Mass., the income
to be used in aid of a student studying for the ministry, preference to be given to colored students.

BUTTON (SUSAN S.) FUND   (T) $ 291.95
Established in June, 1900, by bequest of Miss Susan S. Button, of
Litchfield, Ohio; the income to be used in aid of young men preparing for the ministry or young women preparing for missionary service.

CALLENDER COLLECTION FUND   (L) $ 200.00
Established in September, 1916, by members of the Class of '91
in memory of their classmate, Guy Stevens Callender. The income
is designated for purchases of books for addition to the Callender
collection.

CAROLINE SCHOLARSHIP   (U) $ 1,000.00
Established in February, 1881, by Mrs. Caroline Phelps Stokes,
of New York, for aid of self-supporting women.

CARROTHERS (CLARA E.) FUND   (U) $ 100.00
Established in January, 1909, by gift from the estate of Miss Clara E. Carrothers, of Findlay, Ohio, unrestricted.

CASTLE (HENRY N.) SCHOLARSHIP   (U) $ 1,000.00
Established in June, 1900, by the family of Mr. Henry N. Castle, of Honolulu, H. T., as part of the Reunion Fund of 1900.

CHAPIN (WILLIAM C.) FUND   (T) $ 17,205.75
Established in December, 1904, from the proceeds of a life insurance policy given by Mr. William C. Chapin, of Providence, R. I., for endowment of the School of Theology.

CHURCHILL (LEWIS NELSON)
SCHOLARSHIP   (U) $ 750.00
Established in February, 1890, by gift of Mrs. Lewis Vance, of Oberlin, in aid of indigent students.

CLARK (JAMES F.) PROFESSORSHIP   (C) $ 25,000.00
Established in May, 1883, by gift of Mr. James F. Clark, of Cleveland, Ohio, and brought up to the full amount by bequest after his death.

CLASS OF 1858 SCHOLARSHIP   (U) $ 1,025.00
Established in 1900 by members of the Class, the income to be used in aid of descendents of members of the Class, or by the College when not used otherwise. The scholarship constituted the subscription of the Class of 1858 to the Reunion Fund of 1900.

CLASS OF 1869 SCHOLARSHIP   (U) $ 1,060.50
Established in 1900 by members of the Class as their subscription to the Reunion Fund of 1900.

CLASS OF 1885 FUND   (L) $ 887.00
Gift of the members of the Class of 1885 to Library Endowment begun in 1886. The income is designated for the purchase of periodicals.

CLASS OF 1889 FUND   (U) $ 2,525.41
Gift of the members of the Class of 1889 at their twenty-fifth reunion in June, 1914. The income is designated for use for purposes other than those covered by the budget in such way as the President and Prudential Committee may decide.

CLASS OF 1898 FUND   (U) $ 2,371.35
Gift by the members of the Class of 1898 in the year 1905 and subsequently, the income designated for general university purposes. At present it is assigned for use as scholarships.

CLASS OF 1898 SCHOLARSHIP   (U) $ 1,000.00
Established in 1900 by members of the Class as their subscription to the Reunion Fund of 1900, the income to be used in aid of worthy students in securing an education at Oberlin College.

CLASS OF 1900 SCHOLARSHIP   (U) $ 407.00
Established in October, 1910, by members of the Class of 1900.

CLASS OF 1916 (GRADUATE SCHOOL OF
    THEOLOGY) LOAN FUND   (T) $ 50.00
    Established in June, 1916, by members of the graduating class.

COBURN (HELEN G.) FUND   (L) $ 9,980.10
    Established in October, 1905, by gift of Mrs. Helen G. Coburn, of
    Boston, Mass., and increased to its present amount by bequest of
    $10,000.00 (less the inheritance tax) and assigned to Library
    Endowment as part of the Carnegie Fund.

COCHRAN FUND   (L) $ 500.00
    Established in October, 1886, by gift of Mr. W. C. Cochran, of
    Cincinnati, Ohio, the income to be used for the purchase of books
    concerning philosophy.

COFFIN (C. A.) FUND   (U) $ 1,000.00
    Gift of Mr. C. A. Coffin, of New York, to the Endowment Fund
    raised in the years from 1909 to 1911 to meet the conditional gift
    of The General Education Board of New York.

COLLEGE ENDOWMENT FUND   (C) $ 67,934.59
    Established in the year 1852 by the sale of scholarships. When
    it was found desirable to call in these scholarships, the amounts
    expended for that purpose were charged against this fund. Some
    small gifts for endowment of the College Department have been
    added in recent years.

CONSERVATORY LOAN FUND   (M) $ 4,047.31
    Established in September, 1885, by gift of Dr. Lucien C. War-
    ner, of New York, to be loaned without interest to students of
    more than average musical proficiency.

CONSERVATORY OF MUSIC
    ENDOWMENT FUND   (M) $ 6,000.00
    Established in February, 1909, by gift of Miss L. C. Wattles, of
    Oberlin, as the beginning of an endowment for the Conservatory
    of Music.

COOPER FUND   (U) $ 3,028.26
    Established in December, 1901, by gift of Mr. Samuel F. Cooper,
    of Campbell, Cal., of which $1,000.00 was counted a part of the
    Half Million Endowment of 1901. The income is available for
    general university purposes.

COWLES (LEROY H.) SCHOLARSHIP   (T) $ 1,250.00
    Established in June, 1897, by gift of Mr. J. G. W. Cowles, of
    Cleveland, Ohio; the income to be used in aid of students prepar-
    ing for the ministry.

COWLES MEMORIAL SCHOLARSHIP   (U) $ 1,000.00
    Established in June, 1884, by Mrs. Asa D. Lord, of Oberlin, in
    memory of Rev. Henry and Mrs. Alice Welch Cowles.

CULVER (HELEN F.) FUND   (L) $ 1,000.00
    Established in July, 1909, by gift of Miss Helen F. Culver, of
    Chicago, Ill., to Library Endowment. The income is designated
    for the purchase of books for the Departments of German and
    French.

DASCOMB PROFESSORSHIP   (C) $ 19,634.41
Established in the year 1878 from the proceeds of a canvass for
endowment named in memory of Professor James Dascomb.

DASCOMB SCHOLARSHIP   (U) $ 1,000.00
Established in November, 1879, by friends of Mrs. M. A. P.
Dascomb for aid of self-supporting young women.

DAVIS FUND   (L) $ 586.49 •
Established in December, 1882, by the Misses Caroline M. and
Rebecca W. Davis, of Mantua, Ohio, assigned to Endowment of
the Library.

DAVIS (JULIA CLARK) SCHOLARSHIP   (U) $ 1,000.00
Established in July, 1905, by Rev. Howard H. Russell, in memory
of Julia Clark Davis who assisted Mr. Russell while he was a
student, the income to be paid toward the support of a worthy
student.

DEE (MRS. THOMAS J.) SCHOLARSHIP   (U) $ 500.00
Established in July, 1915, by gift of Mrs. Thomas J. Dee, of
Chicago, Ill.

DICKINSON (JULIA) FUND   (U) $ 38,000.00
Established in March, 1893, by bequest of Miss Julia Dickinson,
of Fairport, N. Y., in which $20,000.00 was designated for the
endowment of the chair of ''Lady Principal''; and the interest
on $20,000.00 to be used in the payment of the regular salary of
the Director of Physical Culture for young women. The payment of the inheritance tax reduced the bequest to $38,000.00.

DODGE (GRACE H.) FUND   (L) $ 2,000.00
Established in May, 1906, by a gift of Miss Grace H. Dodge, of
New York, to Library Endowment.

DODGE SCHOLARSHIP   (U) $ 1,000.00
Established in November, 1881, by Mrs. M. P. Dodge, of New
York, for aid of self-supporting women.

DREW (ALVAN) LOAN FUND   (U) $ 1,000.00
Established in April, 1916, by gift of Mrs. Lizzie Arianna Drew
Copp and Mrs. Lunette Angie Drew Chamberlain, of Richwood,
Ohio, in memory of their father. The income is to be loaned to
self-supporting men in Oberlin College.

DUTTON FUND   (U) $ 4,674.25
Established in September, 1881, by gift of Mr. A. C. Dutton, of
Eaton Rapids, Mich., unrestricted.

EMERSON SCHOLARSHIP   (T) $ 1,250.00
Established in May, 1892, by gift of Mrs. Mary F. Emerson of
Lafayette, Ind., in memory of her husband, Thomas B. Emerson,
and completed by bequest received in 1905; the income to be used
in aid of students preparing for the ministry.

ENDOWMENT UNION FUND   (U) $ 1,650.25
Established in September, 1907, by payment of the principal upon which a subscriber to the Living Endowment Union based the annual payment. As others have paid up the principal the amounts have been added to this fund. The income is available for general university purposes.

FACULTY FUND   (L) $ 2,152.50
Established in the year 1902 by the gifts of certain members of the faculty to the Half Million Endowment that was being raised in that year. The income is designated to be expended under the direction of the Library Committee.

FAIRCHILD (JAMES H.) PROFESSORSHIP (U) $ 37,242.19
Established in the year 1888 from the proceeds of a canvass for endowment among the alumni, named in honor of President James H. Fairchild.

FAIRFIELD (EDMUND B.) FUND   (T) $ 5,016.38
Established in April, 1911, from the proceeds of the sale of property in Chicago, Ill., the gift of Rev. Edmund B. Fairfield, D.D., of Mansfield, Ohio. The income is designated for the use of the School of Theology.

FINNEY FUND   (U) $ 242.70
Established in September, 1882, by gift of Mrs. Rebecca Finney, of Pilot Rock, Oregon, unrestricted.

FINNEY PROFESSORSHIP   (T) $ 21,371.10
Established in the year 1870 from the proceeds of a canvass for endowment for the School of Theology, named in honor of President Charles G. Finney.

FINNEY SCHOLARSHIP   (U) $ 1,250.00
Established in May, 1877, by Mrs. Caroline Phelps Stokes, of New York, the income to be used in aiding colored students to prepare for missionary work in western Africa.

FIRESTONE (ROSE P.) FUND   (U) $ 13,645.76
Established in July, 1902, by gift of Mrs. Rose P. Firestone, of Castalia, Ohio, and increased by bequest to present amount.

FOLTZ TRACT FUND   (U) $ 500.00
Established in October, 1881, by gift of $100.00 by Rev. Benjamin Foltz, of Rockford, Ill., and increased to $500.00 by bequest to erect a fund, the income of which to be used for the purchase and free distribution of tracts to students in Oberlin College, the public schools of Oberlin and out-lying towns and to the freedmen of the South.

FOWLER (CHARLES E.) SCHOLARSHIP   (T) $ 1,000.00
Established in March, 1903, by gift from the Estate of Charles E. Fowler, of Oberlin, to found a scholarship in the School of Theology.

FOWLER (KATE) FUND   (U) $ 2,525.00
   Gift of Miss Kate Fowler, of New York, to the Endowment Fund
   raised in the years from 1909 to 1911 to meet the conditional gift
   of The General Education Board of New York.

FRESHMAN WOMEN'S FUND   (U) $ 584.09
   Established in October, 1907, by crediting to a separate account
   amounts repaid by women for scholarship aid allowed to them in
   previous years.

GENERAL EDUCATION BOARD   (U) $125,000.00
   Established in December, 1911, by gift of The General Education
   Board of New York for the purpose of endowment. This gift
   was conditioned upon raising $375,000.00 from other sources, mak-
   ing a total of $500,000.00 of which $250,000.00 could be used for
   buildings and $250,000.00 to be held as endowment. The income
   of this fund may be used for general university purposes but
   may not be used for specifically theological instruction.

GILCHRIST BANKING FUND   (U) $ 12,509.47
   Established in May, 1906, by bequest of Mrs. Ella J. Gilchrist
   Potter, of Alpena, Mich., as a memorial to her father and mother.
   The bequest was for $9,500.00 (inheritance tax deducted) to
   provide a fund for loans to indigent self-supporting young people
   for a period not exceeding five years with interest at lowest legal
   rate as established by the laws of the State of Ohio. Interest
   paid on loans is added to the fund and reloaned as principal.

GILCHRIST FUND   (U) $ 4,271.00
   Established in October, 1892, by gift of Mr. Albert Gilchrist, of
   Oberlin, unrestricted.

GILCHRIST-POTTER PRIZE FUND   (C) $ 7,030.39
   Established in December, 1912, by bequest of Mrs. Ella J. Gilchrist Potter, of Alpena, Mich.; the income to be appropriated
   each year to a self-supporting girl who has completed a full course
   in Oberlin College and desires to study further.

GILCHRIST-POTTER SCHOLARSHIP FUND (C) $ 4,750.00
   Established in May, 1906, by bequest of Mrs. Ella J. Gilchrist
   Potter, of Alpena, Mich., the income to be used in aid of self-sup-
   porting young women.

GILLETT FUND   (T) $ 4,908.13
   Established in September, 1905, by Mr. Alfred Gillett, of Oberlin,
   for endowment of the School of Theology.

GILLETT FUND   (U) $ 709.68
   Established in March, 1880, by gift of Mr. Alfred Gillett of
   Oberlin, unrestricted.

GOODNOW SCHOLARSHIPS   (U) $ 5,000.00
   Established in May, 1906, by bequest of Mr. Edward A. Goodnow,
   of Worcester, Mass., who requested that the fund be called the
   ''Goodnow Scholarships'' and that the income be used to assist
   young women in obtaining an education but no one person to
   receive more than one hundred dollars per year.

GRADUATE SCHOOL OF THEOLOGY
ENDOWMENT (T) $ 26,767.60
This fund was established in January, 1859, and represents the accumulated gifts for the Department of Theology which have not been erected as separate funds.

GRADUATE SCHOOL OF THEOLOGY
(SPECIAL FUND) (T) $ 700.00
Established in July, 1916, by gifts of Anonymous Friends for endowment.

GRADUATE SCHOOL OF THEOLOGY FUND (T) $ 2,845.69
Established in July, 1876, by gifts of various donors for aid of Theological students. The fund is loaned to students supplementing the aid allowed them from scholarship funds.

GRANT FUND . (L) $ 500.00
Established in June, 1886, by the gift of Miss Elizabeth Grant, of Chicago, Ill., in memory of her sister, Miss Barbara Grant; the income designated for the purchase of books of American poetry.

GRAVES PROFESSORSHIP (C) $ 30,000.00
Established in April, 1881, by gift of Mr. R. R. Graves, of Morristown, N. J. The fund has been increased by gift of $10,000.00 from other members of the family.

GRAVES (MARY JANE BISHOP)
SCHOLARSHIP (U) $ 1,000.00
Established in January, 1894, by Mrs. Elmira Hammon of Dryden, N. Y., in memory of her sister, for aid of self-supporting young women.

GREEN (MRS. MARY POMEROY) FUND (U) $ 50.00
Gift of Mrs. Mary Pomeroy Green, of Chicago, Ill., to the Endowment Fund raised in the years from 1909 to 1911 to meet the conditional gift of The General Education Board of New York.

HALL FUND (L) $ 500.00
Established in June, 1886, by gift of Mr. Thomas A. Hall, of Chicago, Ill. The income is designated for the purchase of books on physical training, physiology and hygiene.

HALL FUND (L) $ 1,350.00
Established in June, 1906, by gift of Mr. Thomas A. Hall, of Chicago, Ill., for endowment of the Library.

HALL (CHARLES M.) FUND (L) $ 9,000.00
Established in May, 1906, by gift of Mr. Charles M. Hall, of Niagara Falls, N. Y., to endowment of the Library.

HALL (CHARLES M.) FUND (U) $ 10,175.00
Gift of Mr. Charles M. Hall, of Niagara Falls, N. Y., to the Endowment Fund raised in the years 1909 to 1911 to meet the conditional gift of The General Education Board of New York.

HALL (CHARLES M.) FUND   (U) $100,000.00
    Established in May, 1917, being part of the bequest of Mr.
    Charles M. Hall of Niagara Falls, N. Y., to establish a fund the
    income of which is to be used to pay taxes on lands given by him
    and for the care, maintenance, and development of the College
    campus and other lands.

HALL (SARAH M.) SCHOLARSHIP   (C) $ 500.00
    Established in June, 1905, by gift of Mrs. Mary H. Johnson, of
    Akron, Ohio, in behalf of her deceased sister, Miss Sarah M. Hall,
    for aid of needy young women.

HANDY (TRUMAN P.) FUND   (U) $ 2,000.00
    Established in April, 1899, by bequest of Mr. Truman P. Handy,
    of Cleveland, Ohio, unrestricted.

HASKELL (CAROLINE E.) FUND   (U) $ 31,019.63
    Established in December, 1905, by gift of Mrs. Caroline E. Has-
    kell, of Michigan City, Ind., and increased to the present amount
    by bequest. The income is available for general university pur-
    poses.

HASKELL LECTURESHIP   (T) $ 20,000.00
    Established in December, 1905, by gift of Mrs. Caroline E. Has-
    kell, of Michigan City, Ind., to establish a lectureship on Oriental
    literature in its relation to the Bible and Christian teachings.

HAWAII SCHOLARSHIP   (U) $ 1,500.00
    Established in August, 1911, by gift of thirty-four friends of
    Oberlin College living in Hawaii.

HAY (C. S.) FUND   (L) $ 2,000.00
    Established in May, 1908, by gift of Mrs. Clara S. Hay, of Wash-
    ington, D. C., to which was added her gift of $1,000.00 received in
    1910. The income of the fund is designated for the purchase of
    foreign books and maintenance of the Library.

HAYDEN (FERDINAND V.) SCHOLARSHIP (U) $ 1,000.00
    Established in May, 1888, by gift of Mrs. Emma W. Hayden, of
    Philadelphia, Pa., in aid of self-supporting young men.

HAYNES (CELIA MORGAN) FUND   (U) $ 1,500.00
    Established in August, 1911, by Dr. Celia Morgan Haynes, of
    Chicago, Ill., and assigned to the fund to meet the conditional
    gift of The General Education Board of New York.

HENDERSON FUND   (L) $ 100.00
    Established in October, 1886, by gift of Miss A. M. Henderson,
    of Minneapolis, Minn. The income is designated for the pur-
    chase of books on the subject of temperance.

HENDERSON (THOMAS) FUND   (U) $ 100.00
    Gift of Mr. Thomas Henderson, of Oberlin, to the Endowment
    Fund raised in the years from 1909 to 1911 to meet the condi-
    tional gift of The General Education Board of New York.

HILLYER (APPLETON R.) FUND (U) $ 100.00
Gift of Mr. Appleton R. Hillyer, of Hartford, Conn., to the Endowment Fund raised in the years from 1909 to 1911 to meet the conditional gift of The General Education Board of New York.

HINCHMAN FUND (U) $ 1,045.00
Established in January, 1872, by bequest of Miss Anna W. Hinchman of Philadelphia, Pa., for the benefit of indigent young women.

HOBART (L. SMITH) FUND (T) $ 1,000.00
Established in May, 1908, by bequest of Mr. L. Smith Hobart, of Springfield, Mass., for the Department of Theology.

HOLBROOK FUND (L) $ 11,176.63
Established in December, 1888, by gift of Mr. Charles V. Spear, of Oberlin. The income is designated for the purchase of books for the Library.

HOLBROOK (LAURA C.) FUND (U) $ 7,763.75
Established in February, 1917, by bequest of Miss Laura C. Holbrook, of Cleveland, O., undesignated.

HOLBROOK PROFESSORSHIP (T) $ 25,000.00
Established in December, 1878, by gift of Miss Mary W. Holbrook, of Boston, Mass., for endowment of a professorship in the School of Theology. Miss Holbrook preferred to have her gift connected with the chair of Homiletics and Pastoral Theology.

HOTCHKISS (HELEN M.) FUND (U) $ 854.00
Established in August, 1902, by gift of Miss Helen M. Hotchkiss, of Oberlin, unrestricted.

HUBEL (F. A.) FUND (U) $ 200.00
Gift of Mr. F. A. Hubel, of Detroit, Mich., to the Endowment Fund raised in the years from 1909 to 1911 to meet the conditional gift of The General Education Board of New York.

HUDSON FUND (T) $ 133.39
Established in November, 1859, by gift of Mrs. B. B. Hudson, of Oberlin, for endowment of the School of Theology.

HULL (FREDRIKA BREMER)
PROFESSORSHIP (C) $ 55,881.37
Established in March, 1889, by gift of Mr. Charles J. Hull, of Chicago, Ill., in memory of his daughter, a graduate with the Class of 1870, for endowment of a Professorship of the German and French languages and literature. The income of this fund is restricted to the payment of the annual salary of the professor or professors in this department.

IRWIN (JEAN WOODWARD) SCHOLARSHIP (U) $ 1,000.00
Established in January, 1902, by Mrs. Hannah B. Irwin, of Wheeling, W. Va., in memory of her daughter, in aid of self-supporting women.

JAMES (D. WILLIS) FUND (L) $ 10,000.00
Established in July, 1906, by gift of Mr. D. Willis James, of New York, for Library Endowment.

JAMES (ELLEN S.) FUND   (U) $ 10,000.00
Gift of Mrs. Ellen James, of New York, to the Endowment Fund raised in the years from 1909 to 1911 to meet the conditional gift of The General Education Board of New York.

JAMES (ELLEN S.) FUND   (T) $100,000.00
Established in December, 1915, by gift of Mrs. Ellen S. James, of New York. An unrestricted gift for the use of The Graduate School of Theology.

JENISON (ANGELINE FISHER) FUND   (U) $ 2,000.00
Established in May, 1907, by gift of $1,000.00 of Mrs. Angeline Fisher Jenison, of Spokane, Wash., and increased by additional gift in 1911.

JESUP (MRS. M. K.) FUND   (U) $ 1,000.00
Gift of Mrs. M. K. Jesup, of New York, to the Endowment Fund raised in the years from 1909 to 1911 to meet the conditional gift of The General Education Board of New York.

JOHNSTON (ADELIA A. F.)
    PROFESSORSHIP   (C) $ 12,524.33
Established in November, 1898, by friends of Mrs. Adelia A. F. Johnston as the beginning of a professorship which should bear her name.

JONES LOAN FUND   (U) $ 2,835.02
Established in March, 1859, by bequest of Miss Jones, of Syracuse, N. Y. The original gift was $529.47 and was increased to $1,000.00 by gifts of other friends. During the years, those who have had the benefit of the use of the fund have made gifts bringing the fund up to the present amount. The fund is available for loans without interest to needy and deserving women.

KEEP (ALBERT) FUND   (U) $ 1,000.00
Gift of Mr. Albert Keep, of Chicago, Ill., to the Endowment Fund raised in the years from 1909 to 1911 to meet the conditional gift of The General Education Board of New York.

KEEP-CLARK FUND   (L) $ 500.00
Established in July, 1886, by gift of Mrs. Fannie Keep Clark, of Chicago, Ill.; income designated for the purchase of books on Modern History.

KEITH FUND   (U) $ 2,997.97
Established in August, 1904, by bequest of Mr. Charles H. Keith, of Chicago, Ill., unrestricted.

KENDALL (ABBIE R.) FUND   (L) $ 475.00
Established in April, 1906, by bequest of Mrs. Abbie R. Kendall, of Conneautville, Pa., assigned as part of Library Endowment.

KENNEDY (JOHN S.) FUND   (U) $ 48,558.45
Established in July, 1909, by gift of Mr. John S. Kennedy, of New York, to endowment, to which was added the proceeds of his unrestricted bequest of $50,000.00.

KIMBALL (EDWARD D.) FUND   (U) $ 3,871.25
Established in April, 1907, by bequest of Mr. Edward D. Kimball, of Watertown, Mass., unrestricted.

KIRBY (MARTHA A.) FUND   (U) $ 1,000.00
Gift of Mrs. Martha A. Kirby, of Detroit, Mich., to the Endowment Fund raised in the years from 1909 to 1911 to meet the conditional gift of The General Education Board of New York.

LATIMER FUND   (U) $ 79.14
Established in July, 1876, by gift of Miss Ann Latimer, of Westfield, N. Y., unrestricted.

LAWSON (VICTOR F.) FUND   (U) $ 1,000.00
Gift of Mr. Victor F. Lawson, of Chicago, Ill., to the Endowment Fund raised in the years from 1909 to 1911 to meet the conditional gift of The General Education Board of New York.

LEWIS (HANNAH SNOW) FUND   (U) $ 500.00
Established in August, 1902, by Mrs. Hannah Snow Lewis, of Oberlin, the income to be used for purchase of literature for the reading room at Lord Cottage.

LIBRARY ENDOWMENT   (L) $ 42.00
Established in November, 1889, from the balance of a subscription to the Library Endowment Fund started in 1886.

LINCOLN (ANN) SCHOLARSHIP   (U) $ 200.00
Established in March, 1891, by Mrs. Ann Lincoln, of Oberlin, in aid of self-supporting young women.

LORD (DR. A. D.) SCHOLARSHIP   (U) $ 1,100.00
Established in February, 1882, by Dr. Asa D. Lord and Mrs. Asa D. Lord, of Batavia, N. Y.

LORD (ELIZABETH W. R.) SCHOLARSHIP (U) $ 1,000.00
Established in February, 1882, by Dr. Asa D. Lord and Mrs. Asa D. Lord, of Batavia, N. Y.

LYMAN (C. N.) FUND   (L) $ 33,395.56
Established in February, 1907, by bequest of Dr. C. N. Lyman, of Wadsworth, Ohio, assigned to Library Endowment.

LYON (MARCUS) FUND   (U) $ 10,000.00
Established in May, 1902, by gift of Mr. Marcus Lyon, of Wauseon, Ohio, to the Half Million Endowment of 1901.

McCALL (MARY TILDEN) FUND   (U) $ 1,094.83
Established in January, 1914, by bequest of Mrs. Mary Tilden McCall, of San Jose, Cal., unrestricted.

McCLELLAND FUND   (U) $ 800.12
Established in August, 1903, by gift of Mrs. Mary C. McClelland, of Benzonia, Mich., unrestricted.

McCORD-GIBSON SCHOLARSHIP   (T) $ 1,000.00
Established by bequest of land by Mr. John Gibson of London-
derry, Vt., the sale of which yielded $500.00, to which was added
$500.00, the gift of Mr. Joseph McCord. The gifts were com-
bined to form the above named scholarship by vote of the Prudential Committee under date of December 27, 1884, the income
to be used for education of men studying for the ministry.

MAGRAUGH FUND   (U) $ 1,166.67
Established in December, 1908, by gift of Mrs. Sarah Magraugh,
of Oberlin, undesignated.

MARTIN (CAROLINE M.) FUND   (U) $ 3,056.97
Established in October, 1912, by bequest of Miss Caroline M.
Martin, of Dover, N. H., unrestricted.

MEARS (HELEN GRINNELL)
      SCHOLARSHIP   (M) $ 1,200.00
Established in November, 1914, by gift of Dr. and Mrs. David
O. Mears, of Essex, Mass., as a memorial to their daughter. The
income is to be used for the benefit of a contralto singer of
promise.

MELLON (A. W. and R. B.) FUND   (U) $ 5,000.00
Gift of Mr. A. W. Mellon and Mr. R. B. Mellon, of Pittsburgh,
Pa., to the Endowment Fund raised in the years from 1909 to 1911
to meet the conditional gift of The General Education Board of
New York.

METCALF (EDITH ELY) LOAN FUND   (U) $ 200.00
Established in February, 1915, by gift of Miss Edith Ely Metcalf, of Chicago, Ill., to provide loans for young women.

METCALF SCHOLARSHIP   (U) $ 1,000.00
Established in March, 1881, by Mr. E. W. Metcalf, of Elyria,
Ohio, for aid of self-supporting women.

MIAMI CONFERENCE SCHOLARSHIP   (T) $ 1,000.00
Established in December, 1879, by gifts from the Churches of the
Miami Conference of Ohio; income to be used in aid of students
preparing for the ministry.

MICHIGAN PROFESSORSHIP   (T) $ 25,158.68
Established in 1881 from the proceeds of a canvass for endowment for the School of Theology among residents of the State
of Michigan.

MILLER (AMOS C.) FUND   (U) $ 700.00
Gift of Mr. Amos C. Miller, of Chicago, Ill., to the Endowment
Fund raised in the years from 1909 to 1911 to meet the condi-
tional gift of The General Education Board of New York.

MONROE PROFESSORSHIP   (C) $ 23,748.25
Established in 1882 from the proceeds of a movement to endow a
Professorship of Political Science and International Law to which
Professor James Monroe should be appointed.

MORGAN PROFESSORSHIP   (T) $ 8,935.84
Established in 1873 from the proceeds of a canvass for endowment for the School of Theology in honor of Professor John Morgan.

MORGAN (JOHN) SCHOLARSHIP   (T) $ 1,000.00
Established in June, 1883, by gift of Mr. William Hyde, of Ware, Mass.; the income to be used for the assistance of young men studying for the ministry.

MOULTON (MAY) LOAN FUND   (U) $ 500.00
Established in May, 1904, by gift of Mrs. Susan A. S. Moulton, of Oberlin, in memory of her daughter. The fund is to be used under the direction of the General Faculty of Oberlin College for the purpose of making loans to deserving students at the rate of interest paid by Savings Banks (at present 4%).

MOULTON (MAY) MEMORIAL FUND   (U) $ 1,000.00
Established in April, 1902, by Mrs. Susan A. S. Moulton, of Oberlin, and her friends for the benefit of worthy and needy young women with preference given to those living at Lord Cottage. The fund is in memory of the daughter of Mrs. Moulton.

NEWBERRY (HELEN HANDY)
    SCHOLARSHIP   (U) $ 1,000.00
Established in June, 1912, by gift of Mrs. Truman H. Newberry, of Detroit, Mich.

NICHOLL (LIZZIE) FUND   (U) $ 10,000.00
Established in January, 1915, by bequest of Mrs. Jane K. Nicholl of Amherst, Ohio, for an endowment fund in memory of her daughter.

NICHOLS (HOWARD GARDNER)   (U) $ 1,750.00
Established in June, 1902, by Mr. J. Howard Nichols, of Boston, Mass., in memory of his son.

NOAH (A. H.) FUND $ 11,000.00
Established in June, 1915, by gift of Mr. Andrew H. Noah of Akron, Ohio. The income of the fund is to be used in making loans to young men, students in Oberlin College.

OBERLIN FIRST CONGREGATIONAL
    CHURCH SCHOLARSHIP   (T) $ 1,000.00
Established in 1881 and completed in 1894 by gifts from the Church for a scholarship in the School of Theology.

OBERLIN SECOND CONGREGATIONAL
    CHURCH SCHOLARSHIP   (T) $ 1,000.00
Established in 1878 and completed in 1892 by gifts from the Church for a scholarship in the School of Theology.

OLNEY FUND   (U) $ 10,000.00
Established in April, 1904, by bequest of Mrs. Charles F. Olney, of Cleveland, Ohio; the income designated for the care, maintenance, repair, and improvement of the Olney Art Collection.

OSBORN (WILLIAM E.) FUND   (U) $ 38,500.00
    Established in August, 1901, by bequest of Mr. William E. Osborn, of Pittsburgh, Pa. Mr. Osborn asked that the fund be called ''The William E. Osborn Foundation for the Chair of the President of Oberlin College.''

PAINESVILLE SCHOLARSHIP   (T) $ 1,000.00
    Established by various gifts by the Congregational Church of Painesville, Ohio, in the years from 1873 to 1879, the income to be used in aid of students studying for the ministry.

PARKER (LEONARD F.) FUND   (U) $ 1,000.00
    Established in December, 1903, by gift of Professor Leonard F. Parker, of Grinnell, Iowa. The gift provides that income of the fund shall be loaned to Juniors and Seniors, men or women, who look forward to the ministry or to some distinctly benevolent or Christian service. Interest on loans to students to be added to the principal until a second $1,000.00 has been accumulated. Fund of $2,000.00 then to stand and the income loaned and reloaned.

PERKINS LOAN FUND   (U) $ 283.92
    Established in April, 1912, by gift of $250.00 by Mrs. Mary F. Perkins of Santa Barbara, Cal., for the benefit of young women. The fund is loaned with interest at 4%; amounts received as interest are added to the principal.

PERKINS (MABEL H.) FUND   (U)   . $ 100.00
    Gift of Miss Mabel H. Perkins, of Hartford, Conn., to the Endowment Fund raised in the years from 1909 to 1911 to meet the conditional gift of The General Education Board of New York.

PERKINS PROFESSORSHIP   (C) $ 20,000.00
    Established in July, 1888, by gift of Mr. W. A. Perkins, of Windham, Ohio.

PERRY FUND   (L) $ 340.25
    Established in July, 1873, by gift of Mrs. Minerva M. Perry, of Brownhelm, Ohio, assigned to Library Endowment.

PHELPS (ANSON G.) SCHOLARSHIP   (T) $ 1,000.00
    Established in May, 1890, by gift of Miss Olivia E. P. Stokes, of New York, in memory of her grandfather; the income to be used in aid of colored men studying for the ministry.

PLACE FUND   (T) $ 4,750.00
    Established in July, 1895, by bequest of Mrs. Sarah B. Place, of Gloversville, N. Y.; assigned to Seminary Endowment.

PLUMB FUND   (L) $ 1,000.00
    Established in June, 1887, by gift of Mrs. L. H. Plumb and children, of Wheaton, Ill., in memory of Mr. Samuel H. Plumb; the income designated for the purchase of books on American History.

PLUMB (RALPH) FUND   (U) $ 20,000.00
    Established in February, 1881, by gift of Mr. Ralph Plumb, of Streator, Ill., for endowment, the income of which was to be used to increase the salary of the President and certain teachers.

PRUNTY (MARY) FUND   (U) $ 2,994.39
    Established in August, 1888, by gift of Miss Mary Prunty, of
Castalia, Ohio, unrestricted.

RANSOM (CHARLES A.)
    SCHOLARSHIP FUND   (C) $ 3,750.00
Established in March, 1910, by gift of Mrs. Amanda A. Ransom,
of Plainwell, Mich., in memory of her husband; the income of
$1,250.00 is to be used for the aid of women only and the income
of $2,500.00 for either men or women in the College of Arts and
Sciences.

RANSOM (CHARLES A.)
    SCHOLARSHIP FUND   (M) $ 1,250.00
Established in March, 1910, by gift of Mrs. Amanda A. Ransom,
of Plainwell, Mich., in memory of her husband; the income is
to be used to aid indigent men or women in the Conservatory of
Music.

REAMER (CORRELIA L.) SCHOLARSHIP   (U) $ 5,000.00
Established in August, 1910, by bequest of Mrs. Correlia J. L.
Reamer of Oberlin; the income to be used to assist young women
who are in part or wholly self-supporting in getting an education.

REUNION FUND   (U) $ 47,270.85
Established in 1900 from the proceeds of a canvass for endowment among the alumni by classes. Several classes established
funds for scholarships and other special purposes. Those funds
not specially designated are included in this fund, the income of
which is used for general purposes.

RICE (FENELON B.) PROFESSORSHIP   (M) $ 30,419.50
Established in December, 1901, by gift of various donors to the
Half Million Endowment Fund being raised that year, to which
was added $20,000.00 set over from surplus income from the
Conservatory of Music. The fund is named in memory of Pro-
fessor Fenelon B. Rice.

ROCKEFELLER (JOHN D.) FUND   (U) $200,000.00
Established in March, 1902, by gift of Mr. John D. Rockefeller,
of New York; the income to be used for the expenses of the
College department and the general administration of the whole
institution. The terms of gift specify that no part of the income shall be used for post-graduate work, the School of Theology,
the Academy, or the Conservatory of Music.

ROGERS (J. R.) FUND   (U) $ 500.00
Gift of Mr. J. R. Rogers, of Brooklyn, N. Y., to the Endowment
Fund raised in the years from 1909 to 1911 to meet the condi-
tional gift of The General Education Board of New York.

ROSSETER (JENNIE M.) SCHOLARSHIP   (T) $ 1,500.00
Established in January, 1881, by bequest of Mrs. Caroline H.
Rosseter, of Great Barrington, Mass., the income to be used for
education of students preparing for the ministry.

SANDUSKY SCHOLARSHIP   (T) $ 1,000.00
Established by gifts from the First Congregational Church of Sandusky, Ohio, from 1880 to 1887; the income to be used in aid of students preparing for the ministry.

SCHOLARSHIP LOAN FUND   (U) $ 2,333.82
Established in 1898 by crediting to a separate account amounts repaid by students to whom aid had been allowed in previous years.

SEVERANCE (L. H.) FUND   (L) $ 5,000.00
Established in July, 1906, by gift of Mr. L. H. Severance, of New York, for Library Endowment.

SEVERANCE LABORATORY MAINTENANCE
    FUND   (C) $ 10,720.00
Established in January,.1902, by gift of Mr. L. H. Severance, of New York; the income to be used for repairs, maintenance, and care of the Severance Chemical Laboratory.

SEVERANCE (L. H.) PROFESSORSHIP   (C) $ 45,000.00
Established in January, 1902, by gift of Mr. L. H. Severance, of New York, the income to be used for the payment of the salary of the Professor of Chemistry; any income in excess of the amount necessary to pay the salary of .the Professor of Chemistry is to be added to the principal of the fund for the care and mainte- nance of the Severance Chemical Laboratory.

SHANSI PROFESSORSHIP   (T) $ 40,000.00
Established in April, 1907, by gift of Mr. D. Willis James of New York, to endow the chair of Practical Theology in the School of Theology.

SHAW FUND   (U) $ 85.06
Established in March, 1882, by gift of Mr. and Mrs. Luther Shaw, of Tallmadge, Ohio, unrestricted.

SHEDD (E. A. and C. B.) FUND   (U) $ 10,000.00
Established in February, 1902, by gift of Messrs. E. A. and.C. B. Shedd, of Chicago, Ill., as part of the Half Million Endow- ment of 1901. The donors requested that this fund be loaned with interest to deserving students.

SHEDD (E. A. and C. B.) FUND   (L) $ 5,000.00
Established in December, 1906, by gift of Messrs. E. A. and C. B. Shedd, of Chicago, Ill., for Endowment of the Library.

SHERMAN (JOHN) FUND   (U) $ 5,000.00
Established in May, 1902, by bequest of Mr. John Sherman, of Mansfield, Ohio. This bequest was counted as part of the Half Million Endowment of 1901.

SMITH (CLARISSA M.) FUND   (U) $ 4,846.10
Established in October, 1896, by bequest of Mrs. Clarissa M. Smith, of Rochester, N. Y., unrestricted.

SPELMAN (HARVEY H.) SCHOLARSHIP   (C) $ 1,000.00
Established in May, 1899, by gift of Mrs. John D. Rockefeller, of New York, for aid of a self-supporting young man.

SPELMAN (LUCY B.) SCHOLARSHIP (C) $ 1,000.00
Established in May, 1899, by gift of Mrs. John D. Rockefeller, of New York, for aid of a self-supporting young woman.

STANLEY (HELEN TALCOTT) FUND (U) $ 50.00
Gift of Mrs. Helen Talcott Stanley of New Britain, Conn., to the Endowment Fund raised in the years from 1909 to 1911 to meet the conditional gift of The General Education Board of New York.

STARR (COMFORT) SCHOLARSHIP FUND (C) $ 3,339.40
Established in July, 1902, by gift of $2,500.00 by Mr. Merritt Starr, of Chicago, Ill.; the income to be used (first) to pay the term bills and College charges of every kind other than those for board and lodging of the children of Merritt Starr in any department of Oberlin College; (second) to pay for the education of deserving scholars in the College Department in the studies of Civics, Economics, Political History, and kindred subjects, as a reward for excellence in such studies. When not used the income is to be added to the principal of the fund.

STOKES (OLIVIA E. P.) FUND (U) $ 1,000.00
Gift of Miss Olivia E. P. Stokes, of New York, to the Endowment Fund raised in the years from 1909 to 1911 to meet the conditional gift of The General Education Board of New York.

STONE PROFESSORSHIP (C) $ 50,000.00
Established in September, 1880, by gift of Mrs. Valeria G. Stone, of Malden, Mass., in memory of her husband. Mrs. Stone requested that this fund be assigned to the professorship of Mental Philosophy and Rhetoric which was at that time the Chair of Professor John M. Ellis.

STUDENT EMPLOYMENT FUND (T) $ 50,000.00
Established in July, 1912, by gift of Mrs. Ellen S. James, of New York, the income to be used for aid of students in the School of Theology.

STURGES (TRACY) SCHOLARSHIP (C) $ 500.00
Established in August, 1881, by gift of Mr. Stephen B. Sturges, of Brooklyn, N. Y., in memory of his son Tracy; the income to be granted in aid of students with a reputation for truthfulness.

SUNDRIES-LIBRARY ENDOWMENT (L) $ 24,855.14
This fund is made up of gifts received as part of the funds being raised for endowment of the Library since 1906 which have not been established as separate funds.

TALCOTT SCHOLARSHIP (U) $ 1,000.00
Established in March, 1881, by Mr. James Talcott, of New York, for aid of self-supporting women.

TERRELL (H. L.) FUND (L) $ 4,570.00
Established in August, 1909, by gift of Mr. H. L. Terrell, of New York, for Endowment of the Library.

THOMPSON (LUCY M.) SCHOLARSHIP (U) $ 2,000.00
Established in August, 1905, by bequest of Miss Lucy M. Thompson, of Oberlin; the income to be applied for the payment of tuition and board of two students.

THOMPSON (ROSA M.) SCHOLARSHIP (U) $ 155.00
Established in June, 1913, by members of the Class of 1886 in
memory of their classmate.

THOMPSON (MRS. W. R.) FUND (U) $ 500.00
Gift of Mrs. W. R. Thompson, of New York, to the Endowment
Fund raised in the years from 1909 to 1911 to meet the condi.
tional gift of The General Education Board of New York.

TRACY SCHOLARSHIP (T) $ 1,250.00
Established in April, 1890, gift of Mrs. F. E. Tracy, of Mans.
field, Ohio; income to be used in aid of students preparing for the
ministry.

TRACY (MRS. F. E.) FUND (U) $ 100.00
Gift of Mrs. F. E. Tracy, of Mansfield, Ohio, to the Endowment
Fund raised in the years from 1909 to 1911 to meet the condi.
tional gift of The General Education Board of New York.

TRACY (MRS. F. E.) SCHOLARSHIP (C) $ 1,000.00
Established in January, 1899, by gift of Mrs. F. E. Tracy, of
Mansfield, Ohio, the income to be used in aid of a self-support-
ing woman.

UNIVERSITY ENDOWMENT FUND (U) $175,588.86
Established in August, 1894. This fund represents the accumulated gifts for general endowment not erected as separate funds.

VAILE (JOEL F.) FUND (U) $ 1,000.00
Gift of Mr. Joel F. Vaile, of Denver, Colo., to the Endowment
Fund raised in the years from 1909 to 1911 to meet the condi-
tional gift of The General Education Board of New York.

VALENTINE (HOWARD L.) SCHOLARSHIP (U) $ 1,000.00
Established in August, 1880, by Mrs. Lucy H. Valentine, of Moun-
tainville, N. Y., for the aid of self-supporting women.

WALWORTH FUND (T) $155,275.00
Established in January, 1877, by gifts of the Misses Ann and
Sarah Walworth, of Cleveland, Ohio. To the combined gifts of
the Misses Walworth received from 1877 to 1891 there was added
the gift of Miss Ann Walworth to the Half Million Endowment
of 1901 and her gift of business property on Central Avenue,
Cleveland, Ohio; also her bequest for the Department of Slavic
Education. The fund as a whole has been assigned by the Trustees for the use of the School of Theology, including the budget
of the Slavic Department.

WARDLE (MARY E.) SCHOLARSHIP (U) $ 1,250.00
Established in January, 1896, by bequest of Miss Mary E. Wardle,
of Elgin, Ill., the beneficiaries to be designated by the First Congregational Society of Elgin.

WARNER FUND (T) $ 427.74
Established in December, 1891, by gift of Mrs. Anna G. Warner,
of Clifton Springs, N. Y., for endowment of the School of Theology.

WARNER (DR. and MRS. LUCIEN C.)
FUND (M) $ 5,000.00
Established in January, 1916, by gift of Dr. and Mrs. Lucien C. Warner of New York, to provide an endowment fund, the income of which is to be used for the benefit of the Conservatory of Music with a preference expressed that the income be used to keep up and extend the Conservatory Loan Fund.

WARNER GYMNASIUM FUND (U) $ 16,000.00
Established in October, 1902, by gift of Dr. Lucien C. Warner, and Mrs. Keren Osborn Warner, of New York, for endowment of Warner Gymnasium.

WARNER (LYDIA ANN) SCHOLARSHIP (U) $ 5,000.00
Established in November, 1888, by Drs. Lucien C. and I. DeVer Warner, of New York, in memory of their mother, for aid to students; preference to be given to young men who are fatherless, but this preference not to exclude others who may be judged more needy or more deserving.

WARRINER (ELIZABETH L.)
SCHOLARSHIP (T) $ 1,000.00
Established in February, 1909, by bequest of Mrs. Elizabeth L. Warriner, of Springfield, Mass.; the income to be used for aid to students in the School of Theology.

WEBB (MRS. REBECCA) FUND (U) $ 100.00
Gift of Mrs. Rebecca Webb, of St. Louis, Mo., to the Endowment Fund raised in the years from 1909 to 1911 to meet the conditional gift of The General Education Board of New York.

WEST FUND (U) $ 1,033.77
Established in September, 1902, by gift of Mr. Edward West, of Wellington, Ohio, unrestricted.

WEST (E. A.) FUND (U) $ 1,000.00
Gift of Mr. Edmund A. West, of Chicago, Ill., to the Endowment Fund raised in the years from 1909 to 1911 to meet the conditional gift of The General Education Board of New York.

WEST (E. A.) FUND (L) $ 2,850.00
Established in June, 1905, by gift of Mr. Edmund A. West, of Chicago, Ill., for Endowment of the Library.

WEST (E. A.) SCHOLARSHIP (C) $ 1,500.00
Established in April, 1897, by Mr. Edmund A. West, of Chicago, Ill., the income to be used for the benefit of self-supporting students of ability and good character.

WESTERVELT (W. A.) SCHOLARSHIP (C) $ 1,500.00
Established in April, 1916, by gift of Mr. W. D. Westervelt, of Honolulu, H. T., in memory of his father.

WESTON (JOSHUA W.) FUND (T) $ 1,000.00
Established in December, 1902, by bequest of Mr. Joshua W. Weston, of LaCrosse, Wis., assigned to the School of Theology.

WHIPPLE FUND   (L) $ 158.45
Established in May, 1880, by gift of Mrs. E. A. Whipple, of Lodi, Ohio, assigned to endowment of the Library.

WHITCOMB (ELLEN M.) SCHOLARSHIP   (C) $ 6,000.00
Established in July, 1884, by gift of David Whitcomb, of Worcester, Mass., in memory of his daughter; the income to be granted each year to six self-supporting young women, preference being given to daughters of missionaries and clergymen who shall be chosen by the Trustees upon the recommendation of the Prudential Committee and Faculty. The gift also requires that the terms of the gift pending the appointment of the beneficiaries shall be read by the Prudential Committee and the Board of Trustees.

WHITCOMB (JANET) SCHOLARSHIP   (C) $ 1,000.00
Established in October, 1899, by gift of Mr. Homer H. Johnson, of Cleveland, Ohio, the income to be used in aid of young women.

WICKHAM (DELOS O.) FUND   (U) $ 1,000.00
Gift of Mr. Delos O. Wickham, of Cleveland, Ohio, to the Endowment Fund raised in the years from 1909 to 1911 to meet the conditional gift of The General Education Board of New York.

WILDER (J. C. and ELIZABETH E.)
    SCHOLARSHIP   (C) $ 2,000.00
Established in April, 1902, by gift of Mrs. Ella M. Wilder Metcalf, of Baltimore, Md., in memory of her father and mother; the income to be used in aid of students of character and ability.

WILLIAMS (JENNIE MORTON)
    SCHOLARSHIP   (C) $ 1,000.00
Established in June, 1883, by Rev. Edwin S. Williams and Mrs. Frankie Lee Williams, of Saratoga, Cal.; the income to be used by the "Principal and Ladies Board in assisting self-supporting young women in special emergencies in their College course."

WRISLEY (ALLEN B.) FUND   (U) $ 50.00
Gift of Mr. Allen B. Wrisley, of Chicago, Ill., to the Endowment Fund raised in the years from 1909 to 1911 to meet the conditional gift of The General Education Board of New York.

WYETT (ANNA M.) SCHOLARSHIP   (U) $ 500.00
Established in February, 1916, by gift of Mrs. Caroline S. Johnson, of New York.

Y. M. C. A. READING ROOM FUND   (U) $ 1,150.00
Established in December, 1907, by gift of $1,000.00 by Mr. William A. Bowen, of Honolulu, to which have been added gifts by two anonymous friends. With the consent of the donors the income is devoted to the purchase of papers and periodicals for the Reading Room in the Men's Building.

ZOOLOGICAL LABORATORY FUND   (C) $ 4,000.00
Established in June, 1911, by gift of an Anonymous Friend for the purchase of books for the Department of Zoölogy.

INDEX OF FUNDS

REFERRED TO IN THE REPORT OF THE TREASURER

In the Index the following abbreviations are used: (U), University; (C), The College of Arts and Sciences; (T), The Graduate School of Theology; (M), The Conservatory of Music; (L) The Library.

REPORT OF THE AUDITING COMMITTEE FOR THE YEAR ENDING AUGUST 31, 1917

To the Board of Trustees of Oberlin College:

Your committee devoted the business day of November 15 to a detailed personal inspection of all the securities in which the endowment funds of Oberlin College are now invested. These papers are kept in safe deposit boxes under the joint control of the Treasurer of the College, representing the Investment Committee, and of officials of the Cleveland Trust Company, and the details of collections and interest and principal, and of reinvestment are subject to the very complete daily auditing system of the Trust Company through the entire year in addition to the annual examination of the Auditing Committee of the Board of Trustees of the College.

We find that all securities called for by the Treasurer's books and annual report are in hand, and the accounts and records of the College Treasurer, as kept in his office in the Administration Building at Oberlin, have been audited by the Public Accounting Division of the Audit Department of the Cleveland Trust Company, which your committee have employed for this purpose, their work in Oberlin occupying the time of two accountants for an aggregate of one hundred and seventy-six hours. They report to us that the Oberlin office is conducted with thorough system and accuracy and efficiency.

We certify also that we have examined the surety bond of the Treasurer, which is kept in the custody of the President of the College.

We submit as a part of our report the report of the expert audit of the business done in the Treasurer's Oberlin office :

Pursuant to your request, we have made an examination of the Accounts and Records of the Treasurer of Oberlin College for the year ended August 31, 1917, in the following manner:

Disbursements: All disbursements were examined and found to be supported by receipted vouchers on file or bank checks properly endorsed.

Cash Account, as shown by General Ledger August 31, 1917, was found to consist of:—

Cash on Hand...............................		$ 3,201.56
Cash in Bank		
Oberlin Bank Company...........	$ 1,721.43	
State Savings Bank Company.....	1,165.73	
Peoples Banking Company........	101.75	
National Park Bank, N. Y........	51.01	
Cleveland Trust Company.........	21,074.38	
Garfield Savings Bank............	339.40	24,453.70

Total Cash on hand and in Bank...............$27,655.26

Bank accounts were reconciled as of August 31, 1917, and were supported either by Bank Statement or Pass Book.

Cash on Hand was verified by actual count at close of business November 14, 1917.

Investment Day Book and Cash Book were verified as to footings, and all postings were checked from Investment Day Book to Cash Book and General Ledger.

Trial Balance as of August 31, 1917, was verified, the balance footing being $3,144,171.23. We also verified all additions in the General Ledger.

Real Estate, $408,549.99.

Loans and Investments, $1,750,888.03; same were evidenced by detail lists, totals of which were verified and found to correspond with balances as shown by General Ledger.

Bills Receivable were evidenced by notes on file aggregating $18,426.27, this being the amount as shown by General Ledger.

Loan Funds: Notes representing various Loan Funds as of August 31, 1917, were on file, with the exception of those paid subsequent to that date, in which case investigation was made to see that proper entry had been made for same.

In conclusion, we are pleased to report that no irregularities were revealed in connection with our investigation. We also wish to commend the accuracy with which your accounting is conducted.

(Signed) IRVING W. METCALF,

THOMAS HENDERSON,

C. H. KIRSHNER,

Auditing Committee.

Oberlin, Ohio, November 16, 1917.

THE ANNUAL MEETING OF THE BOARD OF TRUSTEES, NOVEMBER 16, 1917

Judge Alexander Hadden, of the class of 1873, of Cleveland, Ohio, Mr. Homer H. Johnson, of the class of 1885, of Cleveland, Ohio, and Mr. Charles H. Kirshner, of the class of 1886, of Kansas City, Mo., were reëlected to membership on the Board of Trustees for the term of six years, beginning January 1, 1918.

The ballot of the Alumni for the choice of alumni trustee resulted in the election of Professor Robert A. Millikan, of the class of 1891, of Chicago, Ill., for the term of six years, beginning January 1, 1918.

To fill the vacancy in the Board caused by the death of Dr. Charles J. Ryder, the Trustees elected Professor E. Dana Durand, of the class of 1893, of Minneapolis, Minn., for the term ending January 1, 1923.

Dr. Charles S. Mills, of Montclair, N. J., resigned his place on the Board after a period of service of twenty-one years, and the Trustees elected in his place Dr. Hubert C. Herring, of Boston, Mass., for the term ending January 1, 1922.

The Trustees examined the drawings for the new group of buildings for the Graduate School of Theology, prepared by the College Architect, Mr. Cass Gilbert. The School of Theology now has on hand $100,000 toward the necessary $300,000 for the erection of these buildings.

The Trustees approved a recommendation from the General Faculty that the limit of one thousand students in the College of Arts and Sciences be continued for two additional years, the further consideration of the matter to come up in the year 1919-20.

THE COLLEGE ADMINISTRATION, 1917-18

GENERAL OFFICERS

President, Henry Churchill King
Assistant to the President, W. Frederick Bohn

Treasurer, Hiram B. Thurston

Secretary, George M. Jones
Assistant Secretary, John E. Wirkler

Librarian, Azariah S. Root

Director of Men's Gymnasium, Fred E. Leonard
Director of Women's Gymnasium, Miss Delphine Hanna
Director of Athletics—C. Winfred Savage

Director of the Art Museum, Clarence Ward

Acting Secretary of the Bureau of Appointments, Louis E. Lord

Superintendent of Buildings and Grounds, Charles P. Doolittle

THE FACULTY

EMERITUS PROFESSORS

Harmony of Science and Revelation—G. Frederick Wright
Sacred Rhetoric and Practical Theology—Albert H. Currier
Chemistry and Mineralogy—Frank F. Jewett
Pianoforte—Miss L. Celestia Wattles
Greek—John F. Peck
Church History—Albert T. Swing

The names of the members
of the Faculty are arranged
according to subjects taught

THE COLLEGE OF ARTS AND SCIENCES

Chairman of the Faculty, Henry C. King
Dean and Vice-Chairman, Charles N. Cole
Clerk of the Faculty, George M. Jones
Dean of College Women, Miss Florence M. Fitch
Acting Dean of College Men, Carl C. W. Nicol
Assistant Dean of College Women, Miss A. Beatrice Doerschuk
    (Absent 1917-18)
Registrar, Miss F. Isabel Wolcott

Bibliography, Language, Literature, and Art

Bibliography—Azariah S. Root, Professor

English—   Charles H. A. Wager, Professor
            Philip D. Sherman, Associate Professor
            R. Archibald Jelliffe, Associate Professor
            Arthur I. Taft, Assistant Professor
            Miss E. Louise Brownback, Instructor
            Miss Mary M. Belden, Instructor (Absent 1917-18)
            Miss Esther C. Ward, Instructor
            Lester M. Beattie, Instructor
            Rudolph F. Brosius, Instructor

Oratory and Rhetoric—
            William G. Caskey, Professor

Latin—   Louis E. Lord, Professor
            Charles N. Cole, Professor
            John T. Shaw, Associate Professor
            Miss Frances Hosford, Associate Professor
            Leigh Alexander, Assistant Professor

Greek—   Charles B. Martin, Professor
            *Leigh Alexander, Assistant Professor

German—   William E. Mosher, Professor
                Miss Arletta M. Abbott, Professor
                Frederick C. Domroese, Assistant Professor
                Miss A. Beatrice Doerschuk, Instructor (Absent 1917-18)
                Miss Emma O. Bach, Instructor
                Miss Louise Rodenbaeck, Instructor

Romance Languages—
                John R. Wightman, Professor
                Kirke L. Cowdery, Associate Professor
                Russell P. Jameson, Associate Professor
                Edwin L. Baker, Assistant Professor
                Mrs. Mary T. Cowdery, Instructor

Hebrew—   *Kemper Fullerton, Professor

Fine Arts—   Clarence Ward, Professor
                *Charles B. Martin, Professor
                Miss Eva M. Oakes, Associate Professor
                Miss Jessie Stephen, Instructor

Music—   See Faculty of the Conservatory of Music

Musical History—
                *Edward Dickinson, Professor

Mathematics and the Sciences

Mathematics— Frederick Anderegg, Professor
                William D. Cairns, Associate Professor
                Miss Mary E. Sinclair, Associate Professor
                F. Easton Carr, Instructor

Physics and Astronomy—
                Samuel R. Williams, Professor
                Edward J. Moore, Associate Professor

Chemistry—   Harry N. Holmes, Professor
                William H. Chapin, Associate Professor
                James C. McCullough, Associate Professor
                Edward H. Cox, Assistant Professor
                Paul H. Fall, Assistant

---

* Major teaching in another department

Geology—   George D. Hubbard, Professor
Zoölogy—   Robert A. Budington, Professor
                 Charles G. Rogers, Professor
                 Lynds Jones, Associate Professor
                 Robert S. McEwen, Instructor
Botany—   Frederick O. Grover, Professor
                 Miss Susan P. Nichols, Associate Professor
Physiology and Hygiene—
                 *Fred E. Leonard, Professor

History and the Social Sciences

History—   Lyman B. Hall, Professor
                 *Louis E. Lord, Professor
                 David R. Moore, Professor
                 Harold L. King, Assistant Professor
Economics—   Harley L. Lutz, Professor
                 Howard H. Preston, Assistant Professor
                 Hiss Hazel Kyrk, Instructor (Absent 1917-18)
Political Science—
                 Karl F. Geiser, Professor
Sociology—   Herbert A. Miller, Professor

Philosophy, Psychology, Education, and Bible

Philosophy—   Simon F. MacLennan, Professor (Absent 1917-18)
                 Miss Ethel M. Kitch, Associate Professor
                 Carl C. W. Nicol, Assistant Professor
                 Miss C. Hyacinthe Scott, Assistant
Psychology—   Raymond H. Stetson, Professor
                 *Carl C. W. Nicol, Assistant Professor
                 Edward S. Jones, Assistant Professor (Absent 1917-18)
                 J. Frederick Dashiel, Instructor
Education—   Edward A. Miller, Professor

Bible and Christian Religion—
                 *Henry C. King, Professor
                 *Edward I. Bosworth, Professor
                 Miss Florence M. Fitch, Professor
                 *William J. Hutchins, Professor (Absent first semester
                     1917-18)

---

* Major teaching in another department

Hygiene and Physical Education

Hygiene and Physical Education—
Fred E. Leonard, Professor
Miss Delphine Hanna, Professor (Absent second semester 1917-18)
C. Winfred Savage, Professor
Miss Helen F. Cochran, Associate Professor
Jacob Speelman, Assistant Professor
Mrs. Ellen B. Hatch, Instructor
Miss Mabel C. Eldred, Instructor
Miss Lucy T. Bowen, Instructor
Louis F. Keller, Jr., Instructor (Absent 1917-18)
D. Paul Maclure, Instructor (Absent 1917-18) .
Harold C. Spore, Instructor
Miss Mary I. Dick, Assistant

THE GRADUATE SCHOOL OF THEOLOGY

Chairman of the Faculty, Henry C. King
Senior Dean and Vice-Chairman, Edward I. Bosworth
Junior Dean, G. Walter Fiske (Absent 1917-18)
Secretary and Registrar, Kemper Fullerton

Systematic Theology—
Henry C. King, Professor
*Eugene W. Lyman, Professor

New Testament Language and Literature—
Edward I. Bosworth, Professor

Church History—
Ian C. Hannah, Professor

Old Testament Language and Literature—
Kemper Fullerton, Professor

Homiletics— William J. Hutchins, Professor (Absent first semester, 1917-18)

Practical Theology—
G. Walter Fiske, Professor (Absent 1917-18)

---

* Major teaching in another department

Comparative Religion and Christian Missions—
          *Simon F. MacLennan, Professor (Absent 1917-18)
          *William J. Hutchins, Professor (Absent first semester 1917-18)
Philosophy of Religion and Christian Ethics—
          Eugene W. Lyman, Professor
          *Simon F. MacLennan, Professor (Absent 1917-18)
Elocution—   *Miss Frances G. Nash, Professor
Slavic Department—
          Louis F. Miskovsky, Principal

• THE CONSERVATORY OF MUSIC

Chairman of the Faculty, Henry C. King
Vice-Chairman and Director, Charles W. Morrison
Dean of Conservatory Women, Miss Frances G. Nash
Clerk, Mrs. Mabel D. Brown
Librarian of the Conservatory, Miss Edith Dickson

Pianoforte—   Howard H. Carter, Professor
          William K. Breckenridge, Professor
          J. Arthur Demuth, Professor
          Charles K. Barry, Professor
          William T. Upton, Professor
          George C. Hastings, Professor
          Orville A. Lindquist, Professor
          Bruce H. Davis, Professor
          Mrs. Ada M. Hastings, Assistant Professor
          Mrs. Amelia H. Doolittle, Assistant Professor
          Mrs. Bertha M. Miller, Assistant Professor
          Miss Margaret H. Whipple, Instructor (Absent 1917-18)
          Miss Lelah E. Harris, Instructor
History and Criticism of Music—   ˵
          Edward Dickinson, Professor
Singing—   Arthur S. Kimball, Professor
          Edgar G. Sweet, Professor
          Herbert Harroun, Professor
          Charles H. Adams, Professor
          William J. Horner, Professor
          Mrs. Margaret J. Adams, Assistant Professor

---

* Major teaching in another department

Organ—   George W. Andrews, Professor
J. Franklin Alderfer, Professor (Absent second semester 1917-18)
Frederic B. Stiven, Associate Professor
John E. Snyder, Instructor

Violin—   *J. Arthur Demuth, Professor
Maurice Koessler, Professor
Mrs. Charlotte D. Williams, Assistant Professor
Donald Morrison, Instructor

Violoncello—   Friedrich A. Goerner, Professor

Wind Instruments—
*J. Arthur Demuth, Professor

Theory—   *George W. Andrews, Professor
Arthur E. Heacox, Professor
Friedrich J. Lehmann, Professor
*John E. Snyder, Instructor
Miss Gladys F. Moore, Instructor

*School Music—*Karl W. Gehrkens, Professor

OFFICE ASSISTANTS

General Offices

President's Office—
Miss Mary L. Fowler, Secretary
J. Anthony Humphreys, Assistant

Treasurer's Office—
H. Wade Cargill, Assistant
Miss Dora Cargill, Assistant

Secretary's Office—
Miss Eunice L. Foote, Assistant
Miss A. Gertrude Ransom, Assistant
Miss Ruth Easton, Assistant
Mrs. Charlotte J. Ormsby, Stenographer

Office of the Dean of the College—
Miss Grace E. Nickerson, Secretary

Office of the Chairman of Deans of Women—
Miss Frances J. Hosford, Assistant

Office of the Director of the Conservatory—
Mrs. Mabel D. Brown, Registrar and Secretary

Office of the Bureau of Appointments—
        Miss Ruth M. McFall, Assistant
The Olney Art Collection—
    Mrs. A. A. Wright, Custodian
Office of the Director of the Art Museum—
        Miss Dorothy E. Birkmayr, Assistant

The Library

Reference Librarian—
        Miss Annette P. Ward
Head Cataloguer—
        Miss Eoline Spaulding
Assistants—   Miss Mary J. Fraser
        Miss Hattie M. Henderson
        Miss Edith M. Thatcher
        Miss Esther A. Close
        Miss L. Nell Chase
        Miss Helen B. Morton
        Miss M. Ione Shepherd
        Miss Elizabeth J. McCloy

ALUMNI ASSOCIATIONS

GENERAL ASSOCIATIONS

College Association

President—Mr. Franklin H. Warner, of the class of 1898, 30 Ridgeview Ave., White Plains, N. Y.

Vice-Presidents—Gen. Wilder S. Metcalf, of the class of 1878, 1236 Massachusetts St., Lawrence, Kan.; Mr. Homer Abbott, of the class of 1888, 1526 Edgewood Ave., Chicago Heights, Ill.; Mr. Frank O. Koehler, of the class of 1908, 4537 Xerxes Ave., S., Minneapolis, Minn.

Secretary—Mr. George M. Jones, of the class of 1894, Oberlin, Ohio.

The membership includes all graduates of the College, the School of Theology, the Conservatory of Music, and all holders of honorary degrees bestowed by the College.

The annual meeting is held in Oberlin on Tuesday morning of Commencement Week. The Alumni Dinner occurs on Wednesday, Commencement Day.

Six of the Trustees of Oberlin College are elected to their office by the ballot of all Alumni of the College, one vacancy occurring in the Board at each annual meeting.

Theological Association

President—Rev. Frederick L. Fagley, t'11, 3920 Glenway Ave., Price Hill, Cincinnati, Ohio.

First Vice-President—Rev. Watts O. Pye, t'07, Oberlin, Ohio.

Second Vice-President—Rev. Lawrie J. Sharp, t'13, 3654 Shaw Ave., St. Louis, Mo.

Speaker—Rev. William A. Knight, t'00, Brighton Parsonage, Boston, Mass.

Alternate—Rev. Herbert O. Allen, t'89, Osage, Iowa.

Secretary—Professor Louis F. Miskovsky, t'91, Oberlin, Ohio.

The annual meeting is held at 9:00 o'clock in the morning of the day of the Commencement exercises of the Graduate School of Theology, in May of each year.

LOCAL ASSOCIATIONS

New England Association, Founded in 1877

President—
Vice-President—Mr. Donald S. King, '12, 77 Addington Road, Brookline, Mass.
Secretary-Treasurer—Mr. Louis D. Gibbs, '98 1 Billings Park, Newton, Mass.
Corresponding Secretary—Miss Mary E. Coughlin, ex-'92, 340 Belgrade Ave., West Roxbury, Mass.

New York Association, Founded in ——

President—Mr. E. Allan Lightner, '03, 343 Tecumseh Ave., Mt. Vernon, N. Y.
First Vice-President—Mr. Orville C. Sanborn, '02, 31 Nassau St., New York, N. Y.
Second Vice-President—Mrs. A. Augustus Healy, '92, 198 Columbia Heights, Brooklyn, N. Y.
Corresponding Secretary—Mr. Herman E. Nichols, '15, 386 Stuyvesant Ave., Brooklyn, N. Y.
Recording Secretary—Mr. T. Nelson Metcalf, '12, 104 W. 174th St., New York, N. Y.
Treasurer—Mr. J. Howard Wilson, '12, 70 Franklin Ave., New Rochelle, N. Y.

Oberlin Association of Illinois, Founded in 1870

President—Professor Robert A. Millikan, '91, 5605 Woodlawn Ave., Chicago, Ill.
Vice-President—Mr. Frederick W. Chamberlain, 2845 Sheridan Place, Evanston, Ill.
Secretary-Treasurer—Miss Ruth G. Nichols, '03, 6925 N. Ashland Blvd., Chicago, Ill.
Annual meeting in March or April of each year.

Midland Association, Founded in 1889

President—Mr. Roy V. Hill, '02, 3435 Central St., Kansas City, Mo.
Secretary-Treasurer—Dr. George F. Pendleton, '10, 605 Bryant Building, Kansas City, Mo.

Western Pennsylvania Association, Founded in 1893

President—Mr. Arnaud C. Marts, '10, Standard Life Building, Pittsburgh, Pa.
Vice-President—Mr. Carl A. Zeller, '99, 1601 Westfield Ave., Pittsburgh, Pa.
Secretary and Treasurer—Miss Helen Hudson, '15, 151 Ridge Ave.,
,   Ben Avon, Pa.
Annual meeting in April of each year.

Central New York Association, Founded in 1903

President—Rev. Nathan E. Fuller, '88, 108 Fitch St., Syracuse, N. Y.
Secretary and Treasurer—Professor A. S. Patterson, '95, 415 University Place, Syracuse, N. Y.
Annual meeting in March or April of each year.

Northwestern Ohio Association, Founded in 1903

President—Mr. Jason A. Barber, '79, 1519 Nicholas Building, Toledo, Ohio.
Vice-President—
Secretary—Mrs. Dorothy R. Sargent, 2840 Scottwood Ave., Toledo, Ohio.
Treasurer—Mr. Philip C. King, '10, 2013 Lawrence Ave., Toledo, Ohio.
Assistant Treasurer—Miss Elmina R. Lucke, '12, Scottwood Apartments, Toledo, Ohio.

Cleveland Association, Founded in 1905

President—Judge George S. Addams, '90, 1902 Wadena St., East Cleveland, O.
Vice-President—
Secretary and Treasurer—Mr. William S. Cochran, '06, 3303 Warrington Road, Shaker Heights, Cleveland, Ohio.

Northern California Association, Founded in 1905

President—Rev. Francis J. Van Horn, '90, 1551 Madison St., Oakland, Cal.
Secretary—Mrs. Irene S. Fisher, '94, 553 El Dorado Ave., Oakland, Cal.

Oberlin Association of Summit County, Ohio, Founded in 1905

President—Mr. Edwin W. Brouse, '01, 600-601 Permanent Title Building, Akron, Ohio.
Secretary Treasurer—Mr. McConnell Shank, '05, 104 Paige Ave., Akron, Ohio.

Ohio Valley Association, Founded in 1906

President—Rev. Seeley K. Tompkins, '01, 832 Oak St., Cincinnati, Ohio.
Vice-President—Mrs. Edith C. Shattuck, '93, 4007 Floral Ave., South Norwood, Cincinnati, Ohio.
Secretary-Treasurer—Mr. Oliver M. Nikoloff, '12, 3323 Spokane Ave., Cincinnati, Ohio.

Nebraska Association, Founded in 1906

President—Miss Lucy M. Haywood, c'94, 719 S. Sixteenth St., Lincoln, Neb.
Secretary—Mr. Charles L. Mattson, '09, 117 South 37th St., Omaha, Neb.

Oberlin Association of Puget Sound, Founded in 1909

President—Mr. Dan Earle, '01, White Building, Seattle, Wash.

Vice-President—Mrs. Julia R. Chapman, c'93, 3611 N. Washington St., Tacoma, Wash.

Secretary-Treasurer—Mr. Charles H. Niederhauser, '11, 2715 Belvidere Ave., Seattle, Wash.

Spokane Association, Founded in 1910

President—Dr. Arthur T. R. Cunningham, '96, S. 1220 Division St., Spokane, Wash.

Vice President—Mr. J. Lawrence Breckenridge, Spirit Lake, Idaho.

Secretary—Mr. Fred G. Fulton, '07, E. 1107 32nd Ave., Spokane, Wash.

Treasurer—Mr. Earl W. Pettibone, '01, 1624 11th Ave., Spokane, Wash.

Oregon Oberlin Association, Founded in 1910

President—Mr. Walter S. Jelliff, '08, 619 Corbett Building, Portland, Ore.

Vice-President—Miss Jean McKercher, c'10, 634 Halsey St., Portland, Ore.

Secretary—Mrs. Ora-Bess M. Seeberger, c'11, 190 Lovejoy St., The Royal Arms, Portland, Ore.

Treasurer—Mr. Thaddeus W. Veness, '06, 1016 Spalding Building, Portland, Ore.

Corresponding Secretary—Mr. G. Earl Murphy, '11, 517 Chamber of Commerce Building, Portland, Ore.

St. Louis Association, Founded in 1910

President—Mr. C. Harold Sackett, '04, Windermere Hotel, 5601 Delmar Ave., St. Louis, Mo.

First Vice-President—Mrs. Mary W. Crossen, ex-'92, 5423 Bartmer Ave., St. Louis, Mo.

Second Vice-President—Miss Georgina B. Allison, '09, 5660 Kingsbury Blvd., St. Louis, Mo.

Secretary-Treasurer—Mr. Griffin R. McCarthy, ex'14, 521 N. Clay Ave., Kirkwood, Mo.

Oberlin Association of Southern California, Founded in 1910

President—Mr. Harry A. Ford, '98, 231-232 Bryson Building, Los Angeles, Cal.

Vice-Presidents—Mr. John E. Koster, ex-'06, 1855 Whitley St., Los Angeles, Cal.; Miss Alma E. Stickel, '99, 1632 Reid St., Los Angeles, Cal.

Secretary-Treasurer—Dr. H. Waldo Spiers, '07, 520 Brockman Building, Los Angeles, Cal.

Executive Committee—Rev. L. F. Bickford, '68, 6032 Monte Vista St., Los Angeles, Cal.; Miss Helen S. Pratt, '06, 245 W. Ridgeway Ave., Eagle Rock, Cal.; Miss Estelle A. Sharpe, '84, The Richelieu, Los Angeles, Cal.; Dr. W. M. Burke, '96, 432 Laughlin Building, Los Angeles, Cal.

Oberlin Association of North China, Founded in 1910

President—
Secretary-Treasurer—

Oberlin Association of Dayton and Vicinity, Founded in 1911

President—Dr. Joseph B. Stewart, 615 Grand Ave., Dayton, Ohio.
Vice-President—Miss Mildred K. Emrick, '10, 578 W. Second St., Dayton, Ohio.
Secretary-Treasurer—Miss Winifred M. Ryder, '97, 17 Miami Apts., Dayton, Ohio.

Minneapolis and St. Paul Association, Founded in 1912

President—Mr. Pliny L. Solether, '10, 3749 Elliott Ave., Minneapolis, Minn.
Vice-President—Mrs. Jessie S. Funsett, '10, 3637 Oakland Ave., Minneapolis, Minn.
Secretary-Treasurer—Mr. Clarence C. Young, '13, 1507 Hennepin Ave., Minneapolis, Minn.

Oberlin Association of Western Massachusetts and Connecticut, Founded in 1914

President—Mr. Ralph L. Cheney, '98, 129 Westford Ave., Springfield, Mass.
Vice-President—Mr. Francis E. Regal, '87, 91 Elm St., West Springfield, Mass.
Secretary—Mrs. Elizabeth W. Hope, '03, 95 Grand St., Springfield, Mass.
Treasurer—Mr. George C. Bliss, ex-'92, 27 College St., Springfield, Mass.

Colorado Alumni Association, Founded in 1914

President—
Secretary-Treasurer—Mrs. Marguerite W. Curtis, '10, 941 S. Williams St., Denver, Colo.

Mahoning Valley Oberlin Alumni Association

President—Mr. Dahl B. Cooper, '03, 703 Wick Building, Youngstown, Ohio.
Vice-President—Mrs. Ruth G. Cooper, ex-'15, 252 Poland Ave., Struthers, Ohio.
Secretary-Treasurer—Miss Marie Soller, '13, 118 Berlin St., Youngstown, Ohio.

Oberlin Association of Central Iowa

President—Mr. Arthur W. Brett, '88, 1506 13th St., Des Moines, Iowa.
Recording Secretary—Miss Charlene E. Sperry, '01, 1305 West 9th St., Des Moines, Iowa.
Corresponding Secretary—Miss Edith B. Malin, '15, 1544 10th St., Des Moines, Iowa.
Treasurer—Miss Joyce E. Lapham, '15, 1544 10th St., Des Moines, Iowa.

Oberlin Association of Lima

President—Dr. James E. Dexter, '97, 904 W. Spring St., Lima, Ohio.
Secretary-Treasurer—Mr. Russell I. Watkins, '13, 840 W. Spring St., Lima, Ohio.

Oberlin Association of Rochester

President—Mr. Edwin Fauver, '99, 246 Park Ave., Rochester, N. Y.

Vice-President—Miss Emily P. Hartshorn, Cons. '91, 63 Grape St., Rochester, N. Y.

Secretary-Treasurer—Mr. William A. McKinney, '11, 40 William St., Rochester, N. Y.

INDEX

9 781528 077767